THE FORGOTTEN

EXPLORER

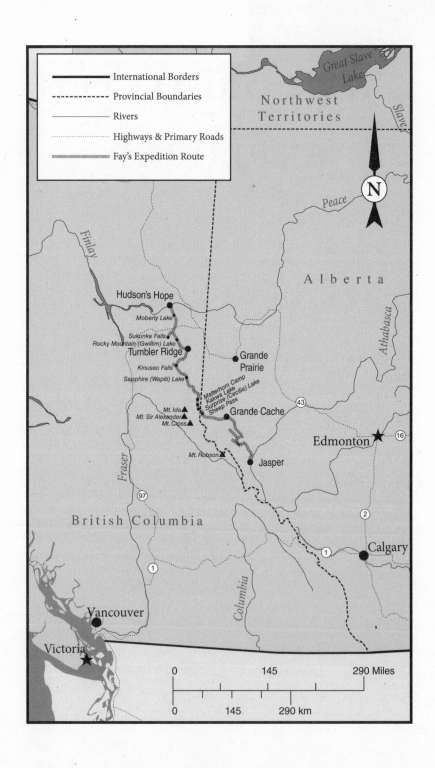

International Borders
Provincial Boundaries
Rivers
Highways & Primary Roads
Fay's Expedition Route

Great Slave Lake

Northwest Territories

Slave

Peace

N

Alberta

Finlay

Athabasca

Hudson's Hope

Moberly Lake

Sukunka Falls
Rocky Mountain (Gwillim) Lake
Tumbler Ridge

Grande Prairie

Kinuseo Falls
Sapphire (Wapiti) Lake

Matterhorn Camp
Kakwa Lake
Surprise (Cecilia) Lake
Sheep Pass

43

Mt. Ida
Mt. Sir Alexander
Mt. Cross

Grande Cache

Edmonton

16

Mt. Robson

Jasper

Fraser

2

British Columbia

97

1

Columbia

1

Calgary

Vancouver

Victoria

0		145		290 Miles

0		145		290 km

THE FORGOTTEN EXPLORER

Samuel Prescott Fay's 1914 Expedition to the Northern Rockies

Edited by

CHARLES HELM & MIKE MURTHA

RMB
Victoria Vancouver Calgary

Rocky Mountain Books
#108 – 17665 66A Avenue
Surrey, BC V3S 2A7
www.rmbooks.com

Rocky Mountain Books
PO Box 468
Custer, WA
98240-0468

Library and Archives Canada Cataloguing in Publication (hardcover)

Fay, Samuel Prescott, 1884-1971
 The forgotten explorer : Samuel Prescott Fay's 1914 expedition to the northern Rockies / edited by Charles Helm & Mike Murtha ; foreword by Robert William Sandford. — Limited ed.

Includes bibliographical references and index.
ISBN 978-1-897522-56-1

 1. Fay, Samuel Prescott, 1884-1971—Travel—Rocky Mountains, Canadian (B.C. and Alta.). 2. Fay, Samuel Prescott, 1884-1971—Diaries. 3. Rocky Mountains, Canadian (B.C. and Alta.)—Discovery and exploration. 4. Rocky Mountains, Canadian (B.C. and Alta.)—Description and travel. 5. Packhorse camping—Rocky Mountains, Canadian (B.C. and Alta.). 6. Explorers—United States—Diaries. I. Helm, Charles, 1957- II. Murtha, Mike III. Title.

FC219.F39 2009   917.1104'3   C2009-903723-8

Library and Archives Canada Cataloguing in Publication (softcover)

Fay, Samuel Prescott, 1884-1971
 The forgotten explorer : Samuel Prescott Fay's 1914 expedition to the northern Rockies / edited by Charles Helm & Mike Murtha ; foreword by Robert William Sandford.

Includes bibliographical references and index.
ISBN 978-1-897522-55-4

 1. Fay, Samuel Prescott, 1884-1971—Travel—Rocky Mountains, Canadian (B.C. and Alta.). 2. Fay, Samuel Prescott, 1884-1971—Diaries. 3. Rocky Mountains, Canadian (B.C. and Alta.)—Discovery and exploration. 4. Rocky Mountains, Canadian (B.C. and Alta.)—Description and travel. 5. Packhorse camping—Rocky Mountains, Canadian (B.C. and Alta.). 6. Explorers—United States—Diaries. I. Helm, Charles, 1957- II. Murtha, Mike III. Title.

FC219.F39 2009A   917.1104'3   C2009-904337-8

Printed in Canada

Rocky Mountain Books acknowledges the financial support for its publishing program from the Government of Canada through the Book Publishing Industry Development Program (BPIDP), Canada Council for the Arts, and the province of British Columbia through the British Columbia Arts Council and the Book Publishing Tax Credit.

Canada Council   Conseil des Arts   BRITISH COLUMBIA
for the Arts   du Canada   ARTS COUNCIL

This book has been printed with FSC-certified, acid-free papers, processed chlorine free and printed with vegetable based inks.

Mixed Sources

FSC

Contents

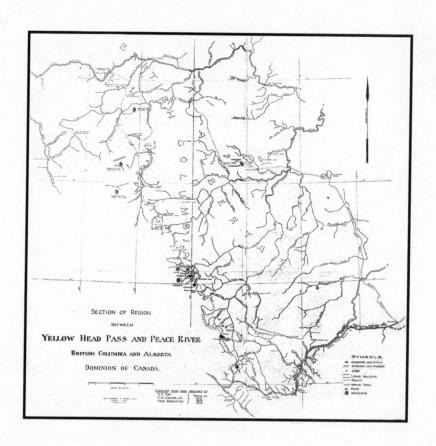

SECTION OF REGION

BETWEEN

YELLOW HEAD PASS AND PEACE RIVER

BRITISH COLUMBIA AND ALBERTA

DOMINION OF CANADA.

SYMBOLS.

The Publisher wishes to acknowledge Peace River Coal for their support of this project.

PEACE RIVER
COAL

A MEMBER OF THE ANGLO AMERICAN PLC GROUP

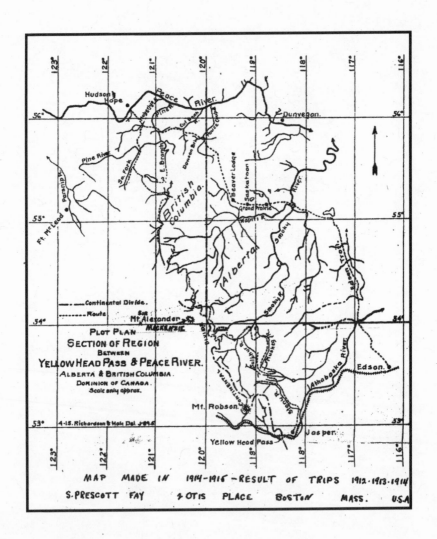

PLOT PLAN
SECTION OF REGION
BETWEEN
YELLOW HEAD PASS & PEACE RIVER.
ALBERTA & BRITISH COLUMBIA.
DOMINION OF CANADA.
Scale only approx.

MAP MADE IN 1914-1915 — RESULT OF TRIPS 1912-1913-1914
S. PRESCOTT FAY   4 OTIS PLACE BOSTON MASS. U.S.A

Acknowledgements

We would like to gratefully acknowledge the assistance of the following individuals: Robert W. Sandford for suggesting the concept of and need for this book, and for the continuing confidence he showed in us throughout its production; Samuel Prescott Fay's daughter Sarah Fay Baird, his granddaughter Fay Baird, and his daughter-in-law Caroline Fay; Don Bourden and Elizabeth Cundert-Cameron of the Whyte Museum of the Canadian Rockies; Gerry Clare of the Dawson Creek Archives; Glenda Cornforth and the always helpful staff of the Jasper–Yellowhead Museum & Archives; Bill Cox of the Smithsonian Institution; Sherman Gray (son of Prentiss Gray) for his inspiration and support; Daniel Helm; Janet Mason, Provincial Toponymist of British Columbia; Mark Phinney of the South Peace Bird Atlas Society; and Jovanka Ristic, Librarian of the American Geographical Society, University of Wisconsin-Milwaukee Libraries.

We would also like to thank the following for permission to reprint Fay's articles: Alpine Club of Canada and the *Canadian Alpine Journal*; *Appalachia Journal* and the Appalachian Mountain Club, Boston; and *Outdoor Life* magazine.

Our families have been wonderfully tolerant of the research and writing time this book has demanded, and their support has been unflagging.

— CHARLES HELM AND MIKE MURTHA

The publisher gives thanks to *Appalachia Journal* and the Appalachian Mountain Club for supplying the image at the top of page 159, to the Smithsonian Institution for the image at the top of page 158 and to the Jasper–Yellowhead Museum & Archives for providing all other photographs in this book.

MAPS, MYTHS & MEMORY IN THE NORTHERN ROCKIES

Because of the way history has been recorded, fully half of the Canadian Rockies lie outside the awareness of most Canadians. One of the central reasons for this – for why the northern Rockies are not as well known as the mountain parks farther south – is that the British Columbia Rockies north of Mount Robson have not had literary champions who were capable of elevating the region's stories of exploration adventure to the level of popular myth. *The Forgotten Explorer: Samuel Prescott Fay's 1914 Expedition to the Northern Rockies* is an important book that over time will contribute significantly to correcting this long-standing historical shortcoming.

Landscapes become legendary only when the stories that arise from them cast into high relief the myriad ways in which the experience of place profoundly shaped the identities of people who lived in or visited those landscapes. The northern Rockies have not had, at least until now, a Walter Wilcox, an A.P. Coleman, a James Outram, a J. Norman Collie or any other widely read early historical literary figure to light the landscape's way into the broader collective imagination of the world. With this book, that just changed.

The Forgotten Explorer affirms the powerful nature of the northern landscape in two ways. The book introduces into the public domain a missing written account of early adventure in the northern Canadian Rockies. The sudden appearance of these long-forgotten exploration records is like a lightning flash revealing something meaningful we didn't know about our western Canadian past. Samuel Prescott Fay is important, not just for his explorations but for his detailed natural-history accounts, which now form a baseline against which we can measure how the landscapes of the mountain West have changed in the last century.

The second reason this book is remarkable is that it introduces two important contemporary figures, Charles Helm and Mike Murtha, who are not only keeping history alive in the northern Rockies but are working to constantly renew that history based on the same fundamental appreciation of place that brought Samuel Prescott Fay back again and again to explore the region's natural charms.

Ultimately this book is about the enduring power of maps and dreams. In addition to remembering Fay and providing a missing piece crucial to public understanding of the history of the northern Rockies, *The Forgotten Explorer* does what all great adventure books aspire to do. Reading this forgotten account makes you want to go there, to experience for yourself what Helm and Murtha discovered when they followed Fay's footsteps back into time. There are not many places left in the world where the experience of adventure offered today remains anywhere near the equivalent of myth and memory. We are running out of places where you can create your own stories. The northern Rockies, however, remain one of those places. Here you get a sense of what Banff and Jasper must have been like a century ago.

In reading Samuel Prescott Fay's account, perhaps you too will be drawn northward, as I was the summer after Charles Helm introduced me to Fay's forgotten journals. Following in Fay's footsteps to Kinuseo Falls, I noticed that the weather in the northern Rockies seems to change even faster and more often than in the south. As we made our way down the switchbacks to the Murray River, we heard thunder in the distance that wasn't from the falls. Soon the sky clouded over. As the river was in full spate, the rough trail that existed along its banks was submerged. We were soon forced back up into the forest, where we followed game trails that took us upward in the direction of a viewpoint atop a steep ridge from where it looked like it would be possible to view the falls – which many argue is the most spectacular natural feature in northern British Columbia.

As the sky darkened, the game trails up the cliff face became steeper and less well defined. Soon we were clinging to the roots of bushes and pulling ourselves up narrow rock chimneys. What suddenly astounded me, however, was the realization of what I was climbing through. Only the day before, in the canyon of Flatbed Creek, I had wondered whether there were enough plants lingering into our time from the Mesozoic Era to establish a direct connection between modern plant communities and the kinds of plants that dinosaurs of the species that had left their footprints on the trackway by the water might have known and fed upon. I laughed when I suddenly realized that in the rainforest created by the mist of the Kinuseo cascade, I was almost completely surrounded by plants that would have formed part of the forest backdrop, in one place or another, for all the dinosaurs that ever lived. There were tall pines and fragrant spruces. There were horsetails and lycopodium and there were ferns and mosses everywhere. Climbing up the mist-drenched wall of the gorge, we were working our way up and out of the forests of Middle Time. Though different species would have existed in the Jurassic, and the horsetails might have been the size of trees, the same basic families of plants forming the living community covering that wall today would have surrounded the dinosaurs that had left their tracks in Flatbed Creek. Samuel Prescott Fay would have approved, I concluded. For it was only by following him north that I found those tracks.

It was all falling into place when I stumbled onto the top of the cliff to find myself surrounded by the flowers and grasses whose petals and seeds had so changed the world. The sky was now completely dark, and when suddenly the wind changed, our words were lost in the thunder of the falls. The rain began to fall in wind-driven sheets. But it didn't matter that we were getting wet. We had found our way to a platform that jutted out over the white tumult of the cascade. I stepped to the lip and peered into the boil of the water. There was a sudden deafening crash directly above us and for a moment we felt the thunder of the falls rising up through the rock and through us to meet the thunder from the sky. For an instant I was a reed playing thunder's song and in all the woods around me the downpour sang along. And then the thunder ceased, leaving us with the roar of the falls and a fine warm rain.

In that moment it occurred to me that all that separated me from Samuel Prescott Fay, or from first Indigenous peoples or even from the dinosaurs that had left their tracks up the valley in Flatbed Creek, was time. That is what a place should be – a window back into place-time – and any book that beckons you to that window, as *The Forgotten Explorer* most certainly does, is a book worth reading.

— BOB SANDFORD
CANMORE, ALBERTA
JULY 2009

Editors' Foreword

FAY AND THE NORTHERN ROCKIES

North of Jasper, in the Canadian Rockies, is a large, roadless and spectacular wilderness of alpine flower meadows, glaciated peaks, canyons, waterfalls and abundant wildlife. Compared to Banff and Jasper National Parks immediately to the south that are visited by millions each year, this northern area sees few visitors. Fewer still attempt to travel through this wilderness in one continuous trip. The first to do so was Samuel Prescott Fay in 1914. His exact route has never been duplicated.

In contrast to the Rockies south of Jasper, little was formally known about the mountains to the north until well into the 20th century. Perhaps they suffer to this day because they are not quite as rugged, their summits not quite as lofty, their glaciers not quite as big. Even now, remarkably little has been published about them, and the subject matter in books on the "Canadian Rockies" often tends to end mysteriously somewhere just north of Mt. Robson. This represents one of the great gaps in North American alpine history. Fay helps fill this void.

It remains impossible to cross these mountains by vehicle between the Yellowhead Pass in the southeast, where Fay's journey began, and the Pine Pass in the northwest, close to where the mountain section of his route ended. Over this distance stretch magnificent parallel mountain ranges, punctuated by largely forgotten passes. And in the middle of this wild country lies the last group of really high mountains in the Rockies – the 10,000-foot peaks dominated by the "Big Mountain," Mt. Sir Alexander, reached and named by Fay.

Fay and his party made a five-month pioneering horse trip of 1200 kilometres along the Rockies from Jasper to Hudson's Hope, cutting trail much of the way because none existed. He had three objectives: to collect and record wildlife for the US Biological Survey, to determine the northern limit of Rocky Mountain bighorn sheep and to reach the "Big Mountain." Undoubtedly also, the exhilaration and challenge of exploring an unknown landscape must have been a big attraction, with the possibility of stumbling on new discoveries, of never knowing what was over the next pass, of being completely self-reliant in the face of dangers and accidents.

Fay kept a detailed journal during the trip, which he provided to the US Biological Survey and various Canadian government authorities. He also published several articles about his discoveries. He remains an obscure figure in Canadian Rockies exploration, however, partly because the journal in its entirety, with all his day-to-day observations, has not previously been published. Similarly, his maps, photographs and wildlife records have been preserved in various archives but never shared with a wider audience. Together these materials provide an early record of an area that remains little known, and they are brought together here for the first time.

Why is it worthwhile to publish this material almost a century after the event? First, in this part of North America, a century takes us back virtually to the beginning of recorded history. First Nations people had undoubtedly travelled through and hunted in the area for unknown generations. Fay noted evidence of trails and food caches as far north as Kakwa Lake and then after Kinuseo Falls. For non-Native people, however, Fay was on the leading edge of discovery and settlement. As late as 1879, George Dawson, the eminent geologist and explorer, had marked the area on his map as "Unexplored Territory." The town of Jasper, where Fay began his trip, was only three years old; Hudson's Hope, where he finished the trip, was an old Hudson's Bay Company post, but the surrounding agricultural land in the Peace River region was only just then beginning to see its first pioneer settlers. The two towns that now lie on his route came much later – Grande Cache in the 1960s, Tumbler Ridge in the 1980s, both as planned coal-mining communities. Fay's journal, then, is the beginning of recorded history for the people who now call this region home. His detailed descriptions, maps and photographs form a baseline against which to compare and appreciate the landscape today, both the continuing natural rhythms of the southern wilderness and the agricultural and industrial changes of the northern half.

Fay also provided the first accounts of what are today the outstanding parks and scenic highlights of the region. He is responsible for the names Mt. Sir Alexander, Kinuseo Falls and Kakwa, which are the spectacular attractions for modern visitors. He described the beautiful scenery of what is now Willmore Wilderness Park and the stunning view of Mt. Ida from above Jarvis Lakes. In articles he wrote at the time, he drew attention to the grandeur and challenges of Mt. Sir Alexander and Mt. Ida, thereby luring climbers to attempt the first ascents of these most northerly 10,000-foot peaks in the Rockies.

His detailed record of wildlife observations, plus the specimens he collected, enriched scientific knowledge in his time and provide a baseline for modern comparative studies.

Fay gives us a window into the past, to a time when the land was unknown and unmapped, when it was possible to truly be an explorer and make important new discoveries. He carried northward the work of Wilcox, Coleman, Outram, Stutfield and Collie and deserves a place alongside them as a pioneer in the Rockies.

Fay's route was unusual and unique, and his party paid the price for it in terms of the privations and frustrations they endured. Aboriginal hunters, timber cruisers, hunters and most explorers would have used the lay of the land, travelling along river corridors or through passes. Fay chose, instead, to follow close to the spine of the Rockies, crossing the many tributary valleys immediately to the east, and his trajectory along these slopes, against the grain of the land, is notable for its boldness and its geophysical challenges. Decades later, this type of adventure travel would become more popular, and the Fay expedition in a sense anticipated the emergence toward the end of the 20th century of the breed of long-distance backpacker that occasionally traverses the same mountain slopes.

He and his party passed through this arrestingly beautiful part of the planet when it was in a virtually pristine condition, and in doing so they seemed to appreciate that they had been blessed with a special privilege. Thankfully, in spite of industrial development, the land is recognizably the same today, and it continues to inspire us and instill the sense of wonder that Fay so eloquently described. When we experience this land, we can be keenly aware of Fay's historic presence, and delighted by the poignancy of his first descriptions of the landscapes and features we cherish.

TRAVELLERS BEFORE FAY

The mountains were surrounded by natural corridors for First Nations people. To the east lay the prairies (and the possible ancestral migration route for the first North Americans). To the west lay the Rocky Mountain Trench, to the south the Yellowhead Pass, and to the north the Peace River Canyon. For early travellers, both Native and non-Native, the Rocky Mountains were a barrier between the prairies and the BC Interior, and there was little reason for travel along the length of the mountain chain.

Despite a moderate amount of archaeological material, especially in the northern part, there does not appear to be evidence of a permanent presence in these mountains. Instead, a seasonal round has been postulated, in which groups would winter on the prairies, then enter the mountains in summer by a variety of routes, only visiting specific sites perhaps every five or ten years so that the stocks of sheep, goat and caribou would not be wiped out.

In the 19th century the Smoky River area became a popular hunting ground for Cree and Métis parties from Hudson's Bay Company posts at Jasper House and along the Peace River, as evidenced by a description by Henry Moberly, factor at Jasper House in the 1850s. By contrast, in the northern part of the area, a variety of determinants may have combined to diminish the oral history potentially available from the countless generations of mountain visitors. The westward expansion of the Cree had displaced the Sekani to the west of the mountains, and diseases like smallpox had ravaged the First Nations, causing a loss alike of elders with their precious knowledge, and young hunters to follow the traditional routes. A further factor was a great fire that swept along the eastern flanks, and the resulting blowdown might have obliterated the trails beyond easy recovery. The pioneer explorers of the late 19th and early 20th centuries apparently felt as though they were entering an untrodden land.

This was not yet true a hundred years earlier at the time of Alexander Mackenzie's 1793 expedition through the mountains via the Peace River Canyon. His exploration was so successful partly because he understood that being guided by the local inhabitants was his best option. Mackenzie, naturally, was focused more on finding the easiest way through the mountains, rather than searching for their peaks. However, once his party had navigated the Peace River Canyon and emerged west of the Rockies, his route, which was dictated by navigable waterways, first took him parallel to the mountain ranges in a southeasterly direction. He was therefore able to obtain a view of a glaciated summit, the Parsnip Glacier on Mt. Vreeland. His journal description of this "valley of snow" represents the first written record of any Canadian Rockies glacier. Mackenzie's and Fay's routes did not overlap at all, except for the Fay party reaching the Peace River at Hudson's Hope.

For almost a century after Mackenzie, the presence of western explorers was infrequent and fleeting – a party of deserters from Simon Fraser's party recorded crossing the Pine Pass in the north in 1806, and Ignace Giasson's Hudson's Bay Company party, guided by the famed Iroquois hunter Yellowhead, crossed Sheep Pass in the south in the winter of 1819–20. Then all was quiet until the search began for railway passes through the mountains. The only precedent to the Fay expedition – of a diarized extended overland trip in these northern Rockies – was by E.W. Jarvis and C.F. Hanington in 1875. Their west–east route was perpendicular to that of Fay. They received instructions from the Canadian Pacific Railway (CPR) to find and survey a pass through the mountains, and set off from Fort George (now Prince George) in January. They struggled up a tributary of the McGregor River and eventually crossed the mountains by what is now known as Jarvis Pass in Kakwa Provincial Park. To their dismay, they found that rivers on the eastern flanks of the mountains flowed northeast. On the verge of starvation, they decided to head south to Jasper House. When they arrived there it was deserted, and they were rescued by a small band of Indians. They then travelled east to Lac Ste. Anne, a mission 60 kilometres west of Edmonton, and once again were nearly starving by the time they arrived. From here on to their final destination of Winnipeg they had more support. They concluded that the route they had found was impractical for a railway.

In the north Joseph Hunter passed through the Pine Pass in 1877, also on the instructions of the CPR. Two years later the route was surveyed by George Dawson. His map records the mountains to the southeast of Pine Pass as a blank area, with the notation "Unexplored Region."

The Canadian Pacific Railway was built in the mid-1880s to the south through the Kicking Horse Pass. Consequently, Banff and Lake Louise quickly developed as tourist resorts and climbing centres. But the Yellowhead Pass and areas beyond were too far from the CPR for exploration by horse parties.

Then, in a flurry of activity in the early 20th century, rival railway companies raced to build a second transcontinental route in Canada, north of the CPR. They sent explorers from both sides of the mountains, surveying routes like the Wapiti Pass, and timber cruisers like Spencer Tuck would try to tie up timber rights along the prospective routes. Little was published about these explorations, possibly due to fear of competition. The most thorough survey was by R.W. Jones, working for the Grand Trunk Pacific Railway. During 1905 and 1906, Jones and his crews explored most of the major passes between the Yellowhead and Pine passes. His 1906 maps, never published and only recently rediscovered, show all the routes they traversed, and identify a preferred rail line via Pine Pass. It is not known which, if any, of the subsequent explorers had access to the Jones map, with the exception of Mary Jobe, who was also in the Mt. Sir Alexander area in 1914. One copy of the Jones blueprints contains relatively late in life and was raising a young family, he was still as involved as ever in wilderness preservation, and was the unquestioned authority on North American sheep.

The letter is merely an apology for having mistimed a previous meeting with Fay, and in it Sheldon confesses that his distracted state might have been due to the arrival of a new infant at the time. But the missive shows that Fay and the renowned scientist knew each other and enjoyed a correspondence of which we today know next to nothing. The new infant, of course, was none other than William Sheldon, who in 1932, at the age of 19, would undertake the first formal exploration for sheep in the upper Sukunka River valley, immediately west of Fay's route.

Sheldon Sr. was closely allied with the US Biological Survey, and was a great friend of Edward Nelson, to whom Fay would be reporting within a year once he was appointed field assistant to the survey. We can speculate that it might have been Sheldon who alerted Nelson to Fay's proposed trip, although Nelson's first letter to Fay indicates that it was Robert Cross who had formally brought it to his attention (Cross had been in west central British Columbia in 1913 and submitted a report to the Biological Survey). Was it advice on wilderness travel that Fay wished to glean from the older man, or his theories on the sheep question? Unfortunately Fay's letters to Sheldon have not been traced, but it is known that Sheldon suggested to Fay that he contact Bryan Williams, BC's chief game guardian. Possibly being able to cite the great man as a reference helped Fay obtain Williams's support and permits for the planned trip.

The US Biological Survey was a section of the Department of Agriculture in Washington, DC, now known as the US Fish & Wildlife Service. Its collections went into the National Museum, and in time it became connected with the Smithsonian Institution. In the early 20th century, recognizing that data and specimen collection required a continental rather than a national focus, the Biological Survey began sending collectors to Canada and Mexico. Inhibited by the small size of its in-house staff, it realized the enormous potential of private naturalists. Adventurers like Fay, even though they were not specifically trained, could go into a previously unsampled area and record the wildlife they encountered, and thus make valuable contributions to science. In turn, the support of the US Biological Survey fired up such intrepid explorers with added enthusiasm and facilitated the granting of permits and access.

Fay was given the title of "field assistant" and wrote how the support of the Biological Survey allowed his exploration to change from a big-game hunting trip to "one combined with obtaining some information of scientific value, [that] made the expedition of much greater interest to all of us."

Fay's communication with the Biological Survey was through Edward Nelson, the survey's assistant chief in charge of its biological collections. Nelson had a wealth of field experience behind him, including time in Alaska studying sheep populations. In time, he would go on to become chief of the survey. When he called the area Fay was proposing to explore a "blank spot on the map," he knew what he was talking about.

In his introduction Fay succinctly sets out the issue of sheep distribution that stimulated the imaginations of hunters and naturalists in the early part of the 20th century. Specifically, did the distributions of the Rocky Mountain bighorn sheep in the south and the Stone sheep in the north overlap, or were they discontinuous? Edward Nelson expressed the problem in a May 1914 letter to Fay:

> This piece of country is extremely interesting to us from the fact that we are greatly in need of accurate information concerning the distribution and relationships of Mountain Sheep, Caribou and Moose of that area and, also, desire information concerning the smaller mammals and birds . . . The sheep immediately north of Peace River are *O. stonei*. What they are immediately south of Peace River and from there down to the border of Alberta to the head of the Smoky, we have no information. This is an extremely interesting question.

FAY'S ROUTE

The natural direction of travel in these mountains would have been to head up one of the major river valleys, cross a high pass and descend down another drainage – thus either crossing the Rockies or else describing a roughly circular route. Fay would write that the latter was a typical First Nations practice. The Fay party's chosen route would lead them in a specific direction which did not take into account the lay of the land – they were obliged to continue northwest toward Hudson's Hope, along the eastern flanks of the mountains. This route was often against the grain of the land, with multiple obligatory valley and mountain crossings.

The country through which the Fay party travelled is very different from the well-known parts of the Canadian Rockies around Banff and Lake Louise and along the Icefields Parkway to Jasper. For most visitors, rugged peaks, glaciers and steep cliffs created by the tilted rock strata typify the

Rockies. For those who venture away from the roads, there are flower-laden alpine meadows and exquisite turquoise lakes cupped in the glacier-carved rock basins. Waterfalls grace many creeks as they tumble from the high mountain basins to the river valleys.

A short way north of the Yellowhead Pass, this landscape changes. High mountains still line the north side of the pass, and in fact the highest peak in the Canadian Rockies, Mt. Robson, towers above the western entrance. But just beyond here, north of Mt. Bess and Mt. Chown, the high mountains end abruptly. The snow-capped peaks rising to 10,000 feet or more are replaced by undulating alpine ridges and basins averaging 7000 to 8000 feet in elevation. For almost 100 kilometres, especially north of Big Shale Hill, the Continental Divide resembles one long alpine meadow. To the east, parallel valleys channel the waters along the strata of the mountains – the Jackpine, Muddywater, Smoky and Sulphur rivers. Their combined flow breaks out of the mountains at Sulphur Gates, next to the modern-day town of Grande Cache, where the Fay party crossed the Smoky River. The valleys are flat, forested and often boggy.

Further north, the terrain is even gentler and the rivers generally flow more directly out of the mountains, cutting across the main grain – the Kakwa and the Wapiti, Murray and Pine rivers with their numerous tributaries, which caused considerable trouble for Fay's party. Elevations are lower still, with peaks rising to only 6000 or 7000 feet on average. But as the mountains lie farther north, the tree line is lower and alpine meadows drape most of the ridges. Fay and his party travelled through this lower country after leaving "Matterhorn" camp and noted how they crossed from one headwater valley to the next, making their way through a confusing maze of isolated ridges and valleys. Even today, with detailed maps available, experienced travellers have become disoriented in this same area.

Breaking this great length of undulating country is the isolated group of high mountains around Mt. Sir Alexander – the "Big Mountain" which first caught Fay's attention in 1912. In this group, Mt. Ida (3180 m, 10,439 feet) and Mt. Sir Alexander (3274 m, 10,738 feet) are the most northerly of the 10,000-foot peaks in the Canadian Rockies. Fay was a hunter and explorer rather than a mountain climber and he made no attempt on the summits. He was content to get close enough to admire and describe them. He published some of the first photographs of these peaks in the *Canadian Alpine Journal*. (Mary Jobe also visited the area on her separate expedition in August 1914 and published her account and photographs in the same issue of the *Journal* as Fay.)

The Fay party travelled east of the spine of the Rockies except for a short section in the Kakwa area. (This spine is also the Continental Divide as far as Mt. Vreeland in Monkman Provincial Park, beyond which the Divide diverges to the west of the mountains to include the Peace River drainage.) Starting from Jasper, they rode northeast to the Stony River (now the Snake Indian River), which led them northward and on to the Sulphur River in present-day Willmore Wilderness Park. At the beginning of the trip, Fred Brewster's brother Jack was in charge of the outfit until Fred could catch up with them a few days later. Jack was unfamiliar with the route and missed the obscure branch trail to the Sulphur (as did Fay, who had been over this route with Fred in 1912). As a consequence, they lost a couple of days heading up to Snake Indian Pass and then backtracking. A similar mistake occurred a few days later when they initially went too far down the Sulphur Valley before turning around and finding the correct route via Eaglenest Pass. But they obtained their sheep specimens in the Sulphur Valley and sent them back to Jasper with Jack Brewster. They also discovered that the erroneous route ended at a coal deposit staked by the Canadian Northern Railway Company, an early indication of the coal-mining interests which developed along the eastern slopes of the Rockies and which continue to this day.

After Eaglenest Pass, they followed one of the better defined Native trails, which led them to Grande Cache through beautiful green valleys and al-pine passes. "It was a magnificent pass," Fay wrote of the South Berland Pass, which prompted him to note in his journal: "Coming along a fine trail with such beautiful scenery on a cool, crisp day with a bright, warm sun is something long to be remembered."

At Grande Cache they had the good fortune to meet Ewan Moberly (whose name Fay spells "Ivan," as it is pronounced), a well-known Métis hunter and outfitter. The Moberly family had moved into the area a few years earlier, from near Jasper. The meeting was fortuitous, as the Smoky River was in flood and the party was able to rent Moberly's canoe for transporting their gear across. As it was, some of their horses were swept down to the mouth of the Sulphur Gates canyon while attempting to swim the river.

The Smoky River marked a major milestone for the expedition – beyond this point they were unlikely to meet anyone else until reaching the Peace River region. In one of his many indications of his love for wild, untravelled areas, Fay noted:

> Now that we are across the Smoky I feel that our trip has at last begun, as we are out of the "tin can" district and beyond the reach of any out-fits except Indians

The party had been on the trail for one month at this point. It would be almost three months before their next encounter with another human being.

From the Smoky River, the party followed the Muddy Water River and ran into a bad stretch of downed timber, the result of a large forest fire in times past. Fay and Brewster had chopped their way through this section in 1912 but many more trees must have fallen in the intervening two years. Fay marvelled at Brewster's "seventh sense" in finding faint signs of the old trail. Again it was a test of endurance for the men, compounded by the hot weather.

The going was no easier for the horses – scrambling over logs all day, with packs that were still heavy with four months' supplies and with little feed.

> The horses were all so tired today that it was hard to drive them and poor old Macloud, the strongest of them all, laid down at frequent intervals, groaning and sweating.

When they reached a small clearing with nice feed later in the day,

> The horses appreciated it and all the afternoon in the broiling hot sun they lay stretched out in the cool grass of the muskeg and ate without getting up, a sure sign of fatigue.

The men spent the time in bare feet and underclothes to keep cool: "It certainly was an extremely informal party." Later in the trip, when they endured a long spell of cold, wet weather, they looked back on this period nostalgically.

But a view of the distant "Big Mountain," their first objective, lifted their spirits. A little further north, they diverged from their 1912 route, on the advice of the Moberly family, and followed a narrow limestone defile, now known as Dry Canyon, which took them in a direct line to Sheep Creek. They were now in mostly open alpine country for the next ten days, with easier travelling and several layover days for hunting, exploring and enjoying the scenery.

While passing through Sheep Pass, Fay reminisced about exploring the Intersection Mountain area on foot in 1912 with Brewster – they had gone further than planned, run out of supplies and had to shoot a "disgustingly greasy" marmot for food. Regrettably, there is no journal from that earlier trip and Brewster's diary contains only practical one-line notes of distance and direction. But undoubtedly there would have been stories around the campfire.

On August 3, while crossing the high, open alpine of Surprise Pass, Fay wrote: "We have a perfect day for the finest scenery of the trip – over the pass to Porcupine Lakes." Modern travellers would not disagree. The party had reached the heart of the Kakwa area and immediately met with success by bagging the caribou specimens Fay wanted for the Biological Survey. Shortly after arriving at Providence Pass and enjoying a closer view of the "Big Mountain," Brewster spotted a group of the animals in an alpine basin. A short stalk resulted in a bull and a cow caribou for the collection.

While still at Providence Pass, on August 5, Fay enthused:

> Our big mountain came out of the clouds in the middle of the morning all glistening with snow and ice after the storm and was magnificent. There is no question about its size and we get more and more enthusiastic about camping close to it.

The following day, after climbing to a high shoulder near camp, Fay wrote of "our wonderful high mountain":

> It has rather a flat, long top with a heavy ice cap and cornice one or two hundred feet thick. Below it, is a large and magnificent glacier with ice cliffs several hundred feet high. It is without question a magnificent mountain and towers far above all the others about.

By August 8, the party was camped at "an ideal spot" at Kakwa Lake – still today the prime campsite at the Kakwa Park headquarters. From here, Fay and Brewster hiked to Babette Lake ("named for a young cousin who took an interest in my explorations") and over an alpine pass for a close-up view of

> the big mountain which, by the way, we have named Mt. Alexander after Alexander Mackenzie, who, in 1793, was the first man to cross the Rocky Mountains and passed west of here up the Parsnip River.

Thus came about the origin of the name of Mt. Sir Alexander.

By August 11, the expedition had passed Kakwa and Jarvis lakes and was beginning the steep climb to cross the alpine ridge north of Jarvis Pass. It was a tough section:

We all toiled up and up, pulling our horses behind us, cursing and
urging horses ahead of us, until from fatigue and thirst and hunger
our patience entirely gave out. Why any sane man comes into these
mountains is a mystery to me when he knows the misery he has to
endure, – yet we all do it, again and again.

Fay's rhetorical question was answered shortly after, when the summit
was attained:

As we turned around there lay a sight that not one of us will ever forget and which more than made up for the seven and a half hours on
the trail. Across the deep valley we had come from rose a high pyramidal mountain, fully 11,000 feet, with nothing but sheer unscalable
cliffs on every side we could see. On both sides were other mountains
over 10,000 feet, with big glaciers and ice and snow in all directions.
Probably no other white man has ever looked on all these mountains
before, – certainly not from this summit. This is without doubt the
most magnificent, the grandest view we shall ever have from a camp
and it is something worth going thousands of miles to see.

Fay was not exaggerating. They were gazing at the north face of Mt. Ida,
one of the most spectacular views in the Rockies. And they had the good
fortune to be there, at the prime viewpoint, in perfect weather. They named
their camp "Matterhorn camp" because of Mt. Ida's resemblance to the
Matterhorn in Switzerland. A scramble to a nearby mountain the next day
opened up views of both Mt. Sir Alexander and Mt. Ida. Fay was able to
provide more information about Mt. Sir Alexander and wrote the words that
inevitably attract climbers: "Undoubtedly it will be a mountain extremely
difficult to climb but not as hard as our other unnamed peak." (He was un-
aware at this time that Mt. Ida had been named by Jarvis and Hanington
in 1875). Fay's articles in alpine journals caught the attention of climbers
– Mt. Sir Alexander was climbed in 1929 but Mt. Ida not until 1954.
   Then it was off into unknown country – beyond where they had been
in 1912 and beyond Native hunting trails. They forded the Narraway River,
thinking it was a branch of the Porcupine (Kakwa) River, thus setting the
stage for their later confusion about the various branches of the Wapiti and
Pine rivers. Now they were on the east slope of the Rockies again but in a
region without the parallel valleys they had followed south of Sheep Creek.
Now they had to cross the grain of the land, from one valley to the next:

It certainly is fascinating work going through a new section of the country without trails. In past trips we have always followed the river valleys but now we are cutting across country from one stream to the next via the best summits we can find. After climbing a mountain to get our direction and set our course we go for three or four days in the heavy timber not being able to see our way but only keeping in the general direction by now and then catching a glimpse of some mountain through the timber by which we set our course.

They were now starting the northern part of the trip, which Fay summarized this way:

From (Kakwa) on to the Peace River we had to depend on our own resources. Had we known what difficulties lay ahead of us, I doubt if we would have attempted the trip, for after leaving the (Kakwa) lakes we spent two months of steady travelling, cutting our way for the most part through a jungle of fallen timber, making actually in distance not over 100 miles in a straight line.

In crossing from the Belcourt to the Red Deer watershed (via Whatley Creek), the Fay party headed over an alpine ridge. One of the most haunting photographs from the expedition is of the horses descending a particularly steep scree slope. Looking at the photo one might tend to assume that the photographer was facing southeast, but it has now been shown that the photo was taken looking north. In retrospect and with the advantages of topographical maps and helicopter access, it was an unusual route to choose and an unnecessary slope to descend.

In the valley west of this ridge, an abandoned exploration track is encountered nowadays, which eventually leads down the Red Deer valley. This old road mirrors the Fay experience in which frustrating trails were encountered that ran up the valleys, perpendicular to his line of travel.

Crossing from the Red Deer to the Wapiti watershed, and into Wapiti Lake Provincial Park, the most likely sign of human life nowadays would be a party from the Royal Tyrrell Museum of Paleontology or the Tumbler Ridge Museum Foundation looking for fish and reptile fossils. Beyond, on the shores of Wapiti Lake, stands an attractive cabin for hikers, close to where Fay penned his first description of what he called Sapphire Lake: "... a delightful glacial lake set in behind a typical terminal moraine and hemmed in by steep mountains . . ."

Fay and Brewster may have known that the Wapiti River system had four main branches. From south to north these are the Narraway, Belcourt, Red Deer and Wapiti. Not having recognized the Narraway as the first, they believed the Wapiti was the third rather than the fourth, and when they ascended the valley to the northwest, and re-entered high country, they believed they could see another main branch of the Wapiti to the north, flowing east. Thus arose one of the few errors in Fay's excellent map.

Climbing what they called an "observation mountain," now known as Mt. Comstock, they then saw a long valley leading north, and descended into it. It was the Murray, then known as the East Branch of the Pine, but they were unsure of this and thought it might be the Sukunka, then known as the Middle Branch of the Pine. Here, the first drivable road since Grande Cache is crossed. From here northward to Hudson's Hope, Fay's route can be approximated by vehicle much of the way.

The Fay party did not understand which river they were on for weeks, thinking they were most likely on the Sukunka (Middle Pine). They cursed the deadfall, rain and tough going, which was a contrast to the easier travel and fine weather of the southern half of their expedition. Yet the river valley did provide them with a reliable conduit of travel and welcome fish to supplement their diet. It also yielded an unexpected bonus: Kinuseo Falls.

Although they did not enter what is now the backcountry of Monkman Provincial Park, Fay commented on the confluence between Monkman Creek and the Murray River. Downstream from here he was inside the present park boundary. For the visitors who journey long distances nowadays to see Kinuseo Falls, and already have a reasonably good idea in advance of what they are going to see, it is difficult to imagine the feelings that must have been aroused in the hearts of the Fay party when they unexpectedly came upon this magical waterfall. There are simply no large waterfalls left to discover like this, anywhere. Wrote Fay:

> There were some big falls roaring ahead and a canyon below . . . They had a drop of about 250 feet and were very magnificent. Such a thing as a big falls was certainly an unexpected sight . . . They cascade over the rocks and are extremely beautiful. It gave me an inspired sensation as I stood there alone at the bottom of the falls, covered with spray . . . They are fine enough if they were accessible, to be a sight such as tourists would travel a long distance to see. They and our Mt. (Sir) Alexander are the two scenic wonders of the trip and they in themselves are worth it.

Fay's height estimate was close; the height is currently given as 225 feet. There were many fish above and below the falls, and Fay later engaged in an ultimately successful correspondence with the Geographic Board of Canada to have the falls officially named "Kinuseo," Cree for "fish."

The later explorer Prentiss Gray learned of the falls through Fay's article in the journal *Appalachia*, and in 1927 made a significant detour to see them. He took the first motion picture of the falls (miraculously, the film has been preserved) and recorded a mellifluous First Nations name from his guides: "Kapaca Tignapy," or "the place of falling water."

Fay never claimed to have discovered the falls, and readily acknowledged that two or three parties might have beheld them previously. He had no knowledge of the archaeological sites that have subsequently been discovered just a few kilometres upstream, but there was evidence of a party that had left a trail some years before him. This coincides with two known visits to the falls: a 215-foot-high cascade at the site of Kinuseo Falls was marked on the 1906 Robert W. Jones map compiled for the Grand Trunk Railway as part of the search for railway passes through the mountains, and there is an anecdotal oral report from a Jim Dixon, who claimed to have seen the falls in 1907.

After some disconsolate days descending the Murray River, during which they found increasing traces of a First Nations presence, they climbed to the top of Mt. Hermann and enjoyed the view of the flat land to the east. Fay commented how somewhere near that distant horizon, homesteaders were coming in to take up land, and how strange it felt to be so close to civilization, yet many weeks away from it. From this subalpine summit today the most striking feature would be the remains of the Quintette mine, part of the largest industrial enterprise in the history of British Columbia: the Northeast Coal Project.

Finally, the party celebrated finding a horse trail and a blaze on a tree, having cut trails through 200 miles of trackless wilderness in two months. Two days later Fay described what he called the "Big Flat," just below present-day Tumbler Ridge, close to where the Lions campground is now situated, and wrote enthusiastically that "It is without doubt the finest flat I have ever seen in the foothills."

In either 1913 or 1914, the first settlers arrived in this area, and the Fay party must have narrowly missed encountering the first two pioneers, Victor Peck and Kate Edwards. As it turned out, they heard the blows of an axe near the Bullmoose Marshes that night, and the next morning made contact with the Danish trapper Neilsen (Fay referred to him as Nelson), who led them to his cabin on Rocky Mountain Lake (now Gwillim Lake).

As with Wapiti Lake, Fay left an evocative first description of this appearance of the lake, and added:

> . . . Seen in the morning light it was certainly a lovely spot; the kind
> of lake you read about and such a place as you would pick out to
> build a house and live . . . Not a breath of air stirred and the surface
> mirrored the surrounding hills.

The party headed along a trail to the Sukunka River and made the mistake of heading upstream, believing they had entered the main valley of the Pine River. This allowed Fay to encounter and describe Sukunka Falls, ". . . a series of very pretty cascades, and small, symmetrical falls, so much so as to be almost artificial looking."

Comparing his photo of the falls with current ones shows how much the topography of the falls has changed over 90 years.

They next encountered the trapper Treadwell, who turned them around and set them right about the route to Hudson's Hope. From here on the journal becomes an intriguing commentary on frontier life in the Peace Region of British Columbia and Alberta. Their brief sojourn in Hudson's Hope provides an entertaining extra chapter in the story of this historic community, and they happened to meet two important fellow explorers, Swannell and Copley, who had completed a government survey of the Finlay River, an upstream major tributary of the Peace.

Some of the men they met in the region, such as Harry Garbitt, Charlie Paquette, Joe Calliou, Hector Tremblay and Rutabaga Johnson, are legendary names in the annals of the Peace region. Most of the other early settlers they encountered, such as Knutson, Borden and Kelly, are traceable through historical records.

On the return trip, before reaching Grande Prairie, the party split, with Brewster, Jones and Symes taking the horses to Jasper via Grande Cache. Fay and Cross, superfit by this stage, walked all the way to Edson, and much later Fay wrote a good description of the Edson trail which adds to the literature on this famous route. From Edson, he shipped the precious scientific specimens to Washington.

Fay and Cross returned to Jasper, missing Brewster, Jones and Symes by just three days. They then caught a train to Edmonton, where they met with Robert W. Jones, the engineer who had searched the same mountains for railway passes for the Grand Trunk Pacific Railway in 1905 and 1906. It must have been a fascinating meeting, with Fay, Cross and the engineer comparing notes on their mountains, in particular Mt. Sir Alexander, which Jones had simply called the "Big Mountain." Jones indicated to Fay that he had not paid much attention to the big peaks, being more interested in the lowest passes through the mountains. The 1906 Jones blueprints, in addition to correctly indicating Mt. Ida, incorrectly show a second Mt. Ida which is actually Mt. Sir Alexander, and note a "large glacier field" alongside it. It is not known whether Jones and Fay discussed Kinuseo Falls, and whether it had been Jones or one of his assistants who had been in the party that had left the trail that Fay had noted at the falls.

The specimens arrived safely at the US Biological Survey in Washington. They were well received, as was Fay's report, and Fay was complimented on helping to fill in a blank space on the North American map. He began writing about the successful expedition, for *Appalachia* and the *Canadian Alpine Journal*. But he was unable to present these papers in person, as within two months he was serving in France in the First World War. In his absence, his namesake (and possibly distant relation) Charles Fay read both papers to the American Alpine Club. The map Pete Fay produced was of a high standard, especially given the limited equipment the party had at its disposal.

THE EXPEDITION MEMBERS

Fay was the ideal person to undertake the expedition. He developed his love of wild places and wildlife early in life. While at Harvard he had climbed in the Alps and sailed the New England coast. He was an avid duck hunter, actively involved with Ducks Unlimited from its establishment in the 1930s. He climbed in the Lake Louise and Lake O'Hara areas for six summers prior to his 1912 trip to Kakwa Lake with Fred Brewster. In 1913, he was exploring and hunting with Brewster. He revelled in the beauty of wild places and frequently referred to views and sunsets in his journal. Even the inevitable challenges and frustrations of strenuous trail travel only briefly dimmed his enthusiasm.

This passion never waned. Writing to Brewster in 1967, in reference to an article he had read about the Stikine country of northwest British Columbia, Fay commented "I wish there were more such inaccessible wilderness areas left."

In retrospect, Fay's choices for companions seem obvious. Brewster was a natural as outfitter, a member of a pioneer outfitting family who are still closely associated with the Rockies to this day. Charles Robert (Bob) Cross was a long-time friend and an experienced climber and hunter who shared

Fay's interest in the goals of the expedition. They required a packer and cook, and Bob Jones and Jack Symes, both experienced men in the bush, were chosen for these tasks. Puzzlingly, Fay referred to them as "green at trail work," yet Jones had wrangled horses on previous trips with the Alpine Club, and Symes had patrolled with the North-West Mounted Police.

Fay ignored advice from British Columbia's chief game warden not to take horses into the area. Likewise he did not follow up on suggestions to take local guides with him, as he knew of no one who would be familiar with more than a small portion of the planned route.

In 1957 Fay had two articles published in *The Beaver* magazine, co-authored by Bradford Angier. Over 40 years had passed since the expedition. This time, Fay commented on the nature and camaraderie of the party:

> It was altogether a fortunate group of men. Never once had there been any misunderstanding or unpleasantness between any of us during our five consecutive months in the bush, during three of which we saw no other human being.

Yet there is one occasion in the journal when Fay was annoyed with Jack Symes, who had allowed their precious lean-to to catch alight and be destroyed, while the rest of the party was trying to retrieve a moose on the Albright Ridge. He vented his frustration in the journal: "I was furious at this new example of his carelessness for now we have only a tipi that is full of holes and leaks like a sieve."

Perhaps the intervening years had dulled the unpleasant memory of this unfortunate incident, perhaps the comment in *The Beaver* was simply the gracious thing to say about these dedicated men, two of whom, including Symes, had given their lives in the war. Or perhaps the journal, rather than the men, had been the recipient of Fay's frustration at the time.

One of the more engaging threads in the Fay story relates to the First World War. It was certainly what the regional press focused on immediately after the end of the expedition – how these five men toiling through unexplored wilderness had come across the lone trapper Neilsen, the first human they had seen in months, and how he had told them about "the war," which they initially assumed referred to a conflict between the US and Mexico.

All five men on the expedition went on to serve in the war. Within two months Fay and Cross were volunteering with the American Ambulance Field Service in France (a voluntary organization that provided humanitarian services such as removing wounded troops from the front), and a year and a day after their chance meeting with Neilsen, Cross was killed in a vehicle accident while helping remove wounded soldiers from the trenches. When the US joined the war in 1917, Fay received his commission and served as an aerial observer. Bob Jones and Jack Symes left Jasper for the recruitment office just three days after returning from their five month expedition and enlisted in January 1915. Jack Symes was killed in action in northern France in May 1917, soon after receiving his commission. Fred Brewster enlisted later in 1915 and, because of his background as a mining engineer, was assigned to a tunnelling division. He served with distinction, became a major and was decorated with the Military Cross and Bar.

Fay's enduring friendship with Brewster is enlightening. We can only imagine how their friendship with Bob Cross would have unfolded over the years had the latter not been killed in the war. Fay wrote of them:

> Major Fred Brewster . . . was the most resourceful man I have ever met. You always had the most complete confidence in him, no matter how bad things ever got. As for C.R. Cross, I can say just as much. As a friend of mine back home in Boston, he had originally interested me in hunting and exploring in difficult and inaccessible parts of the Northwest. He and Fred Brewster were as perfect a pair as any man could want to be with in the wilderness. The three of us together worked out our plans, and every decision was in our hands jointly.

In Brewster, Fay found a lasting soulmate. They corresponded regularly, and met at least once again, in Jasper in 1940. There are endearing letters from Fay to Brewster from as late as the 1960s, when both were well into their eighties. In February 1967, Fay wrote from a hospital bed toward the end of a three-month admission complicated by a fall and pneumonia. In a wistful and alert letter full of reminiscences, he enquired after a rumour of a sheep sighting at the head of the Murray River, and told Brewster how he had come across a reference in a recently published book, *Peace River Chronicles*, to the trapper Treadwell, whom they had encountered in the Sukunka valley. He also spoke of the loneliness of having been the only surviving sibling for the preceding 13 years.

In June 1967, he replied to a postcard of Lake O'Hara from Brewster. He wrote of an incredible day he had experienced there in 1906:

> I was there on that very spot. There is no lake anywhere in the Rockies that is more perfect in its setting . . . That day I set out from

Lake Louise at five o'clock to climb Mt. Victoria, cross Abbot Pass, camp at Lake O'Hara, then climb at Mt. Stephen and descend to Field. When my Swiss guide & I reached the top of Abbot Pass we found the rocks on Mt. Victoria were glazed with ice, and my guide said it was unsafe to climb it, too late in the season. So we descended to Lake O'Hara . . . All we could do was take the trail down to the railroad . . . I went to Field & walked alone into the Yoho & saw the Tackakaw Falls, Emerald Lake, & back to Field for dinner & bed! I think I went forty miles that day!!

FAY'S DISCOVERIES

The findings of the Fay expedition (bolstered by the opinions of the experienced trappers they met as they approached Hudson's Hope) seemed to provide a fairly reliable answer: bighorn sheep were found no further north than the Kakwa area, and Stone sheep were not known to occur south of the Peace River. In between was a sheepless tract of land well suited to caribou.

Yet, in 1917, another explorer for the Biological Survey, Bill Rindsfoos, collected a sheep specimen from the headwaters of a branch of the Wapiti River, throwing the issue into confusion once again. The sheep question was a motivating factor for John Holzworth's 1923, 1924 and 1925 expeditions, and for Prentiss Gray's 1927 and 1928 trips. The exploration of the Sukunka watershed by William Sheldon and Richard Borden, for the American Museum of Natural History in 1932, was also motivated in part by the sheep question.

Holzworth found the northernmost sheep somewhere between the Wapiti and Murray river systems. Gray, moving from north to south, first encountered sheep in the Belcourt Creek drainage a bit further south and took good movie footage. William Sheldon thought he had found signs of sheep in the Sukunka, but in the absence of more substantive evidence this was not considered reliable. In retrospect, the Fay party had passed through the northernmost sheep ranges but had not been fortunate to encounter the animals.

Currently, the most northerly population of bighorn sheep is in the Narraway River area, with occasional sightings as far to the northwest as Wapiti Lake. There is also a small population of Stone sheep at Mt. Selwyn, on the south side of the Peace River. The area in between continues to lack sheep.

The absence of elk from Fay's list of wildlife seen on the trip will strike anyone familiar with Jasper and Kakwa today as noteworthy. It was only in the 1920s that elk were reintroduced to the Canadian Rockies. Likewise, no white-tailed deer were recorded, in stark contrast with the current abundance of this species in the northeastern portion of Fay's route.

Although Fay took pains to record temperature, barometric pressure and elevation, and made detailed records of the animals, birds and fish the party encountered, this was essentially the limit of his natural history descriptions (along with infectious enthusiasm for the hunt). He was entranced by the Mt. Sir Alexander area, but made no detailed geological observations. Perhaps, given the assemblage of 20 horses, the terrain dictated that they would avoid very rocky areas and gravitate to meadows instead. Yet the region through which they passed abounds with dramatic rock strata and formations, and there are sizeable karst areas with caves and sinkholes. The rocks of eastern slopes of the Rockies harbour many fossils, and in some limestone areas, fossilized corals seem more common than bare rock. Subsequent discoveries of Triassic fossil fishes and Cretaceous dinosaur bones and footprints have been of national or global importance, and a paleontological museum of international standard is envisioned for Tumbler Ridge. There is no mention of fossils in the Fay journal. Yet the romantic sensibilities inherent in his appreciation of good scenery and a good sunset are repeatedly apparent, complemented by his sensitive descriptions of wildflowers in bloom in the alpine meadows.

Seemingly unerringly, Fay passed through and described scenic treasures of the region that have subsequently been proclaimed parks. For the first part of the route, he traversed what are now Jasper National Park and Willmore Wilderness Park. He would doubtless be delighted to see his beloved Mt. Sir Alexander, and the surrounding peaks and lakes that he described so vividly, safely protected in Kakwa Provincial Park. From Kakwa northward, he sequentially described the salient features of what are now Wapiti Lake, Monkman, Gwillim Lake, Sukunka Falls and Moberly Lake Provincial Parks, and even made a passing reference to Swan Lake. Kinuseo Falls, a highlight of the Peace River region near Tumbler Ridge, was the second major finding recorded by Fay.

THOSE THAT FOLLOWED

In the years that followed, parts of the region the Fay party had passed through were explored more thoroughly.

The Métis settlement of Kelly Lake, west of Grande Prairie and just inside British Columbia, was established in the years after 1910, and its early residents explored and trapped in the foothills and mountains to the west, which corresponded with the Wapiti and Murray River drainages Fay had traversed. Settlers established a tenuous presence in the Murray and Wolverine valleys near present-day Tumbler Ridge.

In the south the famous Jasper guide Curly Phillips became the acknowledged expert, and the trail north from Jasper, along which he outfitted and guided clients annually, became known as the Phillips Trail. He and Mary Jobe had been around Mt. Sir Alexander in 1914, but did not cross paths with the Fay party. Phillips returned the next year with a party that included Jobe and Caroline Hinman, and led members to within 30 m of its summit. The peak would not be climbed until 1929, by a party led by Andrew Gilmour, outfitted by Phillips. In 1917, Phillips ventured farther north with Jobe, to the Narraway River, where they were beset by early snows. That winter, he ascended the Wapiti drainage from Grande Prairie with Bill Rindsfoos, photographer and naturalist for the Biological Survey. It was Rindsfoos who had secured the bighorn sheep specimen from the same region the previous summer. They spent the winter at a cabin on the Narraway River, and in the spring completed a hair-raising raft descent of its canyon. The adventures of Curly Phillips have been preserved in *Tracks across My Trail*, by the late Professor William C. Taylor. Mary Jobe and Curly Phillips were wilderness sweethearts. Jobe subsequently married Carl Akeley, a renowned wildlife filmmaker, and went on to enjoy a distinguished career in the Congo.

Around the time Fay was exploring the eastern flanks of these mountains, Frederick Vreeland was engaged in similar work from the west. He summarized the spirit of the times by writing: "There is something about the great mountains that enlarges men's souls and inspires them to do great things." Vreeland was an American inventor and manufacturer from New York and already in his forties. In successive summers between 1912 and 1916, he explored the mountains and achieved first ascents of two of the major peaks, Mt. Vreeland and Ice Mountain. He also reached the west side of the upper icefield on Mt. Sir Alexander and provided information and photographs which helped the Gilmour party in 1929. Fay and Vreeland corresponded regularly and used one another's notes and observations to solve the topographical puzzles of the area.

The next documented exploration came in the form of the Interprovincial Boundary Commission. The Imperial Act had defined the eastern British Columbia boundary as extending from the Canada–US border, along the Continental Divide, then due north from where the Divide met the 120th meridian. For years this boundary was drawn on maps without anyone knowing precisely where this meeting spot between the Divide and the meridian lay, nor whether the Divide crossed the meridian more than once. A commission was appointed to explore, survey and define the boundary, and work continued from 1914 until the final publication of the commission's findings in 1925. The director of the Alpine Club of Canada, A.O. Wheeler, represented the BC government, while R.W. Cautley represented the Alberta and Dominion governments. Boundary monuments were painstakingly erected at regular intervals, including on Intersection Mountain, where the Divide and the meridian were eventually found to meet.

The surveyors faced a little known and incompletely mapped area north of Jasper, but exceptions were the information from the 1914 Fay expedition, the 1914 Jobe–Phillips expedition and the 1906 Robert W. Jones maps for the Grand Trunk Pacific Railway. As early as December 1914, Wheeler contacted Fay, having heard from Brewster of the expedition's success. Wheeler asked for information on the Mt. Sir Alexander area and any places where the Fay party had approached the Divide. By January 1915, Wheeler had received details from Fay and was asking for a map. The 1914–15 map Fay and Brewster produced did indeed show the Divide in the Kakwa region, with uncanny accuracy, and the Fay article in volume VI of the *Canadian Alpine Journal* (1914–15) included a map of the Mt. Sir Alexander region. It is therefore puzzling that in the acknowledgements in the Boundary Commission report, Wheeler credited only the Jobe–Phillips map, indicating that it was the only detailed map of the area that had been published by 1922. Likewise, Wheeler referred to earlier surveyors having placed the 120th meridian on the maps incorrectly, just as Jones had done, and it seems likely that he knew of Jones's explorations, but the Jones map is not acknowledged.

Another sheep hunter who followed in Fay's footsteps was John Holzworth, who explored over three consecutive summers from 1923 to 1925. Holzworth too was a field assistant for the US Biological Survey. He too was inspired by Charles Sheldon, and communicated with Edward Nelson, who by this time was the chief of the survey. Holzworth's 1923 trip was the longest, beginning in the mountains on the south shore of the Peace River, and extending southeast to Kakwa. Holzworth was defeated by the rugged country southeast of the head of the Wolverine River that had so challenged the Fay party. When he couldn't penetrate this, he returned all the way north to Pouce Coupe, then circled southeast to Beaverlodge and proceeded from there up the Wapiti River. Despite the detour, his trip bore fruit, and he found and secured specimens of bighorn sheep, including one from between the Wapiti and the Murray rivers. Holzworth marked this site on his map, but unfortunately it had inaccuracies. The site can therefore not be identified other than to say it might have been near the headwaters of Kinuseo Creek. This would be the northernmost record of the species, for sheep are not known to occur in this drainage today.

In 1926, another explorer, Prentiss Gray, followed the southern section of Fay's route into the Smoky River drainage on a hunting trip. In 1927 and 1928, he undertook long expeditions which approximated the northern half of Fay's route, and helped to document its topography, features and sheep populations. Prentiss Gray was a successful New York banker who spent his summers in diverse global locations to pursue his passions for hunting and photography. He wrote detailed journals for his sisters. After his untimely death in a boating accident, they were lovingly preserved by his son Sherman, and eventually published by the Boone & Crockett Club as a coffee-table book, *From the Peace to the Fraser*. The title indicates that of all Gray's exploits, those in these northern Rockies were the most significant.

The Gray expeditions included some of the best-known names in big-game hunting in North America, and employed local guides (notably the Calliou family). In contrast with Fay, Gray travelled from north to south, starting at Hudson's Hope the first year and Grande Prairie the second. His routes were generally a bit east of Fay's route. He then headed west, crossed Fay's route and went through what is still known as Gray Pass, ending up near McBride. As far as is known, Gray was the first to describe and map this pass, in the Kakwa area, although R.W. Jones's 1906 map indicates he too had been there. The place fascinated Gray, and in 1928 he guided a railway engineer through it and proved the feasibility of the route for a railway. Had this become the rail outlet for the Peace region, Mt. Sir Alexander and Mt. Ida would nowadays rival Mt. Robson and the Lake Louise area in the public perception of the Canadian Rockies. For this work, Gray received a fellowship in the Royal Geographic Society.

Based on Fay's article in *Appalachia*, Gray made a large detour to see Kinuseo Falls and was duly impressed. His movie footage of the falls has survived. He carried onerous amounts of camera gear into the mountains, and some of the most endearing of his photos are of this seemingly out of place, cumbersome equipment being used on the mountain summits. Gray used Akeley movie cameras, which had been developed by Mary Jobe's husband.

Gray's trip was not simply Fay's in reverse. In fact, the two routes neatly complemented one another. After Fay and Gray, most of the salient features of the Rockies from Kakwa to Hudson's Hope had been succinctly described.

Mt. Sir Alexander and Mt. Ida were obvious magnets for climbers, but the isolation of the area and the long approach from the nearest departure points along the railway at Jasper or Mt. Robson delayed the first ascents. Jobe and some of her party members made attempts on Mt. Sir Alexander in 1914 and 1915 but they were not experienced mountain climbers and lacked appropriate equipment. Vreeland explored the western side of the high icefield in 1916 but made no attempt to climb the summit ridge. The first ascent was finally achieved in 1929. Mt. Ida waited even longer – the first ascent was in 1954 and this time the party arrived by plane, landing at the nearby Jarvis Lakes.

In the years after, the mountains slowly became more frequented, by hunters, trappers, scientists and surveyors. The Monkman Pass highway construction attempt of 1937–39 lay perpendicular to the Fay route, and helped identify the region's coal and natural gas resources, which subsequently were systematically researched and developed. The fossil fishes were formally reported in 1947, and many paleontologists have since then visited the internationally significant Fossil Fish Lake site in Wapiti Lake Provincial Park.

AFTER THE EXPEDITION

Fay had a distinctive writing style. As the party slowly worked its way northward along the Murray River, for example, the tedium they felt is sometimes tangible in the journal entries, but Fay could still lift himself above this to describe some glorious natural scenes. Loyal to the Biological Survey, he felt compelled to record his wildlife observations in the daily journal, and indicated in the 1956 introduction that this was why he had gone into such detail in it. Certainly his summaries, as expressed in his reports and subsequent published accounts, are more polished. But it is the journal, not the summaries, which provides the reader with a feel for the hardships and challenges of the trip, and thus the magnitude of its achievement.

In contrast to Fay's expansive style, the Brewster diary of the expedition is a model of terse notes that were pragmatic and relevant. It forms an excellent means of corroborating Fay's account, and functions as a reference when details in the Fay journal are not clear. Unexpectedly, it provides significant information that is unobtainable from the Fay journal, in part because Brewster's map sketches detail side trips and indicate campsites with some precision.

Along the northern part of the route, for example, the fact that they saw the Blue Lakes at the head of the Murray River, the sojourn on Albright Ridge, the ascent of Mt. Hermann, and the route up the Wolverine Valley and over the hill to Bullmoose Creek, all come alive thanks to Fred Brewster's attention to detail. Likewise the probability that Joseph, the "laughing Indian" at Moberly Lake, was Joseph Calliou, is confirmed through Brewster's having recorded him as Joe "Cayou."

In many ways, Fay was generous to a fault. Some explorers claim dubious discoveries or are apt to name geographical features after themselves or their relatives, friends or patrons. Fay took the opposite position. He modestly conceded that others had probably seen what his party was recording for the first time, and in some ways his first descriptions are all the more engaging as a result. In his 1956 introduction to the journal, which still deals largely with sheep distributions, he acknowledges the subsequent contributions to the issue by Vreeland, Gray, and Borden and Sheldon.

A possible corollary to this generosity of spirit was an exacting standard when it came to fellow explorers. A few years after the Fay expedition, in 1923–24, a voluminous article by Major Townsend Whelen appeared in four parts in *Outdoor Life* magazine, followed by two articles by Frank Conger Baldwin. They dealt with hunting in part of the area Fay had been through, including the Sheep Pass area in Kakwa. The articles implied that Whelen, and to a lesser extent Baldwin, had broken virgin ground. In his considered reply, printed in full in the January 1925 edition of *Outdoor Life*, Fay systematically destroyed any semblance of fact in Whelen's argument, citing 15 people or parties that had penetrated the area in question prior to Whelen and Baldwin's presence. He concluded: "To find truly 'virgin' country today is virtually impossible."

As for the man who most closely followed in Fay's footsteps, Prentiss Gray, who had shown Fay his stills and movies, it would be nice to think of these two valiant American explorers amiably comparing notes and reminiscing. Yet some of Fay's comments about Gray seem rather uncharitable, referring to the latter's trip to Kinuseo Falls as "hurried" in a March 1941 letter to the editor of *Natural History* magazine. In a 1957 letter to the secretary of the Canadian Board of Geographical Names, Fay was disparaging about Gray's naming habits and stated that Gray's 1932 *Geographical Journal* article on his trip contained errors. He also criticized the absence of specimens for the National Museum and implied that the pass Gray claimed to have discovered was already known to the railway surveyors, as they knew every pass in the region.

And when it came to the feature that really mattered the most to him, Fay brooked no trespassing on his turf. He and Brewster felt they had earned Mt. Sir Alexander, in part by their shorter 1912 trip. They realized in retrospect that they had erred in not claiming credit for it at the time. On July 14, 1914, Fay referred to the mountain in his journal as "our big peak." After their 1914 visit, they were ready to announce it, but found that Curly Phillips had guided Mary Jobe there in the same season. She was calling it Mt. Kitchi and singing the praises of this exquisite area. Brewster wrote to Fay,

> I hope you do not intend letting them steal that away from us as we first discovered it in 1912 and should have recorded it publicly then. I understand they were surprised to hear we had found it in 1912 and camped near it again this summer and photographed it.

With Brewster's encouragement, Fay steadfastly made his case. The articles of both Fay and Jobe appeared in the *Canadian Alpine Journal* of 1915. It appears that Fay won the popular battle, and his success in having the peak officially named Mt. Sir Alexander cemented this sentiment.

It must therefore have rankled that one of the few references to previous explorers in the Whelen *Outdoor Life* articles was to Mary Jobe. In his criticism of the articles, Fay was dismissive of Jobe's "short, hurried trip."

As with many explorers who were touched by the beauty of the Rockies wilderness in their younger days, Fay maintained an abiding interest throughout his life in the area he had explored. His subsequent writings are of necessity somewhat repetitious, but all convey the breathtaking amplitude of the expedition.

His initial report was obligatory, the Wildlife Report for the US Biological Survey. The 1915 article in *Appalachia* XIII, 3, read on April 14, 1915, to the American Alpine Club by Prof. Charles Fay, remains the definitive summary against which others are measured (at the time the club did not yet have its own journal). His article in the *Canadian Alpine Journal* 6, 1914–15, was also read to the American Alpine Club by Charles Fay. Entitled "Mt. Alexander," it dealt more with the Mt. Sir Alexander area and less with the expedition as a whole. Mary Jobe's article on the same mountain, which she called "Kitchi," appeared in the same journal.

Soon after the expedition Fay was communicating with Arthur Oswald Wheeler, founder and president of the Alpine Club of Canada, and with Frederick Vreeland, the fellow explorer who was tackling the same mountains from the west. They compared notes and peaks, were able through this means to clear up some remaining mysteries about the area's topography, and could calculate the latitude and longitude of prominent peaks by combining their observations. Fay and Vreeland made plans to meet in New York in February 1916; it is not known whether this meeting took place. One recently discovered copy of Fay's map contains barely legible 1915 pencil annotations by Vreeland.

Fay's 1925 rebuttal in *Outdoor Life* of the claims made by Major Townsend Whelen was lengthy and eloquent, bringing forth the historian in Fay and his fair-mindedness.

There is then a long break in the Fay record until the 1950s. The report on the last two weeks of the 1914 trip was written in 1956, along with an introduction, and it can be postulated that in thus completing the journal, he may have been preparing it for publication.

The most lavishly illustrated articles were the two-part series that appeared in *The Beaver* in summer and autumn of 1957, co-authored with Bradford Angier, a freelance writer who had moved to Hudson's Hope from near Fay's home in Massachusetts. The piece was called "The Big Mountain," and, as the title implies, it dealt mainly with Mt. Sir Alexander.

In 1959, Fay wrote to Gerry Andrews, surveyor general for BC, in a letter full of interesting tidbits, reminiscences and mutual acquaintances. At the age of 20, Andrews had started the first school at Kelly Lake. Fay enclosed a copy of his *Appalachia* article and clarified the process that had led to the naming of Mt. Sir Alexander.

During the few days spent at Hudson's Hope at the end of the trip, the Fay party had met two surveyors who had completed work on the Finlay River to the northwest. Fay had recorded one as Copley but hadn't recorded the name of the leader. Fay was an avid reader of *The Beaver*, and in 1957 he came across an article, "Ninety Years Later," written by Frank Swannell. He was amazed to discover that Swannell was the unrecorded surveyor, and a correspondence with both Swannell and Copley ensued. One letter to Swannell, politely chiding him on the absence of a Christmas card, was written in 1965, when Fay was in his eighties. A well-known photo of Swannell negotiating his dugout canoe through Long Canyon on the Finlay River is in the possession of the Fay family.

PLACE NAMES

One of Fay's notable legacies is the place names he provided for prominent features. In contrast to many explorers, he mostly avoided names of family members or associates and, instead, sought names that were descriptive (Surprise Lake, Fortress Mountain, Sapphire Lake) or that commemorated a worthy explorer, such as Alexander Mackenzie, the first white person to cross the continent north of Mexico, in 1793 (Mt. Sir Alexander). He added two Native names to the map for important features – Kinuseo Falls ("little fishes" in Cree) and Kakwa Lake ("Kakwa" is an approximation of the Cree word for porcupine, the original name for the lake), as well as Lake Wapamun ("mirror"). In fact, Fay and Brewster shared an interest in Cree etymology, and on one occasion Fay sent Brewster a Cree dictionary. Not all of Fay's names were accepted but some of the most prominent names in the region owe their existence to his initiative and to his perseverance with the Geographic Board.

Only two place names deviate from Fay's usual practice. Babette Lake, close to Kakwa Lake, commemorates "a young cousin who took an interest in my explorations." Mt. Cross is a memorial to Fay's friend and fellow expedition member Bob Cross, who was killed while volunteering in France in 1915.

Fay's correspondence with the Geographic Board of Canada was protracted. Soon after the completion of the expedition, he sent copies of his maps of the area to the Board, and had the support of A.O. Wheeler regarding the "Big Mountain." Alexander Mackenzie had passed 30 to 40 miles west of the massif, but had not seen it, due to intervening mountains. Fay was at the forefront of the sentiment that the mountain be named in Mackenzie's honour. Fay suggested Mt. Alexander, but this could have created confusion with Mt. Alexandra in Banff National Park. Wheeler argued for Mt. Alexander Mackenzie, supported by Charles Fay, the president of the American Alpine Club. This name was initially accepted before being changed to Mt. Sir Alexander in 1924.

In December 1915, Edward Deville, the chairman of the board, wrote to Fay, acknowledging the expedition's success, lamenting the death of Cross and suggesting that Fay might want to name a peak after his deceased friend. Fay replied quickly, suggesting that a mountain named Thunder Mountain be changed to Mt. Cross, and this change was initially approved.

Just prior to this, Fay had written Wheeler a letter, telling of his experiences in France, and of the death of Cross. Wheeler had replied: "We appreciate very greatly the splendidly humane instincts that have taken you and the late Mr. Cross on this work. Mr. Cross has died the death of a hero."

Wheeler, clearly touched, brought Cross's death to the attention of the Geographic Board, and in February 1916 he wrote to Fay, implying that it was his letter to Deville that had prompted the board's offer to Fay regarding Mt. Cross.

Unfortunately, much confusion about Mt. Cross ensued over the years. It appears that the co-ordinates of the peak originally so named were incorrect, and that Wishaw Mountain became the name in common usage. When the Canadian Board of Geographical Names (the later name of the Geographic Board) reappraised the situation in 1957, it decided to keep the name Wishaw Mountain and to apply "Mt. Cross" to an adjoining peak in the Kakwa region. Fay reluctantly lent his support to this.

At Fay's instigation, the name Kinuseo Falls was accepted in 1920, and "Kakwa" was also accepted, replacing the unofficial "Porcupine," which had long been in use. Following these successes, the secretary of the board, one R. Douglas, unwittingly guaranteed himself subsequent notoriety by pointing out in 1925 that Fay was lucky in having these four names accepted, "as the board generally looks with disfavor on names suggested by tourists." One can only wonder how Fay must have felt on hearing these sentiments.

THE NORTHERN MOUNTAINS TODAY

Fay's observations about the beauty of his route were shared by other visitors over the years, and as a result the first 640 kilometres (400 miles) the party covered are now protected in one long series of wilderness parks along the Continental Divide – from south to north: Jasper National Park, Willmore Wilderness Park, Kakwa Wildland Park, all in Alberta, and Kakwa Provincial Park in British Columbia. Modern adventurers can still enjoy the land and the wildlife as Fay did, dependent on their own resources as he was. From Yellowhead Pass to Kakwa Lake, a modern hike along the Continental Divide, partly west of Fay's route, takes a minimum of ten days, all through wild country with few visitors. A little farther north, between the Belcourt Valley and Wapiti Lake, much of the land is still wild, with occasional seismic lines and rough exploration tracks as evidence of more recent activity. It is only beyond here, nearing Tumbler Ridge, that dramatic change is encountered.

One of British Columbia's largest industrial initiatives was the Northeast Coal Project, which saw the development in 1981 of two large mines and the creation of the community of Tumbler Ridge, just above the "Big Flat," which Fay had described so vividly in 1914. The coal market collapsed at the end of the millennium, but subsequent revival led to the development of new mines. There is an enormous amount of Cretaceous coal lying in a band along the length of the eastern foothills of the northern Rockies. A multitude of coal licences have been granted, and only the remoteness of the terrain, the absence of infrastructure and the vicissitudes of the price of coal appear to stand in the way of the coal's eventual extraction. Some of these licences lie close to the Fay route, but they do not encroach upon it.

The Tumbler Ridge–Hudson's Hope section is one of the most developed parts of the Rockies. A flight over this section will show an expanding number of seismic lines, roads, gas wells and logged areas, as well as the coal mines and farms. Yet this region is large, and its wild areas are the most easily accessible in the northern Rockies. Monkman, Gwillim Lake, Sukunka Falls, Mt. Lemoray and Bocock Peak provincial parks provide enclaves of official protection. Visitors are beginning to discover this part of the Rockies, with its beautiful scenery, splendid waterfalls, new parks, expanding trail system and recently discovered dinosaur fossils and tracks – and the contrast it offers to the well-known national parks farther to the south.

The other area that has seen change is Grande Cache, on the northeast edge of Willmore Wilderness Park. The modern-day town of Grande Cache was developed as a planned coal-mining community in the late 1960s. It is laid out on a plateau downstream of the Sulphur Gates canyon where some of Fay's horses were briefly trapped during the river crossing. The original Grande Cache was named by Ignace Giasson, an Iroquois working for the Hudson's Bay Company post of St. Mary on the Peace River, who, in about 1820, established a large fur cache (storage depot) here while hunting and trapping west into British Columbia.

The Fay party reached here on July 25, 1914, and met Ewan Moberly, whose canoe they used to cross the Smoky River. The Moberly family were among the first permanent settlers – they and other Native families moved to the Grande Cache area in about 1910–11, after their relocation from the Athabasca Valley following the creation of Jasper National Park. The family has had a long association with exploration in the nearby Rockies (Adolphus Lake, near Mt. Robson, is named for Ewan's brother) and descendants still live at Grande Cache.

On the doorstep of Grande Cache is the spectacular Willmore Wilderness Park, which was designated in 1959 thanks in part to the lobbying of Fred Brewster. Following his 1912 and 1914 expeditions with Fay, Brewster frequently visited the area over a period of 40 years, guiding visitors and trophy hunters, and using many of the Native trails that he and Fay had followed. In a February 22, 1959, letter to Brewster, congratulating him on his role in the designation of the park, Fay reminisced about his favourite Mt. Sir Alexander area, "which being in BC is not part of this park. This is too bad as that area just off the map on the extreme northwest corner is so magnificent that it ought to be in this park." Fay would have been delighted that Mt. Sir Alexander is now a highlight of Kakwa Provincial Park, which was designated in 1987.

The majority of those who appreciate the northern Rockies today limit themselves to one or two segments per visit, and extended overland travel remains rare, largely because the terrain remains remote and challenging.

MODERN TRAVELLERS

Pioneer long-distance explorers like Fay have been succeeded by a few modern-day counterparts, and it is interesting to see how they fared. One of these was Chris Townsend, who achieved a reputation as Britain's foremost long-distance hiker and completed a remarkable trip in 1987. He walked the length of the Canadian Rockies, from the US–Canada border in Waterton Lakes National Park to Liard Hot Springs in the north. He recorded this journey in his book *High Summer*. He remarked on the significant contrast between the developed trails of the south and the difficulties he got into in the less developed (for the hiker) north. Armed with inadequate maps and questionable information, he struggled from Grande Cache, straying north rather than heading northwest. He got lost in the forested foothills for eight days and had to cross numerous canyons before finding a BC–Alberta boundary monument and thus locating his whereabouts. Days later, he was rescued by a pair of hunters.

After a brief respite in Tumbler Ridge, Townsend returned to his rescue point and hiked along the initial part of the old Monkman highway. Here, he got so absorbed in his walking that he forgot to detour the kilometre necessary to see Kinuseo Falls. Then he bushwhacked through the wet forest and deadfall of Hook Creek, in descriptions reminiscent of those of Fay in the same area 73 years earlier. Passing Hook Lake, he headed down the Sukunka, a route the Fay party had considered after one of their mountaintop reconnaissances. Townsend, however, had the advantage of roads and highways to walk on, and took just six days to get from the upper Sukunka to Hudson's Hope, after which he headed back into the wilderness.

A Californian, Peter Vacco, passed through the area in the late 1990s. His aim was to hike from the US–Mexico border to the Arctic, and he made this into a long-term project, resuming each spring where he had finished the previous fall. In his second year of hiking the portion covered by Fay, Vacco had some narrow escapes, first almost drowning while crossing the Narraway River (some distance east of Fay's route). When he reached Tumbler Ridge, he heard of the Monkman Pass highway epic of the late 1930s and became enthralled with this adventure. Displaying remarkable flexibility, Vacco changed tack and started hiking southwest through Monkman Pass, tracing the historic route. He built himself a raft to float down the Herrick River but got sucked under a logjam and again was almost drowned. He picked up his journey the following year.

In 1999, another long-distance traveller approximated much of Fay's route. Karsten Heuer embarked on an adventure to draw attention to the threats to the integrity of the Rockies ecosystem "from Yellowstone to Yukon." Travelling different sections of the route with different companions and sometimes alone except for the company of his faithful dog, Heuer skied from Jasper to Kinuseo Falls, then resumed his trip a few months later and canoed past Tumbler Ridge down to the Peace River before hiking north to the end of the Rockies. His travels have been recorded in his book *Walking the Big Wild: From Yellowstone to the Yukon on the Grizzly Bears' Trail.*

In summary, although these explorers and travellers approximated parts of Fay's route, or followed it exactly in places, no one has repeated the journey. It remains an epic adventure, along an enticing and awe-inspiring route, which can be mapped out accurately. It begs to be reattempted by a latter-day adventurer.

FAY'S LEGACY

Even now, almost a century after the Fay expedition, geography continues to dictate travel patterns. Highways are still confined to the few low passes through the Rockies. Few venture more than a day or two's travel from the highways. The Icefields Parkway ends at Jasper and the adventurous traveller who ventures north, on foot or on horseback, can still experience the land just as Fay did in 1914, at least as far as Tumbler Ridge. The southern trails still exist, the rivers must still be forded; the trackless wilds north of Kakwa still confound backpackers, the sheep and caribou still roam the same ranges. Glaciers have receded and forest fires have swept through some areas, but in the large expanse of protected parkland the mountains and valleys and rivers remain just as Fay described them. His journal was the first description of them and remains a timeless record.

Along the southern part of his route, Fay's journal records the very begin-
nings of the town of Grande Cache and the initiative of the pioneering
Moberly family, long before coal was discovered and developed. It is one of
the community's earliest records.

The northern half of Fay's route has changed: today there is farming in
the Peace River country and development of coal, forest and oil and gas
resources in the Foothills and around Tumbler Ridge. Here, Fay's journal
becomes a vital record of what once was, an historical legacy for a new
community establishing its identity and seeking its roots.

Tumbler Ridge was planted on the North American map out of nowhere
in 1981. In a region whose recorded history stretched back only to the time
of Alexander Mackenzie, it seemed initially that this new community in the
forested foothills had no history at all. However, research has revealed a fascinating historical human presence. Most visitors were transient; some settled
for various lengths of time. But Fay's written record remains, the first for the
area, and the way he described many of its geographical highlights establishes
his place firmly near the beginning of recorded history for Tumbler Ridge.

Edward Nelson of the US Biological Survey wrote to Fay:

> You have cleared up one of the blank spaces on the map of North
> America, which we have long desired information from. I congratu-
> late you on having made a successful expedition ... Many of your
> photographs are gems. You have my sincerest thanks from the Survey
> as well as my personal appreciation for your kindness in doing such a
> completely satisfactory job.

Indeed, he and his men had achieved this, but their legacy extends well
beyond this undoubted accomplishment. In being the first to write in detail,
and write well, about the magnificent mountainous country he travelled
through, Fay assured himself a place as a giant in the annals of the northern Rockies. His expedition serves as a timeless example of fortitude and
camaraderie, and enhances the cherished sense of place of those who are
fortunate to live in these foothills or who are in increasing numbers choos-
ing to visit these mountains.

Another of Fay's legacies is undoubtedly the apt place names he advanced
for notable features: Mt. Sir Alexander, Kakwa Lake and Kinuseo Falls, all
of them attractions for modern visitors.

One of the few who had penetrated the mountains before Fay was Major
C.F. Hanington, who along with Jarvis crossed the Rockies in the winter

of 1875 via what is now known as Jarvis Pass. They showed the CPR that the route was impractical for a railway. Fay was aware of their expedition and, in 1926, sent Hanington some photos of the area he and Jarvis had traversed 50 years earlier. Thanking Fay, Hanington concluded his letter by noting: "I won't bother you with a lot of stuff, which might interest you, or it might not; but is of little use to modern people, who don't give a Damn for what has happened in the past." How wrong he was!

One of the region's historians, Gerry Andrews, in his book *Métis Outpost*, writes of the Jarvis–Hanington expedition: "That epic journey should be prescribed reading for all Canadian high schools."

The same could be said for the Fay expedition. What would men like Jarvis, Hanington, Fay and Brewster give to know of the resurgence of interest in their beloved mountains, and the reverence with which their adventurous exploits are viewed today?

Fay more than achieved his three objectives. He collected many wildlife specimens for the Biological Survey and meticulously recorded his observations; he established the northern limit of bighorn sheep as it was known at the time; and he reached, described and named the "Big Mountain." But he also produced a thorough journal, prepared a detailed and largely accurate map with basic equipment, published numerous articles to share the information with others and ensured that all the data was carefully preserved in archives. When writing the introduction to his journal in 1956, Fay summarized his satisfaction with the expedition in a typically modest way:

> Having definitely located our "big mountain" and placed it on the map and having accomplished all of our objectives after five months going through difficult country and living off the land and all this without any accident to ourselves or serious one to the horses gave us the satisfaction of knowing that our trip had ended successfully.

Fay had the vision, plus the resources of time and money, to seize an opportunity available to few – to explore a new area and to share his discoveries with others. His thorough journal, his published articles and his lifelong interest in the area all attest that Fay recognized his responsibility to record his experiences for posterity and to provide a foundation for the historical record. We are enriched by his foresight.

INTRODUCTION TO JOURNAL OF S. PRESCOTT FAY OF 1914
EXPEDITION HUNTING SHEEP AND OTHER BIG GAME
BETWEEN THE YELLOWHEAD PASS AND THE PEACE RIVER ALONG
THE CONTINENTAL DIVIDE OF THE ROCKY MOUNTAINS
IN ALBERTA AND BRITISH COLUMBIA.

In 1912 and 1913 I went in north of Jasper and the Yellowhead Pass, down the Smoky River and over to Sheep Creek; from there over a high pass to the headwaters of the Kakwa River, Kakwa Lake and Jarvis Pass. From there we returned to Jasper after crossing the Smoky River at Grande Cache. As I was hunting for sheep in order to determine the northern limits of *Ovis canadensis* (the bighorn sheep) we went up all the tributaries of Sheep Creek and covered most of the high country. We did not hunt the mountains on the upper Sulphur River, but along the head of Sheep Creek where we knew sheep should be found we saw trails on the mountains but saw no sheep. We fully hoped to find sheep further north and expected to get some specimens around the head of the Kakwa River, but bad weather, heavy snows and lack of food forced us to return late in October without proving anything regarding the sheep question.

In 1914 we determined to cover the entire country between Jasper and the Peace River, so we set out from Jasper in June with twenty horses and grubstakes for four months. We would have to "live off the country" as regards meat, as we could only carry enough bacon for one month. We felt sure there would be enough game in the country to support our party of five men. Mr. E.W. Nelson, assistant chief of the Biological Survey (now the US Fish & Wildlife Service) in Washington, heard of my plans and wrote asking for my help in securing specimens for him for the National Museum of birds and mammals, because the area to be covered was still "a blank space on the map" as regards any scientific knowledge of its fauna. As I was glad to do this, he appointed me a "field assistant" and secured for me special permits for collecting any mammals or birds, in or out of season, from the chief game guardians of both British Columbia and Alberta, as our trip in following the Continental Divide would take us into both of these provinces. This change in our objective, from a big-game hunting trip merely, to

1

one combined with obtaining some information of scientific value, made the expedition of much greater interest to all of us. In carrying out the securing of specimens for him of the larger game animals we were able to do this and at the same time provide our party with the necessary meat for our sustenance and without killing any more game than our ordinary hunting licences allowed us. The above explains the reasons why I often went into such detail in my Journal. On my return in November, we shipped our collection of heads and skins of birds and mammals to Washington and I rendered a detailed report of each species found in the area, with full information as to its habits and range as well as all dates when seen.

To bring this area up to date (1956) regarding the sheep problem, mention should be made of three other expeditions during that same time and since then. From 1912 to 1916 Frederick K. Vreeland covered the west slopes of the Rockies from the Yellowhead Pass to the Peace River by ascending by canoe and on foot the Parsnip River to its source, going up many of its tributaries and also ascending the Fraser River in a similar way. He found no evidence of any sheep. North of the Peace River in the vicinity of Laurier Pass, however, he found Stone sheep (*Ovis stonei*) as did Borden and Sheldon in 1931. In 1926 Prentiss W. Gray hunted the south branches of the Wapiti River and found on the lower mountains bighorn sheep (*Ovis canadensis*). On our way north in 1914 in going through this area, but further to the west near the Continental Divide, we purposely did not hunt here although we felt we might find sheep, as we fully expected to get specimens further north and also because this area was too close to the known ranges of sheep along the streams on the north side of Sheep Creek and the Smoky and Sulphur rivers. So finding sheep here would not be of any particular value.

In 1931 Richard Borden and William Sheldon (son of the late Charles Sheldon, who contributed more than any other man to the knowledge of the varieties of North American sheep and their ranges) hunted the headwaters of the Sukunka and Pine rivers (south of Peace River) going in from Hudson's Hope. As we were unable to cover this corner in our 1914 trip because of the lateness of the season and with supplies exhausted, they wanted to make sure that there were no sheep in there. We had based our conclusions as to this area, in our report to the Biological Survey, from information given us by the Indians and trappers around Hudson's Hope who had hunted that entire country at the headwaters of the above two rivers, and had never seen sheep there, – only caribou, which require a different type of range. Borden and Sheldon also found no evidence of any sheep there. This upheld the results of our investigations and hunting of 1912, 1913 and particularly 1914, namely, that the only sheep in the mountains between the Yellowhead Pass and the Peace River were the bighorn (*Ovis canadensis*) and the only ranges where they were to be found, on the eastern side of the Continental Divide, were in the southern half of this area. As for the Stone sheep (*Ovis stonei*), they do not seem to come south of the Peace River. However, north of it they have been found around Laurier Pass by Vreeland, Borden, Sheldon and others. They also are found in the Butler Range ten miles northwest of Hudson's Hope, and in fact Stone sheep have been shot in recent years by Bradford Angier on the very edge of the north bank of the Peace River within one mile of Goldbar only thirty-four miles due west of Hudson's Hope.

S. PRESCOTT FAY

7 CEDAR ROAD

CHESTNUT HILL, MASS.

MAY 25, 1956

FRIDAY, JUNE 26. CLOUDY – WARM.

Fred had to go off for a week, so Jack[1] is coming along for a week or so and then Fred will hurry along and catch up to us near the Sulphur River. We left Jasper at 3.15 p.m. with sixteen pack horses – a big outfit – and five saddle horses. Most of the horses had been running for a month and they were a pretty wild bunch but we managed to pull out without much fuss. Bob Jones is coming as packer and Jack Symes, recently of the Northwest Mounted Police, as cook. Both are green at trail work but are a good type to get on to things quickly. Saw killdeer, killdeer plover, sparrows, juncos and robins along the trail which led past Swift's.[2] I stopped to ask him if he got the pictures I sent him last winter.[3] He settled here twenty years ago, long before the railroad was ever planned, and is quite an interesting character.[4] Several packs slipped and we had to stop to adjust them but on the whole the outfit went along finely. The horses were heavily packed, from 150 to 200 pounds apiece, and that kept them quiet. It seemed good to be on the trail once more and especially good to have Bob Cross along. We crossed the Snaring River and it was a mean stream, swift and deep, almost deep enough for the horses to swim, so that some of the packs got wet. At 8.15, about five hours on the trail, we camped at Moberly's flat, where the log house of the families of the Moberly half-breeds and some graves showed where they once lived.[5] There was some excitement unpacking the horses; lots of bucking and tearing around, but the only thing that happened was a broken halter. It was such a beautiful night that we didn't put up the tipi[6] but just unrolled our blankets on a little knoll looking up and down the valley, as pretty a camp site as could be found, and turned in for the night. It wasn't dark until about eleven, when we rolled into our blankets. Distance 15 miles, altitude 3500 feet.

SATURDAY, JUNE 27. CLEAR – HOT.

Up at 5, to find a beautiful day. Found the horses quickly although they had gone back a mile or two. Made use of an old log railroad construction stable and drove the horses into it, where we put the halters on and took off the hobbles. We found in the grass outside a mass of enormous mushrooms and we picked a large two-gallon pot full in a few minutes. I fried them for supper and they certainly were delicious. Nobody seemed to mind them at all! They were the largest I have ever seen. We packed in two pairs, Bob Cross and Jack Brewster working together, while Bob Jones and I paired off. At 9 we left, while Bob Jones went back across the Snaring after the horses we couldn't find yesterday. About noon, without event, we reached the Stony River[7] which was rising rapidly and after awhile Jack found a good ford and we all got across without wetting a single pack. On the other side we at last were on a trail and away from the wagon road and it seemed as if the trip had really begun. We camped in a beautiful little flat covered with flowers, the purple blossoms of the pea vine and the red tiger lilies predominating. In fact, these two flowers were massed everywhere. An hour later we heard bells and found Bob Jones across the river with the four horses and we showed him the ford. Now we have all but one of the horses we want and shall not bother about him. There are twenty-five horses feeding on the flat about the tipi and it makes quite a fine-looking camp. Having the tipi up makes things look homelike, and tomorrow night, if all goes well, we will be out of reach of civilization once more and well on our way to the head of the Sulphur. We had a merry chase lasting an hour rounding up the four head of new horses and Jack finally roped them from a saddle horse. Bob and I walked up the hill back of camp and got a fine view up and down the valley. Pyramid Mountain[8] showed up well with its coat of fresh snow and appeared well named. Found part of the skull and core of the horns of a ram. Distance 10 miles, altitude 3000 feet.

SUNDAY, JUNE 28. SHOWERY – WARM.

During the night two of our horses swam the river and a bunch of four others came over to our side and led our horses away down river, so it took Bob some time to locate them. Finally, the four horses swam back and then we had to drive four of our horses into the river, as we now have more than we need, so we drove them into the water but they came out on a bar in midstream and when we left two hours later they were still standing there. Got the horses packed without difficulty, as they are quieter now, and left at 10.30, on the trail at last. It led through small growth of Jack pine on a ridge back from the river with here and there some very steep-sided "coulies"[9] to go down into and out again. One bad piece of muskeg afforded the only difficult place and it was a mean stretch while it lasted. Today the predominating flowers were the paint brush and wild rose, and they were everywhere. We had several short, heavy showers and one came with a terrific thunderstorm and the lightning struck right over the top of our heads so that Bob Cross felt it distinctly. Then it turned cold quickly and we had a terrific hailstorm, the stones stinging our hands, and the horses so much that they refused to face it and turned into the brush back-to. There was lots of down timber but much of it had been cut away last year. The trail was one that probably the Moberlys used for years on their hunting trips. Only one pack horse slipped all day long. Saw lots of moose tracks, and some goat wool on a tree, also a lick in the mud near the trail. Made camp at 4 p.m., five and a half hours on the trail, distance 12 miles, altitude 3500 feet, on a little flat by the river with plenty of fine feed for the horses and tipi poles. The rabbits were so thick that they ran around the tipi and gnawed at our grub pile almost between our feet, – quite a sight. I got several fine pictures at six or eight feet focus. Quite a lot of excitement was caused by a grizzly and her cubs coming down to the opposite bank of the river. We were attracted by the cub squealing, – apparently the old lady had hit him over the head. They ran into the spruce and while we watched for them to come out a goat appeared just above (not over 400 yards from us) and went along the edge of the cliff, frightened probably by the bear scent. He soon disappeared in the timber above and the bears never showed up again although we watched for them a long while. They must have stayed in the timber as they could not have come out without being seen, as bare rock slides were on both sides and above. It certainly was an interesting afternoon. Now, while I am writing, the hares are running about me and one is eating grass within an actual distance of three feet of my body! I never saw them thicker or tamer before. There must be lots of young ones around. This is certainly a good game country, as there are deer, moose, sheep, goat and bear tracks all around us. This is a pretty spot on the river. Across the cut bank is steep and about 400 feet high, with seams of poor-looking coal along it. If we were across we would be burning it for fuel. A duck, apparently a goosander,[10] flew up the river. Saw sharp-tailed grouse along the trail. Soon things began to get interesting. As I was looking at the high cut bank for signs of coal the first thing I knew was that there were two sheep, – a ewe and a yearling, hard at work licking the rocks about 200 feet above the river, just in front of me. Shortly an upward current of air brought them my scent and they ran up about 100 feet before they turned to look at me from a broken crag. It was wonderful the way they went up the side of what looked like a sheer rock cliff. On closer inspection it was possible to see little footholds here and there. I ran back to camp to tell the others and found Bob had picked up a bunch of eight ewes and lambs with his glasses on a mountain several miles off. As soon as the sheep got to a place just under the top of the bank, our former friend the goat appeared headed for the sheep. Awhile ago we were expecting to see an encounter between the goat and the grizzly, – now it looked as if there might be something between the goat and sheep, but as the former came over the face of the cliff the sheep backed away and the goat went down toward the river, not coming within fifty feet of them. It was an interesting sight to watch them eye each other and then to see the sheep turn around and move off, leaving undisputed the way to the lick below. The goat descended very rapidly and stayed at the lick an hour before he continued over the face of the cliff, going with the greatest of ease over the most impossible looking places, finally disappearing in the timber beyond. The sheep were the most forlorn-looking objects I ever saw as they were in the process of shedding and they appeared moth-eaten. There are a dozen spots on the face of the cliff where little rocky trails and footholds lead down to the licks. The sheep continued up and soon lay down under a clump of spruce trees under the bank, and at dark they were still there. The goat looked not white but his coat was stained yellowish, while the sheep were extremely light coloured. Certainly we are in the midst of the game country and soon ought to have fresh meat. Never before have I seen sheep, goat and grizzly bear within an hour of each other and all within range of a long shot. The rabbits soon became a pest and gnawed away at pack covers and the grub pile right at our feet. Often we could count twenty or more within a few feet of us. Certainly a remarkable camp! Heard a red-bellied nuthatch.

MONDAY, JUNE 29. CLEAR – HOT.

We awoke to find a beautiful day. Last night we covered up everything with pack covers carefully and weighted the sides and top with heavy logs to keep the rabbits out and hung our boots up. But in spite of the trouble they carried off the grease pot and mush pot, – the latter we were unable to find at all. They came into the tipi and pulled out Bob's lash rope for his bed and gnawed it through in a dozen places. He was wild this morning. Bob Jones laid his gauntlets down last night during supper and when he went to pick them up they were almost gone, – this morning there was nothing left but the buttons! Pretty hungry lot of hares. The horses were nearby and before we ate breakfast they were driven into camp and tied up, ready for an early start. Left at 9.45 and all day the horses went well, only one pack slipping. Went through several bad pieces of muskeg, but on the whole the trail was good, going through park-like groves of Jack pine and poplar. Thought we saw goat on another cut bank a mile above camp where a swift creek came in on the east side. Saw golden eagles, a horned owl etc. In a muskeg we came upon a pair of solitary sandpipers, where they apparently had a nest or young, as they flew around me in a great excitement, giving a soft "peep" continually, now lighting on the edge of a little pool, now on the branches of a spruce tree. It was an interesting as well as a pretty sight. There is very little known about their nesting habits, and I would like to have stayed around to watch them longer. We came upon a cow moose in the low willow brush and for a long time she stood (about 300 yards away) watching our outfit go by. We found on the same flat a fine camping spot with tipi poles waiting for us and good feed for the horses, right on the Stony River. Bob and I walked up the trail a mile but saw no game, – only tracks of moose and deer. Some fresh horse tracks going both ways, so someone has been down here recently and turned back. Morse and Hutchinson, Forestry Department men whom we met last summer at Robson,[11] have their names on a tree August 8, 1913.

Travelled five hours, distance 15 miles, altitude 4000 feet.

TUESDAY, JUNE 30. HOT – BRIGHT.

Another wonderful day, although very hot. Last night it was quite cool so that the water in the pail froze, – wonderful for sleeping. All the mouse traps that Bob set out last night were found except one. Probably a hare stepped in and walked off with it! Forgot to say that the cow moose we saw yesterday was very light coloured and the porcupine was very black except his tail, shoulders and head, which were tawny. Left about ten and the trail all day was the finest I ever saw, mostly through park-like groves of Jack pine. We came to the other trail coming in from Rock Lake[12] about noon.

The country looked familiar and here and there I recognized a mountain but saw no landmarks along the trail. Camped about four, after six hours on the trail; distance 15 miles, altitude 4400 feet. All along on both sides and ahead are wonderful-looking sheep hills. Saw a deer and a cow moose with twin calves close by each other in the same willow covered muskeg. The former was wild and jumped quickly but the moose watched our outfit a long while before she ran, followed by her two calves. Camped on a little spruce point, a wonderful vantage point to look over the sheep hills but no level spot to put up a tipi. Lots of mosquitoes around but they aren't as vicious as those at home. Shot two male and one female Franklin grouse,[13] all in beautiful spring plumage. There were no young birds around. Also got an American three-toed woodpecker. Saw Canada jays,[14] myrtle warbler and white crowned sparrow. Spotted one sheep on the hills about five miles away, probably a ram. Today was an awfully hot day – a real scorcher – on the trail and we were glad to make camp and sit around in the shade. Turned in without the tipi, rolling up in our blankets under the spruces.

WEDNESDAY, JULY 1. BRIGHT – HOT.

Left about the usual time, – 9.45. Saw no game at all. Birds seen were juncos, some kind of owl with two nearly full grown young, Canada jays, Franklin grouse, female, spotted sandpiper and white-crowned sparrow. The trail was very different from yesterday; – some bad muskeg but nearly all day we were in bad down timber, nearly bad enough to call for an axe. In some places the timber was large; in others the ground was criss-crossed a foot high with small, two-inch Jack pine and spruce, – too small and springy to break, it would just fly up every time you stepped on it. Everybody soon got in a bad humour and it was not until we got supper that we were in a peaceful frame of mind. Bob saw two more sheep on a hill north of the trail. Shot a pine squirrel and Canada jay. Bob and I spent the rest of the afternoon skinning birds. Signs of beaver near camp. Moose and deer and bear tracks along the trail. Camped at 3.15, five and a half hours on trail; distance 12 miles, altitude 4700 feet. The sandflies put in an appearance at sunset. Did not put up the tipi. The strawberry blossoms are everywhere and in about two weeks more there ought to be lots of strawberries around. From the looks of the grass in the meadows the snow hasn't been gone about here for more than two weeks. Yesterday we passed a creek coming in from the north and today about three miles below our camp tonight a heavy creek came in from the northwest. Right here is another creek (probably Deer Creek,[15] the one we are looking for) coming from the north. Just before rolling into my blankets I listened to the beautiful song of a hermit thrush, – a wonderful song to hear by the banks of a rushing stream far off in the mountains. There was no other sound except the tinkling of the horse bells from the meadow nearby. Everybody suffered from the mosquitoes during the night and hardly anyone got much sleep.

THURSDAY, JULY 2. BRILLIANT – HOT

Heard red-bellied nuthatch and hermit thrush after breakfast. Another scorching hot day, destined to be an ill-fated one. Left about 9.30 and most of the day the trail was fine, through open Jack pine timber where the footing was dry and good. All along were familiar spots, as two years ago I was over this part of the trail with Fred Brewster and Beau Gaetz[16] on our way to the Porcupine lakes.[17] Saw Canada geese, mallards, golden-eye ducks, juncos and Canada Jays. No game sighted but tracks and signs of moose, deer, bear and sheep. It was a hot day and the horses came along slowly. The upper Stony River is pretty country, fine rocky mountains with snow and ice on one side and fine-looking sheep mountains on the other. For a day the down timber is bad and country all burnt, but fine, open green timber prevails. Goat ranges on one hand and sheep hills on the other, with moose and deer in the valley, as well as bear. We have been looking for a certain spot for two days where our trail forks but not until 3 p.m. did we find that we had passed it about twenty miles back. Jack has never been through here, – I came two years ago – so that is the reason we couldn't find the other trail. Now we know we have gone too far, as we are close to the head of the Stony and are camped at the spot from where we crossed the Stony summit[18] over to the Smoky[19] waters two years ago; so tomorrow we will have to go back and return through all the down timber once more. The mosquitoes are terrible and we are almost eaten alive, but it is just one of the numerous incidents of trail life. It's hard to keep from thinking of the luxury of home life with wire-screened porches, but such thoughts won't do here! Bob Jones and Jack Brewster climbed a hill about 1500 feet above camp and saw seven goats (three billies). They were shedding and presented a very moth-eaten appearance. They saw no sheep hills, only wonderful goat ranges. Returned about 10.30 through the brush. The horses have taken the back trail and we may have trouble in locating them tomorrow. Bob and I suffered misery after supper skinning mice and squirrels, being nearly devoured by the mosquitoes. Distance 12 miles, altitude 5000 feet.

FRIDAY, JULY 3. BRILLIANT – HOT.

Sleeping was bad again last night, as the mosquitoes were terrible. However, my sleeping net was a lifesaver and I managed to get a good night's rest. Symes seems to suffer more than anyone and has hardly slept for two nights. It is absolutely necessary to keep on gloves and a head-net and keep in the wind or in the smoke of the fire to be able to rest in peace. I owe an apology to these mountain pests for not giving them due credit for their energy. I said they were not vicious, but now I realize that mosquitoes never were more so. Heard a pine warbler and saw a beautiful pair of harlequin ducks at close range. They were swimming in a "sloo"[20] close by the river. There is a beautiful glacier and mountain[21] west of here about six miles where the Stony River heads.

It is next to impossible to appreciate this ideal little spot on account of these pests. Bob went off to get the horses at six o'clock and was gone all day while we sat around unable to do anything on account of the mosquitoes. It was nothing to count fifty or a hundred on a man' s leg and back at a time. Made a smudge down by the river and the combination of the smoke and a fresh breeze from the glacier down the valley just about made it possible to exist. The heat was terrific. Two female and one male harlequin duck were swimming in a "sloo" and I shot the latter for the collection. He was in beautiful full plumage. Curiously enough the male golden-eye seen at close range the other day was in immature plumage or else had already moulted. At 3.45 Bob arrived with all the horses but Pat. He found them in three different bunches, some as far as the previous camp across the river. He had a hard day of it, with nothing to eat since last night. At 5.15 we pulled out and I took the lead and at 9.15 we reached our old camp, having done in four hours what it took five and a half hours before, but this time we drove the horses as fast as possible. The only event was seeing a beautiful swan swimming gracefully in the river. I had not realized they were ever seen up here in the mountains but Jack said he saw two at Jasper in June 1913. Hardly any mosquitoes around and we all had a wonderful sleep, rolled up in our blankets in the brush. Distance 12 miles, altitude 4700 feet.

SATURDAY, JULY 4. BRILLIANT – HOT.

No rain after all, last night, although it looked showery about eleven o'clock. Another broiling hot day. Left about ten and came through all the miserable timber once more. The Stony River was very high as a result of these hot days and warm nights after the heavy snowfall and the back water was over the trail in many places back from the river. There were one or two bad spots where the trail cut down close to the riverbank and was covered with the dirty water so that it was only guesswork where the bank ended and the river began. Fortunately, the horses were not cranky and we got by without mishap. It would have been just like one of them to have jumped into the river and swum to the other side, followed by some others, as happened to us two years ago. Then, it was the middle of August and the river was lower, so there were little "sloos" all along. Now the meadows are so flooded that it looks like a big lake. Saw spotted sandpiper, kingfisher, juncos, Canada jays. The latter two we see daily. Some kind of a hawk lit in a tree nearby but I couldn't tell what kind. We reached camp after four and a half hours, – distance 12 miles, altitude 4400 feet. Bob and Jack went up so-called Deer Creek and after a short distance the trail improved. Four days ago Jack decided it hadn't been used for a great many years but he didn't go up far enough. Now we know this is the right trail and tomorrow will bring us up to the summit and over to the Sulphur River[22] headwaters and in the midst of the sheep country. Although we have lost four days we can make up for lost time provided we have any luck with the sheep. It will be an interesting hunt for a pair for the Biological Survey[23] to determine what species range around here north of the Athabasca River.[24] Pat, the lost horse, has gone on ahead of us, as his tracks are plain in many places, and probably he is in Jasper by this time. Fred may head him off and bring him back as he is due here any day now. Heard a ruffed grouse drumming today and saw several young rabbits and fluffy young grouse.

SUNDAY, JULY 5. HEAVY RAIN – COLD.

Left early – before 9 – and the weather looked very bad. Within half an hour the rain began and all day long until late afternoon it poured hard. The brush was wetter than I ever saw it before. My rain shirt kept me perfectly dry except from my knees down, which of course were soaked. We were all as cold as could be and didn't enjoy the day a bit. It was too cloudy to see the mountains and the trail was so old and dim that it was nearly impossible to follow, so most of the time we were pushing our way through muskegs covered with a growth of willows about four feet high. The only way to keep partly warm was by walking. After the last few hot days it didn't seem possible that it could be so cold. The changes are quick and sudden here. However, it was a great relief as I was done up by the heat. We finally came on a long willow flat and found to our surprise the stream was flowing toward us, – where it goes to is more than we know, as it surely does not flow into the Stony toward which it heads.[25] Signs of old camps and tipi poles showed it was a great hunting ground once of the Crees,[26] long since given up. At 1.30 made camp in a spruce grove where the trees were about two to three feet thick and high; up here, where they grow slowly, they are probably four to five hundred years old. Unpacked in the downpour and put up the tipi, then the weather cleared and the sun came out. It was fine to dry off. After a meal Bob and I climbed a ridge about 1000 feet above camp and found on all sides of us as fine sheep country as the hills in the valley of the Brazeau River.[27] Heavy sheep trails all mossed over showed that once the sheep were plentiful. No sheep or recent signs appeared. We plan to hunt ahead tomorrow and then take the outfit over the summit to the Sulphur River. Distance 10 miles, altitude 5800 feet.

MONDAY, JULY 6. COOL – SHOWERY.

It stormed soon after we were up but it cleared immediately and we started off for the day to hunt. Bob went with Bob Jones, intending to go down this valley about two miles and then cut across the range over to the valley beyond and return by following it down and back over by the summit of this stream and the Sulphur. I went off with Jack B. over the summit. We were among the finest of sheep hills all day, yet never saw a sign of any sheep nor even a fresh track. It was discouraging work, as it was a strenuous day, and when we once started for home we came at a good pace, yet it took us over two and a half hours before we reached the tipi, – glad to be back after our first day's hike over the hills. We saw horned larks, white crowned sparrow, golden eagles and beautiful pair of willow ptarmigan, the male bird being very red indeed. The finest thing in these mountains at this time of year is the quantity and variety of wildflowers, which grow in profusion everywhere. Probably the prettiest of all is the mountain forget-me-not, and it was a sight that I shall always remember to see these little blue flowers all over the hillsides. Then there were patches of buttercups, the yellow contrasting with the patches of the purple flowers of the wild pea vine. A flower that grows like a hyacinth and has blossoms like sweet peas grew in large numbers. Lots of strawberry blossoms and heather, also flowers like strawberry blossoms. One of the prettiest sights of all was the little purple flowers that grew in clumps of green moss always on the bare rock slides.[28] In fact, most of these flowers grew among rocks where there was scarcely any vegetation at all. The only animal life we saw was now and then a ground squirrel[29] and a large porcupine, very black except for his tawny quills. He was very tame and we watched him at a few feet scuttle through the willow brush. No signs of Fred, which seems queer. Bob and Bob Jones returned at 9.30 soaked to the skin, miserable and cold, having climbed all over the mountains and seen what we saw, – fine sheep hills but no sign of life.

TUESDAY, JULY 7. COOL – SHOWERY.

Yesterday on our return Jack and I saw fresh sheep tracks on the side of the mountain beyond camp where Sunday Bob and I had seen well worn old trails, so it looked as if some sheep were around. I made up my mind it was worth investigating, so off Jack and I went at 9.55 and at 10.55 I had killed three fine rams. The largest one had horns 38 and 39 inches, respectively, with a base measurement of 16 and 17 inches; the next was 31½ and 29½, 17½–18; the third 29 and 29½, 15¾ –16.

As we came over a shoulder Jack and I both dropped on our knees simultaneously, for there on the slide rock about 400 yards away was a sheep. Jack put the glass on him to find a good ram. Then we backed down a way, circled the hill and came up on a ridge where he would be below and about 100 yards off. I crawled up and there was a ram, but not the same one.

I fired and wounded him badly. Then another one appeared and I fired again, but missed twice before the third shot took effect. In the meanwhile other sheep appeared and ran off to our left. Then Jack suddenly said, "Look at that big one." Sure enough, not fifty yards off were three rams, – a yearling, a four-year-old and a buster, the leader of the flock. I had emptied my gun, so I reloaded quickly, running up the hill as the rams disappeared from sight, shortly reappearing further off. I fired and they ran, then fired again and missed, but the third time the big ram fell. I had hit him far back in the hind quarters as he was trying to run off. None of them needed to be shot over, as they were all vitally shot, and by the time I had reached them, one after another, they were dead. It was all over so quickly and I was so successful in getting some fine rams for the Biological Survey at Washington that it hardly seemed possible. Jack was as pleased as I was. They were all fine heads – one particularly so – the kind that I have been after for three years. Jack returned to camp for the others to help skin and cut up the sheep and while he was gone I measured them, and climbed to the ridge above me, where I could look down the whole length of the valley to the distant mountains on the Athabasca River. I looked in the other direction, and there on the ridge above me, outlined against the sky, were three of the five remaining rams (there were eight in the flock). It was a wonderful sight to be up among the sheep hills and fine mountains looking down into the valleys on one side and on the other to have three fine rams walking along the skyline, now disappearing over the edge, only to reappear again. For half a mile I watched them until finally they went out sight, not to be seen again. There is no grander or wilder scene than a flock of rams among the rocks. The flowers were beautiful on this ram pasture and everywhere were the beautiful little forget-me-nots. A bird flew around, – new to me, – very similar in build to a thrush, back grayish, long tail, but no spots on his breast. Soon Jack returned with Bob and we set to work measuring the sheep. Then Bob Jones and Symes appeared leading three horses, which they left below the rock slide in the timber. It was three hours work before the carcasses were ready to be put on the horses. The smell of the fresh meat frightened them so we blindfolded them as we packed the meat. The three men led the horses back to camp as Bob and I followed, carrying the remaining odds and ends. I found a fine set of horns and top of skull which the Indians had apparently cut off and left on the mountain. It looked several years old. Three horses, each loaded with a carcass and a fine head, made a great sight. The rest of the day was spent in skinning heads, salting scalps, cutting up the meat and getting the work underway. We celebrated this our first event (the twelfth day out) with a draught of HBC[30] rum.

WEDNESDAY, JULY 8. COOL – CLOUDY.

We all started early with the work on hand. The most interesting discovery of all was that the sheep that we plan to send to the Biological Survey has an incipient case of lump jaw. The only other locality where this seems to occur is in the Klappan region of the upper Cassiar Mountains in British Columbia,[31] where the Ashcroft Trail[32] runs through, and some think it has been introduced by the cattle. The lump on the jaw was prominent but the case was not sufficiently advanced to have the teeth turning black and falling out. The other two rams were OK,– only the old one had his teeth well worn down on one side from age. He was probably nine or ten years old, – the others, five and seven, respectively. Last night I forgot to say we had a feast of fresh liver and kidney and after our two weeks' steady diet of bacon and beans we ate all there was.

THURSDAY, JULY 9. COOL – CLOUDY.

The work continued again today. We salted the hides yesterday and now they are OK. We are preparing all the meat that it is possible to cut off the bones, by a formula – 3 lbs. salt, 4 tablespoons allspice and 5 of pepper, well mixed and rubbed on the moist flesh, off which are cut all sinew, muscle, tissue and enveloping membranes. This is hung to dry in the wind and sun, if not too hot. When thoroughly dry we will pack it in alfocuses [sic; probably 'alforjas,' 'saddlebags'] to be used later on as a reserve supply. Now between our bacon and cured meat, we have about 200 pounds, enough to last five men six weeks. However, this is for reserve only and we will get all the fresh meat possible.

Nothing of interest seen or heard today. Jack left on his saddle horse with the heads and hides packed on Punch, intending to go to Horseshoe camp tonight, and if he doesn't meet Fred he will continue on down the Stony and find out what the trouble is. Had a fine feast of marrow bones and soup of rice and sheep tongues! The mountains were beautiful in the late afternoon light and we all sat outside as the shadows lengthened.

Total, second week, 125 miles.

FRIDAY, JULY 10. COOL – SHOWERS.

This fine, cool weather continues, good for drying the meat. Some mosquitoes around but not enough to make life miserable. Attended to the meat and did the chores around camp so as to have everything ready when Fred returns. Bob went after the horses, to see if they are all right, and returned about noon with a moulting adult white-tailed ptarmigan which he killed with a rock, and a shed caribou antler. Bob says it has both the characteristics of the woodland, from its palmation, and of the Osborn, from its general shape, but does not resemble the barren ground species.[33] Just as we were getting dinner ready Fred appeared, having come from Jasper in two and a half days. He met Jack and camped with him last night. The Stony was so high that he had to wait five days before crossing. The Athabasca is higher than in years. We walked up the hill behind camp to show Fred the "ram pasture." Saw the most wonderful rainbow – a double one – that I ever saw, a complete circle, not 200 yards away. Dug a large chipmunk out of his hole for the collection.

SATURDAY, JULY 11. WARM – CLEAR.

Last night as I walked through the big spruces at twilight, which was about 9.30, the mountains were beautiful in the late afternoon light. It was quite still except for the rushing of the creek below. Here and there the hares bounded up and down the hill. Suddenly a note fell on the evening air and the woods were filled with the wild, vibrant song of the hermit thrush. Such beautiful, ventriloqiual notes amid such surroundings can be better imagined than described. Another good day and Bob and I left for the day at 9, not returning until 8 in the evening. Had an extremely interesting day.

Before we had been gone long, just at the edge of the timberline we heard a grunt. It sounded like a bear but turned out to be a cow moose, not 100 yards away. I walked toward her to get a picture, but she turned and ran. We kept on all day; were in the finest of ram country. Saw what looked like a bear on the top of a mountain a long way off and we went after him, but found he was nothing but a large marmot on top of a rock. Shot two birds, one a kind of sparrow,[34] the other a grey-crowned leucosticte. The former has a beautiful song with a thrill to it. Bob nearly stepped on a willow ptarmigan on her nest, high up about 8000 feet, on a rock ridge. She left it but we chased her back and she sat on her ten eggs while I photographed her. We lit a fire from the dead boughs of the summit balsams and boiled a pot of tea and ate a slice of bannock before we went on. At 4 we reached our farthest point, a rock peak overlooking one of the finest sheep valleys and prettiest spots imaginable. The upper half was a beautiful green pasture, while lower down the spruce and balsams dotted the landscape which was backed by fine rock mountains. This is the true head of the Sulphur. Came around the mountain by a pass and returned home by the old Sulphur trail, well worn and extremely old.[35] Saw two rams, one small and one medium, in the far valley, and nearer home saw a yearling or a two-year old which we watched for a long time to make sure it was not a ewe. Returned to a fine supper of corn bread and roast mutton, – signs of Fred's presence in camp! Saw golden eagles, sparrow hawk[36] and sparrows; also four dark porcupines, – three at one spot.

SUNDAY, JULY 12. HOT – BRILLIANT.

After five days' stay we decided, as long as the meat is cured and the country covered as far as the sheep are concerned, it is time to move over the summit and camp near some hills that look like good ranges for ewes. We got started at 10.15. Alice kicked up a big row by bucking at the outset and tearing through the timber, trying to get rid of her pack, but she found that it was too securely put on. The horses were feeling good and pretty wild after their long rest by themselves away up on the mountain side. The summit was a mass of wild flowers, – each day we seem to find a new kind blooming, the variety is so great. However, nothing can compare with the mountain forget-me-nots that cover the hillsides with their little clusters of blue flowers, among the bare rocks as well as in the green meadows. Two things I shall always associate with these sheep hills, one is the forget-me-nots, the other the sweet song of a species of yellow-crowned sparrow which I am unable to identify. These two seem inseparable, for the song is always heard in the alps where these flowers abound. As we came over the summit the trail improved, becoming very heavy, showing that in years past there were many Indians hunting through here. Saw lots of willow ptarmigan, the male birds being in fine plumage, though from the specimen I shot they are moulting, not having assumed their complete summer plumage yet. We had a fine view way down the Hay River[37] for it heads here. We came over the summit, finding a tremendously well-beaten trail, the main one between the Athabasca Valley and the Grande Cache on the Smoky River. Made camp after four hours having come about 10 miles, altitude 6100 feet, on the exact summit between the waters of the Sulphur and Hay rivers. We can look way down each valley and it is a beautiful spot, fine open country and lots of feed. I spent three hours skinning birds while Bob and Fred climbed a mountain, only to find good sheep country with no signs of any kind of any living creature, – very discouraging.

Saw a buffalo skull along the trail.[38] The mosquitoes are frightful tonight and are nearly eating us alive. The sunset tonight was certainly magnificent, very brilliant and one of the most beautiful combinations I have ever seen.

MONDAY, JULY 13. WARM – OVERCAST.

There seem to be quantities of ground squirrels all through this country. A grizzly bear sometime recently has been through here digging them out of their holes. It was showery when we awoke this morning and I was rather glad, as I felt ready for a day of rest, for we have had none since we left Jasper, – either being on the trail, hunting or working in camp every day. However, it looked clearer so Fred and I set out leaving the two Bobs behind to go in another direction (to the main valley of the Sulphur) on their saddle horses. We didn't get started until late, about 9.30. Hunting sheep in stormy or wet weather is only wasted time, as they are lying in some shelter or lee and not feeding, and besides, it is difficult to see far on cloudy days with the glasses. We went down the trail about two miles and then up the hills through the down timber, for the whole valley of the Sulphur has been burned over. It was a steady steep climb for an hour or two before we reached the top of the first ridge. Scattered here and there were old sheep signs, a year or two old, an occasional old track and a few trails over the slide rock and grassy summits, but nothing recent. We reached the top of a hill about 8000 feet (2000 feet above camp and sat down to eat our bread.[39] We overlooked miles and miles of magnificent sheep country, both ram and ewe ranges of the finest kind. Below us was a large valley with small side valleys, all fine places for ewes, well out of the way, and almost inaccessible, yet no signs of any sheep. However, it is far away the most likely looking spot of all we have yet seen for ewes. An old trail, quite heavy, ran through it and we thought it was the pack trail over to Trail Creek and the Grande Cache, but when we later investigated we discovered it was a very old hunting trail, probably used by game too. We came off the mountain and through a couple of miles of frightful down timber, walking and jumping logs to the valley below where we struck the main trail, and two hours later were back in camp feasting on corn bread, oatmeal, tea and stewed peaches, a perfect meal after a long, hard day in the hills. Saw golden eagles, a sparrow hawk and white-tailed ptarmigan at 8000 feet. Fred baked a lot of bread yesterday and it is a great change after a long spell of bannock.

TUESDAY, JULY 14. COOL – RAIN.

Robin around camp as well as a song sparrow singing this morning, which seemed very homelike. There are numbers of willow ptarmigan close to camp and we hear the male birds calling about ten o'clock at night, toward dusk, and again at daylight. Heard a flicker and a red-breasted nuthatch before we left. Decided not to hunt any longer for a ewe unless we see some especially fine country below. Left with the outfit at 10.30 and before we had gone two hundred yards, we got into a piece of muskeg. Alice broke her cinch and started to buck, giving one of the finest exhibitions I ever saw, not stopping until she had thrown off her packs which consisted of the flour sacks. These she deposited with much abandon in the muskeg, – however, without ill effects to their contents. She soon quieted down after leading everyone a merry chase before she was captured and then repacked. Our progress downstream was resumed. Saw tracks of a doe, moose and a large wolf, also saw a flicker, two sparrow hawks, female harlequin duck flying up river, chipping sparrows and numerous spotted sandpipers. There seems to be a number of them breeding here as we get lower down. We passed one especially pretty meadow which was a mass of buttercups and the bank enclosing it was covered with forget-me-nots, the yellow and blue forming a beautiful bit of contrasting colour. The rain started early in the afternoon and kept up until long after reaching camp. The trail was practically no trail at all, as it kept in the river bed and along the gravel flats all day. All kinds of incidents took place as we recrossed the river continually, and the water being extremely high, there were lots of deep holes. Several horses lost their footing and got their packs wet, but the funniest of all was Tommy jumping off a bank into an invisible mudhole. He went entirely out of sight and when he reappeared instead of being a white horse he had a black head as he had dived into a mud bank. He was an object of ridicule. Some of the horses were up here this spring and Fred let them lead the way and it was remarkable the way they crossed and recrossed the river and followed up the right gravel flats with no trail or guide. It was one of the most interesting cases of horse memory that I have ever seen. I have often heard that a horse will never forget a piece of country if he has only been over it once, trail or no trail, and this certainly was a good proof. Simeon did the leading but it was old Buzzard who led at the finish and crossed the river at an impossible-looking place and led us to a hidden flat, an old camping site of the Indians. We reached here at 5.30 after seven hours on the trail, making about 15 miles, the altitude being 4600 feet, as we came down about 1500 feet, the river dropping very fast here. Poplar, cottonwood and Jack pine all about, and we are once more in the so-called banana belt. Forgot to say that Bob said he saw a bluebird yesterday, also that I found a Jack pine growing above timberline near a clump of summit-stunted balsams at about 7500 feet, also that I found a balm of Gilead[40] tree at 6500 feet. There is an Indian grave on the flat here.[41]

The flat is covered with larkspur, just starting to bloom; also some paint brush blossoms. I forgot to mention that yesterday from the top of the hill we climbed we saw a big mountain about sixty-five miles distant northwest by north from us which we immediately recognized as our big peak[42] seen from the mountains at the head of Sheep Creek[43] September 12, 1912. About thirty miles away south by west from us rose the snowy top of Mt. Robson[44] and it looked magnificent, shimmering under the brilliant sun. This was a rare opportunity to compare these two giants, and though our big peak was double the distance we were from Robson it suffered nothing in comparison to it, which justified our former belief in its great height. We regretfully descended the mountain, as we knew it would be fully two weeks more before we should again catch a glimpse of the distant peak.

WEDNESDAY, JULY 15. COOL – BRIGHT.

Curious weather, – it is as cold as fall and blowing a gale this morning. Temporarily the rain has stopped; the thermometer only 44F at 9 o'clock. It was a fine night for sleeping. This has been a very old Indian camping ground and is still used as such. The flat has the only horse feed for miles and it is in the center of fine hunting grounds. It is a real boneyard here, as the ground is covered with bones of deer, moose and sheep. Found a very large ram horn in the creekbed, nearly as large as my best head. The blankets got so wet yesterday that we didn't get started until late, as we tried to dry them out first. Trail similar to yesterday, following the riverbed most of the time, crossing and recrossing. Nothing of interest occurred. Camped at 4.30 (only three hours on the trail) in burnt timber. Found a buffalo skull. Opened the sacks to dry contents, as the dried fruit, bacon etc. may get musty and spoil. Hares very tame again and I photographed them eating bacon etc. at six feet. One came to me and gnawed my trousers until he finally got his teeth too far in and bit me, – that settled it and I chased him away. Distance 6 miles, altitude 4000 feet. harlequin ducks, sharp-tailed grouse, spotted sandpipers, eagles.

THURSDAY, JULY 16. WARM – BRILLIANT.

We passed a sulphur spring, which accounts for the name of this river. The odour was very strong. The young of the sharp-tailed grouse seen were nearly half grown and the chipping sparrows able to fly. Left about ten, down the river trail, crossing as often as usual. Here the river goes through a narrow canyon but we managed to get along although the water is pretty high. We came to tracks on a little mud flat which were very numerous which turned out to be those of a ewe and lamb. While I was examining them from my horse Fred called out, "There's a ewe." I jumped off and ran forward, loading my gun, and fired, as we want a ewe for the Biological Survey. She was 200 feet above us on a cliff. The first shot apparently went through her vitals but she ran forward a few paces. Then Bob fired, breaking a leg, and my next shot went through her shoulder, bringing her to the ground. As it would only mean starvation to the lamb Bob put a bullet through her heart the second shot. All of which was fairly decent shooting amidst the excitement of twenty horses and five men running around. The range was about 200 yards and it was a difficult mark, being uphill. Altogether it was a piece of luck getting our specimen so handily. We all climbed up on the cliff, brought the two sheep down, gralloched them, loaded them on a horse and continued on our way. The location was apparently a sheep lick, as the flat was heavily tracked up and the signs and trails were numerous all around and under the overhanging ledges of the cliff. We came to a fine-looking coal seam and shortly saw a "discovery stake" showing the CNR[45] interests have taken up all the coal here. Our trail became poorer and poorer, for very little travel has gone over it. Soon we came to a 1912 location stake and our trail ended, showing that it was only cut to stake out the coal two years ago. So we have missed our cut-off over Trail Creek to the Grande Cache.[46] We turned around and returned to our camp of last night. Again we have gotten on the wrong trail and will lose several days by it, but it was lucky, as by doing so we got our ewe, and our meat supply is assured for another week. The valley bottom is filled full of alders, replacing the willows. Saw cliff swallows, robin and harlequin duck. Saw beaver pond and fairly recent cottonwoods cut down by them. Distance 6 miles, altitude 4000 feet. Third week, total distance 162 miles.

FRIDAY, JULY 17. HOT – BRILLIANT.

A wonderful stretch of weather. We are beginning our fourth week, and so far, the weather hasn't interfered with our hunting or moving on the trail. We have had several bad rainy days but they were clear enough early so that we were able to start and not be held up in camp. The rabbits are so numerous here that they are a pest. All leather straps, food, ropes etc. have to be put well out of their reach to prevent their being chewed up. Most of the time there are half a dozen running around camp. During the night they are at their worst. Fred woke up to find one chewing his hair! Symes says he is going to set a place for them at meals to keep them from chewing up our outfit. Bob went off early for the horses but he hasn't returned yet and it looks as if they have left us and crossed the river to go several miles to our previous camp, where the feed was so thick. He returned after a couple of hours with all the cayuses, having had to ford the river on foot, a dangerous proceeding in such a rapid stream as this. Our start was delayed, – it was 11.45 before we were ready to start. Yesterday near the lick we found a lamb (a ram) drowned in the river. Either he had lost his footing and fallen in from the rocks or had been drowned in swimming the river, crossing to the lick on the far side. Only case of this kind I ever saw. Bob says he heard of one being drowned years ago north of Banff on Panther Creek. We made fast time and in two and a half hours reached the big flat where we camped before. Here we thought our trail might turn off but we found no signs of it so we decided to camp here. The river has gone down over a foot since the rain but this hot weather should bring it up again. This was another very hot day, similar to the weather we had our first week, but the air is clear and dry; no mosquitoes and almost no flies, so conditions are ideal, with a fresh breeze. Saw lots of spotted sandpipers and chipping sparrows and two harlequin ducks. Got to camp early (distance 8 miles, altitude 4000 feet) and had a wonderful long afternoon to loaf in with some washing and mending to do. Saw chipping and white-crowned sparrows and what appeared to be a yellow palm warbler.

SATURDAY, JULY 18. WARM – CLOUDY, LATE SHOWERS.

Went through the usual routine and left at 10.30, up the river. Saw a female harlequin duck, white-crowned sparrow, chipping sparrow, golden eagle and juncos. There seem to be no grouse in this part of the country at all. We crossed the river continually, as usual, which has given most of the horses sore feet. The water keeping their hoofs soft, they consequently have very little to resist the hard sharp rocks on the riverbank . During the last few days the water has gone down a foot or more, making the fording easy and we have no more trouble with wet packs. Symes kept count and found we crossed the stream twenty-two times. Saw tracks of a cow and calf moose, a ewe, a doe, and a coyote. It is very interesting keeping a lookout for the tracks along the trail and so finding out what game there is about. Camped after five hours (distance 12 miles, altitude 5000 feet) on a little grassy flat on which there is what appears to be a child's grave. This has been a favourite camping ground for the Indians, and lots of sheep and deer bones lie scattered among the bushes. Fred went off to look for the trail over to Trail Creek but found only a very old one. Heard hermit thrush singing at midday.

SUNDAY, JULY 19. HOT – AFTERNOON, COLD – RAIN.

The horses pulled away from camp as usual soon after daylight and Bob had to go several miles upstream after them. We made a quick getaway, only taking an hour and a quarter from the time the horses arrived until we left, – speedy work with twenty horses. Saw numerous golden eagles, willow ptarmigan, chipping sparrow, – a spotted sandpiper at over 6000 feet, the highest I have seen one. Also saw flicker and sparrow hawk; fresh tracks of a deer and old ones of a moose. It was hot all the morning but early in the afternoon the rain began, first as showers, then as a heavy downpour with a strong wind back of it. We found a pass through the range north of us and one of the prettiest spots I have seen.[47] The trail led through a narrow break in the hills, ending in a grassy summit not 200 yards wide with sheer rock walls rising several hundred feet to a bare rocky peak 2000 feet above us.

A little waterfall with a drop of 100 or more feet made the scene perfect. It was in reality a pass in miniature – the kind that you read about in fairy books, where the brigands live in hiding. We thought of camping just below the summit but the wind blew too heavy for comfort, so we continued on and about an hour later stopped in the pouring rain to camp among the wet spruces on rough, rocky ground. After the tipi was up, the ground levelled off, and supper ready, things looked very cheerful. I never saw it rain harder or look less like clearing for another day or so. Everything was soaking wet but we managed to dry out pretty well before turning in for the night. The wildflowers were beautiful again today and I wish I knew something about them, as nearly every day some new variety appears in bloom. Some of the little hillside meadows were carpeted with buttercups while others were covered with masses of forget-me-nots. One place where the timber had been burnt out the ground seemed to be aflame with the brilliant blossoms of the "paint brush." Just before reaching camp we came upon quantities of orange columbines growing among the spruces and they were a pleasant sight, very cheering in the cold, miserable storm. We were six hours on the trail and made about 18 miles, altitude 5900 feet.

MONDAY, JULY 20. COLD – BRIGHT; LATE SNOW SQUALLS.

To our great surprise we awoke to find a cloudless day and cold as late autumn! The thermometer was only thirty-six at 7.30 and everything frozen stiff, the tipi and pack covers being like boards as the rain froze on them solidly. It is a fine-feeling day and a pleasant change after the heat of the last few days. The snow is low down on the hills about us but won't last more than a few hours with this strong sun. We stayed in camp all the morning to dry the outfit after yesterday's wetting and to bake some bread. There were lots of birds around, numerous juncos and chipping sparrows, as well as a hermit thrush, Canada jay and a pair of pretty little Wilson warblers. It was like an Indian summer day at home. The air was clear and crisp, the sun was bright and warm and there was a fresh breeze blowing. It was just such a day as I have spent often at Edgartown[48] sitting in the blind watching the ducks fly about the pond. At 1.15 we left, going down the little valley whose stream flowed into a large valley at right angles to it, which proved to be a branch of the Hay River.[49] Here we turned west along a well-worn trail which we feel without a doubt leads to the Grande Cache, as it has been recently travelled on. I have never seen a prettier valley than this. It runs nearly east and west and is so straight that it is possible to see to its summit in one direction and miles down it the other way. It is about a mile wide. On the side our trail was on is a long line of rounded, grassy hills covered with loose rock above. On the opposite side the green timber runs up about 300 feet; then comes the grassy lower slopes showing very green in the afternoon light, surmounted by high, rocky peaks. About fifteen miles in each direction this chain extended. Coming along a fine trail with such beautiful scenery on a cool, crisp day with a bright, warm sun is something long to be remembered. Here we saw a marsh hawk[50] scaling over the meadows and willow-covered flats. Then a large brown hawk of some species flew off from a dead tree and later a golden eagle soared on extended wings high up. We kept on climbing more and more, crossing the summit between the waters of the Hay and Muskeg rivers.[51] It was a magnificent pass, about 6800 feet, well above timberline. On one side was range after range of high, rounded, grassy hills – magnificent sheep ranges – and on the other side were high, sheer, rocky peaks towering several thousand feet above the grassy summit. We saw a pair of willow ptarmigan with a brood of young chicks from which they tried to draw me by pretending they were injured and could scarcely get out of my reach, – the typical trick of the grouse family. Soon we came to a flock of half a dozen grey-crowned leucosticte feeding under a snow bank. About this time we had a heavy snow squall. We now descended to the waters of the Muskeg River[52] and after dropping down through past the spruces we camped at 7.30 on a little flat where some Indians have been within a few days, there being bones and hair of sheep around, showing there are sheep here. Saw a sheep on the hills near the summit; either a ewe or a small ram.

Distance 18 miles, altitude 5400 feet.

TUESDAY, JULY 21. COLD – WINDY – CLOUDY.

Another bitterly cold morning, but at present the sun is bright and its warmth helps a lot. However, it didn't last long and all day it was cloudy and windy, making it so cold that I wore my mackinaw and had my warmest mittens on to keep warm, and even then walked quite a lot leading my horse. Left our windy camping spot at ten and went over another summit, the highest yet, as it was about 7000 feet. This took us from the waters of the Muskeg River to another stream that runs parallel to the Sulphur and into the Smoky River.[53] Saw a sparrow hawk, golden-crowned sparrow, eagle, a Canada jay, juncos and a pair of harlequin ducks, the male apparently already having moulted and assumed the plumage of the female. Came through the fallen timber a few miles and camped in it, after three and a half hours on the trail. Distance 6 miles, altitude 5400 feet. Tracks of a large bull caribou along the creekbed, only a day or two old. Dried out the sheep hide and our supply of cured meat, which has suffered from the recent wet weather. It looks as if we were going to have a storm. Fine-looking sheep country on all sides.

WEDNESDAY, JULY 22. WARM – CLOUDY.

The down timber, although hateful stuff, has its compensations and here the flowers are growing in profusion, the two predominating blossoms being the purple "fireweed," very similar to our phlox, and the clusters of large lavender asters with here and there patches of bright red "paintbrush" flowers. Undoubtedly we are on the right trail now as we can see the low foothills below us and should be at the Smoky River in a couple of days if the weather permits. Caught a white-footed mouse[54] in one of the traps. It is only the second mouse we have managed to get so far, our specimens chiefly consisting of chipmunk, ground squirrel etc., besides a number of birds. In saddling my horse I found to my disgust that my canoe shirt (rubber waterproof) had been chewed to pieces during the night in spite of the fact that it was tied to the saddle in the usual way and that the latter was placed on top of the outfit pile which was covered with pack covers with a heavy log on top. Three big holes were chewed out of the coat, – one under the arm, one in front and a big one over my shoulders, all rather important places. This is the third year I have carried one and they are the most useful article of clothing I have ever carried. I'd rather my boots or any other clothes had been eaten up. In taking down the pile we found a pack rat at the bottom where we had him cornered. Bob chased him out and I killed him with a stick as he appeared, – bitter revenge. He skinned him and his skin is now in the collection. We left about eleven and found nothing but down timber all day, very tiresome indeed. The trail led to a little flat where the Indians who are a few days ahead of us camped. Here the old trail continued down the river while a more recent one led over the hills about due north through the down timber. We first followed it, then decided the old trail was safe so turned down the creek. Saw a very interesting event take place. I was watching a hawk perched on top of a dead tree when Fred's horse started a spotted sandpiper, – apparently her young were nearby. She fluttered over the ground as if hurt to draw us away. Apparently the hawk took all this in from his lofty perch and in an instant swooped down but just missed the sandpiper, which saw the hawk in time to get away. It was all over in an instant but an interesting event to have seen at only a few feet distant. Soon we came to a large flat where the trees had been chopped down over a large area, showing a great deal of camping had been done here. We separated to see which way the trail led and came on a lick where we found tracks of caribou, moose and sheep. It was a wonderful sight and explained why so much camping had been done here. The lick was in a mudhole where a little water oozed out from under the bank, undoubtedly saline. We kept on downstream and camped after six hours in the down timber, – distance 15 miles, altitude 4400 feet. We are out of the mountains now and nothing but low hills with the timber all burnt off on all sides. Saw tracks of a band of rams in the creekbed. Also saw the first robin since leaving Jasper. A Franklin's grouse, juncos, white-crowned sparrows and a flicker comprised the birds seen.

THURSDAY, JULY 23. WARM – CLEAR.

We now think the new trail we passed yesterday is a cut-off to the Smoky River, and apparently the reason this one is no longer used is owing to the amount of down timber. It begins to look as if this might be a branch of the Muskeg River[55] but in another day or two we ought to know. This is the end of the fourth week and the time certainly has gone fast. A well-travelled trail comes in from the east nearly a mile below here.[56] We are on the right track all right again. Jack Symes suggested last night that the pack rat be dissected and the pieces of my shirt returned to me! However, his idea was not carried out. Had showers during the night but the spruces were thick overhead and no one got wet. Only put up the shelter tent, as it was too late to cut tipi poles. Heard a partridge drumming last night at eleven o'clock, – just about dark. Up at 6 and on the trail by 9. It was a long day, seven hours before we made camp, but with the exception of a few patches of bad down timber where the axe was required, the trail was fine, either through open meadows along the creek or high up on Jack pine ridges. This is probably the oldest trail in this part of the country, yet it has been so little used lately that we frequently lost it for awhile. In one meadow I counted six deep furrows. As one trail became too deep from use another was made a few feet away and so this was accounted for. Came through the finest moose country I ever saw – mile after mile of willow-covered flats with green spruce along the edges next to the hills and one fine little lake.[57] Saw lots of tracks. The birds consisted of eagle, sparrow hawks, a whistler, harlequin duck, red-bellied nuthatch and what I thought was an American merganser. Passed a very old Indian grave, the logs having rotted away and fallen down; also two old log cabins, or at least the remains of them, which were used by the Indians trapping in winter. Numerous old deadfalls for trapping marten all along the trail. Distance 18 miles, altitude 3800 feet. Saw the first tamarack, or larch, trees and passed numerous old Indian camping grounds. A kingfisher is sitting in a tree near camp making his usual noise. Symes went in swimming in the river. How he stands the ice cold water is a mystery to me. Fourth week, total distance 257 miles.

FRIDAY, JULY 24. WARM – CLEAR.

Although it is a month since the longest day of the year, the evening twilight is long and it is eleven o'clock before it is pitch dark. For four weeks we have been on the trail, yet the weather has not interfered once with our plans and we have not yet been held up by the rain. This is the longest stretch of fine weather I ever saw in the mountains , – usually two weeks is considered a long time. However, it will probably change soon and we will make up for all this. We are entirely out of the mountains now and even the hills are no more than little elevations about us. The hares are very plentiful everywhere, – last winter they were thicker than they had been for years. They say that every seventh year they get so numerous that a disease sets in which causes an enormous mortality so that for years they are very scarce. We find numbers of them dead along the trail, which points to the fact that the disease has undoubtedly appeared. Bob Jones went fishing last evening and in a very short time appeared with five pound-and-a-half trout and one buster that weighed fully four pounds. He caught them in a little "hole" in the Muskeg River close by. We had some for supper late and everyone agreed they never tasted better fish. They were extremely rich, juicy and tender, with a fine flavour. The meat was quite pink and we decided they were Dolly Varden trout. We left about ten and found the "bulldog" flies very bad, worrying the horses continually. After a mile we came to a familiar spot, – an old camp ground with the remains of a log cache. We stopped here two years ago on our way home and found two fire rangers camped, the first white men we had seen for three months. We had been out of tea, coffee, salt pork etc. for some time and they very generously dug down into their cache to give us enough of the necessities to see us through to Hinton, – about a week off. From here on, the trail led along and across the Muskeg River, all of which was familiar. Passed one of our 1912 camping places, which brought back many amusing memories. After six and a half hours we

camped at an old Indian site near the little fenced grave, the spot where we
found the main trail to Hinton in 1912, which was a good sight to us at the
time. Another day will see us camped on the banks of the Smoky River. Saw
white-throated sparrows, chipping sparrows, eagles, cliff swallows, spotted
sandpipers, a flicker, crows, and a pair of nighthawks flying around the tipi
giving the familiar harsh cry. It showered early in the evening but the sun
set clear. As we turned in at eleven, about dark, a pack of coyotes began to
yelp across the stream and it sounded good to hear them once more.

Distance 18 miles, altitude 3400 feet.

SATURDAY, JULY 25. HOT – BRIGHT.

A kingfisher, chipping sparrows and some kind of warbler seem to be our
only bird neighbours this morning. Got away about 9.30 so as to camp near
the Smoky River early. The nighthawks here seem to feed or fly about during
the day as much as during the night. The trail was different from any previous day as it led through open poplar woods with scattering groves of balm
of Gilead trees. The grass and tall flowering plants grew under the trees and
the growth was very luxuriant, the fireweed (wild phlox) and larkspur often
reaching a height of four or five feet. At times it seemed as if we were going
through gardens, the flowers were so thick. This continued for the three and
a half hours we were going. We passed several very pretty little lakes[58] but
our view of the mountains was cut off as we were in the poplar woods all
the time. Came to a tipi where we found a young fellow named Mason – a
fire ranger – the first person we have seen for a month. He told us not to
go down to the Smoky about five miles away but to camp near a lake a mile
beyond, where there is plenty of horse feed. Shortly we came to what is
known as the Grande Cache settlement, where three families of Moberlys
and some other Cree half-breeds have settled and built log shacks. They
came here four years ago, being driven out of the valley of the Athabasca
when Jasper Park was planned.[59] They have a number of horses and cattle
and live here all the year, going to Hinton, where the railroad is, 100 miles
away, once in a great while for supplies or going into the mountains to get a
supply of meat, as there are moose and sheep around. We only made about
10 miles and our altitude of 3500 feet was a little higher than last night. After
making camp Fred, Bob and I rode down to the river. We got our first view
of it from the top of a steep bank 400 feet above it.

The Smoky looks deep and heavy, too much so to ford. It splits up in
numerous channels, so while I stayed behind with the horses the others

went down but found this trail led to the low-water ford, – impassable at this time of the year. While I brought the horses back to camp they went upstream and returned later to say that they had found where the river runs in one stream and here is where the crossing is made at high water by rafting. So our scheme is to build a raft, and possibly two, and to swim the horses and raft the outfit tomorrow. It rained hard all night and the tipi leaked so that we all got pretty wet, but dried out after awhile.

SUNDAY, JULY 26. WARM – BRIGHT.

It was raining early so we slept late. Later on Fred, Cross and Bob Jones went off down to the river with one horse (Macloud), some rope, a big auger etc. to build a raft. Jack and I stayed behind in camp. This is one of the prettiest spots I have seen for some time. We are camped on a small lake and at the other end rises a green-timbered mountain about 3000 feet above us.[60] It looks like a scene in the White Mountains at home and reminds me a lot of Chocorua.[61] There is quite a lot of bird life around, which makes it all the more interesting. A pair of Great Northern Divers, a female Golden Eye with four young ducks, a flock of "peep," two pair of winter yellow legs with half grown young, a pair of killdeer plover, a robin, least fly catcher, tree swallows, song sparrows, a ruffed grouse with well grown young and sparrow hawks. Jack and I started off to look up Ivan[62] Moberly in order to buy some flour and baking powder, as we want to add to our supply before leaving the Smoky. Ivan keeps a few things for trading with the Indians that pass through here. We walked past his house and went up the Sulphur River along the high bench above it to find him.

There are numerous little meadows where he has been cutting hay (mostly weeds) to feed his cattle during the winter. To our surprise we found a mowing machine, big hay rake and wagon. Later on he told us he packed everything in on his horses from Edmonton, over three hundred miles away. That was four years ago, when that was the nearest point where the railroad was. He said his horses got sore backs from the heavy wagon wheels and big pieces of machinery. It seems funny to see their squaws, children and all putting up hay, with snow-covered mountains in all directions. We went on through numerous little meadows and finally came to a tipi where we called for Ivan. The man who came out turned out to be his brother Adolphus,[63] who was in a very sorrowful state as his two-year-old child died of a fever only a few days ago. Ivan, he said, was further back so we returned and met him shortly. He was very pleasant and talked quite freely and although his

English was rather broken it was intelligible. Once in a while he couldn't understand us and he would say "me no savvy." He had flour etc. and said he would come back later to our camp, so we left him carrying his axe with his rifle done up in a buckskin case slung over his back.

They have picked out an ideal spot for their horses, – on a big, green, grassy hill looking right down into the deep valley of the Sulphur River and up the valley of the Smoky, with green sheep hills on one side and snow mountains on the other. No one could have chosen a more ideal spot. We returned to camp and it drove me crazy to sit around listening to the yellow legs whistling. It seemed so natural to see them running around feeding on the mud flats at the edge of the lake, calling frequently to each other, and so tame that they would let me come within a few feet of them that it made me homesick, and I thought of Chatham[64] and the big flats where the shore birds feed. I watched one yellow leg feeding for some time and saw him catch a fish nearly two inches long, too big to eat at once, so that he spent a long time in cutting it up with his bill. The killdeer had a beautiful mellow note, yet rather mournful, like that of the piping plover. Ivan came later and Fred and I went over to his house, a log shack plastered with mud, and got the supplies. Although flour is three dollars a sack (fifty pounds) at Hinton, all he charged us was five dollars! Yet, he packed it in here, over a hundred miles from the railroad. It was a beautiful evening, without a breath of wind, and not a sound until one of the loons started to give his lonely call. That was a fitting sound for this wild, beautiful spot. Later; when it was dark, the coyotes began to yelp and we went to sleep with their wild cries ringing in our ears.

MONDAY, JULY 27. WARM – BRIGHT.

Again it rained last night and we got wet. However, it cleared early and so we planned to go to the river and cross. Forgot to say the men found a cottonwood dugout canoe near where they planned to build a raft, so they returned early and we bargained with Ivan for seven dollars for the use of it. He is one of the nicest and most willing Indians I ever saw. He came over to the tipi and down to the river with us. Here we unpacked the horses and piled up the packs etc. on the gravel flats at the edge of the river. At this spot all the water flows in one stream about one hundred yards wide and the current is nearly eight miles an hour – a good, deep, heavy stream, yet no rapids and perfectly safe although several men who have rafted here in the past have gone down and lost all their things. Bob and Fred took the packs etc. over in five loads, and it was bitterly cold work walking in the water pulling the canoe along the bank. It was an eighteen-foot dugout, capable of carrying a thousand pounds, but in this stream it didn't seem safe to carry more than five hundred pounds at one time.

Ivan and I crossed over as passengers, – ready to look after the horses when they landed. I walked up and down the shore to attract the horses' attention while Ivan sat in the bushes ringing one of the horse bells for the same purpose. Amid loud yells, hooting and cursing the men on the other side drove the twenty horses into the river. Some went one way, some another, and all was mixed up.

Most of them turned back, three only coming across; then another bunch was driven in and arrived safely, but the last lot turned back, landing downstream at the base of a cliff where they couldn't get up it was so sheer.[65] Here they stood in the water up to their knees for half an hour until Fred drove them in again. I was on the other side leading Bruce up and down to attract their attention and this time they came finely. So the crossing took place without any mishap and we cooked up a meal and drank to the health of the Smoky. We offered Ivan some of the powerful Hudson Bay rum, but he said "me no touch," which impressed us greatly. Mason crossed with us and will go along for two days, as he is going up the Jack Pine River.[66] We will leave the Smoky sooner, as we go up the Muddy Water. We shook hands with Ivan and he pushed off his dugout from shore, landing speedily on the other side.

Distance 4 miles, altitude 2800 feet.

TUESDAY, JULY 28. COOL – SHOWERS; CLEAR – WINDY.

We camped last night right on the riverbank where we landed our outfit among the big cottonwoods and spruces. The ground was soft and springy, making as comfortable a spot to sleep on as the best of mattresses. Saw a fresh bear track close by camp, – looks like a small grizzly. Now that we are across the Smoky I feel that our trip has at last begun, as we are out of the "tin can" district and beyond the reach of any outfits except Indians. Fortunately, it was clear all night but at the time we got up the rain came and we had several heavy showers before it cleared up, about eleven. We decided not to move but spend the day in camp as there is so much for us to do after steady travelling and before we get started again. Today was the general clothes washing we have had planned for some time, and the trees are covered with articles of clothing drying in the wind. I suppose now we will date events from the day of the "wash-up." Recently we have calculated the time since we last "baked bread," just as if it were some festival such as the "Passover." Had big feed, in the nature of a cranberry and a prune pie, both of which were huge successes and were speedily consumed. A kingfisher and flicker were the only birds seen today and of course the ubiquitous spotted sandpiper.

WEDNESDAY, JULY 29. HOT – BRILLIANT.

A beautiful cloudless day greeted us at sunrise and we are off again up the Smoky and by tonight or tomorrow will be on familiar ground again as far as the Porcupine lakes,[67]- about a week. There we will hunt for goat, moose and caribou. From there on we know nothing about the country and the trails will all be new to us and probably poor ones at that. During the last few cool, rainy days the snow has come down extremely low on the mountains, way below timberline, so the effect is more like October, especially so as the sky has been a cold grey exactly like a late fall effect. The river has gone down about a foot during the last two days as a result of the cold weather. My foot has been troubling me so much the last week that I have had to give in to it and do as little walking as possible. I have put on a loose pair of Barker boots and soak it night and morning in hot water to try to get rid of the soreness and swelling. The buckskin mare Alice jumped on my foot nearly a month ago and instead of its getting better it has steadily become worse until it has almost laid me up and my only chance of getting it well enough to get on my hunting boots and go after the sheep is to give in to it altogether. I hate lying around a half invalid but it is a necessity. We started about 10.30 and most of the day were in bad fallen timber which meant plenty of chopping so that the outfit moved slowly, – in fact, it took us six hours to make our 10 miles (altitude 3200 feet). We never saw a single bird except an owl which looked like a hawk owl, but I was not sure. We camped alongside an old cache belonging to Fred Kvaas and Tom Monagan [sic], who have been trapping the country up above here the last three years.[68] The ground is covered with rabbit skins (killed for food, not for their fur), also marten and lynx skeletons. If the skulls weren't so "fragrant" we would carry them along for the collection. There are some fine-looking sheep hills across the river, but there doesn't seem to be anything moving on the slopes, – it is too near this settlement of breeds. However, there is part of a sheep hide here, killed last winter, which points to the fact that these hills on this side (west) of the river are a winter range, which is likely, as there is good feed, a southern exposure and very little snow lies here. Turned in about dark, with the drumming of a partridge and the hooting of an owl resounding through the timber.

THURSDAY, JULY 30. HOT – BRILLIANT.

Another perfect day after a wonderful, cool night for sleeping. Birds were plentiful around camp early this morning and I saw several new varieties for this trip. There were several cedar waxwings feeding on the saskatoon berries and a humming bird sipping honey from the larkspur and fireweed. A red eye vireo and young bird lit within a few feet of me, so close that I was able to see his red eye without the glasses. Also there were song sparrows and some kind of warbler which I was unable to identify. Soon after we left which was at ten, I saw a lone barn swallow flying over the horses. What he was doing here is a mystery to me, as we are many miles from any kind of a building, the nearest being the log houses at Grande Cache, ten miles away, but not a barn or likely resting place within a hundred miles. In about two hours we reached Muddy Water River, which was quite a little stream, no doubt very bad at very high water but today it was easy to ford. Now, it is nearly August and the highest water of the year is over and all our streams are past for some time, except some very small ones which we will cross near their sources. Soon we got into bad fallen timber and our troubles began in earnest. It looks hopeless at times and it certainly was. Saw one of our large chipmunks sitting in the rocks. We found the old trail but no one had been over it for years, – probably not since the big fire burnt it over. It has all fallen in, so anyone coming this way avoids it. The only people who go this way are breeds and one or two trappers. Fred and Bob Jones went ahead to chop the trees away and it was slow work.

Signs of the old trail appeared now and then, and how Fred followed it the way he did was a mystery to all of us. It was a fine exhibition of a guide's seventh sense. Finally, we decided to hit across the top of the hill to find the old trail and here was our mistake, as the trail turned out to be ahead of us some ways. From here on we had lots of chopping and it was slow, tiresome work. Packs came off and sometimes three or four horses had to be repacked at once. Roachy fell under some logs and could not move until the logs were cut away. Snowball's pack went clear over his head but the ropes held him so he couldn't move. One trouble after another turned up and it was 8 p.m. before we made camp in a mess of down timber, with no feed for the horses. After a while we picked out spaces between the fallen logs, unrolled our blankets and were soon asleep. Distance 10 miles, altitude 3700 feet. Fifth week, total distance 309 miles.

FRIDAY, JULY 31. HOT – BRILLIANT.

The flowers have been very pretty lately. In this burnt timber there are acres and acres of fireweed, making beautiful patches of purple between the trees, thus making up for the desolate effect of the fire. Found some columbines – the same colour and variety as we have at home. The bunch-berry flowers are about over, here. Through this burnt piece there are lots of berries, but they are not yet ripe. The raspberries (the true wild ones, not our thimbleberries of the East) are very numerous as well as the black currants. In another two weeks there should be lots of ripe berries and I hope by that time we will find some more good patches. The horses had a miserable day of it with ten hours on the trail and it was the most trying day of all on our nerves, as there was something going wrong continually. After a halt to cut the trail the horses were almost impossible to move they were so discouraged and tired.

The horses went back this morning and it was two hours before Fred and Bob returned with them. The chief trouble was that the horses split up in two bunches and Macloud, who was in the lead of one bunch, had lost his bell and it was slow work following their tracks, especially as they had left the trail. This place where we camped is the same spot where we were forced to stop two years ago. Today we are here because we had to rest the horses although there was next to no feed at all, for the nearest flat with de-cent grass is about five miles away. Two years ago this spot was a paradise to us, as for three weeks we had been cutting our own trail through the burnt timber and until we found this old trail we hadn't seen during that time a single sign of man or horse. The horses were all so tired today that it was hard to drive them and poor old Macloud, the strongest of them all, laid down at frequent intervals, groaning and sweating. He has had the heaviest load and because of his strength he pushes through everything, tearing up trees by the roots, so that it has been a heavy tax on his strength. In two hours we came to a little flat with nice feed, though not very much of it, and old tipi poles, – making a short day. The horses appreciated it and all the afternoon in the broiling hot sun they lay stretched out in the cool grass of the muskeg and ate without getting up, a sure sign of fatigue.

We spent the afternoon in bare feet and underclothes in order to keep cool and it certainly was an extremely informal party. This is the last day of July and we have been out over five weeks; the time has certainly gone fast. Some mountain ash trees along the trail. Distance 5 miles, altitude 4700 feet.

SATURDAY, AUGUST 1. HOT – BRILLIANT.

The country certainly looks familiar all around here. Saw again yesterday the high mountain between the head of Sheep Creek and the Porcupine lakes, the same one that we saw recently from the hills along the Sulphur and from Sheep Creek two years ago.[69] But we could not find it later. Some of the members of the Alpine Club saw it from the Mt. Robson region in 1913.[70] We plan to try to locate it and if possible get near enough to photograph it. For a guess it must be over 12,000 feet,[71] and probably in the center of the last high group of mountains in this section, for from there on, the mountains become lower.[72] Left camp early, about 9.30, and all day the going was uninteresting as we were in burnt timber continually, at times necessitating a lot of cutting, while at others the fires had been so recent that the dead timber had not yet had a chance to get blown down. Came to the spot where we camped two years ago and instead of going over the mountain to Sheep Creek we continued on up the valley of the Muddy Water, as the Indians told us, – following the old trail which only showed up now and then. Since the fire it has scarcely ever been used and probably no white man has ever been over it. Once, it must have been a fine trail and used a great deal by the Indians. After a couple of miles it turned into a narrow pass between the mountains and led through the defile for about three miles. It was an unusual little pass, being extremely narrow and the sides sheer about a thousand feet above to the top.[73] If it hadn't been for the burnt timber it would have been a beautiful spot. As it was, it was very fine. The floor was a succession of little flats with here and there a pool of water, a little lake. For the first time magpies put in an appearance and we saw several in this pass. Franklin's grouse, juncos, Canada jays, spotted sandpipers, red-bellied nuthatches, least flycatchers, humming birds and numbers of cedar waxwings were seen. It was another extremely hot day and early and late in camp the mosquitoes have been very bad, – the worst since the Stony River. Besides, the "no-see-ums" (as the Indians call our little midges) and sand flies (black flies) are very bad too. In another two weeks the insect season will be over. Camped after six and a half hours on Sheep Creek in a beautiful little pine grove. Our friend (?) Mason must have had enough of the down timber and turned back, as he hasn't appeared yet![74] Distance 12 miles, altitude 4100 feet.

SUNDAY, AUGUST 2. HOT – BRILLIANT.

Bob Jones and Fred had to cross the creek after the horses this morning and they found it cold work. Left promptly at ten with another long day ahead of us. It was a pretty valley all day, but it was a scorcher as far as weather was concerned. The trail led through muskegs all day so that it was soft going and rather hard on the horses, as there was scarcely any let-up. However, it is not as bad as down timber. Both Andy and Macloud, the two that were played out two days ago seem to have recovered and came through finely. Fine hills on both sides of us that look good for sheep, but as a matter of fact these are goat ranges. Saw song sparrows, an eagle, juncos, cedar birds and I think a grey-crowned leucosticte. The country all looked familiar, especially one spot in the spruces where we camped last time. Finally we came out of the timber onto the familiar open summit country of Sheep Creek,[75] – as pretty a summit as there is in the mountains – and put up the tipi after six and a half hours on the trail, on the same spot as 1912.

Saw very fresh moose tracks on trail made this morning and some goat wool on the trees. Our names are still legible on the tree near camp but our cache in the grub boxes in the tree is no more, as the Moberlys took it, – a curious thing for an Indian to do, as they regard a cache as something never to be touched, but the present generation of breeds is a poor lot. The mosquitoes were worse this evening than for a long while. Distance 18 miles, altitude 4800 feet.

MONDAY, AUGUST 3. HOT – BRILLIANT.

We found to our surprise that we have managed to consume over one-third of our supply of dried fruit though we have only been out a quarter of our time, and our supply of condensed milk has gone even more rapidly so that we will have to be more saving from now on. This camp of ours is in an ideal spot, on a little knoll of open timber above the creek. In front and on both sides are summit meadows of fine feed for the horses and opposite a row of rugged rocky peaks. The left-hand one[76] in 1912 we climbed on a hike from camp with packs on our backs, off for a two days trip which lasted four owing to getting further off than we intended. We returned dead tired and hungry, as our food had given out shortly and we were driven to shooting a marmot to eat. It was a young one and so disgustingly greasy that it all but made us sick. So this spot has all sorts of memories for us. It was a fine night for sleeping, as it was cold, – in fact, cold enough for the water to freeze in the pail. The stars were out as clear as could be and it was still and beautiful.

Quite a number of birds are around, – the grey-crowned leucosticte seem to breeding here – also chipping sparrows, juncos and golden-crowned sparrows. Strange to say no willow ptarmigan seem to be around, yet it is an ideal spot for them. The mosquitoes are so bad again this morning as to be almost unbearable. This continued hot weather with no wind seems to bring them out in thousands. We have a perfect day for the finest scenery of the trip – over the pass to the Porcupine lakes.[77] Our course is due north and will be mostly from now on. As we came out of the timber going over the pass we had a magnificent view of the mountains far to the south around the head of the Jackpine River with Mt. Bess,[78] as we thought, high above the others. It is a beautiful pass,[79] all rocky going, hard for the horses, with here and there patches of green, and countless wild flowers.

Once more we were in the land of the beautiful little mountain forget-me-not, the prettiest flower that grows in these mountains. The rock mountains rose sheer several thousand feet on both sides of us and at the base of the largest and most impressive peak lay a wonderfully coloured little lake, perhaps a mile long.[80] It certainly was a gem in its wild setting. The colour seemed to change from an emerald green to a turquoise blue depending on the way the light affected it. Here we stopped the outfit for a few minutes and glassed the country for any sign of game. We looked over Sheep Creek pass into British Columbia, and as far as the eye could see, mountain towered above mountain until they were lost in the distant haze. On we went, leading our horses, making it easier on their unshod feet over the cruelly sharp rocks, up to the top of the summit above the line of perpetual snow, – well over 7000 feet. Here we saw a goat and we stopped to watch him as he crossed a very steep snow slide. He was a billy, all by himself, and although a mile away seemed to be very much frightened by our outfit. He continued up the steep snow slope as we carefully watched him through our glasses. The going was heavy through the soft snow and he found it tiring work for his mouth was open and his tongue hanging out from the exertion. Finally, he reached the almost perpendicular cliff and started up its face, which seemed to us an utter impossibility. All of a sudden as he reached up with his forefeet and tried to jump up with his hind feet he slipped and went over backwards. It looked as if he would fall to the base of the cliff but, marvellous to say, he turned in mid-air like a cat and landed about ten feet below perched on a sharp bit of rock with all four feet close under him. It was a wonderful sight, especially so because I have never heard of a goat falling from the rocks before. Here we left him and went on our way. All the mountains through the pass and on both sides are fine goat ranges, – in fact, the cliffs and mountains on the north side compose the most beautiful goat ranges I ever saw. Last time (1912) we saw here 14 nannies and kids, but today we saw only recent tracks. The brilliant green of the grass caused by the luxuriant growth of weeds and other flowering plants makes a pleasant contrast to the deep green of the spruces. Above these alpine meadows tower the bold mountains of rock and ice. Here one of the branches of the Porcupine River (a tributary of the Smoky) heads.[81] We went back into the timber and on emerging a mile further came suddenly upon a view unsuspected to those who hadn't been here before, and it was so beautiful and so sudden that it called forth exclamations from them.

About a thousand feet below us, surrounded on all sides by green timber above which were the rocky peaks, lay a lovely lake three to four miles long of a most beautiful emerald green. This is one of the sources of the Porcupine.[82] The trail, if it may be so called, led straight down as steep as possible through the timber for some ways, then branched off and up again.[83] Apparently no one had been through here since our outfit two years ago and what was left of the trail was not much, as the big spruces and balsams had fallen across it, borne down by the spring snowslides from the mountains above. Once out of this we had a last look at our lake behind us. Then over another open summit[84] where the going was soft, for the snow had not all melted yet and one little pool was not even free from ice. As we came to the highest point, there about 15 miles away, towering above all the other peaks, rose a beautiful mountain, all snow and ice – our long-looked-for big mountain.[85] It looked to be fully 12,000 feet high. All around were familiar peaks and shortly we were unpacking the horses at the spot where we camped before, with tipi poles to greet us and the remains of our camp – a pile of wood and several tin cans, not to mention a bottle still hanging by the neck to a spruce tree. After our meal Fred discovered some animals in a basin on the shoulder of a mountain opposite camp, above timberline. We ran for the glasses and found a bunch of caribou, – two bulls, two cows and two calves. Here was our chance to get specimens for the Biological Survey at Washington. For a few minutes things were in a mess as we got together guns, cartridges, glasses, skinning knives, stones etc. I put on my heavy boots for the first time in ten days and found them more comfortable for my sore feet, as they were tight and held the bones securely. In a few minutes we were off, climbing the hill as rapidly as possible after our big meal, – deciding the best method of stalking them and arranging a code of signs with the men back in camp, to be used in case the caribou moved away. Bob took the lead owing to his greater experience in hunting caribou. The wind was in our favour and we soon saw the backs of the caribou lying down. My hands shook so from the climb that I missed my first shot. They ran a short way and I fired again, hitting the bull. He ran a hundred yards and dropped, dead – shot through the heart as we later found out. Bob got the larger cow on his first shot as she ran off. The rest of the caribou ran about in confusion, giving us many opportunities to get more, but we had our Biological Survey specimens and were satisfied. The storm had begun now and it was bitterly cold as it rained and blew heavily. We gralloched both animals and while we were doing it the little calf ran back grunting for his mother, making a pathetic sight, but as it is usually the case they are taken care of by another cow we did not shoot it as we felt sure it would not starve. We ran over a ridge to watch the caribou as it was a sight worth seeing, – there they were all four watching us, not over 200 yards off, circling around, until suddenly they got our scent. In a second their heads went up and off they ran, full speed. With their peculiar gait and tails sticking straight up they presented a funny sight. When they reached a patch of snow they stopped and looked around at us, and a prettier, wilder sight I never saw, – truly an Alaskan scene, as Bob said! It was cold and we were soaked to the skin so we ran down the mountain to camp, bringing the liver, heart, kidneys, etc. with us and within an hour of leaving the tipi we were back again. As the men saw the caribou running around they didn't think we had killed any, so they were pleased at the news. Jack said on making camp that he wanted meat right away, and he certainly did not have long to wait. Saw our first hawk owl, also jays and four robins at 6500 feet~ Distance 12 miles, altitude 5500 feet.

TUESDAY, AUGUST 4. SNOW – COLD, CLEAR.

Awoke to find wind and snow and very cold, but after a couple of hours the snow stopped and the sun came out. All day, however, it was cold. Yesterday we found a lot of wild onions, which we picked. The roots have only a very small bulb half an inch through but they are strong of onion flavour. Today we lived like kings; for breakfast we had liver and kidney and onions fried; for dinner roast heart; and for supper, boiled tongue and baked marrow bones! How could anyone live higher than that. After breakfast we took four horses up to the basin, skinned and cut up the caribou and brought about 400 pounds of meat to camp. We now have over six weeks' supply of meat, consisting of fresh caribou, cured sheep and bacon, so if it all keeps it will be fine. The caribou evidently live on grass above timberline at this season. The clouds were low, so the view of our high mountain was poor.

It has a big hanging glacier similar to Mt. Victoria at Lake Louise. Counted seven lakes[86] and saw our way clear via the pass[87] north to the very foot of the big mountain, so we have an interesting time ahead of us. Spent all day until pitch dark skinning the caribou, drying the meat, fleshing skulls and salting hides. Saw grey-crowned leucosticte.

WEDNESDAY, AUGUST 5. HOT – BRILLIANT.

Our big mountain came out of the clouds in the middle of the morning all glistening with snow and ice after the storm and was magnificent. There is no question about its size and we get more and more enthusiastic about camping close to it. The weather changed and it became hot. Spent all the morning working in camp over the results of our hunt and remaking the grub boxes, as they are too big, and also cutting down our fibre-collecting chest, which is altogether too clumsy. The bull caribou, judging from the worn condition of his hoofs and teeth, is older than we thought in spite of his small horns, probably six to eight years. Some kind of thrush about, as well as willow ptarmigans, robins etc. The flies (every known variety) and mosquitoes are very bad and we are having trouble keeping them away from the meat which is hanging up drying. Went over all the sacks and repacked everything, as we have about 400 pounds to add to our outfit and we are going into unknown and untravelled country. Cross went up to the caribou hills to look at the mountains and pass ahead. Breakfasted on liver; dined on the finest and juiciest of caribou steaks and supped on tongue soup!

THURSDAY, AUGUST 6. HOT – BRIGHT – RAIN IN AFTERNOON.

Cross came back last night so enthusiastic about the wonderful view of the fine mountains he got from above the caribou hills that we decided to stay here another day. He saw what he thought was Mt. Robson. It was not as clear today and later it all clouded up. Before starting I saw a cow caribou on the skyline coming into the basin, so we tried to stalk her to get a picture, but the wind was wrong and she scented us, so when we reached the basin we saw her running away over the shoulder of the mountain back of it. This shoulder was our objective point and the view certainly justified the climb. Below us was a beautiful basin covered with the greenest grass I ever saw. Below it lay the two Porcupine lakes;[88] above them another lake[89] behind which rose our Fortress Mountain with its two high snow peaks at either end.

Then to the north lay our pass to the Wapiti River, in which were two more lakes.[90] Thunder Mountain,[91] a sharp peak, came next, behind which is our wonderful high mountain.

It has rather a flat, long top with a heavy ice cap and cornice one or two hundred feet thick. Below it, is a large and magnificent glacier with ice cliffs several hundred feet high. It is without question a magnificent mountain and towers far above all the others about. It was too hazy to see Mt. Robson or the far peaks. Found that the caribou feed on grass and a low-growing weed with a rounded leaf. Jack and I came down while Fred and Bob stayed up to do some more climbing and later returned to say that the clouds lifted enough so that they could see Mt. Robson and another very high mountain which lay about 60 miles south by west from us, while Robson lies nearly south southeast and about 80 miles distant. This should have been plainly visible from the Robson group when the Canadian Alpine Club were camped there last year. It looks from here to be as high as Robson itself and lies in British Columbia near the Beaver River.[92] All the afternoon it rained and we worked in the tipi repacking the collecting chest and its trays and making a drafting board etc. to be prepared to map the country from now on, which undoubtedly will be the cause of numerous heated discussions in the future as to the distances and directions. Our meals were still as varied and delicious as the past two days, – liver fried for breakfast; large, thick, tender, juicy steaks for dinner; and roast heart for supper. The cow caribou appeared in the basin after we had all returned to camp. She must have been there while we were crossing it. Sixth week, total distance 356 miles.

FRIDAY, AUGUST 7. COLD – RAIN, SNOW.

Mean weather today but there is so much to do in camp again that it is not lost time. We all had plenty to keep us busy during the morning, during which time it snowed and rained a bit at intervals, with the sun now and then appearing for a minute. I spent a couple of hours on the meat, which has suffered much the last two hot days from the flies. Symes was busy preparing to bake his bread. Cross had a long job sewing up and patching his duffle bag – a long, tiresome job – while Bob and Fred sewed pack covers and made a bell from an old copper pot we picked up along the trail to take the place of the one Macloud lost recently.[93] We planned to go to look up our goat and moose lick[94] we found in 1912, but about that time in the afternoon it stormed worse than ever, so that we spent all the afternoon in the tepee reading the works of Alexander Dumas as I brought along three of his best works in small editions. Everyone was absorbed in his particular book and so the day passed. Bob went out to look for the horses and it was long after dark before he returned. Thinking he had lost his way Symes gave his lungs a little exercise and Bob fired some shots to attract his attention, but he soon returned not having lost his way at all, only having a little difficulty in finding Macloud.

SATURDAY, AUGUST 8. COLD – CLOUDY.

In dissecting the heart of the cow caribou, we found it contained a piece of bone at the upper end as I had once read stated as a fact although it sounded at the time very peculiar. Waited all the morning to see what the weather would do for if it cleared Bob and Fred wanted to get another view of their mountain. However, it didn't and we can't afford to waste any more time so we packed the horses and moved down to the Porcupine lakes, camping in an ideal spot, a good piece of ground right on the creek that runs from the upper lake to the lower one.[95]

Lots of fresh tracks of moose, mostly bulls, and an old, rather small grizzly track along the lakeshore; also numerous ducks swimming about, mostly golden eyes. Saw a marsh hawk skimming over the muskegs, also a spotted sandpiper along the creek and jays and song sparrows. A large flock of birds, at least 200, flew about restlessly among the spruces, – must have been pine siskins.

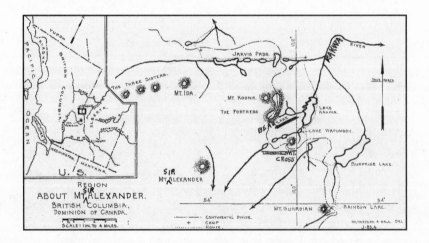

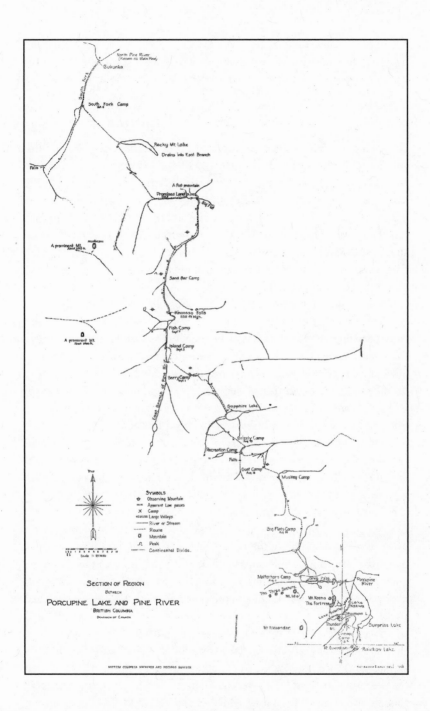

SECTION OF REGION
BETWEEN
PORCUPINE LAKE AND PINE RIVER
BRITISH COLUMBIA
DOMINION OF CANADA

When we reached camp it became warmer and the mosquitoes swarmed again to our misery. Two years ago today we started on our long three months' trip from Hinton. Distance 6 miles, altitude 5000 feet.

SUNDAY, AUGUST 9. HOT – BRIGHT.

No one has been here since we camped in 1912 and our tipi poles and firewood were just as we left them. Fred and I left for the day to visit our little lake discovered in 1912[96] and to try to get over the pass west of it to the other valley[97] that runs from camp to the big mountain which, by the way, we have named Mt. Alexander[98] after Alexander Mackenzie, who, in 1793, was the first man to cross the Rocky Mountains and passed west of here up the Parsnip River. The lake was as pretty as ever, backed as it is by the high rugged cliffs at each end of which is a snow peak about 10,000 feet high. This, I think, should be called The Fortress.[99]

Saw several porcupines and I got my boot filled with one's quills. The moose tracks were everywhere, some being very fresh. We looked around the lake with glasses and as I was using them Fred called for them in a hurry for he had discovered an object at the far end of the lake about a mile away. "It's a grizzly" he said as he shoved the glasses in my hand. The bear was so far off and the willow brush so thick that we could only see his back, so it was some time before we made sure it was not a moose. But finally he came out into an open space and elevating his head moved it from side to side as he sniffed the air for any dangerous scent, a characteristic habit of a bear, owing to their very poor eyesight, and repeated very frequently while feeding and travelling. Here we saw cedar birds and harlequin ducks. Our stalk was decided on and we hastily crossed the creek and made our way along the shore of the lake, thus losing sight of the bear, and lessening our chances of seeing him again on account of the thick brush, but it had to be done on account of the direction of the wind which was favourable for us as it blew down the lake from him, – apparently it was a "he" bear, as there were no cubs about. He was a good grizzly though not a very large one and probably was about five years old; an adult but not up to his full size, reached probably at seven to nine years. We came along the shore carefully and when within a third of a mile a goose honked and a flock of goslings taking the warning swam out into the lake behind her. Then a puff of wind blew toward where we last saw the bear. Either one of these may have alarmed the bear, showing him the presence of danger, for we never saw him again though we sat down for a long while where we overlooked the entire flat and hillsides, and while we ate our lunch of cold caribou steaks we watched everywhere with the glasses. His hide would of course be poor at this time of year but he would be desirable for the Biological Survey collection. We went on over our pass, up over the rocks and steep snow slopes, digging our feet in to prevent slipping. There are fine goat basins and ledges all about under the cliffs of the Fortress but all we saw were old goat and caribou signs on the grassy summit about 7500 feet, – probably a spring range for it would undoubtedly be windswept and so free of snow early. Saw a white-tailed ptarmigan and a golden eagle. Soon Mt. Alexander appeared and though the top was hidden in a cloud we had a magnificent view of it.

A range carrying an enormous glacier, – one fine hanging one forms the base and the mountain itself rises from this big mass fully 3000 feet above it, pyramid-shaped on both of the faces we have seen, apparently unscalable from these two sides. It has a curious lot of ice hanging on the bare face and what keeps it from falling is a mystery. Three lakes lay below us, the western one draining into British Columbia, where the timber looked dense and impassable.[100] Dropped down to the valley and returned to camp, seeing more signs of bear or moose. Song sparrows, juncos, jays and golden-crowned sparrows were in abundance. Saw golden eye with flock of six full grown young ones but unable to fly. Three sandpipers, either semi-palmated or least, I could not tell which, were at the mouth of the creek.

MONDAY, AUGUST 10. COOL – RAINY.

We planned in case of a fine day to go up the valley to a high ridge close by Mt. Alexander to get a good view of it and some photos as well, but being an uncertain day with the clouds low and also uncertain as to the next few days we thought it best not to waste any more of our valuable time, so we packed up the horses, leaving late, about noon.

Saw some more pine siskins and among the numerous ducks on the larger lake, which is between three and four miles long, were golden eyes with their young, Holboel's grebes[101] and surf scoters with nearly full-grown young. The males of the two latter were in fine full adult plumage. We were only on the trail four hours and the going was good although there was some muskeg with one very bad deep hole where every horse had all he could do to wallow through, up to his belly in mud. Packs had to be readjusted but no damage was done and no horse needed to be hauled out. Buttercups, violets, columbines, purple asters and paintbrush predominated, – the latter has faded from a scarlet to a pale rose, simply beautiful. Camped a mile west of our camp of 1912 – on a dry Jack pine ridge. It showered at intervals all day. No one has been here since we were except Griggs, a trapper, the last two years. A beautiful rainbow just before sunset. Distance 10 miles, altitude 4500 feet.

TUESDAY, AUGUST 11. COOL – CLOUDY, SHOWERS.

All kinds of signs of moose, one old coyote track and old signs of bear. Below our camp on the creek is a little mudhole, a lick used by the moose, and a heavily used trail leads to it. Left about 10, by the trail we found in 1912, which we believe leads over to the Wapiti River. For several miles we followed it, now and then losing it. No one has been over it for at least five years and doubtless it is much longer since the Indians have used it. It led through the balsam timber and the only reason it is at all passable is that the moose use it as a highway. I never before saw such moose country any-where in the mountains. Fresh signs, tracks or beds are everywhere. Once in awhile we came to a little grassy, weedy meadow of an acre or two and nearly every one had half a dozen places where the moose in lying down had flattened the grass. Now and then we would come to a little lake, some of them a mile or two long and of the most exquisite emerald green I ever saw.[102] The contrast of the colour with the dark green of the spruces along the shores, in turn contrasted with the lighter green where the sunlight fil-tered through to the underbrush beneath, – all these as a foreground to the massive peaks of sheer rock and ice beyond was a sight not easily forgotten. Saw a golden eye with brood of young ducks on one lake. Pine siskins, jun-cos and jays were the only other birds seen. There were half a dozen lakes in all in a string through this pass that drain undoubtedly into the Wapiti River.[103]

Soon we lost our trail altogether and we had a miserable time over the fallen timber and big rocks, slippery from their covering of moss. In going over one large one, Queen, Fred's saddle horse, fell, luckily without hurting him. She was in such a position that we had to unsaddle her and then roll her over before she was able to get to her feet. Fortunately, she was unhurt. We found one very bad piece of muskeg where several horses got badly mired but all got through safely. Little Cigar, the roan mare, got in up to her belly and she presented a funny sight as she floundered through, plough-ing her nose through the mud, now on one side and then flopping over to the other. Ahead of us we saw across one of our beautiful emerald green lakes one of the high mountains. It is a sharp-pointed peak similar to the

Matterhorn, with a snow cornice on top.[104] Soon a cloud came along and hid the top. Further on we saw a sight that was worth a long trip in itself. There, through a long vista in the spruces and balsams towered our high mountain (Mt. Alexander).[105]

Its top is generally flat but with a heavily indented ice cornice from one end to the other. Without a doubt it is 12,500 feet,[106] judging from the way it towered above us, fully 15 miles away. For some time we watched it through the glasses. Then we left and our troubles began. Finally, we came to the crest of a ridge and for the first time all could see the country around us. Below was a deep canyon valley,[107] impassable to us, so our only choice lay in going up to a summit above timberline on our right. The climb began, and up and up we went, over and around the fallen logs that tried to block our progress, through the heavy, slippery underbrush and over the rocks hidden by the moss. Not a horse had a fall or an accident, wonderful to say, although we had the most dangerous going I have ever seen. The rocks were big and all hidden so the chances were against them in seeing their footing. We all toiled up and up, pulling our horses behind us, cursing and urging the horses ahead of us, until from fatigue and thirst and hunger our patience entirely gave out. Why any sane man comes into these mountains is a mystery to me when he knows the misery he has to endure, – yet we all do it, again and again. There's an end to everything and soon we were above timberline and on a fine large open summit with several basins and one or two little lakes. As we turned around there lay a sight that not one of us will ever forget and which more than made up for the seven and a half hours on the trail. Across the deep valley we had come from rose a high pyramidal mountain, fully 11,000 feet, with nothing but sheer, unscalable cliffs on every side we could see.[108] On both sides were other mountains over 10,000 feet, with big glaciers and ice and snow in all directions. Probably no other white man has ever looked on all these mountains before, – certainly not from this summit. This is without doubt the most magnificent, the grandest view we shall ever have from a camp and it is something worth going thousands of miles to see. The mountain south of us is a splendid replica of the Matterhorn, and I think nearly as inspiring.

Our Mt. Alexander is hidden from view behind it, but we can't have everything. A climb to one side of us up a shoulder of one of the nearby mountains should reveal the high snow-capped mountain once more. The pyramid-shaped mountain across the valley seems unscalable, as about 500 feet from the top there are perpendicular cliffs on all three sides we can see, and the last 200 feet the slope varies from 50 to 90 degrees, with snow and ice.[109] The very summit is ice-covered and has the most overhanging cornice I ever saw; it must be 50 to 100 feet. With the late afternoon sun the effect was magnificent and the pink glow later on the snow was as fine as any on the Swiss peaks, – an attraction that draws people from thousands of miles away. About midnight I awoke and went out to find the moon shining brightly on the snow and just above the peak was a brilliant planet set in the sky like a beacon to mark its position. Very large bull caribou track along trail. Distance 12 miles, altitude 5300 feet.

WEDNESDAY, AUGUST 12. HOT – BRILLIANT.

We awoke to find a day in a thousand, – clear, bright sun, a wonderful blue sky and not a cloud to be seen. Before breakfast I rushed around taking pictures of the peak from several viewpoints and getting two panoramas of three photos each, one of which was taken across a little lake nearby with all the mountains reflected in it.

We made up our minds to stay here until we should have a fine day for this wonderful panorama of snow and ice so we were lucky in having such weather for the first day.

After eating we all climbed the mountain east of us to the top, about 2000 feet above camp, and long before reaching the top Mt. Alexander appeared, rising white and clear without a cloud to conceal it. We feel sure that it is fully 12,500 feet high and the other peak well over 11,000 feet. It is tremendously impressive and carries more snow and ice than Mt. Robson, with a wonderfully jagged snow crest, probably corniced all the way. The three arêtes we have so far seen are about of an angle of 45 degrees, though lower down not over 30 degrees, and the sides are probably 60 degrees at least. Undoubtedly it will be a mountain extremely difficult to climb but not as hard as our other unnamed peak. Snow and ice, glacier and peak stretched far to the south, west and northwest, while to the east and north lay bare rocky ridges, a perfect succession of them. Below us on the snow we saw three caribou, a bull perhaps four or five years old, a cow and calf. They doubtless did not see us and could not have seen us but probably heard Bob shout to us calling our attention to them. We rolled a large rock down the mountain toward them but so used are they to rock falls that they scarcely paid any attention to it. Far below us lay our string of six lakes, the longest over two miles and of the most exquisite emerald green. After taking numerous photos we returned. Lots of caribou tracks and old goat signs, indicating this as a winter range, which accounts for our not seeing any around in such likely looking country. Glissaded down a steep snow slope and so returned to camp speedily, leaving Fred and Bob still on the mountain. As we were eating dinner we spied a cow caribou going over a snow slope not more than a mile away. There were tracks all over the snow; apparently they prefer the going to the rough rocks. She lay down shortly on the snow, apparently eating some of it, and soon disappeared over the ridge. Saw willow ptarmigan, golden crowned sparrow and golden eagle. From our climb we picked out the best way through this trailless country, but it is none too good, as it is all heavily timbered and no signs of feed for the horses. Some moose and goat tracks around camp. Had an hour's snooze after dinner before Fred and Bob appeared, having climbed further along the ridge to the next peak.[110] Later Bob and I climbed the eastern shoulder of the mountain southwest of us and got a fine view of the western side of the sharp mountain where the only possibility of making an ascent seems to be, from what we have seen, though we have not yet seen the southern side of it. A pinnacle of rock separated from the very top knob by about 400 feet of snow ridge whose side nearest us lies at an angle of about 80 degrees, making a dangerous ascent, and still worse just above where it meets the main summit. Our string of six lakes lay east of us and in the late afternoon light were of a beautiful sea green colour. I feel that today was the most perfect I have ever spent among the mountains. Caribou moss is all over these basins and mountains.

THURSDAY, AUGUST 13. WARM – CLOUDY, SHOWERS.

The mosquitoes are still bad though mostly at sunrise and at sunset. During the day we suffer from the big buzzing "bull dog" flies that bite the second they alight on your hand. But almost the worst of all are the sand flies that alight on your forehead under the brim of your hat or in your ear and crawl around and over your anatomy in the most disagreeable way. It would be better if they would only bite and get it over with. I never before suffered so much misery from flies and bugs without any let-up and it will be the end of the month before we get rid of most of these pests; then it will be time for other troubles, so that all is not joy on the trail off in the hills. Heard red-bellied nuthatch at breakfast and shot a fine big blue (Richardson's) grouse[111] for the collection. It was a female with two well grown young which undoubtedly are large enough to take care of themselves. Their plaintive cries as they wandered around the tipi looking for their mother were very pitiful indeed, but such is the result of "in the interests of science." During the night there were several big ice falls from the mountains, but after breakfast they were bigger than ever and the thunder and roar was simply terrific. Unfortunately, it took place on a hanging glacier behind the shoulder of the mountain southwest of us, so we were unable to see the effect, which must have been magnificent. The hot morning sun is what loosened the ice and caused the big falls. Did not leave until late, about 11.30. Dropped down into our valley,[112] where we found open going at first through the muskegs. Then it was all through the timber, chiefly spruce, though we found one or two short stretches of Jack pine and one grove of "white bark pine," similar to Jack pine except that its general outline is bell-shaped and five needles grow in a cluster instead of two. The bark on the ends of the branches is very light coloured, hence the name (*albicola*).[113] Found an old moose trail which we found good and so we followed it some ways though most of the time we were just pushing our way through the timber which for a trailless day's trip was good, fairly open going with very little down timber. Saw a cow moose feeding in a "sloo" with her head under water. We camped by it, as it was the only grass and water in sight, though the camp itself is on the steep hillside. Heard geese honking at camp. Distance 10 miles, altitude 4000 feet. Seventh week, total distance 394 miles.

FRIDAY, AUGUST 14. HOT – BRILLIANT.

The first signs of hares here that we have seen since leaving the Smoky more than two weeks ago. We all had a restless night and we were afraid the horses would go back on us and so awoke constantly and listened for bells. Up at 5, just daylight, and at 7.30 were under way and on the old trail Fred found last night. Someone has been over it about four years ago. A good-sized stream ran close to where we camped, evidently heading in a big ice mountain west of us, – one of the main branches of the Porcupine River.[114] A mile below we found a campground with four large meat-drying racks, signs of the Indians having made a big killing here with the moose. The signs, cuttings etc. appear about two years old and doubtless the Indians we met on Sheep Creek in September 1912 camped here, as they had come from this direction. Here we continued down the river, where there were beaver signs everywhere. Bob saw two in the river last evening when he went to try to get a fish. Then we swung up the side of the mountain, following an old trail, while the Indians apparently kept along the river.[115] Before leaving the stream we had several amusing though nearly serious incidents occur. First Simeon took it into his head to jump off the bank into the river and got in a deep hole and was soon mixed up in a bad swirl and logjam. By the merest chance he managed to get out safely though he was in serious danger of getting tangled up and drowned. Shortly, Roachy jumped in and swam to the other side, followed by Scotty and Jimmy, incidentally wetting the packs containing flour, tobacco and other important items. Fortunately, they had sense enough to stay over until we forded and joined them though we fully expected to see them swim back about the time we reached the other side. Going through the down timber Snowball fell under some logs and was so wedged in that he couldn't move until the packs were removed and the logs cut away. We moved along slowly through muskeg and fallen timber without trail for eight and a half hours before making camp in the muskeg we saw two days ago from the mountain as planned. Saw large grizzly track on river, signs of moose everywhere, spotted sandpiper, Franklin grouse, juncos and jays. It seems slow work only to make five miles in a straight line after eight and a half hours pushing through the timber, but every five miles counts and after ten days or so it amounts up fast. Tomorrow we should be over the summit and possibly on the waters of the Wapiti River.[116] Distance 10 miles, altitude 4500 feet.

SATURDAY, AUGUST 15. HOT – BRILLIANT.

It was such a beautiful clear evening yesterday that we didn't bother to put up the tipi or even the shelter tent but just rolled up in our blankets on the pine needles and moss and slept soundly. Another fine day and we were up early, so that we left camp about 9 and waded through long stretches of open muskeg, finally coming to a nice dry meadow with fine feed where we found an old trail that hadn't been used for six or eight years at least. Then we lost it again and followed an old moose trail and finally found the pack trail fortunately going through the very pass we were headed for. Here the signs were as old as before. Hardly any cutting to do at all, which made it pleasanter. After four hours we came over the summit, which was low (below timberline), about 5000 feet, and found a fine clear stream with green timber everywhere and a nice flat with good feed where we camped. There is a fine-looking goat basin and mountain west of us and we soon were examining it with the glasses to find two goats (billies) high up on the most inaccessible kind of cliffs, so we plan to stay over a day to hunt them.[117] Saw no birds. The meat has all gone bad owing to the flies and hot weather, so we will have to kill something soon. Camped at 1 p.m. and had a pleasant loaf at last. Distance 10 miles, altitude 4600 feet.

SUNDAY, AUGUST 16. HOT – BRILLIANT.

Moose signs as numerous as ever, with fresh beds on the flat we are camped on. At last we have one thing to be thankful for, – the mosquitoes are on their last legs owing to the continued cold, frosty nights, which have also turned the foliage of some of the more delicate weeds and leaves of rasp berry bushes. Bob Jones and Fred started off to cut out the old trail and climb a mountain northeast of camp[118] to see the best course to keep the next few days, as we have reached the point we picked out four days ago and want to get our course straightened out again with another objective point in view. Cross and I went off on a goat hunt, up the steep cliffs west of us. The hill was so steep through the timber that we had to pull ourselves up using the spruce branches and bushes. There was much down timber, which made it worse. The last 500 feet of about a 2000-foot climb was above timber but as steep as ever, with rocks and cliffs to make it more interesting. Saw lots of old signs and tracks of goats but no sign of the two we saw last evening. Sat down to eat lunch on top of the little ridge which, being iso-lated, makes a fine basin between it and the main mountain, with a way out at each end. The goat trails were numerous and well worn all along the rock slide, showing it must be fine goat country. Spent about two hours glass-ing all the mountains and valleys in sight. Saw two goats a couple of miles away, high up on the sheer cliffs, feeding peacefully, but it would have been useless to go after them, as it was next to impossible to climb to where they were, as well as out of the question to make the stalk out of sight, as there was no cover, and if one was killed he would likely roll down the mountain a thousand feet or more before stopping and get so smashed up as to be of no use to us. So under the circumstances we satisfied ourselves in watching them. Below us we saw Symes in camp baking bread and the horses feeding along the creek. Downstream are several "sloos" and lakes where we saw two cow moose with their calves, each pair in separate lakes. Finally, one cow with her offspring swam the lake, went through the brush and joined the others. While the cows fed peacefully together with their heads under water the calves were playing in the reeds and willows along the shore. One cow didn't seem to care for her calf associating with its companion, so she left the lake to chase it away and it was an amusing sight to see her run after it as fast as she could through the mud and reeds. The calf was not anxious to leave its playmate and returned several times, only to have the cow dash madly at it again. All this did not seem to please the mother of the abused calf and she became so irritated at the treatment of her offspring that she left the lake too in order to offer protection. She and the other cow made a few feeble antagonistic movements which resulted in all four of them going off into the timber, each family by itself, and so this amusing incident ended. Shortly afterwards we saw one pair feeding peacefully in a nearby "sloo." We left the mountain, seeing the uselessness of hunting under such adverse conditions as described. It was interesting to find that the moose had worn a trail up the steep hillside to above timberline to the open weedy pastures, but whether to feed or to keep away from the flies I don't know. The elevation was about 6000 feet. All along on both sides of this stream are the deepest and most used moose trails I ever saw, – as heavy as well-travelled pack trails. Saw a magpie at 6000 feet, and at last our first Hudsonian chickadee[119] and a warbler, at 5500 feet. I suppose the former, as well as the black-capped, must nest here but they never appear until the middle of August so well do they hide themselves. Also saw Franklin grouse and a winter wren. Returned to find the others had just reached camp having seen the most extensive view Fred ever saw in the mountains. He saw the prairie to the east, Grande Prairie to the northeast, the valley of the Wapiti and the east branch of the Pine[120] to the north and to the south Mt. Alexander towered far away above everything. For three to four more days' travelling our course is picked out via a summit we saw from our mountain with no burnt timber in that direction. Fred saw a cow and calf moose in the "sloo" below, tracks of goat and caribou and four goats on the mountain opposite. They brought back a caribou horn. Saw spotted sandpiper along creek.

MONDAY, AUGUST 17. HOT – BRILLIANT.

Concerning the Hudsonian chickadee I saw yesterday, some say its note is indistinguishable from our black-capped chickadee, but on the contrary there is a marked difference as it is more nasal (as if the bird had a cold), not as loud and by no means as attractive a note in any way. Another perfect, cloudless day. I never saw such a stretch of weather before. This is typical of mid-August in the mountains, – clear, cloudless days with a bright sun and clear, cold nights down below freezing, with heavy frosts, just like our Indian summer days at home. Bob and I slept under the spruce trees and found it much dryer, as the meadow was extremely damp and chilly owing to the heavy frost. The horses found us of course and I woke up to find half a dozen of them standing around looking at me, looking like a lot of sentinels, and had to chase them away. An owl began hooting over our heads under the brilliant stars, adding to the loneliness of the scene. He had another queer note, a sort of a wheeze or a croak that startled us. At last I had a fine night's rest, the best for at least a week, and I feel better for it, as the last few days I have been pretty tired out and yesterday's climb only added to it. It would have been a good day to have loafed in camp. Scotty, one of the bay horses, has been making all kinds of trouble lately by eating and tearing the pack covers to pieces along the trail in his endeavours to lick off the salt from them that got on from the hides being rolled up in them. Nothing seems to have stopped him so Jack made the necessary equipment out of wood and made a strong net of cord which we are going to tie on him today and it looks as if we would have him under control all right now. At last we have found mice. Fred heard them running all around his bed last night and we jollied Bob at being such a poor "mouser" but he found two in the traps after breakfast. Both are very small and of the white-footed species. Today was a repetition of former days, – following heavy moose trails that showed blazing here and there, made by an Indian trapper probably about six to ten years ago. It is doubtful if horses have ever been in this valley before. Lots of old signs of beaver and a dam in the river nearly finished. Saw a trapper's old brush lean-to. No birds at all. More or less chopping had to be done. Camped after six hours, only making about eight miles by trail and in a straight line about four (altitude 4500 feet). Unable to make the summit as planned so camped this side of it on a semi-dry willow flat on the riverbank. Saw 12 goats feeding on the mountain west of us late in the afternoon, – all nannies and kids.

TUESDAY, AUGUST 18. HOT – BRILLIANT.

Only four of our goats appeared on the mountain before leaving, at which time a kingfisher flew about us. First we went down the creek a way, then left it, crossing the willow flats, muskegs and beaver dams etc. and the ascent of the hill began, which turned out to be 1700 feet high. Luckily, the going was not as bad as we expected, as it was less steep and there was less cutting than we anticipated. Saw old cutting evidence of someone having crossed in the dark ages. After three hours we emerged from the timber on a dry summit[121] and shortly made camp on the highest point, in the open with no timber about us, so it is a pretty exposed camp for stormy weather, – nothing but stunted balsams about three feet high, too tough to cut or break and almost impossible to burn. After eating, three of the men left to climb the mountain east of us to pick out our next objective point and the method of reaching it. Ahead we can see a long distance, high, bare, rocky peaks and deep valleys. The main valley of the Wapiti[122] is now in sight about two days off. Lots of caribou tracks about as well as those of a bear. Made only three miles in a straight line. The big "bull dog" flies and other varieties are worse than ever this afternoon. I believe a man consumes at least 50 per cent of his vitality in fighting flies in this country in mid-summer. It certainly is fascinating work going through a new section of the country without trails. In past trips we have always followed the river valleys, but now we are cutting across country from one stream to the next via the best summits we can find. After climbing a mountain to get our direction and set our course we go for three or four days in the heavy timber, not being able to see our way but only keeping in the general direction by now and then catching a glimpse of some mountain through the timber by which we set our course. Then finally, in a few days we emerge from the timber to an open summit and as we look back, see the course we have made, the spot we started from and each successive day's trip. Then we climb another mountain and again lay our course for a few more days. Today we reached camp early and as I was tired I did not go off with the others up the mountain but planned to stay in camp and have a few hours' loaf. But there is no rest for the weary. First I had some washing and sewing to do, then I tried to read but the flies were so bad that it was far from a restful afternoon. The others did not put in an appearance so we ate supper without them, at which time Bob appeared. Two goats, one small and one large one, were sighted high up on the skyline and Bob told us that they had come within a few feet of one and he was so tame that they threw a rock at him before he moved off. Either one they could have shot but they took no guns with them. The goats came down lower and we could see them watching our horses feeding below, evidently puzzled by the strange sound of the bells, but not in the least alarmed. Jack was looking at them with the glasses and said they had lain down, which meant they would not move again until daylight. That was enough, so Jack and I put on our boots, got guns, knives, stones etc. together and were off to get the goats. Our caribou meat is about on its last legs owing to its age and the flies, so we want a further supply and I want a couple of heads. We went up the thousand or more feet speedily, stopping now and then a moment to get our wind and admire the wonderful panorama unfolding in the distance and the colours caused by the setting sun. We were lucky in our stalk and got to within 50 yards of the goats and killed them both. One had horns 7 1/2, the other 9 1/2 inches and their coats were in good condition. Apparently they had been eating caribou moss. The effect of the distant mountains in the fast-fading light was magnificent. We gralloched both goats and returned, reaching camp at dark, having been gone only an hour and a quarter, – a record goat hunt. We lit a big fire and all sat around laying our plans for the next stage of our trip. Distance 5 miles, altitude 6000 feet.

WEDNESDAY, AUGUST 19. HOT – BRILLIANT.

Went up to the top of the mountain[123] about 2000 feet above camp with Bob, as I wanted to see the view on such a perfect, clear, cloudless day, while the men went to skin the goats and bring the meat, hides and heads back to camp. We were able to see fully a hundred miles in every direction and such an extensive view I never saw before and rarely a finer one.

In one direction we could look way off into the rolling prairie until it became dim in the distance, while on all the other sides rose peak after peak, one towering above the other. To the south were our two big mountains, which towered far above everything in sight. The sharp peak has a sharp ridge on the south side which we never saw before, making the first part of the ascent practical but the last 500 to 1000 feet are as sheer on that side as any other. Mt. Alexander we feel rises 13,000 feet, as we are about 35 miles away and it towers far above everything. It is in the shape of a trapezoid and does not look like a difficult mountain to ascend though once on top it would be dangerous work to reach the eastern or higher end over the roughly indented cornice. Returned about noon to work on the hides and heads. Saw a flock of about 50 grey-crowned leucostictes, evidently preparing to migrate, a lark, little chief hares,[124] marmots and chipmunks, all high up in the rocks between 7000 and 8000 feet. The horses were apparently contented, feeding high up on the grassy slopes under the rocks and cliffs about 1000 feet above camp. The heat is terrific today in this unshaded spot and the bulldog flies worse than ever. From the mountain we saw the main Wapiti Valley and thought we could see the east branch of the Pine, our objective point. The mountains ahead look good for goat and bear as well as caribou, but not for sheep. It looks as though we have passed through the moose country. It gave us a queer sensation this morning as we looked into the prairie country perhaps 100 miles away with Grande Prairie city and hundreds of homesteaders within the circle of our vision yet invisible to us. Civilization, with the comforts of home almost within sight, yet in reality still months away from us, a curious anomaly. Thermometer 87 degrees in the shade. A female humming bird flew about camp at noon, and a young spikehorn bull caribou appeared on the ridge above camp, the same one we saw earlier and that Bob got so close to yesterday that he hit it on the shoulder with a rock! A menagerie camp!

THURSDAY, AUGUST 20. HOT – BRILLIANT.

Started as usual but got away late, about 11. Bob found the horses on the ridge west of camp 1000 feet above us, all lying down peacefully sleeping, thinking their retreat was secure. Back they had to come and then all the way up again, this time packed. Down the other side we went, scaring a good sized goat about 300 yards ahead of us. Then along and up another summit, all the time above timberline. Here Fred and Bob left us to climb a ridge to see the possibility of getting down the other side. They evidently found it OK, as they called to us, so we led the horses up. The view was fine, looking down into a big, open, grassy basin. Below us was a young bull caribou feeding. We started the horses down an almost impossibly steep slope of scree which formed a covering to the steep ledges, – a misstep meant a roll of 500 feet over rocks and cliffs and a dead horse without doubt, but we took them along slowly and carefully – without doubt the most dangerous place we have yet taken horses.[125] The sharp rocks cut their feet and they hated to come but they did and without any mishap. On we went through now open stretches and then tangled masses of stunted fir or spruce, until we made camp and were under cover before a heavy shower struck us. Saw willow ptarmigan, golden eagle and lots of small birds. Distance 12 miles, altitude 5500 feet.

End of eighth week, total distance 439 miles.

FRIDAY, AUGUST 21. COOL – CLOUDY.

These summit meadows are still a mass of flowers; at present the purple aster predominates in the rank growth. Higher up on the bare rocks yet where there is plenty of moisture the forget-me-nots are still blooming in profusion, apparently as yet still unaffected by the frosty nights. It showered hard about dark last night but although it was cloudy we had no more rain. This morning I saw a junco and a Hudsonian chickadee. Evidently the sudden change from the well-aged caribou meat to the fresh goat was too much for us as we all have felt the effects of it the last two days. Our breakfasts have been once more of the fat of the land, – fried liver and kidneys. From Fred's report after his return from a short walk ahead to the summit in order to pick out our course down to the valley of the Wapiti[126] there are either deer or sheep around, which fact has caused more than a little interest. We expect to find a trail once more and will be surprised if none exists. It looks as though a change in the weather has come and getting ready for a few days storm as we have had several showers the last two days and it looks like more rain all the time. The horses strayed off and Bob had a hard time in locating them, so it was 11.30 before we got under way over the summit, which does not go above timberline. It looked like about four hours' trip to drop down the steep hill covered with burnt and down timber to the banks of the Wapiti. But appearances are often very deceitful and this certainly was a good example of the old saying. Fred saw a little lick in a mudhole where the trails radiated from it in all directions, like the spokes of a wheel, and Bob and I tried to locate it but were unable to, so went on after the outfit, catching up to them on the steep hillside beyond. Here we found not only grey and black currants, raspberries and blueberries, but, better still, huckleberries and as thick as I ever saw them. Out here the latter berry far surpasses the blueberry (which is the reverse of conditions at home) because of the fact it has no seeds, grows to a large size, often nearly as big as a Delaware grape,[127] and is as juicy and sweet as any berry I ever tasted. We ate them literally by the handful as we walked along leading our horses down the steep rocks. The only other berry here whose flavour is equal or possibly better is the raspberry. Having looked forward to a big feed of berries all summer, at last we ate to our hearts' content, scarcely having to stop to pick them, until we could eat no more and we were hungry too for we had been through breakfast many hours. Here our troubles began and the chopping was incessant to clear a passable way for the horses. A steep descent of a thousand feet, then a level bench, then another drop to a bench below, and so on to the riverbank . But before we reached it the time was about 8 p.m. and by the time the horses were unpacked and supper eaten it was dark. But back to our troubles as they were numerous today and serious ones. First of all, in coming down a very steep slope covered with down timber which necessitated much jumping of logs in steep places, with incessant chopping, Andy caught his hind feet in a clumsy way and fell, rolling down head over heels until he was caught in a jam of logs below. We unpacked him, cut away the logs and he got up, unhurt luckily. In another minute, Tommy, Cross's saddle horse (he was walking, not riding, at the time) fell near the same spot and rolled down the hill. He too was finally extricated unhurt and strange to say neither gun nor glasses, which were tied to the saddle, were injured. So far, so good, but we had one more hill worse than anything yet attempted. It was the only way to reach the flat about 200 feet below. There was very little down timber on it but it was terribly steep, an angle of at least 50 degrees, and covered with loose gravel with rocks underneath. We let the horses come slowly, three or four at a time, so they wouldn't crowd each other. It was an awful-looking hill and it didn't seem possible that horses could ever get down packed as they were. Part way down Cigar's pack slipped onto her neck so that she was in danger of being thrown. I ran out and got her and headed her uphill where Jack and I unpacked her. Then after it looked as if we had saved her from a serious fall she reared, from excitement and probably scared by the insecure footing, and fell over backwards dragging all three of us after her. All managed to scramble from under her, but down the hill she went bounding like a rock until she was stopped in a logjam. We managed to get her clear of nearly everything and still she didn't move and then we discovered that she was held by a snag from one of the trees under her. Finally, we got her up, only to find a terrible tear in her belly, a whole square foot of skin and flesh torn off and hanging. But apparently it had not pierced her. We led her down, bathed it and bandaged it up. Bob led her along while Fred went ahead cutting our way to the river, where we camped. Then we threw her, tied her and washed the wound out and again bandaged it. She was as quiet as a lamb and everyone had sympathy for her as she is the nicest, gentlest and most affectionate little mare in the whole outfit. It was late, about 11, before we rolled into our blankets. Saw signs of a large bear, undoubtedly grizzly. Burnt timber and berries usually spell bear. Saw two bulls (one large one) and a cow moose in the burnt timber. Distance 5 miles, altitude 3500 feet.

SATURDAY, AUGUST 22. COOL – RAIN.

It rained hard during the night but we all managed to keep dry in spite of having no shelter. Before breakfast we put up the lean-to and afterwards the tipi, – the first time in ten days that we have had it up. Sometimes we have slept under the lean-to but the weather has been so good that most nights we have rolled up in our blankets in the open and slept soundly under the stars. However, it is good to have the tipi up once more and sit around the fire again, although the lean-to with a fire in front is as comfortable a shelter as can be imagined. It looks as though the change in the weather has actually come and this is our first day for over eight weeks that we been actually held up in camp by the weather, – a remarkable stretch of fine weather and one that will be seldom equalled in the mountains. At last all the flies have gone, but doubtless will reappear on the first warm, sunny day. Even if it had been good weather today we shouldn't have moved from here as little Cigar has to be attended to and her tear sewed up, which was impossible in the darkness last night although it would have been far better. Then she should have a day or two of rest before going on the trail again. We hope to save her, under Doctor (?) Cross's care, but she will have to go unpacked the rest of the trip. Strange to say, no trail showed up on this side of the river yet it may be across or possibly lower down, as the river may not be travelled so near its source. There seem to be two good passes north-northwest of us that will lead us to a further branch of the Wapiti and into the Pine country. One of these is just inside (and is better and more open going), while the other is just outside of the last range of mountains before reaching the foothills. In spite of all our trials and tribulations of yesterday there certainly was some humour in certain incidents. In leading Cigar after her accident the outfit crossed a muddy creek where the mare would have strained herself badly so Bob tried to lead her by it through the willows and small spruces. As he was doing so Jack called back to see if he could get through all right; Bob's answer came back with a mournful wail to it, "Yes, but I'm cutting down a tree with my knife!" There are a pair of black-capped chickadees around camp in the rain this morning, which makes it seem very homelike, and their cheery note is very pleasant to hear again, as it is the first time we have seen them this summer. After dinner Cigar was thrown and tied securely, when all the preparations were made in boiling instruments, preparing bandages etc. and Dr. Cross washed the wound and took about a dozen stitches in it, leaving a gauze drain as a precaution. She must have suffered a lot but she was very nervy about it. At times she struggled fiercely but luckily we were able to hold her, though it took three of us in spite of her being as securely tied as possible. It was a two hours' job but she seemed to have come through finely and began to walk around to feed as soon as she was free. It was a disagreeable, cold-blooded task and all were glad to have it over and completed, – apparently successfully. Bob Jones returned from down the river on a search for horse feed with the news that there is a trail with last year's cutting on it. However, our plan is to leave the Wapiti a short ways downstream and go over a pass toward the Pine River, and unless there is a trail over it we shall benefit but little from this one. Had a fine feed of wild raspberries this afternoon. They were so plentiful that I sat down and for half an hour feasted until I could eat no more, scarcely having to move from the same spot, – it was as good as being let loose in a cultivated patch at home and was a reminder of childhood days!

SUNDAY, AUGUST 23. WARM – RAIN.

Yesterday was the first real rest we have had for two solid months, during which time it has been pretty strenuous and I don't know when I have
appreciated a day's rest more. I just loafed around and read, ate and dozed
all day except for the two hours we were sewing up the little mare. Today
was a repetition of yesterday – reading, eating and sleeping – and it was fully
as much appreciated. Bob Jones and Fred went down the river separately a
couple of miles but found no feed for the horses and no better camping
place than this gravel bar of ours which is covered with down timber. They
saw fresh bear tracks and a sort of den with goat (?) bones lying around.
All day it showered, with now and then the sun appearing so that it looks
as though the weather was slowly clearing. Saw a pair of harlequin ducks
in the river. Bob Cross shot a chipmunk yesterday, and skinning him was
my only attempt at work. He finished the work on the marmot, which was
a long, slow job. Baked bread again today, enough to last us another week.
For supper, as an example of our bill of fare, we had cold roast goat, cocoa,
bread and butter, with cake and freshly picked berries! Who could ask for
a better meal? Saw eight goats on the mountains west of camp, all nannies
and kids. It certainly is fine goat country all about here.

MONDAY, AUGUST 24. HOT – BRILLIANT.

Our wonderful weather returned again today. Saw three black-capped
chickadees, five harlequin ducks and a spotted sandpiper near camp and
in the afternoon a pair of Hudsonian chickadees. Made a late start, not getting away until nearly 12 o'clock. The weather at first looked doubtful but
the heavy mist was soon cleared from the valley to reveal a cloudless sky.
Followed the river (which is from 50 to 100 feet wide here and one to two
feet deep) for about two hours. In the absence of any bars we went right
down the middle of the stream most of the way. Found a very old trail that
evidently hasn't been used for a great many years, probably not since the
fire that burnt this part of the valley and caused the fallen timber to block
the trail.[128] Then we left the river to follow a little creek and here we found
a heavily blazed trail from ten to 20 years old, – probably only the original
outfit had been over it. As it didn't go our way we soon left it and Fred and
Bob Jones preceded the outfit with their axes and for the next six hours
there was continual chopping as we climbed one heavily timbered ridge
and down the further side only to climb the next one. It was the longest and
most discouraging day of all but finally we emerged from the timber on the

upland meadows and soon made camp, at 8 p.m., about dark, having been eight and a half hours on the trail and climbed more than 2000 feet.

Cigar, the invalid, had a hard day but came through OK. Everyone was dead tired and rolled in early. Twelve hours between meals is too long. Small falls about ten feet high just above camp where the river runs through a canyon. Distance 8 miles, altitude 5000 feet.

TUESDAY, AUGUST 25. WARM – CLOUDY.

Saw a cow caribou and her calf on a high rock ridge 1000 feet above us this morning, apparently not much alarmed by our presence as after watching us a few minutes she continued feeding. As we camped last night another cow caribou was feeding on the edge of the little "sloo" we are camped on. Finally she decided it was unsafe and ran off. Put new bandages on the mare and washed out the wound. She apparently is none the worse for yesterday's hard trip. Bob is not only an accomplished "vet," but an excellent doctor as well, as he has fixed up my finger in good shape. An old cut didn't heal well and the first thing I knew it had become badly infected so that I was afraid of blood poisoning. All one night I lay awake with it, as it was throbbing like a steam pump. Yesterday morning Bob lanced it, which immediately relieved the pain and since then it has steadily improved. Saw numerous small flocks of pine siskins. All stayed in camp during the morning, as we got up late owing to our hard day yesterday. After an early dinner Cross and Fred went off to climb a mountain in order to look ahead to settle our next few days' travel. Bob Jones was sewing pack covers while Jack and I were peacefully dozing after having read for awhile. Suddenly I was awakened by Macloud's bell ringing, as well as the others. Bob suspected trouble and ran out of the lean-to. "There's a bear!" he yelled. "Get your gun." I jumped up and so did Jack who waked up from a sound sleep. There were all the horses rounded up in a bunch, running along, with a grizzly after them; – this all within 300 yards of camp. I ran to the pile and threw off one pack cover after another looking for my gun, which is always left on the outside so as to be handy. Finally, I discovered it in the center of everything and pulled it out, loading as fast as I could with the few cartridges I always carry in my pocket, at the same time yelling to Bob to get more cartridges out of my bag. In the meanwhile the horses went over a knoll but the bear came on slowly toward us, apparently not seeing us. At about 200 yards, probably less, I fired and he rose on his hind legs and turned a back somersault. I thought I had him but he bounced up like a rubber ball. Again I fired and this time he let out a bellow of pain, biting at his shoulder where the bullet struck. He kept on alternately dropping as I fired and bouncing up again. After eight shots he fell dead, but we watched and waited a long time before going near him although Jack had his knife in his hand, crazy to skin the first grizzly. He turned out to be a two-year-old with a splendid, well-furred hide. He was hit four or five times, – all but one being found in the neck and shoulders. Being my first grizzly, when Bob and Fred returned we duly celebrated this event.

WEDNESDAY, AUGUST 26. WARM – CLOUDY, SHOWERS.

A busy day in camp in fleshing and finishing skinning the bear hide and skull, with washing, mapmaking etc. as side issues. A marsh hawk skimmed over the little lake. Heard a red-bellied nuthatch and found a greater yellowleg feeding in the long grass along the lake; quite tame but hasn't whistled at all yet. It has been cloudy and at times gusty all the morning and looks as if the weather might suddenly turn cold and snow. If all goes well we will be down in the lower country again tomorrow in a less exposed place. The country is lower ahead and no summits above timberline in sight, – not good for goat or caribou and no sheep hills in sight, so we will be in poor country for all the game we want. Breakfast of liver and kidneys once more. The kidney of a bear is formed of small rounded masses, differing from sheep, goat, caribou etc., but like that of a steer. At last we caught a long-tailed jumping mouse.[129] The hills around are full of them and we have over 20 traps out. Later caught a short-tailed one. Bob Jones saw another bear but he got away too quickly for us. Migration of warblers and sparrows, – tree, chipping and song sparrows all represented.

THURSDAY, AUGUST 27. COOL – CLOUDY, SHOWERS.

Another bear alarm just before dark last night. The horses were rushing wildly back and forth over the hills, alarmed at something, probably a grizzly, so Bob and I went up with our guns but could see nothing wrong, though by this time it was too dark to see much. It was pretty looking down to the valley below us, stretching far away. In the foreground at our feet was the little lake and our camp and tent at the further end with the blazing campfire. Above the distant range of mountains the evening stars shone brilliantly, completing this lovely alpine picture. Awoke this morning to find a change in the weather but not as we expected, for the storm has passed by in a windstorm and it is clear and cool like an autumn day. Supped last night on very fair bear steak and breakfasted again on liver and kidneys. This has been a beautiful, quiet little spot and we hate to leave but we must keep moving and can't afford to look around for more bear, which certainly are around, – surely no better place in every way could be found in which hunt them. Tonight we have been out nine weeks from Jasper, though it does not seem that long. We plan to be back by November 1st at the latest, as that is the extreme limit of our grubstakes, so that we have been out just half of the trip, and tomorrow the second half begins. Our larder is well stocked for another two weeks, as we have plenty of goat and bear meat. Bob suggested killing a caribou so as to have a greater variety of meat. In that case Symes would have to write out a menu for our meals. It is unusual enough to have two kinds of meat and not know whether we are going to sit down to a meal of roast goat or fried bear steaks. Also we have plenty of grease as an Indian does. We got away late today and planned to make a short drive to the timber on the other side of the pass in order to get in camp early and get well settled, as it looks as though we would get a good storm as a climax to this contin-ued threatening weather. Before we had gone a couple of miles, as I was remarking to Fred that the absence of goat about in spite of the heavy signs looked as if this was a winter range, I saw one and on inspecting him with the glasses decided to stalk him, for although his horns were short he was a very large old billy. He led me up over a steep, stiff slope where it was impossible to step without slipping, making the climbing extremely tiresome. Fred signalled there were two more, both of which I shortly caught sight of. One was lying down on a projecting cliff, the other on the scree slope under it, while the first goat was nervous and climbed up ahead of the steep slope I was on and was quickly out of sight as well as range. I continued on over a series of ledges with the two goat not far ahead. I watched them at intervals closely with the glasses and was very much undecided whether to shoot or not as their horns appeared too short in spite of their size. They became alarmed finally and went down a steep snow slope, sliding down with all four feet set, the snow flying in a cloud about them. It was a very amusing as well as interesting sight. I fired three times, apparently missing entirely. One now climbed up to a ledge above, thinking he was safe, while the other went on over the slopes of alternating rock and snow. I fired at the one on the ledge above me, about 200 yards away and he came out of the air like a rock, falling to the slope below and rolling to the foot of a snow slide several hundred yards below.

It looked as if he would be all torn to pieces and his horns broken but on inspection it proved very little harm had been done. His horns were short, having been previously broken, – not over 8 1/2 inches, but they had a large base of 5 1/2 and 6 inches, respectively. He was an enormous old billy, fully ten years old. His teeth were all loose, but he was as fat as he could be and beautifully furred. Three of the men came up to skin him and Bob said the other goat was one of the finest specimens he had ever seen and advised me to go after him, but I had only two cartridges left. However, it was a great temptation to get my last head, so I climbed up after him as fast as I could go. He acted as if he was hurt or else not alarmed by my presence and I planned to get as close as possible to make the most of my two shells. Finally, he turned his back to me, deliberately lying down and when I got within 75 yards of him he stood up and I shot him. Away he went over the cliff, down to the rocks below, but scarcely was injured by the fall. He too was an old, fat billy and we skinned him out and then went on after the outfit, not catching them until we found them already in camp. Distance 5 miles, altitude 5000 feet. Total distance, ninth week, 457 miles.

FRIDAY, AUGUST 28. WARM – BRIGHT.

Left after the usual preparations, for the valley below, reaching it through the green timber down the steep mountain side with ease. Here we found a beautiful valley[130] with a stream running through and green timber on both sides up to the green alps, which in turn were surmounted by the bare, rocky peaks. We decided there must be a trail and soon found an old one where the cutting appeared to be three different ages but it has been five or six years at least since anyone has travelled it. The sight of a trail through green timber with Jack pine flats was a joy to our hearts, as it has been nearly four weeks since we have been on such a trail with such fine country around us.[131] It certainly is good to get such a breathing spell after the weeks of slow, bad travelling we have experienced. Finally, we came to a beautiful lake about two by three miles of the most wonderful sapphire blue colour, a very rare colour for a lake in these mountains.[132] On two sides it is surrounded by rocky cliffs which run into rocky peaks above, and at the further end there is a gap where the river that drains it runs, one of the forks of the Wapiti. Made camp shortly, surrounded by beaver dams and ponds. Distance 10 miles, altitude 3700 feet. Saw a sharp-tailed grouse along the trail.

SATURDAY, AUGUST 29. WARM – BRIGHT.

At last I have finished fleshing the goat hides, which is hard, tiresome work. For two days each morning until we packed up, and again as soon as we make camp until dark, which is about nine now, I have sat down with a hide in my lap doubled up over it working as fast as possible in order to get it ready for salting before it dried out too much. We kept on about northwest today and our course was very straight so that we made fast time as well as a good distance in the four hours we were on the trail, which still continues. Only a little cutting appeared now and then, but we passed a very old meat rack and tipi poles, showing in years past that the Indians hunted and trapped here, and no wonder, for it is full of moose, caribou, goat and beaver. We will soon find trails that are well used and probably in the big valley ahead of us, which should be the north branch of the Wapiti.[133] Passed lots of low-bush blueberries, the bushes being only about three inches high. Made camp at the edge of burnt country that extends for miles and miles ahead or us and probably the start of more of our troubles. Bob and Fred went over the hills as usual to look ahead and pick out a way through the timber. Saw a pair of mallard ducks and hawk owls. Distance 10 miles, altitude 4000 feet.

SUNDAY, AUGUST 30. WARM – BRILLIANT.

Awoke to find a beautiful clear Sunday, with everything frozen solid. Last night we had a heavy thunderstorm with lots of lightning and a downpour of rain for an hour, during which time we all huddled in the lean-to with a roaring fire in front of us. As soon as the storm was over the men went out to their beds in the open while Bob and I turned in under our shelter. During the night it turned cold and it was very sharp this morning, but an extremely pleasant change and I hope it continues. When the sun reached us about 9 o'clock, we warmed up fast. A red-bellied nuthatch and some kind of warbler are around camp, also some species of woodpecker and chickadees. The men found that it will not be necessary to go into the burnt timber but very little and found a good way over a green-timbered ridge and into the valley beyond, where better-looking sheep country appears, so we are all looking forward with interest to the developments of the next few days. The country here is quite different from that between Jasper and Laggan[134] (the Athabasca and Bow River passes) for here we are camped in a high valley yet it is only 4000 feet above the sea and timberline is but 5000 feet and the mountains, of course, correspondingly low, from 7000 to 8000 feet. Our course today lay first through the tall willows, pushing our way through a moose trail, then up through the green spruces, along a caribou trail above timberline, then along it for several miles. Here we saw a magnificent bull caribou and he seemed very different from those we have been seeing, for he was very much larger, had typical *Osborni* horns and colour, as his neck and shoulders were white, his head and body black. He was not more than 300 yards away and stood looking at us until our scent reached him and then he trotted off. His horns were in the velvet or I would have shot him as they were of good size. Lots of sparrows and juncos migrating. Here we dropped down the steep hillside of burnt timber and followed a caribou trail along the lake to a little lake where we made camp.[135] Fred walked ahead and returned with the report of a large valley and river running north, – surely there must be a trail on it. Can it be one of the branches of the Pine?[136] We are far enough to be on the waters of that river. We have picked out our mountain to climb tomorrow, then we will know more. Distance 10 miles, altitude 3600 feet. So cold that the water froze again in the pail during breakfast at 9 a.m.!

MONDAY, AUGUST 31. HOT – BRILLIANT.

Bob, Fred and I went up the mountain already referred to and found quantities of huckleberries along the hillside in the burnt timber, large juicy and sweet, so that we got a big feed, both going up and returning. Saw white-tailed ptarmigan, rock rabbits, rock chipmunks, prairie horned (?) larks, warblers, a pair of hawks and a bluebird; the latter flew over the top of the mountain and gave his pretty call as he flashed his blue back in the sunlight as he passed us. It reminded me of home and spring. The view from the mountain which is about 6000 feet (2200 feet above camp) was magnificent and very extensive.[137] The air was clear and we could see the mountains west over the divide, those far to the south of us and the prairie to the east. North lay a big valley that swung northeast and it looked like a branch of the Pine. If so, we could see the main valley about 40 miles further to the north. This whole situation is very interesting, as it will take us some time to be sure. Possible sheep hills beyond.[138] Saw a cow and calf caribou a mile away, – lots of tracks and fine hills for them as well as sheep, but not a sign of them. Had a big feast at supper of a fine roast of bear and stewed fresh huckleberries! Shot an adult solitary sandpiper on a mud flat in the "sloo"; a young bird was also around.

TUESDAY, SEPTEMBER 1. HOT – BRILLIANT.

Last night was clear and frosty, cold enough to be perfect for sleeping but as soon as the sun arose all the chill disappeared and later on it was hot and continued so all day. Shot another solitary sandpiper before leaving. The heat brought out the sand flies, which pestered us to death. Two years ago at this time we were cutting our way down the Smoky River through the burnt timber, as we are now, with bright, warm days and then we were also bothered in the same way by these pests. This valley in many ways reminds me of the Smoky, irrespective of the flies, timber and weather. The berries were thicker than ever, comprising nearly all kinds, – low-bush blueberries, huckleberries, black and grey currants, raspberries, mountain high-bush cranberries and saskatoons, not to mention as many more non-edible varieties. They were so thick that, as Symes expressed it, "we had to pick our way through them"! Once we stopped so that all hands could sit down and feast and it only took a few minutes before we all had a B.F. All day long as we went we picked bushes, and ate them on the way. I finally ate and ate until I was tired of seeing berries. We are certainly making the most of them, as in a week or two they will be done for from the frosty nights. Often we picked several kinds from the same spot, eating them together in one handful. We went on cutting our way through the burnt timber, which was fairly open, as the fire was a recent one and so there was very little of it fallen. Saw a fine male Franklin grouse and a winter wren. The moose trails became quite frequent and so we followed one tremendously heavy trail and we knew it would lead to a lick, for it was as heavy as a pack trail. Sure enough, it did and none of us had ever seen such a game lick. Trails came from all directions to it. It was circular, about 150 feet across, and composed of semi-soft clay. Moose and caribou tracks, the latter extremely large, were everywhere so that it resembled in every way a muddy cow yard. It was such a rare and wonderful sight that we unpacked Jimmy to get another film for my Kodak. We finally, after seven and a half hours, reached the spot on the river[139] and camped where we planned to from the top of the mountain yesterday. Passed through several tamarack (larch tree) swamps. Distance 12 miles, altitude 2800 feet.

WEDNESDAY, SEPTEMBER 2. HOT – BRILLIANT.

Is this the east branch of the Pine River? Every indication points that way, – according to the distance we have travelled, the direction of its course, its size, which is as large as the Porcupine half way down its length, and the whole lay of the country and valleys as viewed from the mountain two days ago. If so, we can't be more than 40 miles in a straight line from the main Pine Pass (west branch).[140] The altitude of this valley is very low, as well as the hills above us. In another week at the outside we will surely know where we are; in the meantime things grow very interesting. Fine looking bear country but no signs, which is strange. Built a big fire after our second late meal and sat around it while the moon (which is nearly full) rose in the east simultaneously with the evening star, – a wild-looking scene made even wilder still. This is the first time we have seen the moon. Its orbit is only just getting high enough so that it can be seen over the mountains from the valley. At last we are back again in the land of the poplar and balm of Gilead trees, though they are not numerous here. Today was a repetition of yesterday, only worse, for it was steady down timber of the worst kind all day, keeping Fred and Bob Jones busy cutting steadily. We were over eight hours on the trail and only made about four miles in a straight line. Berries were plentiful, but not the way they have been. However, we ate our fill over and over again. More kinds still put in an appearance. Among them the salmon berry, similar to our thimbleberry only it is red and very soft with little flavour, so it is poor eating. Then we found real red currants and cranberries, the latter exactly like our cranberry at home except on a very diminutive scale as to leaf and berry. It grows on the damp moss in swampy places and I never before saw them. Passed one small swamp and in it were spruces, tamarack, Jack pine, poplar, balm of Gilead, willows and alders, quite a variety for this country. Found wild cherry trees. Very muggy and hot. A big fire must be burning far south of us, as the air is filled with smoke. Saw Canada jay as the only bird. Distance 8 miles, altitude 2600 feet.

THURSDAY, SEPTEMBER 3. HOT – BRILLIANT.

We are camped on an island in the river, a poor spot, as there is no open place or level spot either; the kitchen department is on the rocks of the riverbed. There is also a lack of horse feed of any kind. Here the river is double the size of last camp, as a big tributary comes in from the south-west.[141] It showered several times during the night but our canvas blanket covers kept us dry as a bone and our sleep was undisturbed. Another day similar to yesterday, – sky almost cloudless, but smoky everywhere. First of all, some time ago we found our supply of dried fruit was becoming so alarmingly low that we had to eat it only once in a while; then our sugar supply went so fast and our milk too that we had to cut our consumption down to a third of our past portions. Now our flour at the rate we are using it will scarcely carry us to the middle of October, so we are going to allow ourselves only two slices of bread a meal apiece. In that way it should carry us through until at least November first. This is a precautionary measure, as we don't want to take any chances with the uncertainty there is ahead of us. Today was a repetition of yesterday, – the worst of down timber from start to finish. Saw a cow and a calf moose, Franklin's grouse, Canada jay, spotted sandpiper and a kingfisher. Berries were quite plentiful, and today I got a big feed of raspberries and red currants, – at times it was possible to sit down and eat and eat until you were satisfied. It would be impossible to do better in a cultivated berry garden at home. After seven long, weary hours of trail cutting, making a tiresome day and exasperating work trying to drive the weary horses, we camped on another branch of the East Pine (?),[142] – no feed for the horses, of course, so we put them back and they will go back to a muskeg half a mile away where there is some grass. Camped on the riverbank and saw fish jumping all about us as we forded. In about an hour we had over 30 trout, weighing from one to three pounds. As our meat supply will be gone tomorrow we are laying in enough fish for a few days. The men fished standing alongside of the fire, landing their fish literally in the kitchen department! You could watch the fish swim up and grab the bait, – not actual sport, but we want the food. Distance 10 miles, altitude 2800 feet. End of tenth week, total distance 517 miles.

FRIDAY, SEPTEMBER 4. COOL – SHOWERY.

We started on our trip in June and here it is September, having been out ten weeks. It is quite a long time, yet we are still some distance from Pine Pass and trails with lots more miserable travelling ahead of us. The weather has been with us, which has certainly been a big help. Watched a fine, dark-coloured mink running along among the rocks on the other side of the creek and swimming along in the water as we finished breakfast. Also a little winter wren hopped around close by, very tame. Both of these seemed in their exact place in this wild, lonely-looking stream, and just added the right touch to the scene. These fish here are not very gamey and it is doubtful how much sport a man would have with proper tackle fishing with flies. All that was used last night was an alder rod, string and a hook with meat for bait. At last we are in green timber again, having reached it last night just before camping, after four days of steady cutting through burnt timber. There will be plenty of cutting through this, but it will be a change, at least.

It looks as if this green timber might continue a long way. Another day or two will carry us to the limit of the country we were able to lay our course through and then we will have to climb another mountain and map the region ahead once more. Now that the day is over, the story is very different. We started without very good prospects. In the first place the horses went way back and it was over two hours before Bob returned to camp with them. This timber is very thick and everywhere the ground is covered with the trunks of old trees fallen from age, some rotted on the ground, others high above it. First of all, after an hour's chopping, we found that in the dense timber with no landmarks to make use of we had made a complete circle, and were back within a hundred yards of camp! That was discouraging but we could only see the humorous side of it and so nobody cared. There were scarcely any berries at all and it was a long, dreary day standing around while the sound of the axes resounded ahead, then after 15 minutes or so, moving ahead a hundred yards! It showered all day and the combination of the dense timber and the damp, wet, moss-covered ground was gloomy. As Bob said, "Dismal Swamp" wasn't in it with this place. After six hours we had to give up and in an hour after turning around we were back at our godforsaken camp, glad enough this time to be here. Distance 6 miles. Saw a harlequin duck flying up the stream.

SATURDAY, SEPTEMBER 5. WARM – SHOWERY.

After eating our supper of fish in the dark last night, having been 14 hours between meals, we piled on the wood and sat around the fire a long while discussing our situation. First of all, our meat supply is nearly exhausted and we must kill a moose or a caribou as soon as possible. Secondly, it is next to impossible to take the outfit to the lake five miles beyond here,[143] as it would require two men a week to chop out a trail and we can't afford to waste that amount of time. Thirdly, the range just ahead of us is the last section of possible sheep country, as beyond we believe none exist. Reports place the sheep about 20 to 40 miles south of the Pine Pass, and here we are about 30 miles from it.[144] Therefore, if we can hunt this country on foot we can both settle the sheep question and as well get high enough up in the mountains to again locate ourselves. Fourthly, we must not wait much longer before starting for home and the only possible route is down the river, chopping our way through the burnt country in the hope of finding a trail further down to get us home. It will be a long job and may require several weeks, but it is now our only way out, as we can't return the way we came.

It is of course a disappointment not to be able to reach Pine Pass and go home via that trail, but it is out of the question entirely, as we will have to content ourselves with trying to reach Grande Prairie city from here, where we can add to our grubstakes before starting on our last stretch home. As it is, it may take us a month to reach this most northern town, and probably most of the time we will be cutting our way through down timber. It rained again during the night. We returned over our trail to the main river in about an hour and a half, having taken six hours to go up, and made camp. We put up the tipi on a nice little flat, for the first time in about a week. Most of our camps lately have been in such miserable places that there was not enough room even to put up our lean-to, so we have just picked out a place for our beds and turned in, with the starry sky overhead. Fortunately, we have had nothing more than a showery night now and then or we would have had a miserable time of it. Cigar's wound is healing wonderfully and before we reach home she ought to be entirely well and strong and ready to carry a pack once more. Four geese flew over just before dark and I honked to them. I called them back three times. Each time they circled lower with their wings set, anxious to alight in this "sloo" but the tipi scared them and they went off down the river. Everybody had roast goose in their mind, but it turned out to be extremely visionary. A flight of robins and warblers. Distance 6 miles, altitude 2600 feet.

SUNDAY, SEPTEMBER 6. WARM – RAINY.

Rested and loafed in camp all the forenoon, while preparations were made to bake bread in the bean hole, our usual custom. The afternoon was passed in a similar way, reading and dozing, so that altogether it was an extremely peaceful and enjoyable day. Bob brought the map up to date and it certainly has turned out well. We feel that it is very accurate and reliable, as much as can be made from careful compass directions and estimating distances. We have the satisfaction of knowing that no one else has ever made this trip across this section of the country and so this map of ours should prove a very valuable piece of work.[145] That, combined with our specimens of sheep, caribou, bear and small mammals collected, as well as the addition to the knowledge of the range of the large mammals, forms a nucleus of facts that are of great scientific value to the Biological Survey.[146] It remains now for us to complete our work by getting another pair of caribou, a grizzly, a pair of deer and determining the existence or non-existence of sheep in the hills about us. This is the last possible range for them this side of the Peace River, and when this work is done we can turn our faces homeward and begin the task of cutting our way out to the trails that surely must exist east of here.

MONDAY, SEPTEMBER 7. WARM – RAINY.

Found the same weather today. The clouds are low down, about 4000 feet, and no present prospect of any change. Spent the morning as yesterday. Heard robins again. It is time any day for the bluebird migration south to begin, and it will be cheerful to hear their warbling notes about camp. Our supply of meat is at last exhausted and we are compelled to draw on our reserve supply laid up for emergencies only. We hate to dig into it but necessity forces us to it. All of the forenoon we discussed future plans and decided finally what our next move will be. Bob and Fred are going off on foot with necessary food and outfit packed on their backs for a week and will hunt the country ahead to determine the existence of sheep and caribou. The rest of us will stay behind. Bob Jones and I will hunt moose and caribou as we must have meat, and in the meanwhile we will catch some more fish to help out the food supply and save our supply of cured meat. Then we will start down the river, and provided we reach good trails within a reasonable time we will go north instead of south to Hudson's Hope, a Hudson's Bay Company post on the Peace River, and there replenish our grubstakes to carry us the six to seven hundred miles home. Flight of rusty grackles[147] and pectoral sandpipers (grass birds).[148]

TUESDAY, SEPTEMBER 8. WARM – SHOWERS.

As there is no use in the men starting until it clears, owing to the impracticality of hunting in cloudy, wet weather, it was decided to stay in camp. Their grubstakes are laid out and all is ready so that they can start at a moment's notice. Bob and I went down a mile below, to where the creek runs into this river, to get some fish. On the way down we saw three green-wing teal, eight harlequin ducks and some warblers, – also moose and a small grizzly track. Found some more chopping, showing that about ten years ago someone came up here from downstream, but whether with horses or in a canoe is the question; we think the latter. Where the creek comes in there is a big backwater and swirl of foam. Here we fished and in three hours we had landed 45 of the finest Dolly Varden trout that ever were caught, running from three quarters of a pound to two pounds apiece. I never had more sport in my life. It was not strictly fishing, from a sportsman's point of view, and it may seem that we took more than our share, which certainly would be the case if it were not for the fact that we are fishing for food.

Now we have enough to last the three who are staying behind nearly a week, and when the supply gives out we can get plenty more. The fish were very gamey and with light tackle would have given a real fisherman as good sport as he ever had. It was a pretty spot, as we cast from a gravel bar that commanded a view of the river both up and down stream, while behind us we were able to look up the creek bed. Occasionally, the clouds lifted sufficiently so that we could see the range of mountains beyond, which Fred and Bob will hunt first on their trip. It seemed strange that this pool should be full of Dolly Varden trout while that up the creek had a different variety, common to the waters that flow into the Arctic Ocean. They are larger, running from one to three pounds, have almost black backs, a long head, large mouth and teeth and the meat is soft and hasn't much flavour; neither are they a gamey fish.[149] Found a few blueberries on the way home and they are the first that have had as good flavour as those we get at home. They are the only variety of berry, strange to say, whose flavour is inferior to our corresponding berry at home. We both agreed that by closing our eyes we could easily imagine ourselves seated at the counter at Thompson's Spa[150] eating our lunch of blueberries, perched as we were on a pile of fallen timber.

WEDNESDAY, SEPTEMBER 9. WARM – SHOWERS.

This valley is a great migration route for birds, and every day there are sparrows, warblers and other varieties about, but in their present plumage identification is difficult. Several times a day we hear the grass birds (pectoral sandpipers) chirping as they pass. It is an interesting spot from that standpoint. We have now been out the same length of time (75 days) that our 1912 trip lasted, which was the longest single trip I had been on, as last year we took several trips. Yet we are not even at our farthest point, though we do not know where that will be, but another week ought to see us started out of here, either home, which will be a matter of six weeks by the shortest route, or toward Hudson's Hope, which will prolong the trip until December 1st. On leaving here before completing the trip I am anxious to get a pair of deer for the Biological Survey, as well as a pair of caribou from east of here, as the latter may be the barren ground type. As to just what species range there we do not know and it will be interesting to find out. However, our grubstakes are getting low, our tea and coffee having been going so rapidly that we are economizing on them also now. We had fully expected to find fairly well-travelled Indian trails with good camping places, horse feed and tipi poles through most of this country, so that in this respect it has been a great disappointment to us. We have decided that a fitting title to the expedition should be "A search for the elusive tipi poles"! Very appropriate, I think. The rain and damp weather of the last few days has moistened the ground and loosened the trees to such an extent that the high wind of yesterday caused many of the standing dead timber to fall and we frequently heard loud crashes about us, showing the danger of having to camp in burnt country. So far none of the horses have been hurt and I hope they will escape entirely. Weather today similar to yesterday and useless to attempt anything. Bob and Fred got all ready to go but the weather was so doubtful they put it off. Fred and I went downstream to try for a moose but of course saw none. Saw robin, sheldrake, red-breasted merganser, American pippit, Brewer's blackbirds, song sparrow, spotted sandpiper and winter wren, also another English snipe[151] back of the tipi.

THURSDAY, SEPTEMBER 10. COOLER – RAINY, CLEARING.

It was very hot all night, which made it poor for sleeping. At times it blew a hurricane but the old worn-out tipi seemed to stand it pretty well. The rain came down in torrents, so that altogether it was a wild night listening to the rain beat on the tipi and the wind howling through the timber, tearing up the trees by the roots or breaking them off close to the ground and crashing them to earth. The lean-to pulled out its stakes and I went to fix it. The men hesitated about starting, for although the sun was out for breakfast it drizzled continually, and in every direction it was storming hard. Black clouds hung low over the mountains and the wind continued to howl. Finally, they decided to make a start and with our best wishes were off and lost to sight amidst the brush along the river, each heavily laden with a pack on his back. They both look forward to a miserable time but are anxious to put this trip through as it will be the climax to our trip and decide the sheep and caribou question definitely. They will be gone from five to ten days and it will be a long wait for us in camp though we have plenty to do in chasing moose and fishing. However, we will be mighty glad to see them returning up the river and by that time will be more than ready to start our homeward journey. Watched a mink among the rocks across the river. He would dive into the water and return with a fish four or five inches long which he was not slow in devouring, then the performance was continued. We are going to set some traps for both mink and beaver – the latter are below here at the junction. It is time for the bluebird migration south any day now and I am looking forward to seeing them once more, – probably this mild weather has delayed them, but from the recent snow on the mountains above us it looks as if the cool fall weather would shortly begin and then they should come along. The leaves are turning fast and there is a fine bit of colour among the trees; the high cranberry bushes are bright red, the fireweed is brilliant orange and red, and the willows are assuming a dull ochre, which makes the effect very fine indeed. However, it makes me long for home and the unsurpassable beauty of our Massachusetts autumn foliage, which nothing of its kind can excel. Went upstream in the afternoon but saw no signs of moose or bear, very discouraging, – not even a fool hen or a porcupine in this godforsaken valley! A kingfisher appeared along the river. Saw a varied thrush.

End of eleventh week, total distance 528 miles.

FRIDAY, SEPTEMBER 11. WARM – SHOWERY.

Fish again for breakfast; we have lived on nothing else for a week now and I am getting pretty tired of them as they have not the flavour or firmness that our brook trout of the East have. Furthermore, there isn't much nourishment to them and I never feel as if I had had a meal. Long before the next meal I am hungry again. All of us have taken in our belts a hole or two as a result! A large flock of about 50 geese flew northwards this morning. Apparently they lit on the river above here last night and were circling around to get their bearings. It was cold last night and we had the first frost for some time. This morning the air is chilly, more like autumn, and the sky is full of snowy-looking clouds so that the probability is that we will have snow yet. The mountains are covered with it. The barometer has again gone down, so the weather surely has not yet changed for good. Lots of Bohemian waxwings around camp this morning, also a robin, a winter wren and harlequin duck. The men went down to the big pool but only caught eight fish. Bob and I went upstream in the afternoon with two guns and two lines and returned late with but one fish. However, he was a good one and we had a good afternoon's fun.

SATURDAY, SEPTEMBER 12. WARM – SHOWERY.

Ate our last fish for breakfast, so it is up to us to catch a big supply if possible. We are getting too much in the habit of first eating up our scanty supply of fish and then having to catch our next meal! So Bob and I are going off for the day, well equipped with fishing tackle, to the big pool about an hour downstream from here to try and make a big haul. We probably won't equal our big day but with luck should return with 20 fish. They caught one of the so-called Arctic trout among their fish (Dolly Varden) yesterday. Heard a partridge[152] drumming this morning steadily from 7 until 9. Either a pack rat or a weasel disturbed our slumbers greatly early by running up the side of the tipi and then sliding down. Whether he took it for a toboggan slide or not is the question; at any rate, he apparently got more enjoyment out of it than we did. Once he stuck his head under the edge of the tipi but not long enough for me to identify his species in the dim morning light. It was cold enough last night to freeze everything, – even the water in the "sloo" was covered with ice. Although the sun warmed things up considerably, there is a crispness to the air indicating that fall is undoubtedly here for good. Bob and I went off for the day fishing to the big pool below. On the way we went to look up the horses and found them about a mile from here, in good feed and very fat. We managed to get a good feed of saskatoons and blueberries (saw a new variety of the latter which is very dark coloured and has a different leaf). Saw harlequin ducks, black-capped chickadees, northern hairy woodpecker,[153] Bohemian waxwings, flicker, kingfisher and robins. On the muddy shore where the moose and grizzly tracks were we found the tracks of a small goat, very fresh, probably early this morning. Apparently, he came down to the shore at this point for a drink and then returned. Undoubtedly he was crossing from one range to another. Our first attempts at fishing were without much result, as the fish were out of reach of our short poles and lines, so we resorted to the casting spoon, an excellent device to reach fish farther out and get them started coming in. I caught one and Bob five (he using the spoon). Then we ate our bread and chocolate. The fish bit poorly while the sun was out, better when it was cloudy and later during the light showers best of all. Then there were lots of winged creatures on the surface of the water beaten down by the rain but on our side of the river we saw no fish rising. Later on across the stream the fish came to the surface continually. Now came my turn and I began to land the Dolly Varden better than Bob. We were in the water half way to our knees in our efforts to reach the fish hole and it was cold work. For four to five hours we stood without moving in this icy water so that our feet felt like icebergs, – I say "felt" but should have said, in the absence of any feeling, "were" like icebergs. Some of the fish were as small as half a pound, while one old grandfather which I landed would go three pounds without a doubt. He was a beauty and the largest of this species we have yet landed. Finally, a fish broke the long line of the spoon, a great disaster as our stock of any kind of line is very low, so we both resorted to poles. At 5.30 we stopped, having caught 21 fish averaging a pound each, which was as successful as I had hoped. That makes 74 fish caught in this hole. There are lots more across the stream but not many left on this side. Started home in a drizzle – wet, cold and hungry. Passed the cutting that we have found from time to time on our way up and down the river to this fish hole. Across are some stumps cut off high above the ground, which indicate the winter chopping of a trapper. On our side we found a piece of deadfall cut out which is the first and only sign of any cutting done which looks as if horses had been the cause. Then there were four or five small trees cut down with their tops chopped off and lying nearby on the ground. This puzzled us more than anything else at first but as there is a fish hole along the bank there, someone had apparently cut them with the object of fishing, which pointed to summer travel. At the big pool is a log 50 to 60 feet long and two feet at the butt end where it was out. This must have drifted down from above and probably was felled in order to get across the river higher up where it is more narrow or else in winter to cross the stream where it had an open channel in the ice at a wider place. Across the stream are some meat racks. All this cutting etc. is extremely interesting to me and gives us something to argue about at mealtimes or in the evening around the campfire. Several outfits have been up here, one up the ice in winter, another up the river in a boat and possibly one with horses. None have been up within the last ten years and probably only three or four parties have ever been up here. The signs look like Indians mostly but possibly one outfit were white men.[154] We haven't seen a single fresh moose track in all our roaming around the last week. A lonely place, practically no game, not even a sign of a wolf or sound of an owl. The only birds here are migrants and nothing seems to really live here except one partridge and a few mink, except the fish of course! A godforsaken spot indeed![155] Nothing but tamarack (larch) wood to burn and it sparks so badly as to keep us picking off burning sparks from our beds continually. The tie rope of the tipi caught on fire this evening but luckily no more serious damage was done. It might have caused the whole tipi to burn up if I hadn't discovered it in time to throw water on it and get it out. My big Dolly Varden trout measured 18 inches in length, 10 inches in girth and was probably 3 pounds in weight.

SUNDAY. SEPTEMBER 13. WARM – SHOWERY.

It poured hard during the night so that Bob and Fred must have had a mean night of it, camped on the top of some hill. Today the clouds are so low that it will interfere with their hunting and mapping, as they will not be able to see any distance at all. Yesterday we picked up a moose horn whose point was just sticking out of the gravel bar on an island in the river and to our surprise found it to be of enormous size. On reaching camp I measured it and found that its spread was 31 inches; provided the other horn was as large it would give a total spread, allowing for the width of the skull, of about 70 inches! Truly, a giant head and up to the Alaskan moose in size. Its height is 44 inches, length of longest tine 22 inches, girth of base above burr 10 inches. Its type is distinctly that of the Alaskan moose and will interest Bob Cross I am sure, as he remarked to me that the moose in this country did not appear very large. Here is a horn that belonged to a veritable giant of his race. Everything about the horn is as heavy and as massive as can be. The moose was undoubtedly in his prime and the horn shed last winter, so that this bull may be in our vicinity now. I would certainly give a lot to see him and be able to bring his head home.

This makes another unlooked-for scientific problem to solve. First we had the Smoky River sheep, which we settled; then the caribou, also settled, and the bear the same way, although an adult grizzly would be more desirable than a two-year-old. Then we saw a caribou which had all the appearances of the "*Osborni*," which we had no reason to believe ranged east of the Parsnip waters or at any rate east of the continental watershed of the Rocky Mountains. Now, to cap the climax, we have a giant race of moose similar to the Alaskan. I never knew that even west of here in British Columbia the moose were anywhere near this size. If we can solve these two additional problems as well as settle the caribou species east of here out in the lower foothills and get specimens of the deer in that section too, we will have accomplished an amount of work that the Biological Survey at Washington would be tickled to death with, but I am afraid that is trying to do more than is possible considering the lateness of the season and the scantiness of our grubstakes. More geese went by again this morning. We see a flock in the air nearly every day now. I said we have settled three problems of scientific interest – the Smoky River sheep, new race of caribou and bear. But there are two more, – the non-existence of sheep between Sheep Creek and the Peace River (unless Bob and Fred find them in this last possible range), also as a fifth problem the existence of goat as far as the head of the middle branch of the Pine

River or within 20 miles of Pine Pass or 40 of the Peace River. A pair of redstarts (the male in beautiful plumage) feeding about camp make it appear very homelike. It is strange no bluebirds have passed by yet, as it is time for their migration. Curious weather, snow squalls on the mountains, which are now white with snow, and rain squalls here. Then it clears for an hour or so and the sun shines so brightly that it is positively hot and our worst enemy, the flies, swarm again. Went upstream with my gun in the afternoon but found on getting up to the only possible place for moose that the horses had worked their way up there so that the constant ringing of the bells would prevent any moose from coming around. During the night our animal friend was at his usual pastime of running up the side of the tipi, then sliding down again, – quite a nuisance.

MONDAY, SEPTEMBER 14. COLD – SHOWERS ALL DAY.

Another poor day. The barometer has gone down three tenths and it looks now as if we were going to get a good cold snowstorm and then a final clear-up and be colder for good. I hope Bob and Fred get back before it hits us. Northern hairy woodpecker, Bohemian waxwings, Brewer's blackbirds, redstarts, Wilson's warblers, hawk owl, white-throated sparrow (first seen this summer) about camp. Nothing of the slightest interest occurred all day, as it was so rainy that we stayed in the tipi all day and read. Bob mended some pack covers. He went out to bring the horses down to the feed that there is along the river on this side below camp. When they appeared I went out to see what the excitement was that seemed to be taking place. Some of the cayuses had already crossed and were standing on the rocky north bank. In midstream were half a dozen horses' heads sticking out of the water, swimming for the other side, while the rest were just entering the water. Bob had intended to keep them here as there is plenty of good grass for them, but Alice decided that she preferred to cross over and of course the rest followed her. As it happened, they picked out one of the deepest places in the river. However, it was a pretty sight to watch them swimming and no harm was done by it.

TUESDAY, SEPTEMBER 15. COLD – SNOW.

Awoke to find a heavy snowstorm underway fulfilling the predictions of the barometer. It has begun to go up a little, so by night it may start to clear, and if all goes well, by another day we may be having fine weather once more. Such a long spell of rain may end in a month of bright yet cool weather. This is the sixth day Bob and Fred have been out so they should put in an appearance any day now. It would have been impossible for them to have had worse weather. Their only piece of luck was that for the first three days the clouds were sufficiently high so as to allow them extensive views necessary for map-making and picking out any possible sheep country. Since then, hunting has been almost out of the question. Once more we celebrated, all hands participating in the ceremony of bread-making. We are now down to our last hundred pounds of flour (two sacks), enough to last us four weeks at our present rate of consumption. No signs of the men although it is time to expect them any day now. During the evening a flock of geese flew over, honking loudly. What a wonderful, wild, lonely sound it is, only surpassed, to my mind, by the howl of a wolf or the call of a loon. The hoot of an owl is another sound I love to hear, but it doesn't carry with it the same feeling of loneliness.

WEDNESDAY, SEPTEMBER 16. COLD – CLOUDY.

The coldest night yet and coming as it did after such warm weather it seemed all the colder. Everything frozen up, even socks, boots and wet clothes. Barometer still going up but still below point it started from. Thermometer at sunrise was only 26 degrees. Bob and I went off for the day fishing, as our supply was so low that only one small fish was left for breakfast. Found a few belated strawberry blossoms, coming so late that no sooner do they open their white petals than they immediately wither. We took our trail up to our former camp, finding a few black and red currants, now and then a raspberry or a huckleberry, with quite a number of blueberries which are about in their prime now. Fished an hour or two opposite our old camp, catching nine Dolly Varden trout, the only ones there. Last time, there were only Arctic trout in that pool. They must have moved lower down into the main river. Here we ate our lunch, toasting our bread and roasting a trout in front of the fire on a stick, a perfect and sufficient meal. Saw our first water ouzels[156] – three in all – also winter wren, Canada jay, pipit and juncos. Followed the creek down to its mouth two miles below. Halfway down, the creek from the western valley comes in, very small. Caught eight more fish. Found some very fine fish holes. In the riffles they were rising to catch flies, with which the water was covered, refusing to take bait. Returned at 7 p.m. via the main river, thus making the circuit.

THURSDAY. SEPTEMBER 17. COLD – SNOW.

Today is just like a day in December at home, when we get our first snow-storm. The thermometer about 25°, it is cold and still with no wind and heavy clouds hanging everywhere, entirely obscuring the sun, giving a real wintery aspect. The snow is falling slowly and the distant mountains are gradually disappearing in the haze. Barometer has gone down a bit. Our only chance of getting good weather once more is to get out of this spot and we certainly will do that as soon as the men return. We look for them today. The river has gone down fully a foot since we camped here. Spent the day in the tipi on account of the storm and nothing to go out for. About 3 p.m. I heard steps and ran out to meet Fred and Bob returning from their eight days' trip.[157] They looked so dirty and Bob so utterly played out that I scarcely knew them. The latter had a severe chill and was very sick for three days so that Fred was very much alarmed about him. However, he says he is OK now. Owing to the bad weather they were in camp most of the time. They killed a fine moose with 51-inch spread, so our meat supply is OK. Saw no bear, caribou, goat or sheep and no signs of any sheep hills, so the absence of sheep in this country is settled to our satisfaction. Fine moose country ahead. They feel sure this is the middle fork of the Pine River, not the east branch.[158] Redstarts, robins, Brewer's blackbirds about. End of twelfth week.

FRIDAY, SEPTEMBER 18. COLD – RAIN.

The barometer still has a downward tendency, which is very discouraging. It was such a miserable day that we decided to stay in camp and sit around the tipi fire. That will probably be best for Bob, as he certainly looks thin and sick in spite of what he says, but he should pick up speedily.

For two weeks we have lived on fish only, a long period for that diet, so we are more than enjoying the fat moose steaks that they brought back with them. The tongue is boiling for supper and once more we will be feeding on one of our favourite delicacies. Made up the packs, allowing three horses to carry the moose meat below here which we hope to pick up on our way down the river. Our grubstakes are at a very low ebb, so we plan to continue north to the Hudson's Bay Company post at Hudson's Hope to get a new stock. Then we will turn south from the Peace River and begin our homeward trip of 500 or more miles to Jasper via Grande Prairie City. We figure on reaching Jasper by November 15th, about two months from now. Bob and Jack went down to cut out a trail and bring the horses near camp to be ready to start tomorrow. Robins, juncos, white-throated sparrows about. It poured all the afternoon so our start tomorrow looks dubious.

SATURDAY, SEPTEMBER 19. COLD – SNOW.

The only change in the weather is that the rain has turned to snow and it is colder. Ever since 3 p.m. yesterday the precipitation has been continuous, without let-up. A quiet, steady rain with no wind, turning to snow, points to the fact that this is the final storm before the clear-up. However, the only real reason for being optimistic on the weather is that since last night the barometer has risen slowly and steadily, though not very much. Everyone was busy reading or playing solitaire all the morning around the tipi fire. I dug out two packs of cards from my bag which I had nearly forgotten and they helped considerably to while away the hours. Two large gulls, probably herring gulls, flew overhead. Yesterday the men in cutting the trail found another large moose horn, which may be the mate to this large one. As we will pass it on leaving we can then measure it and decide. This is the 16th day of rain and we are sick of it, – certainly we must have had our fair share by now and have paid for the remarkable stretch of magnificent weather which prevailed for ten weeks, during which time not once were our plans upset by the weather. The barometer is still slowly rising.

SUNDAY, SEPTEMBER 20. WARM – CLEAR.

Although the weather had not cleared, the barometer had returned to its former place and everything pointed to a good day, so that all hands were strongly in favour of breaking camp. It certainly was a wise move, for before we left the clouds had broken and all during the rest of the day the sun came out at intervals warm and bright. What a charming effect the sun can have after it has been hidden for a week or more. Bob took a long time to get the horses as they were across the river and some way down. Not having been packed for about two weeks they were pretty wild, so altogether it was slow getting started and it was 1.30 before we left. We crossed the river,[159] following the trail the men cut yesterday. For some reason there is almost no fallen timber on this side, so that it was a relief. We met the river, having crossed the point to shorten the distance, and here picked up the large moose horn Bob found yesterday and put on the trail so that we could take it along with us. It is another fine big one (right horn) and almost an exact mate to the first one, so that it undoubtedly is its mate although slightly lighter. Its spread is 29 inches and height 41 inches as compared with 31 and 44 inches on the other horn. This would make the spread fully 68 inches, which is certainly an enormous moose. Runt carried one horn and as he is a little horse, weighing not much more than 500 pounds, he was almost out of sight as the horn of course was put on top of the pack. At this bend in the river is a magnificent big fish-pool[160] and Bob and I let the outfit go on while we tied up our saddle horses by the bank to fish. Trout were rising continually only a few feet from the shore and so we knew we would have no trouble in getting a day's supply or possibly more. We landed them very fast at first, though they bit in a very slovenly way. I tried an experiment after we had made quite a catch. There was an eddy where we were fishing and a long log fully 50 feet stretched from the shore out on the surface of the water. Consequently, there was quite a swirl of foam and bubbles on one side of it. I pushed the log out into the stream, destroying this swirl. It was carried back again to the same spot by the eddy in about ten minutes, and I repeated the process and it again returned in about the same length of time. In the meantime every fish left and I never saw a fish or had a bite until the log had been back in its former position long enough for the swirl to form once more. Then the fish returned one by one and soon they were biting as fast as ever; all of which goes to prove that not only do they want an eddy but they seem to like the protection of the swirl to conceal themselves in the shallow water. This bend in the river was a beautiful spot, – the combination of the peace and quiet, disturbed only by the rising of the fish, with the beautiful colours of the autumn foliage. Across on the other side, which was steep and rocky, were some brilliant patches of yellow where the small poplars were scattered. Just beyond was a little meadow with its grass well browned by the frost and its fireweed brilliant red. For a background was the deep green of the lofty spruces that rose into the air like spires. This viewed from across the level expanse of smooth, dull-greenish water was a composition such as would please the eye of an artist. As I fished, a duck (a harlequin) swam close to me and in spite of my presence and the disturbance I created she was not afraid and continued feeding as I landed my fish. Juncos were the only other birds about. Bob landed one large fish, fully three pounds. We later measured it and found it was 19 1/2 inches in length. Altogether we caught 35 fish in less than two hours, averaging nearly a pound apiece. They were all Dolly Varden trout. It was time to move along, so we started, as much as we hated to leave this beautiful little spot. After fording the river we followed through the timber where the rest of the outfit had preceded us, crossing and recrossing the river, until we caught up with them. Here the outfit was held up while Fred and Bob went ahead to cut a trail over a ridge, as there were some big falls roaring ahead and a canyon below. We walked ahead to a point overlooking the latter but could only see the top of the falls. We did see enough to find out that they had a drop of about 250 feet and were very magnificent. Such a thing as big falls was certainly an unexpected sight. Here we found lots of chopping, indicating that the last outfit up here had portaged their outfit over the ridge and hauled their boat up this steep hill, which must have been quite an undertaking. Soon the cutting was done and we got the horses over safely in spite of the steep slopes. The falls were magnificent without any question. After fording the river we camped on an island. It was pitch dark before the stuff was piled up and our supply of freshly caught trout cooked, but we managed to get by without swallowing any bones in the dark. Saw lots of moose tracks and a small bear track where the berries or at least the remains of them had been plentiful. Saw water ouzel, harlequin duck, juncos, American pipits and Canada jays. Distance 6 miles, altitude 2500 feet.

MONDAY, SEPTEMBER 21. COOL – SHOWERY.

We were up at daylight so as to get the horses as quickly as possible because in the absence of any feed we were afraid they wouldn't want to stay around very long. It rained during the night and looked as if it might be showery all day. While the men were packing up I wrote our names etc. on a blaze on a large conspicuous spruce and went up to photograph the falls. They resembled in a certain way the Shoshone falls on the Snake River in Idaho. Early in the summer when the river would be about three feet higher there would be a tremendous volume of water coming over and probably none of the rocks or ledges would then be visible. Now, the falls cascade over the rocks and are extremely beautiful. In one place there is a big, fan-shaped cascade, while on the right is a little fall by itself falling fully 100 feet sheer to the pool below and carrying even now a good volume of water. The total fall from the river above to the pool at the base is about 250 feet, while the falls themselves are over 200 feet. It gave me an inspiring sensation as I stood there alone at the foot of the falls, covered with spray, to think that probably only two or three parties had ever beheld this magnificent sight. Perhaps no white men have ever gazed upon it, – and yet they are fine enough, if they were accessible, to be a sight such as tourists would travel a long distance to see.[161]

These falls and our Mt. Alexander are the two scenic wonders of the trip and they in themselves are worth it. To complete the loneliness of the scene a water ouzel flew past me and teetered on the rocks near by. Certainly he was in his fitting surroundings, – along a dashing river where the spray flew about. I finally tore myself away, after having taken many pictures and climbed above the cliffs to get some good views, and found all the horses packed up and the men waiting for me to return. Once more we were under way and at first the going was good along the gravel bars, but then our troubles began. The river's banks and bars were muddy and the stream itself became slow and sluggish. We could not ford, on account of the mud and deep holes. Fresh moose tracks, some very large ones, were everywhere, also a fox, caribou and small grizzly track. As we came around a bend we saw a flock of at least 50 geese on a mud bank about 150 yards ahead. Bob and I fired (I on the ground, Bob on the wing) and I managed to kill my bird, so we are looking forward to a roast goose at last, after two years of waiting. Signs of beaver everywhere. A bull moose three or four years old appeared on the other bank as the men were cutting the trail ahead of the horses and although Fred was standing on the bar in plain sight he not only was not frightened but had every appearance of coming over to have a fight. He changed his mind and disappeared in the bushes. Saw raven and bald eagle for the first time; also kingfisher, Canada jays, ouzels, pipits, juncos, Canada geese. There was lots of cutting, so our progress was slow. Macloud distinguished himself by jumping into the river and wetting our small stock of food; also Snowball had a bad time in the river. Distance 8 miles, altitude 2400 feet.

TUESDAY, SEPTEMBER 22. MUGGY – CLOUDY.

It showered at regular intervals all night but the weather looks better this morning, the most encouraging feature being a rise of two tenths more in the barometer. Our camp is in a wet spot, in the long grass which formerly formed the bottom of a beaver pond. In consequence of the rain the ground is soft and soggy. However, we managed to make an extremely comfortable camp, putting up both the tipi and the lean-to, an almost unheard event, as it is some time since that has happened. There is quite a lot of black birch along the riverbank, also some golden birches which make me homesick to look at. These both are scarce in this country, especially the latter. We are camped directly at the base of the mountain[162] where Fred and Bob spent their weekend of misery.

Up there is a whole moose cut up and hanging ready to be taken down, so today we plan to take five pack horses and cut a trail up to timberline and bring every bit of the meat and fat down, – provided some bear hasn't visited the spot in the meantime and been gorging himself or if the ravens which are flying about and croaking in a mournful manner have not made too many meals off it. Bob caught a fish last evening which was a Dolly Varden trout so that the species below the falls is similar to that above. It was very warm last night, so that instead of its snowing on the mountains above us it rained, as it did down here, and so nearly all of the snow has gone off them. We left about 10.30, all except Jack Symes. His last words were to be back at six to sit down to a roast goose, cranberry sauce and corn, and these words were in our minds most of the time. The first hill was very steep and required some chopping, but after we were past that, the going was through open burnt timber except for about half a mile of green balsams toward the end. At one halt I carelessly left my gun and had gone some distance before I discovered it was missing, so had to return. A second delay was caused by the sudden disappearance of Jimmy, who managed to hide in the bushes until we were by, then he started back for camp. Luckily, I discovered his absence in time so that Bob speedily went after him, finding him a short ways back. It was much further to the moose and their camp than I thought and it was not until 3.30 that we reached it. While two of the men cooked some steaks and boiled a pot of tea Fred and I sawed and cut the carcass up into suitable sections for packing. No animal had touched the meat since it had been killed and the cold weather had kept it finely. There was fully 500 pounds of meat and we gloated over it like savages. It is strange how different one's feelings are under different circumstances, for who would ever have such feelings as this at home? To us it meant 30 days' meat and all we want to eat at mealtimes. The steaks were fine and we all had four apiece and numerous cups of tea before we were satisfied. It was 6.30 before we left and in another hour it was dark, making it impossible to see our way any further. After some searching we found an open spot with a little pool of water in it. Here we stopped and made camp. There was nothing to do but tie the horses to the trees, miserable as it was for them; otherwise they would make for camp in the valley below. We built a big fire and ate a supper of moose steaks and tea. Then we unrolled the big moose hide, rolled ourselves up in the saddle blankets on it and slept until daylight. It was mild all night and the stars at last shone brilliantly so the weather has changed.

WEDNESDAY. SEPTEMBER 23. HOT – MUGGY.

We were up at daylight and after a hearty breakfast packed the horses and started for camp. All the way we had difficulty in keeping the trail we had come up by. Then the packs, which were very clumsy, kept slipping, had to be taken off and put on again continuously. The horses were in a bad temper after 24 hours of no feed and they made so much trouble we had to lead them. It was hot and muggy and we were tired and all in a bad temper,[163] so altogether it was an unpleasant trip. We passed through several patches of devil's club, a plant two to five feet high that is covered with long, stiff, barbed thorns that pierce your clothes and dig into your skin. It is without doubt the most miserable and useless plant the Lord ever made. Reached camp in good time and found through Jack's carelessness the lean-to, the most useful article in the whole outfit, was burned up. I was furious at this new example of his carelessness for now we have only a tipi that is full of holes and leaks like a sieve. He had a lonely night, not knowing what had happened to us and thinking we had met with a disaster. We had our postponed goose feast with corn and cranberries, a welcome meal, but under the circumstances not as pleasant an affair as I had looked forward to. Dried the meat and hide in the afternoon, making ready for an early start tomorrow. Flies were back again today, also mosquitoes.

THURSDAY, SEPTEMBER 24. HOT – BRILLIANT.

Even if we were unfortunate enough to have our lean-to go up in smoke we are lucky in having all our food saved, as nearly all of it was inside, and I imagine Jack had to do some hustling to get it out. The men's towels and Jack's new hat were both burnt, the latter only partially. It will, I hope, be a good lesson to him, as he will suffer more than anyone for in the rain and snow (and we will have plenty of miserable days later) he will be compelled to do all his cooking in the open, without any protection. The Canada jays are very tame around camp this morning, eating the bits of meat strewn about. Geese flew overhead, bound south, last evening. Also a hairy wood-pecker was tapping on the dead trees nearby. In spite of this being a wet spot it is pretty nevertheless. The tipi is pitched on an open muskeg, formerly the bottom of a beaver pond. It is covered with long grass, now browned from the frosts. The timber all about is tamarack and the light, feathery effect produced by it is very beautiful indeed. It shows the effect of the frost, for many of the trees have assumed a yellowish tinge so that the trees present many different shades of light green, tawny and yellow. Behind on the steep hills is the burnt timber, dreary enough looking, yet causing the green spruces higher up to look greener than ever. Around this meadow, fringing it, are low willows, bushes and weeds of various kinds, all in their autumnal garb of red and yellow. So altogether there is lots of colour about us, with much variety to it, making the contrasting shades of deep and light green more effective than ever. A pair of Arctic three-toed woodpeckers[164] (the first I have ever seen in these mountains) feeding along the river, also a beaver swimming about, helped pass away the time spent waiting for Bob to bring the horses into camp. A curious echo enabled us to hear the horse bells though the horses are actually two miles away and so every minute we expected to see them appear at the other end of the meadow. At times, when the wind is right, we can plainly hear the roar of the Great Falls above us, which are about four miles in a straight line. In spite of all the timber between, which should prevent the sound reaching us, the hills are so situated that it undoubtedly is the echo that we hear, as with the horse bells. Heard a red-bellied nuthatch. The men didn't return with the horses until nearly two o'clock, so we cooked our dinner and before they arrived Fred and Bob went off with their axes to cut the trail down to a spot near the end of the ridge that runs up to the range of mountains to the west. They plan to spend two days hunting this; then we will start for Hudson's Hope, having completed all of our hunting for the trip, and nothing will stop us excepting stormy weather or an accident. As it was so late we decided to cut the trail out today and move down the first thing in the morning. It is a frightfully hot day and we are sitting around in undershirts, – extraordinary weather for the last week of September way up in the mountains. The men had a bad time in getting the horses as they were across the river, which had risen too much to ford. So Jack swam it with one of the horses but the horse got tangled in a logjam so that Jack had to slip off and swim it alone; he found the water icy cold. Tonight we will tie each horse up so that they can't leave us. Saw water ouzel about 5000 feet along a creek up on the mountainside yesterday. End of thirteenth week, total distance 542 miles.

FRIDAY, SEPTEMBER 25. HOT – BRIGHT.

White-throated sparrow, mallard ducks, kingfisher, ravens, Canada jays, red-bellied nuthatches, Arctic three-toed woodpecker were about camp this morning. Instead of tying the horses up last night as we planned, Fred and Bob took turns, each taking five-hour watches, staying near the horses and preventing them from leaving. Every time they would pull out they would head them off and drive them back, – mean, tiresome work but sometimes it is a necessity. Up at daylight, ready for an early start. Just about sunrise I was down at the river washing and the effect of the early morning light was perfectly magnificent. In the foreground was the dull-green-coloured river from which the morning mist arose. Its banks were lined with tall dark green spruces that shot up into the air as straight, pointed and stiff as so many spires. Mingled among them were the graceful, feathery branches of the yellowish tamaracks and underneath was the brilliant orange and red colour of the willows and weeds. Far down the river in the distance was a range of hills, just high enough to be above timberline, and seeming further off than they were in their haze of purple. Above, the clouds were beginning to assume a delicate shade of pink which became more brilliant as the sun neared the horizon, and as I sat there and watched this exquisite picture the colour faded as rapidly as it had come. We had trouble as usual with the horses, as they were in a cranky mood, but we managed to leave about 9, following the trail cut yesterday, which was frightful going as there was muskeg, fallen timber and bad roots, as bad a combination almost as can be imagined. Saw several meat racks, tipi poles, several boats, camping grounds, a paddle, a log cache, a good deal of chopping and a blaze on a tree covered with Cree writing, the only distinguishable parts being the date 1910 (which is undoubtedly the last outfit that has been up here) and the name Issidore (as it was spelt). A Beaver Indian from the Peace River, north of here, by that name was one of a party that crossed the Pine Pass in 1895 and possibly it is the same man.[165] Every day now we see more signs of hunting and trapping done on this river but in every case the outfits have come in by boats, on foot or up the river on ice, which points to the fact that the valley below down to the mouth must be bad for horses. There is not a single sure indication of there ever having been a horse in this valley except our own. Probably we are the first to ever bring horses through it; others had more sense! However, the increasing signs are encouraging and some day we will find a trail. The colouring was pretty all along the river but the prettiest effect of all was the deep-green spruces that lined the banks with here and there a clump of half a dozen balm of Gilead or cottonwood trees with their brilliant orange foliage, a vivid yet magnificent contrast. Before leaving we took the wise precaution of putting nearly all our tea, coffee and sugar in my waterproof bag and packed it on top of one of the horses, getting it as high as possible. These are our essentials of all our grubstakes that we cannot afford to get wet. It was a wise move too. We forded the river a mile down and followed the gravel bars. The going improved and it was a relief to be able to keep out of the timber. But our troubles soon came owing to the depth of the river. We had to cross and the water was very deep. One by one the horses got deeper and deeper until they had to swim. Even their packs went entirely out of sight and only their heads were visible as they swam snorting to the other side. We followed in the same way. I had just finished a film and in order to keep it dry I took it from my Kodak and put it in my hat for I thought if my horse got too excited I might not be able to stay on his back as he swam and so have to leave him in midstream. However, it never happened, though we had to swim the river three times. All came through without mishap. After going for three hours we camped at the foot of the mountain (which Fred and Bob are going to hunt) on a broad gravel bar. As soon as we unpacked the horses all the saddle blankets were spread out to dry and we unpacked our bags and in fact the whole outfit, as nearly everything was soaked. My bags kept out most of the water and only a few things got wet. Heard a partridge drumming and saw some kind of gulls flying westward.

Distance 5 miles, altitude 2300 feet.

SATURDAY, SEPTEMBER 26. COOL – SHOWERS.

We planned to reach this spot in one day from our rainy camp and it has taken us six, so the conundrum is how many days will it take us to reach Hudson's Hope! Several days ago we made a pool, – Bob Cross said 14 days, Fred 16, Bob 17, I 19 and Jack 21. Travelling days only of three hours or over are to count. Also I bet Bob we wouldn't reach there in 84 hours of travelling, so not a little interest is centered in our progress. In our last camp the Canada jays were so tame that I hung some meat on a line between two trees and sat only eight feet away and photographed them. I quite easily got two good pictures. This gravel bar we are camped on, which is on a bend in the river, is one of the most interesting spots from a game standpoint I have ever seen. It is covered with tracks, all of which are very fresh. There are tracks of moose, grizzly bear, deer, wolves, coyotes, foxes, beaver, muskrat and even geese, which makes it very interesting to study the different tracks. The deer tracks are especially interesting, as they are the first we have seen for a great many weeks, – it must be nearly two months. The wolf tracks are extremely large. The rain came down in torrents last night as a result of a four-tenths drop in the barometer. In the middle of the night I heard the horses nearby and thinking they were getting ready to leave us again I got up and went out to drive them back. The sky had cleared quite a bit and the stars were numerous, yet there was a stormy-looking effect. As I returned to bed an owl hooted across the river, which was answered in turn by one on this side, and as I dozed off the incessant hooting continued. This morning was a dull, miserable, damp day but as our time is limited Fred and Bob shouldered their packs for a two days trip from camp to the hills west of us to make a final try for sheep or caribou.[166] This last hunt will be the climax to the whole trip, as this range is the last possible one that could contain sheep. During the night the river went down several inches and if this cloudy weather continues, which prevents the melting of the glaciers at its source, the drop ought to continue fast. Any real cold spell should send it down fast, and cold weather is what we want more than anything else, both to render the river fordable and to save our valuable supply of meat, which is going bad fast from this continued hot weather. Our grubstakes are getting lower and lower every day and we may have a hard time ahead of us in getting out of this miserable country. Soon we will be reduced to a straight diet of meat, tea and flour. So we are anxious to get started and keep going until we get somewhere! As Jack has a fire in the tipi to bake bread, I didn't dare leave camp, as after our last miraculous escape from fire I don't dare take any chances of leaving him alone. If our whole outfit should get burned up, and we narrowly escaped it the other day, we would have difficulty in getting out even with our lives. I cannot say enough for the beauty of this brilliant orange foliage of the balm of Gilead trees which predominates here. The leaves have begun to fall rapidly now and I am afraid it will be over all too soon. Bob reported seeing some ducks with white breasts in a little cove along the river, so I went down with the .22 automatic gun and managed to get one which proved to be a female Gadwall duck. The other two were frightened and flew off up the river. Our friend the ruffed grouse drummed on his log all day and the ravens flew about croaking in their dismal way. Canada jays and a winter wren are among the poplars. Saw a big grizzly on top of the mountain west of us, and for a long time I watched him digging for mice or ground squirrels of some kind; then he disappeared in the brush. Several times we thought we heard moose or bear and I went out with my gun, but nothing turned up. The last time this happened I heard voices and instead of a moose appearing Fred and Bob turned up. They were able to accomplish all that they wanted in one day. They saw the same grizzly that I did, a black wolf and four caribou, but were unable to get any of them. The latter were large and looked like *Osborni*. No sheep were seen; it was distinctly a caribou range with plenty of moss.

They saw probably Moberly Lake and the main Pine River.[167] Below is better going – open hills and fine feed. They saw two blue (Richardson's) grouse on the summit feeding on bearberries.

SUNDAY, SEPTEMBER 27. COOL – RAIN.

Another magnificent effect at sunrise on the mountains, with brilliant-coloured clouds above, which, with the autumn foliage contrasting with the dark green spruces, was very fine indeed. Yet it was a wild, stormy-looking effect. Before we had finished eating breakfast the howl of a wolf resounded far off from the mountains, and a few minutes later Fred said, "There's a black wolf," pointing to a gravel bar across the river, about 200 yards off. I ran for my gun and fired at him as he sat on his haunches, but it was too far for such a small mark as he made head on. He jumped and ran off at top speed and made a beautiful picture in his fine coal-black coat. I would have given a lot to have shot him, as he must have had a magnificent hide. Apparently he was attracted by the smell of the meat hanging on the racks drying. If I had tried to get nearer he undoubtedly would have run, as he was watching us intently. However, it was worthwhile to have even seen him. Soon three of the men went off to cut the trail out to the good going several miles below here, while Bob Cross and I stayed in camp. I went out to round up the horses and found them above here, gradually getting on their way up river, preparing to leave us again. After driving them back to the "sloo" and their feed I returned to camp and then the rain began in earnest and for awhile it came down in torrents. Black-capped chickadees about. Bob and I stayed about the tipi all day, trying to dry out the small mammal and bird skins etc. Every little while I had to go out and drive the horses back, as they kept working up beyond us either along the gravel flat or behind in the timber. One hour the sun would be out bright and then the next it would pour, so that it was impossible to dry my goat and bear hides, which badly needed to be hung up after their last wetting. About six, during the heaviest downpour of all, the men returned, having cut a trail several miles down to a gravel bar. They saw all kinds of tracks, – moose, caribou, deer, bear, wolves, coyotes, foxes, beaver, geese, in fact everything but sheep and goat. Also they saw a moose. Beaver dams and ponds and rocky ridges caused lots of cutting.

MONDAY, SEPTEMBER 28. WARM – SHOWERS.

The storm has cleared, the barometer has risen three-tenths and at last we have got a real fall day – clear and cold, with a fresh wind. However, when the sun gets up I suppose it will warm up fast. The horses were trouble-some last night and restless so Bob had to go out and round them up in the timber and drive them back. Left about 10, following the trail already cut out and everything went serenely for a long time. But things changed soon. First it clouded over and all day it showered, much to our disappointment after the bright prospects at sunrise. We had several very bad stretches to manoeuvre and with our usual luck we got through without mishap. One mudhole caused nearly every horse, one after another, to get bogged and they had to be dragged out. Then a dangerous, steep rock ridge covered with large blocks of rocks hidden by a mossy covering caused a good many horses to fall. Jack once more distinguished himself by forcing his horses into the river and for five minutes they stood on a bar while we watched them with our hearts in our mouths, wondering whether they would swim to the other side of the river or not, during which time we just sat and cursed them. Finally, the men got to them and drove them back. An owl hooted all the afternoon near camp,[168] which seemed rather strange during broad daylight. Distance 5 miles. altitude 2300 feet.

TUESDAY, SEPTEMBER 29. HOT – BRIGHT.

Another day starting out like yesterday. It rained hard last evening but apparently did not shower during the night. No room for the tipi so we arranged it in the form of a lean-to. In driving the horses down to feed last night, Bruce, with his usual amount of sense, jumped down off the bank onto the river bars while the rest of the horses went along the timber. He refused to follow anything except the river, and being cut off by a logjam, could not return except by the way he had gone down, but he didn't know enough for that. He got excited, ran down along the edge of the river under a cut bank, and being unable to get up, swam the river to the other side, ran about, and in the absence of any scent, swam back again. By that time it was very dark and so Fred decided to trust to luck that he would find the rest of the horses by himself. The men cut trail yesterday afternoon nearly down to the open hill slopes, and if these prove as good as they appear to be we will keep up on them away from the river. An American three-toed wood-pecker[169] was tapping the trees about camp. The wind blew violently all last evening, carrying our lean-to out into the air like a sail but we managed to hold on to it. At intervals we heard big trees crashing to the ground under the influence of the terrific squalls and it had a wild sound as the wind storms tore down the valley. Ahead of us the open hillsides certainly look good and there the sun is shining brightly, a contrast to this spot and what we have passed through. We have looked forward to reaching it for such a long time that we have called it the "Promised Land." Let us hope it will prove to be such and not be a disappointment. The Children of Israel could not have looked forward to their Promised Land any more than we are looking forward to ours. Bruce was not with the horses this morning but Bob soon found him where we last saw him yesterday evening. Got under way as usual, all but Cigar being packed, it being thought best to give her a rest, for her side, although doing finely, has a hard scab on it that keeps breaking open under the strain of jumping logs. After following the trail cut by the men yesterday afternoon and going about a mile further we at last reached our open country, the first of its kind we have seen since leaving Sheep Creek two months ago. It consisted of hillsides with scattered clumps of poplar and willow bushes. The ground was covered with fallen timber but it was low to the ground and only a little cutting was necessary here and there to get through. Grass browned by the frost grew very sparingly, but here and there was a little meadow, a thing we haven't seen for two months. It was a real joy to be in such country once more and we hope it will continue until we reach trails. We call it fine going but anyone accustomed to travelling on trails would consider it frightful country to go through. We can see ahead for another day or possibly two where we will have similar going. After there being so much timber falling we didn't dare camp among the burnt trees so camped on top of a bench covered with second growth Jack pine and willows which had to be cut away before we had a clear space to unpack the horses. In coming down a steep hill Fred and I, who were ahead, had the pleasure of having a bunch of rocks dislodged by the horses following us come down. One large rock first came by Bob, just missing his leg, then it bounded within a foot of me and then it whizzed by Fred's head. It was a miracle that we all three escaped it. This is the third successive day we have made three miles in a straight line from our previous camp. If we can continue at that rate we will soon be in good country. Distance 6 miles, altitude 2200 feet.

WEDNESDAY, SEPTEMBER 30. HOT – BRILLIANT.

As Bob remarked, there is almost a feeling of joy to look back at the miserable stretch of country we have been through. We certainly experience much more pleasure in that than we did some time ago in looking ahead into it. Of course we are not "out of the woods" yet, but we have got some good going ahead and it can't be many days now before we find travelled trails. This valley here resembles the Athabasca above Jasper and is a fine-looking range for deer. There are lots of moose signs but none are fresh; perhaps it is more of a winter range for them. The rocks on the hills about us also are different from what we have been through, as they are a sandstone formation. The last two days we have found lots of the so-called "pea vine" growing through the burnt timber. A good part of it is dead from the frost but some is still green with here and there a purple flower still blooming. This is one of the great favourites of the horses, but as much as they like it the vine is too delicate a growth to be as good staying feed as some of the hardy, stronger grasses. It is good to see an old friend like this once more. Also we are back in the hare country once more and I saw my first one for two months (since leaving the Smoky River valley). Quite a number jumped ahead of us. They are just beginning to turn, as their legs and flanks are white though their backs, sides and heads are still in the brown summer pelage. Yesterday the going was too perfect to continue all day for this kind of country. On reaching camp I got all eight hides out (bear, sheep, goat and caribou), thinking that with the bright sun and warm wind they would dry out finely, but no sooner were they hung up than the wind dropped, the sun disappeared in the clouds and it began to look like rain. The air soon got too damp to do any good so I had to pack them away again. It is discouraging, as they need to be dried out thoroughly owing to their soaked condition acquired from swimming the river several times a few days ago. Saw juncos and either a sparrow or a pigeon hawk. Today is the last day of September and with luck we will be able to see the so-called gap a few miles ahead where the river leaves the mountains and turns from its present easterly course and flows north into the main Pine River, along the outside range of mountains, through the foothills. Barometer steady today but it is still and overcast, yet far in the west is a patch of blue sky which is slowly enlarging so that probably before noon the sun will be out once more and it will be hot again. The sun did come out shortly and all day it was literally hot. The only time we can realize it is fall is when the sun goes under a cloud; then it becomes chilly. The going was similar to yesterday, only better! Every minute was enjoyable! We kept up on the open slopes and after two hours we climbed a ridge and here sat down to appreciate the situation. This was the gap, for at this point the river leaves the mountains and turns north.[170] Behind us was the miserable country we had come through and ahead lay the rolling foothills, and for several miles ahead, up to the next turn in the river, the same open going continued. Not more than two miles away the

Jack pine timber began, and I hope we have come to the end of the spruce. About ten miles east there is a north and south valley. If any trail at all exists between this branch (middle or south) and the east branch of the Pine it will be through this valley, so we should in the course of a few days find a real trail. After everyone had enjoyed this scene with a peaceful smoke, we continued. Saw a pair of golden eagles. Hares plentiful and moose, deer, coyote and wolf tracks abundant. About this time I spotted a moose a mile off and as what little meat remains from our previous moose is going bad fast we decided we wanted this one, so Bob and I left the outfit to make the stalk, having arranged with Fred to wave his hand in the direction Mr. Moose moved as we would be unable to see him until we reached the river. Bob and I set off at a dog trot. We looked at Fred through the glasses but no signal, so on we went until near the river. Again we looked back and Fred waved his hand upstream so we ran that way and I soon saw the moose and in another minute got a shot at him, about 400 yards away. He disappeared as if hit so I fired twice more into the bush. Soon Bob joined me and the moose reappeared. Bob fired and down he went. So we signalled the men, who joined us with the outfit and made camp on the bench just above the river. After eating, three of the men took three pack horses and swam the river to get the moose. At last our food supply is OK and if the weather only stays cool we have 20 days meat in camp. The men found it cold work going for the moose, as in crossing the river, which was narrow but deep, the horses refused to swim but kept pawing for the bottom. Consequently they went in deeper than if they had actually swum. On the return the same process was repeated so that they were wet to the armpits and the water was bitterly cold. On their return there was a mad rush for the fire and a speedy change to dry clothes ensued. Curiously enough, no shot hole was found in the moose but it may have gone undiscovered in the long thick hair. At any rate, the animal was stone dead. We ate the liver for supper but it is not up to sheep or caribou liver, as it is too soft. We have lots of fat once more, which we all take great pleasure in feasting on, like a lot of Indians; also the kidneys, tongue and legs for their marrow bones to say nothing of tenderloin steaks, rumps etc. As we were eating supper the moon, which is almost full, rose over the hills, and later as we sat around the campfire the Northern Lights appeared, getting more and more brilliant until the whole northern half of the sky was brilliantly illuminated while streamers of light shot high up into the heavens, – a sure sign of colder weather. In the northwest, below the third star in the handle of the dipper, we have watched recently with interest a fine comet with quite a tail. Tonight, in spite of the brilliancy of the moon, it showed up conspicuously. What comet it is of course we do not know and it will be interesting to find out when we get home.[171]

THURSDAY OCTOBER 1. COOL – CLEAR.

It was clear and cold last night and everything froze up, including of course all the men's clothes and horse blankets wet yesterday afternoon in going for the moose. The first day of October has come in under auspicious circumstances, for we are out of the mountains, in God's own country once more, and with plenty of meat in camp and cold weather to keep it in. Today is without doubt the finest day we have had in weeks, a typical cold, clear October day, with a bright, warm sun and a cloudless sky. We intend staying in camp to give the meat a good drying, also the hides, and to bake bread as well as wash some clothes, – all necessary proceedings. Bob returned from looking up the horses, having found signs of horses, the first for two months. At last we are in the region of some horse travel, no matter how slight. It is queer how all things come together, – good weather, open country and fresh meat. While watching the hills with our glasses Bob spotted a good-sized black bear high up. For some time we watched him as he came down the hill quite speedily until he disappeared in a gully filled with timber. Then a pair of caribou appeared higher up still, on the skyline. A pair of golden eagles are soaring over the hills and Canada jays are about camp. This sight of game was too tempting to keep us in camp, so Fred and I put a lunch in our pockets, leaving Jack to bake bread, Bob Cross to dry hides, skins and wash clothes, and Bob Jones with various chores. It was a longer climb than I anticipated to the top and it was two hours before we reached the shoulder, where we sat down on a point that overlooked the whole country far and wide, and ate our lunch. In spite of the cold early morning the bright sun made it extremely hot climbing and the perspiration rolled off me in streams. I found that, not having done any climbing for some little time, my wind had not improved from the rest and my leg muscles were not in the best of condition. On the way up we found horse tracks, apparently an outfit of 15 horses, going down the valley. It was a pleasant discovery, as the last tracks we saw were two months ago. On August third coming over the pass between Sheep Creek and the Porcupine lakes we found tracks which apparently were those made by us two years ago. Since then we have seen nothing until today. Undoubtedly this was an outfit of Indians and in that case we can't be far from trails, as they rarely travel far from trails. If they want to hunt in a new country they will go a few miles beyond the limit of trails, then each subsequent trip they may go a little farther. They never penetrate a country unknown to them, or untravelled, for long distances as a white man will do. So this was a very encouraging sign. Up on our lookout point we covered the country with glasses and below us on a flat covered with a three- to four-year-old growth of Jack pines was our black bear, moving along downstream not half a mile away from camp, so if we had stayed below and hunted him, as we once thought of doing, we probably should have been able to get him. No sign of our caribou appeared so we continued on to the top after eating and came out on the summit, with the country spread out all about us like a map.[172] South of us stretched the river valley we had been following so laboriously for a whole month making tortoise-like progress. Far in the distance in the same direction was a semi-circle of peaks, many of which we recognized as having climbed for hunting or mapping the country.[173] Then they were bare and barren masses of rock, but now, covered with snow and ice, they were cold and bleak enough looking to make us glad to think that we were far away from them. To the west and north was a succession of valleys, very confusing indeed, and to the eastward lay first the foothills and then the level prairie country stretching in the distance just as far as the eye could reach. There, within eyesight probably, yet too far off to be visible, stretched the last remaining piece of prairie that is being ploughed up for cultivation, – Grande Prairie and Pouce Coupe prairie. There the country is being homesteaded and people are coming into it almost daily to take up their land. On our way home we shall probably go through this very country. To think how near and yet how far we are from civilization and the land of plenty, for it will be many weeks before we reach it. In the foreground was fine-looking caribou country, a rolling moss-covered upland pasture, with timber here and there for shelter and little lakes dotted about – still frozen over, the warm sun not being sufficient to counteract the effect of the freezing of last night. Altogether it was ideal caribou country. To the west were fine-looking, bare-topped hills, certainly appearing at a glance like good sheep ranges, but being moss-covered and no trails in sight they must be inhabited only by caribou. However, this last little stretch of country, which is too inaccessible for us to hunt during our limited time, we can find out from the Indians as to the nature of the animals that range there. It was bitterly cold lying on the rocks on the summit looking over the country with glasses, although there was no wind. As soon as Fred had finished his map we were ready to leave. What disappointed us most was that the valley which he and Bob took to be the west Pine can't be it after all, which means that the valley we are searching for must be at least ten miles further, – that is, 20 from here. We are extremely puzzled as to our situation. Below, across the river, is a fine, grass-covered flat surrounded by open groves of poplar, an ideal camping spot, and we hope to make it tomorrow by keeping high up on the bare ridges as we have been doing. Here there should be a trail or at least signs of camping. Saw caribou and black bear signs. Had our last feed of frosted low-bush mountain cranberries, blueberries, huckleberries and bearberries. Came down over the steep, bare, grassy slopes, making quick time. Saw three golden eagles and goshawk soaring over the hills; three prairie sharp-tailed grouse on the grass ridges,[174] Canada jays and Bohemian waxwing. By the time we reached camp the barometer had dropped and it looks stormy. Heard a moose across the river while at supper. End of fourteenth week, total distance 565 miles.

FRIDAY, OCTOBER 2. COOL – RAIN.

Again the barometer has accurately predicted the weather. At first it did not look too bad and we almost decided to start and not waste a day, but wisely we changed our minds and it was well for within an hour it settled down to a steady rain. The wind is from the northeast and quite cool. Higher up it is snowing and the mountain we climbed yesterday is white with snow. Again the barometer has returned to its reading before the storm, so tomorrow it ought to be clear again. We are now on our last sack of flour, which is only a two weeks' supply, and it doesn't seem possible we can reach Hudson's Hope by that time, so we may have to get along without bread for a while. However, we have tea and coffee and meat. That is our regular diet, with some beans or fruit about once a week as a treat. Our supply of the last two we are using very sparingly. Spent the day in the tipi and often argued how many days we are from Hudson's Hope. We still maintain this is the south and not the east Pine River, in spite of the looks of the valleys ahead being against it. All day at intervals the discussion would start again. The looks of the country is such that almost any argument, supposition or theory will hold, which makes the discussions all the more heated. Our latest conclusion is that the series of "cut banks" we saw about ten miles north is the junction of the south fork and the main or west Pine. If it is so we should reach it in three travelling days and seven more should take us to Hudson's Hope. These rainy days in the tipi have their amusing and humorous sides, as each one of us seems to have a distinctive occupation or number of occupations. Mine are usually uninteresting, such as writing my diary, sewing, playing solitaire, reading and last but not least watching the barometer at hourly intervals. I have opened it so often now that the catch to the case has finally worn out and dropped off. Next is Jack, who has but one diversion except at mealtime when he is cooking, and that is lying back in a comfortable position reading and smoking. Our five small volumes of Dumas's works which I brought along, with two packs of cards, have proved very popular and helped to while away many an hour. Then Bob Cross, who seems to have more occupations than anyone, – but first of all is his map-making, which consumes much time. Besides that, he always seems to have boots to repair, glass case to put new stitches in, the medicine case to repack, or a thousand and one repairs to his outfit, which always seams to need fixing. Once in awhile his work is actually done and he lies back and reads his book, puffing meanwhile at his pipe in perfect peace. At these times he certainly looks as though he enjoyed his hour's relaxation. Fred, whose outfit is usually in pieces, at present is sewing his hat, the crown having been slowly torn off until it was held by one corner only. Yesterday when he faced the wind his lid stood on end, making him look like some created creature. His trousers are continually in need of repair as his supply is limited to two pair. If he had more, these wouldn't be worth repairing. The ordinary person if assigned to such a job would be at a loss to know which piece to sew on to which, so many are there of them. He spent the morning sewing his socks, the repairing of which was similar to a picture puzzle. However, the results were excellent. Bob washed his underclothes yesterday for him and having but one set he went up on that cold mountain minus his "Jaegars." With his trousers cut off just below the knees (the lower part of the legs being used to patch the upper) he might easily have been taken for a Scotch Highlander in his native costume by some innocent person. However, Highlanders are not very common in these altitudes at this season of the year. Lastly, is Bob Jones, whose clothes are remarkably intact except for his trousers. He started with a pair of corduroys but they quickly fell a prey to the snags and underbrush and soon became a mass of streamers until his trousers resembled those belonging to the stage organ grinder's costume. He is now sewing the streamers together, rather an arduous task. His khaki trousers also were badly torn above the knees so he resorted to Fred's procedure of cutting the lower part off in order to patch them. This left his socks etc. exposed to the deadly underbrush so he ingeniously devised a set of leggings made from strips of the remains of the canvas "lean-to" that was burnt up awhile ago. These he wraps about his calves and tied with another strip of said "lean-to" they answer the purpose very well. One thing is past repair and that is our tipi. However, it hangs together well. It is so full of small (and large) holes that waking up about daylight I imagine myself sleeping out in the open with the stars shining brightly over my head.

SATURDAY, OCTOBER 3. COOL – CLEAR.

Today is the 100th day since we left Jasper and civilization behind us, and as it turned out it was a day long to be remembered as it most certainly was the most eventful day we have yet had. We started out early, soon after 9.30 in a dense fog, so we could see nothing of the hills about us, but as the barometer had been steadily rising we knew it would not be long before it cleared. It did so slowly, until we had an almost cloudless sky. We followed the ridges west of camp and for a couple of miles were able to keep along the tracks of the outfit that was in here about a year ago but then finally lost them where the bushes became very thick and the tracking impossible in the grass. Here we entered the timber and found the going good as it was composed of an open growth of poplar, balm of Gilead, Jack pine, spruce and willow. We followed along the base of a ridge at the foot of which was a piece of swampy ground overgrown with alders and willows. It might just as well have been a patch of woods at home within 200 yards of our house in Dover, it resembled it so much. Here and there were scattered a few white birches. Fred thought this was a good place to look for a trail, for if one was to exist it would be through there, not far off. So we separated, going in opposite directions. In ten minutes he was back, saying the going was better out a little ways, so we took the horses through to an open grassy meadow. To our great surprise here was an unmistakable trail and then the question arose whether it was a horse or moose trail. It certainly resembled the former as it was wide and smooth, being evenly packed, a moose trail being narrower and more cut up. Then it was the exact location for a horse trail, whereas a moose trail would more likely follow the river and any side trails would lead from it to the hillsides, to some lick, "sloo" or muskeg. After everyone had expressed his opinion and had an enjoyable smoke on the strength of it we rode on, following it. In every way it more and more resembled a pack trail, more especially the minor "turn-offs" to avoid trees and the spaces between the trees. Still no signs of a blaze, only scars on the poplars where the moose had torn off the bark in rubbing their horns on the trunks in order to remove the velvet from them. After a mile we found the first blaze and Fred made another one above it and we dismounted while I took a picture of the crowd standing around this famous tree. This was one of the biggest events of the summer. On we went again and it was a pleasure once more, after two months, to see the horses all strung out in single file along a real, perfect trail; they certainly must have enjoyed it fully as much as we did. On we went as the trail took us, first through open groves of Jack pine or beautiful tall poplar trees, then through an open meadow covered with long grass and covered with poplars fully 50 feet tall, their trunks as straight as masts, and their upper branches still covered with leaves, now turned to a deep orange-red. Above, the blue sky was clear except for a woolly cloud that floated lazily along here and there. The landscape effect was very pleasing and reminded me of Corot's pictures, except that the air was a little too clear. With various windings and turnings and losing the trail, when we would stop the outfit while Fred and I went in opposite directions to again locate it, we made rapid progress. We saw a fine golden eagle and a rough-legged hawk, both of them close to us for we surprised them suddenly from their perch on a dead tree. Also an American three-toed woodpecker, Canada jays and a Franklin grouse (the first I have seen for some time) were seen. The trail descended to the river and the chopping along it was six to eight years old, so last year's outfit did not come this way, which was puzzling to us and we want to follow them. Beaver dams and cuttings were as plentiful as usual and caused us trouble. We followed the river for quite a long way and close to the bank all along was a little open lead that made an ideal place for a trail, but no cutting appeared. In one spot the trail separated and we followed the river one, which turned out to be wrong. Here the river was a real river, as it is fordable at this time of the year almost anywhere and in places not above the horses' hocks. All along the edges are narrow gravel bars and the bottom is of gravel so that the fording is perfect, but now there is no need to ford it. Above, where we had to cross, it was nearly impossible, – in fact, it was in most places. Altogether this was the most enjoyable day I have ever spent on the trail, as we feel sure we can reach Hudson's Hope shortly unless some unforeseen obstacle turns up. It is well too, as supplies are getting lower every day. We camped after seven hours, having made fully 14 miles (10 in a straight line), altitude 2100 feet. It was dark before we had supper. Then the moon rose and the owls began to hoot, – a fitting close to such a perfect day.

SUNDAY. OCTOBER 4. HOT – BRILLIANT.

Luckily we decided to put up the lean-to last night. It was well, for it was bitterly cold; the thermometer must have been close to zero, for when we got up soon after daylight it was only ten above. Even by the time the sun had set last night the water froze in the pails and our boots and blankets were frozen stiff after the wetting we got. I forgot to mention that just before camping Fred forded the river again and it was so deep that some of the horses had to swim, and consequently the outfit got soaked, blankets and all. Only yesterday did our hides and skins get comparatively dry after ten days' work, and it is maddening to have had such an unfortunate occurrence. Fred and Bob have gone off trail-hunting, the latter across the river, while we are behind packing up the outfit. Heard a raven around croaking at daylight. The horses stayed around close to camp all night and ringing their bells disturbed our slumbers. Several of them came into camp and had to be driven away. One ate all the grease out of the frying pan and another licked the soup out of the pot. Another time we will rope the camp so they can't get in. After Fred and Bob went we started to break camp, saddling the horses but not packing them, and then we waited for several hours. It was a cloudless day and it is some time since we have felt the heat as here in this shadeless, windless spot. The thermometer registered 63 degrees in the shade at 2 p.m., a change of 53 degrees in a few hours, since this morning when we got up. A golden eagle flew past and half a dozen little black-capped chickadees flitted among the willows about us while we ate our lunch, scolding continually, a reminder of the warm October Indian summer days at home in the woods. About 3 p.m. Fred returned with the news that there is no trail beyond the mountain, but that it must be just back of us but because of the open character of the country impossible to find. He found about fifteen shed moose horns on the ridge west of us. They all were dropped in little spruce muskegs where willows grew scatteringly. A perfect day for travelling lost, yet we have a definite idea of where the trails are and to make sure of that it is a day well spent after all. We went below a little way and found the old trail going along through open timber, – Jack pine, spruce and poplar, a rather unusual combination. Fred and Bob cut away the logs from our camp to the trail while I went down to the river and followed it back in the hopes of getting a shot at a deer. About 5 Bob Cross returned, having covered about fifteen miles across the river on foot. He found about a mile from this stream a well-worn trail similar to the one we followed yesterday and followed it three miles to a big open grassy flat at least a mile square. Here were old tipi poles and meat racks but no signs within five years. Another trail came in from the southeast along a creek[175] just as Fred and I thought while we were on top of the mountain two days ago, so our judgment was correct, as also it was that we should find a trail yesterday. This means three trails converge on this flat, so that one main trail will lead out down the river and should be a fine, heavy trail. Also it looks now as if this were the East Branch and not the South Fork. The situation is certainly getting more amusing every day. However, in two days we should reach the main Pine River and probably then we will know. We celebrated this event with a portion of Hudson Bay rum, which leaves us only one more. Again, it was a beautiful, cold, clear night and soon after the moon rose over the hill we rolled into our blankets, without any tipi or shelter, – only the star-filled sky for a "roof," ready to be up before daylight tomorrow for an early start.

MONDAY, OCTOBER 5. WARM – BRILLIANT.

Another ideal Indian summer day. We were up just at daylight, with the full moon shining in the west, and crawled out of our frosted blankets to find the air crisp and biting, but after the fire got going well we quickly thawed out. As daylight came the moon became silvery and then slowly became inconspicuous in the blue sky. As this change went on, the clouds between it and the distant hills became pinker and pinker from the rays of the rising sun, making a beautiful effect. As we were eating our breakfast the coyotes began their curious musical yelping, a sound I always like to hear although it often is a sign of an approaching storm. We left early, at 9.15, going down the river via the trail we located. It was not very good later on and Fred had to do some chopping; then we forded and found the going better and shortly came to the "big flat" where a creek comes in from the southeast,[176] on which is the trail from the Wapiti, and also a creek from the west.[177] This flat is at least a square mile and covered with the best of grass and pea vine but now all frosted and brown. In the summer it would easily be a sufficient range for 200 head of horses. It is without doubt the finest flat I have ever seen in the foothills. Its edges are mostly fringed with poplar with here and there a clump of spruces. Tipi poles and meat racks were numerous.[178] We forded the river here and, thank God, we left it, with the hope of never seeing it again as for five weeks it has caused us continual trouble, worry and work. Another fine flat nearly as large was on the other side.[179] We crossed it coming to our trail leading up a steep slope to a bench above. Also a trail goes down the east branch of the Pine, for we now feel sure the river is not the south fork. This trail we followed we hope goes to the junction of the south and west Pine. If so, we can't be more than six days from Hudson's Hope. After a short distance we emerged from the timber and about 300 feet below us, surrounded by an amphitheatre of bare grass hills, was a beautiful flat of several hundred acres covered with the finest grass. Three sets of tipi poles were at the far end already set up, a sight we haven't seen for two months. Here we made camp, – at last, our Promised Land Camp! A piece of calico cloth belonging to a squaw lying on the ground is evidence that the last outfit of Indians was here about two years ago. This is the most recent sign we have seen for more than two months. We made about 10 miles, altitude 2000 feet.

TUESDAY, OCTOBER 6. HOT – BRILLIANT.

It certainly seems good to be in God's own country once more and we certainly do appreciate it after all our trials and tribulations. From here to Hudson's Hope and home to Jasper, altogether a distance of over 600 miles, the going should be good and on fine trails. Of course we may have minor trail troubles but nothing like what we have been through. During the two months that we have been without trails, during which time we have come across the mountains, picking out our course in order to hunt the country and cover every possible sheep range, we have been 200 miles and have cut our own trails all that distance, which is a tremendously long way, an average of a hundred miles per month, or a little over three miles per day. Certainly that is a tortoise-like gait, but if anyone could see the country we have traversed they would readily understand the reason of such slow progress. We made an early start today; almost the earliest during this trip, for we were on the trail at 8.45.A hawk owl flew past us as we left this ideal camp and when we reached our temporary home in the evening another flew over. The country the trail traversed was fine, open flats then poplar and most of the day Jack pine ridges alternating with patches of spruce, the former predominating. Continually fool hens (Franklin's grouse) flew up into the trees out of the trail and now and then in some open spot or on some poplar side hills a ruffed grouse jumped up and whirred off out of sight. It made me wish I had my little .22 rifle, as a meal of chickens would be a great change from our steady diet of moose meat. On we went, hour after hour, making fast time, until Fred became interested to know what lay ahead of us, for the thick timber shut off our view, so he climbed a tree from which he sighted probably meadows several miles off in the next valley. [180] Another hour brought us to a growth of small (fifteen to twenty feet high) burnt Jack pine. Apparently there had been a heavy wind storm recently which had filled the trail with these trees. About two miles ahead in a valley bottom were several fine, grassy flats, – that looked like home to us so Fred and Bob went ahead with their axes to hurry our progress as it was getting toward sunset, and considering the amount of chopping we made rapid progress. Just as the sun disappeared behind a distant ridge we came suddenly upon our meadow, a perfect little spot, covered with plenty of good grass for the horses. It was set in a growth of Jack pine and through it ran a stream.[181] Plenty of wood, and dry ground on which to lay our blankets made all the requisites of a perfect camp. We were soon unpacked and eating supper around the fire in the short twilight that we get up here at this season of the year. First the evening star appeared in the east, then one by one all the others came out until the sky was brilliantly illuminated. Our comet is still visible and very plain indeed. Then, to render the scene perfect the moon rose and the hooting of the owls broke upon the stillness of the evening. As we sat talking around the fire Fred said, "There's a moose," and as we listened we heard his horns ringing as he hit the trees through which he was passing. After the first few sounds it was evident the strokes were too regular. Someone said, "It's an axe," and as we listened again we became convinced that it was. Apparently, some Indians had just come into camp late as we guessed, and were cutting firewood for supper. It was a thrilling sound and no-one except those who have experienced it knows what it is to have been away from civilization three and a half months, and been months without having seen or heard a soul except ourselves, and then suddenly to hear unexpectedly, within a few hundred yards, the sound of an axe. It is a feeling that impresses one as nothing else can. In order to let them know of our presence Jack cut down a tree as we thought they might come over to pay us a visit and around the fire in the evening over a pipe and a cup of tea one can get much more information out of an Indian, but no-one appeared and we turned in for the night, still uncertain as to who might be camped on the other side of the creek.

Distance 20 miles, altitude 2700 feet.

WEDNESDAY, OCTOBER 7. HOT – BRILLIANT.

Again we were up at the first streak of dawn in order to get away early. We felt certain that the Indians would call on us early but no one seemed to appear. During breakfast a shot was fired from the direction of their camp, a signal, as we supposed, by which they wanted to let us know of their presence. Bob answered it by discharging his gun, but nothing more happened. Both camps were aware of the other's presence now and the next step was for someone to make a move. As we were anxious to find out more accurately our position and as to the trails and distance to Moberly Lake and Hudson's Hope, Fred and I waded the creek and headed for the column of smoke that rose above the tree tops, indicating the position of their camp. In wandering about through the open spaces we came upon a man with a gun on his shoulder and a couple of traps in his hand. It was a strange sight, to say the least, but notwithstanding the looks of the individual, who turned out to be a white man, apparently a Scandinavian,[182] still he was a welcome sight. He told us he was in there trapping with his partner but they were leaving today to go on foot to their main cabin twenty miles away as their food supply had been exhausted. We urged him to walk back to camp to get some meat, which he did, and as he ate a steak and drank a cup of tea we plied him with questions. Someone said, "What's the news outside?" And he said, "The chief thing is the war." We looked at each other in surprise, thinking that the United States and Mexico had gone to war, but before we had time to put our thoughts into words he told us of the terrific European war. We were completely swept off our feet by this startling news: it seemed like a dream to find out, away off in the mountains, that the five largest European powers have been at war for two months, during which time we have been in complete ignorance of it.[183] He told us the latest news, which was eight weeks old, of the battle of Nurem in France where the French gained a victory, of the big loss of life and of the various naval manoeuvres. It all sounded true and we of course believed it, but the news coming as it did out of a clear sky certainly was somewhat staggering. After awhile our surprise and interest turned from the topic to that which concerned us more vitally. He told us of the trail over to Rocky Mountain Lake[184] and that it was a good one. But as that was not the direction we wanted to take we decided to try to find a trail going northwest to the main Pine River. When he left we hurriedly packed the horses and at 9.10 were on the trail again, but before we had gone a mile we were on foot trail-hunting. The trapper, Nelson by name, turned up again and he advised our going to the lake, then taking a trail from it to the main Pine northwest from there. That decided us and we set out. All day the travelling was good, as there was no cutting and a fine, well-cut-out trail through dry Jack pine ridges, here and there going through a piece of spruce or tamarack muskeg. We saw numerous Franklin's grouse and several ruffed grouse, three of which I shot. An old trail led off in the direction we want to go but we didn't dare take it as we think it safer to stick to Nelson's advice. After over seven hours' travelling we camped, another long day for yesterday was eight and three-quarters hours. It was clear and the sun, shining from a cloudless sky, made it very hot. It was the most miserable day I ever spent on the trail, as I am suffering from a very painful boil on my wrist which has affected me all over as every bone and muscle in my body aches and pains and a long day in the saddle only aggravated it. Distance 15 miles, altitude 2300 feet.

THURSDAY, OCTOBER 8. HOT – BRILLIANT.

I am afraid the cause of this large boil that I have developed must be from feasting on so much fat and grease which we have all been devouring with the delight of Indians, so I have decided to abstain entirely. A week should take us to Hudson's Hope and then we will get a decided change of diet, which should be a good blood purifier. Bob lanced the boil for me but apparently it had not come to a head yet, so it gave me no relief. All I can do is to be miserable for awhile until it is ready to be lanced. I had a miserable night; in the first place, I had an awful chill and couldn't get near enough to the camp fire to keep warm – I almost sat in it. Then, after I got into my blankets, I had a miserable fever that made me roll about in a restless way all night. However, when I awoke, washed and had breakfast I thought I felt better. Apparently, sleeping out in the open on a good dry spot under the trees seemed to have been beneficial. My arm is useless, so I walked up and down to keep warm as I was unable to help pack the horses. We got away early again, at five minutes to 9, and in less than an hour came to Rocky Mountain Lake and the cabin belonging to Nelson and his four partners. A string of whitefish hung on a pole and other signs of life were about, but nobody was in. The lake was a pleasant surprise, not its existence, of which Nelson had told us, but its beauty, and seen in the early morning light it was certainly a lovely spot, – the kind of a lake you read about and such a place as you would pick out to build a house and live. It was about twelve miles long, set in a big depression of the foothills which rose quite abruptly from its shores. Its outline was irregular, and here and there a point covered with green spruce and dotted with clumps of poplar with its bright yellow foliage extended into the lake. The sun was in such a position over the right hand hills that all that part of the lake lay in an obscure haze, which added to the beauty and peace of the scene. Not a breath of air stirred and the surface mirrored the surrounding hills. Just below us was the only ripple, which was caused by a duck that swam slowly along, diving suddenly every little while to catch a fish.[185]

Here was where our trail to the Pine left, that which went to the east branch and we found it without any trouble, so that we were soon climbing the hills on our dash to the Pine River. Nelson said it was twenty miles, which meant a long distance, and that there was four miles of heavy fallen timber but he had sawed a good many logs out this summer and an outfit of Indians from Moberly Lake had been over it within a few months, so we might be able to slip through without much difficulty. Shortly we came to this stretch, and the size of the logs, together with the recent cutting as well as signs of horses, convinced us that we had found the right trail. Luckily, no more trees had fallen and Fred scarcely had to use his axe, so that in two hours we were through and had come to a grass-covered flat in a hollow at the foot of this hill. Soon after we started I began to feel miserable and in a short time I felt so sick that I could scarcely sit on my horse, for the fever of the last two nights seemed to have taken my strength away and the brilliant hot sun overhead only made matters worse. I was frightfully thirsty and longed for a drink of water but every pool and stream was as dry as a bone and I couldn't get a drink anywhere. I planned to call a halt and camp at this flat for it was the last bit of horse feed this side of the Pine, but every bit of water had disappeared and every pool was dried up. As camping here then was out of the question I kept silent and so on we went. It was not a pleasant prospect to look forward to. On we went, mile after mile, through Jack pine and spruce forests and then came a stretch of several miles through a muskeg which slowed us down quite a bit. Today we saw no fool-hens, only two ruffed grouse, and it was a pretty sight as they flushed close to us and tore through the big timber on whirring wings in the dusk. All along we saw deadfalls for marten and one large one for bear. Many trees were scratched by the latter's claws and some of their fur still clung to the pitchy scars they had made. Both cinnamon and black bears are about here. We are now out of the moose country for we saw no tracks at all. We passed two cabins,[186] more evidence of Nelson's trapline. He said it was eight miles from the second one to the Pine. Now, the first one we took by some mistake to be the second and we began to think we would reach the Pine in good season, well before sunset, but to our disgust after we had gone fully four miles beyond the first cabin, and thinking how well we were progressing, we came to the second cabin. For a minute the air was blue with oaths because of our miserable luck. It was now 3.30 and the sun sets at 5.30; the twilight is short and at our present rate of progress it would take us four hours. To try to follow this trail after dark would be nearly an impossibility. However, on we went and about four miles further on we climbed a hill and saw the valley of the

Pine a few miles ahead of us, but we knew by the trail it would take a couple of hours to reach it. Fred called back for everyone to push the cayuses as much as possible and so we sped along on our last lap. It had been a long, hard day and I was just about dead, but the cool of the afternoon gave me a sort of second wind. It was too chilly sitting in the saddle and so I walked the last two hours, as well as quite a lot during the day. The horses were very tired as this was their third very long day but they came along well. We sped along in the dark with the yells and curses of the men urging on the horses behind us resounding in the timber. Finally, we reached the river flat and after apparently following it for some distance saw the Pine at last at our feet. Here was home and we made camp an hour after dark. We had been ten hours and twenty minutes on the trail and had made fully twenty-two miles, – Fred thought twenty-five. It was the longest day we have ever made and considering my condition I was about dead. However, we lit a big fire and ate to our hearts' content and with our last remaining supply of Hudson's Bay Company's rum we drank to the Pine River. It was a beautiful, still, bright evening, and in a few minutes I was rolled up in my blankets. The moon rose over the hills and no sooner was it up than a coyote howled in the distance; then another answered upstream and in a minute they were calling all about us close-by. The chorus increased, but I no longer heard any coyotes for I was sound asleep. Distance 22 miles, altitude 1600 feet. End of fifteenth week, total distance 646 miles.

FRIDAY, OCTOBER 9. HOT – BRILLIANT.

We awoke to another beautiful. cloudless day and before the sun was up we were eating breakfast and again the cries of the coyotes resounded back and forth across the river flats. It certainly is a fitting sound for this wild northern country and is real music to our ears. I have been calling these last days hot, but in comparison to the heat of summer it is different. The thermometer in the shade doesn't go much above sixty degrees, yet the sun shining from a cloudless sky is so brilliant that although we have on the same clothes as when we left Jasper last June it is impossible, for me at least, to even walk without getting in a perspiration. The air is so clear that it doesn't seem cold in the early morning about sunrise, yet the thermometer is below thirty degrees, for it is always freezing. We decided to take a day off. I feel the need of it badly and then it will give me a chance to keep a hot poultice (incidentally made out of bannock in the absence of bread or any other material) on my forearm all day. Further, it will give the horses a good rest and a chance to fatten up on this green grass, the first they have seen for a good many weeks. Bob Cross and Fred went off in different directions to locate the trail to Moberly Lake and Hudson's Hope, which we figure is not over seventy-five miles away now, so that another week should find us there. After a wonderful, restful sleep I feel much better today so that by tomorrow I should be ready to travel once more. Another boil has appeared but the first one is beginning to break so it may not amount to much. This is a very pretty spot here. The valley, which is fully four miles wide, is covered with a growth of poplar and balm of Gilead with here and there some spruces. Everywhere are flats and meadows where there is plenty of good grass. The hills, which do not rise over a thousand feet above us, are covered with spruce and are rounded or flat on top. It is pretty country, – nothing beautiful or magnificent, just what might be distinctly called God's own country, after what we have been through. My forearm and wrist have begun to swell rapidly and the flesh on my wrist is just like dough; I can press it in and a hollow will remain, – a symptom of the most dreaded mountain disease, scurvy. This is not a pleasant prospect. Consequently, I am going to stop eating meat entirely. Fortunately, the remainder of our grubstakes contain some beans, erbswurst (dried pea meal for soup) and dried fruit, so I shall stick to this diet, together with bread and tea, in the hopes of preventing this developing any further. We shall push on fast to Hudson's Hope and there may be able to get some fresh vegetables, which undoubtedly the man in charge will grow. That, with a complete change in diet ought to get me in good shape again. Fred returned at noon reporting no trail across the river, so we will start off tomorrow upstream until we find our trail to the lake. Two flocks of geese went by, honking, one bound north, the other south. The only other bird I saw was a hawk owl perched on the top of a dead poplar. It has been a beautiful Indian summer day and if this weather only lasts another week all will be well. Sometime about the middle of the month the big October storm is due and Hudson's Hope would be a good place to lay up in it. The sand flies are as numerous as on a day in August. Found a strawberry blossom, the last touch of summer. Bob returned in time for supper, having found no trail on the other side upstream, – nothing but the worst of going. Turned in early, before the moon rose.

SATURDAY, OCTOBER 10. WARM – BRILLIANT.

Still the good weather continues. The barometer is high and steady and Bob woke up in the middle of the night to find the Northern Lights lighting up the sky, further indications of clear weather. I found on changing the bandages on my arm that the poultice of yesterday had brought the boil to a head and it had burst, which was both a great physical as well as mental relief. We were under way soon after ten and made good time on a splendid trail for over six hours, – mostly over open poplar flats. The most interesting feature was the number of white and black birches; in places they literally covered the side hills in groves so that it seemed very much like New England. With the poplars and spruces scattered about it was easy to imagine ourselves in Maine. Also in a creek bottom there were several large willows similar to those that grow at home along the brooks. I never saw them before out here. Black-capped chickadees, Canada jays and ruffed grouse were the only birds seen. Camped about a mile east of the mouth of the South fork.[187] It is slow progress to Hudson's Hope and each night we are "one day's march farther from home." Some day I hope we will actually be headed the right way. There was a light easterly wind that kept down the heat of the sun. Distance 16 miles, altitude 1700 feet.

SUNDAY, OCTOBER 11. WARM – BRILLIANT.

It was very misty everywhere early, but about noon it cleared entirely and the sun was as warm as ever. Yesterday I forgot to say we saw smoke near the trail, which on investigation proved to be a prairie fire that apparently had been burning for months. At times it probably would nearly go out but would continue to smoulder until a fresh breeze would fan it into life again. As we were unable to extinguish it in any way, we went on our way. Then later we went through where the big timber had been swept by this fire and it was a black, deserted spot, the big, bare black trunks rising from their beds of ashes which filled the air as we waded through. A thing that puzzles me is that this river flows north-northeast, not east as it should. Still we continue and yet no sign of the South fork, which is very puzzling. Each possible valley we imagine is it and each low pass north seems as though it must be the one carrying the trail to Moberly Lake. Such is the situation. For two hours we continued over the usual open going. First we saw tracks of a moccasined foot, apparently that of an Indian, then tracks on the flats going both ways of a nailed foot, – a white man, probably a trapper. Soon we came to a terrific windfall in the dead timber, the worst we had seen for a long while. However, through it some outfit had been this summer, as the chopping was very recent, yet dozens of trees had fallen across the trail since then. At this point the river goes through a rocky canyon, above which are a series of very pretty cascades and small, symmetrical falls, so much so as to be almost artificial looking.[188]

It was slow, hard work cutting through the big logs and it took nearly two hours. As we came out into the open we saw a trapper's cabin below us. As we approached it Fred gave a yell but no one answered as no one was at home. It was a little, square 8 by 10 log cabin, mud plastered, with a clay chimney and a little window of one pane of glass, a great luxury for a trapper. On the roof was a toboggan for winter use on the frozen surface of the river and outside was a small but strongly built log cache for his grub, near which was a meat rack. On it drying were a number of musk-rat carcasses, but whether to be used for trap bait, to feed his dog with or meat for the trapper I don't know. The latter doesn't sound very attractive but a trapper's life is a hard one and they are willing to eat nearly anything in the absence of good meat. We went on and soon came to more deadfall which had not been cut out. It now looked as if the recent cutting we had passed through had been done by the trapper to get his horses through to bring in his winter's supply of grub. Fred went ahead to look for a way through and as we waited for him we saw a man heavily packed, followed by an Airedale terrier, coming along the creek. Certainly this was a piece of luck, meeting this trapper, as he would be able to further direct us on our course. As he approached, preceded by his dog, barking vehemently at us as he would at any stranger, we saw he was an elderly man, of well over fifty, slim and wiry of build, with a grey beard. His clothes were very ragged and his trousers as well as his undershirt seemed well past repair. We greeted him as he approached and he threw off his pack and sat down on a log. He had gone further yesterday than he had planned to and could not get back so was compelled to pass the night out. He said it was a cold night and as someone made a remark about his clothes he said, "I haven't got enough on me to flag a wheelbarrow." He was a true Yankee and appeared so. Slowly he opened up and became very genial. At first he took us for a band of Soto[189] Indians whom he had been afraid were coming up to trap and hunt and when he found out his mistake he was greatly relieved. This is really the Beaver Indian country but one or two families of Sotos have come in from the east somewhere north of Winnipeg. They are much disliked by the Beavers for coming in to their country after the game. We told him that we were bound for Hudson's Hope and wanted to get fresh directions. He laughed, saying we had come forty miles out of our way! It seemed impossible and we couldn't understand it. Then to our surprise he quietly informed us that instead of our being on the main Pine River, as we supposed, we were on the South fork. That was too much for us. Our trail from Rocky Mountain Lake had come direct to the South fork, yet Nelson had told us it was the main Pine and he didn't know where the forks were. He had only been in this country a year so that partially explained his knowledge, but this man, whose name is Treadwell,[190] has been in seven or eight years. This latest development startling as it was, could not help but strike our humorous side. After having been nearly the whole length of the East Pine and so glad to leave it, then to innocently mistake the South fork for the main river and rapidly hit up it into the mountains. One thing is certain, – we probably know more about the Pine country than any other man, but what little consolation that is![191] He said from there on up the river was impassable for horses and the same with the main, West, or North Pine as he calls it. However, he said three men started from British Columbia last year[192] to come over Pine Pass, but owing to their inability to come to an agreement as to the choice of routes they separated. Each had one horse. One came over the pass on this South fork, another via the West fork[193] (the third route he didn't know). The latter only had five days' grub but it took him fifteen. However, he managed to live on rabbits and birds. He had to literally wade the river the whole way, as did the man on the South fork.[194] Both ways are nothing but fallen timber. Years ago, before the country was burnt, there were good old Indian trails and then matters were very different. Someone wanted to go through from here to British Columbia and tried to hire the man as guide but no inducement was sufficient to hire him to cross that miserable stretch of country again. It was lucky after all that we were unable to get through to the "Pine Pass" as we planned, for we certainly would have had a serious time of it in getting out. He himself has been to the South Pine Pass and says there are lots of caribou (large ones), but not a sheep in the country. He knows them and is sure of it. He has never seen one and says the Indians never have. "But," he said, "there are sheep up by Fort Graham," which is true and his knowledge of that makes us feel all the surer of the correctness of his assertion as to the lack of sheep. It is interesting to us and a great relief to our minds, for it would seem hard to have gone all this way and been blocked from the last corner where the sheep ranges are! He told us there had been no rain since June and he never saw the water so low, which has been a great help to us which we hadn't realized before. Had it been a wet season our troubles would have been increased, if such a thing could be possible. Fred soon returned and then we asked questions about the trail. The man said he would draw us a map in his cabin, so Jack and Bob Jones started to take the back trail with the horses while we three adjourned to the cabin. It was typical of a trapper's shack inside, a table, a bunk and a fireplace being the main features. Mink, muskrat and beaver skins stretched on boards or laced to willow branches hung about everywhere. We remarked about his window. "Well," he said, "there is no reason why a man should make a Siwash of himself just because he's trapping!"[195] He asked us about the war but we only had Nelson's news. He had left Fort St. John before it broke out and his source of information had come from Jack Jarvis, who is trapping the creek below and had been at the Fort more recently to get his winter's grubstakes. He drew us a map of the country (tolerably correct) with the trail to the "Hope," as he calls the Hudson's Bay post. Then we left him, with many thanks for all his valuable information. He had been very glad to see us and showed it plainly; in fact, I think he was sorry to have us disappear almost as soon as we had turned up. As we came along we saw a coyote bounding over the logs about a hundred yards in front of us, crossing the trail at full speed. It was pretty as it sped along without stopping to look at us though we whistled and yelled at him. It was some time before we caught up with the horses and made camp two miles below where we were last night. Distance 15 miles, altitude 1700 feet.

MONDAY, OCTOBER 12. COLD – CLOUDY.

As usual our early start. It is a great relief to *really* know where we are and the exact route to Hudson's Hope. No more cutting to do, so Fred has put up his axe, a thing that hasn't been done for months. Now we will be *surely* on good trails to the "Hope" and all the way home. Today is Farmer's Day at the Hunt Club at Dover and I suppose Bill is having the time of his life with a crowd of people at the house. Also I suppose Joe is on hand for the celebration. It is interesting to picture what your friends are doing at home. Being Columbus Day, a holiday, Bill Long is probably off Cohasset in a dory, coot-shooting, and undoubtedly Chauncey Nash is with him, – but I bet it isn't as cold there as it was here today. All day it was cloudy and chilly. We made quick time, only taking four and a half hours to return to our former camp. Saw Canada jays, golden eagle, black-capped chickadees, ruffed grouse and I think a pine grosbeck, which was perched on a poplar giving his low musical warble frequently. It looks like snow. Distance 14 miles, altitude 1600 feet.

TUESDAY, OCTOBER 13. CLOUDY – LATE RAIN.

This is a great country for great horned owls and coyotes, for every night we hear them regularly near camp. Except for the ubiquitous hares, this big, fine valley of the South Pine is almost uninhabited. Probably a few moose wander through it and of course near its source on the bare hills are plenty of caribou as well as wolves. It should be a splendid deer country, as should the East branch, but neither seems to have any but an occasional one. Yesterday we began our real march to Hudson's Hope and home, a distance of probably 600 miles by trail. If we can average 100 miles per week, allowing for bad weather, it will be fast going, – faster I imagine than we will be able to make. December 1st should be the outside date at which we ought to be back in Jasper. Soon after reaching camp yesterday the weather quickly changed, becoming steadily warmer, so that all night it was quite mild, with a southwest wind blowing. Early this morning it rained hard and in consequence we got quite wet before getting up. This sudden change to warmer weather seems extraordinary but accountable by the fact that we are slowly nearing the famous Peace River farming district, the last piece of wheat land in this northwestern country. Apparently the climate is all [sic; read: 'everything'?] they claim for it. We made very fast time all day through birch and poplar country almost entirely. This travelling on good trails through pretty country has a fascination all its own. As we ride quietly along the leaf-covered trail among the poplars now bare of leaves, there is scarcely anything to disturb the stillness. Sometimes a partridge feeding in the brush will startle us suddenly by flushing almost under our horses' feet and whirr off, dodging the tree trunks, at amazing speed, or a hare will jump close by and tear off on its zigzag course. But oftentimes the partridge will sit still or merely jump to a log and watch us with outstretched neck as we pass, wondering doubtless what strange creatures we may be, or the hare will crouch on his bed of leaves where he has been sunning himself, hesitating whether to try to escape detection in lying low rather than by dashing off. This is all beautiful partridge country and many a brush shot would like to be camped in such country with a pair of good dogs. We came to a piece of heavy spruce timber among which were some giant cottonwoods, some of which would measure six feet in diameter. Such trees would make magnificent dugouts. Before I realized how fast we had come we had arrived at the forks of the south and west (or main) rivers.[196] Ahead of us was a man standing watching us approach, – undoubtedly a trapper.[197] Certainly this is populous country! He was not a very genial person. However, he gave us what little information he was in possession of concerning the country and the trails and we shortly left him, to continue our way, for we planned to push on further to a prairie several miles away where the trail forks, one branch going to the "Hope," the other to Fort St. John. This man and two others had all taken up homesteads here, so we are fast approaching civilization. His house consisted of a log shack, half underground, and a small patch of ground about it which was enclosed by a rude fence. He had planted some potatoes. He said all the potatoes at the "Hope" and Fort St. John had frozen in the ground before they were dug up. Someone asked him about this and he said that his would have frozen too but the Indians had stolen them. He appeared to be soured with the world in general and to have a grudge against everyone, so he was not a particularly genial individual. We left him and after two hours came to the prairie described. As we approached, a tipi loomed up and there, at a fire outside, were two elderly squaws and two kids eating their supper, – a very picturesque scene. We camped close by and it was dark when we finished eating. Then the rain began and it soon became a downpour. We moved into the tipi and as everyone was dead tired we stretched out around the fire, – thus we dozed, not one of us with a thought of bothering about a third meal. Distance 20 miles, altitude 1700 feet.

WEDNESDAY, OCTOBER 14. WARM – BRIGHT.

Daylight saw us up, ready for an early start. As we were at breakfast one of the squaws came over and sat down at the fire, pipe in mouth, looking for some tobacco, which someone gave her. She brought over a pan in which were several dressed rabbits and a sack containing some of our friend's stolen potatoes. It was evident she wanted to trade, and more evident to all of us which articles appealed to us. While this was going on the other squaw came over and joined her. We felt of the potatoes and although they were frozen they were small and real young spuds. We offered her a cupful of tea leaves, which satisfied her, and threw in as additional some moose fat. Our eyes opened wide at the sight of the first fresh vegetables we had seen for four months. But the humorous part of it was that after having begged tea in vain from the trapper below at the forks they had dug up his potatoes during his absence and then traded them to us for the tea. That man seemed half crazy anyway, but I'd have liked to see the expression on his face if he had known of this. The squaws left and packed their horses, following us along the trail, which resembled yesterday's except that we had a mile of fallen timber of which the worst logs had been cut out. This country seems to be full of goshawks, I suppose owing to the great number of partridges, which are their chief prey. It was a beautiful, warm morning after the storm and the fragrance of the balm of Gilead fall buds gave a sweetness to the air. We climbed steadily several hundred feet and finally as we came over a high ridge the country before us lay at our feet like a map and we overlooked the country about which we had been thinking and dreaming for weeks past.[198] Directly below us was Moberly Lake, a beautiful expanse of water, sapphire blue in colour, that stretched more than fifteen miles to a range of caribou mountains that loomed up in the blue haze far off on the horizon. At the east end was prairie country several miles in extent. Here is where the Indians are camped. By degrees we dropped down from one bench to another until finally we reached the rocky shore of the lake whose surface was covered with white caps, for a fresh westerly wind was blowing causing the waves to roll in on the beach. A real expanse of water with waves beating on the shore was a sight that was good to my eyes and I could not get enough of it. On we went to the outlet, which we forded, finding two tipis with their quota of Indians (Sotos, as we later found out, – the Beavers being camped at the other end of the lake). These Indians are not shy like the Crees and Stoneys, who will run to the shelter of their tipis at the approach of a stranger. The Indian spoke broken English. He directed us to camp further along. At the mouth of the creek we saw them tending their nets, for there are whitefish in the lake, and as we have been talking of a feed of these fish for several weeks we told him we would trade, so it is likely he will follow us over to camp. An hour later we camped in a beautiful, big meadow from which the hay had been cut by a mowing machine which had been packed in from Hudson's Hope, where it came by boat etc. up the Peace River. Half a dozen log shacks testified that the Indians had settled here as well possibly as some white men. It was as if we had camped in a hay field but were now on the outskirts of civilization and must accustom ourselves to this kind of thing. We are now within one day of Hudson's Hope. For a whole month we have been talking of this place and of what supplies and fresh grubstakes we will get, so it is almost exciting to be so near to our goal. As we ate supper an Indian came and sat down, but as we gave him nothing to eat he became disgusted with our manners and left. As it happened, we camped in a spot where there was no water and we all set out on a tour of discovery and finally found a little pool three-quarters of a mile off. Such a thing never happened with us before. Soon after the Indian left, a white man turned up, – the first real human white man we have yet seen and it was a pleasure to talk to him. We gathered all the information, possible trails, Indians etc., as well as the war news, but he has heard nothing since our latest information. In talking of hunting etc. he said he has hunted and trapped all the west Pine and has never seen or shot a sheep, and this in connection with Treadwell having said the same as to the south Pine makes us feel our trip is a thorough success, which is so satisfactory to us that we are thoroughly well pleased. He hunted with Vreeland[199] on his trip north of the Peace River at Laurier Pass two years ago, concerning which Bob and I have been so interested, so it seemed strange to meet this man here.[200] It shows how small the world is. He and a man named Charlie Poket[201] are together here, owning a herd of cattle. The latter Fred met eight years ago in British Columbia, so before dark we went over to their shack and had a long talk with them. Fred traded him a horse for a canoe on his trip across British Columbia to the Findlay River.[202] Poket said a crazy Italian got the horse, killed it and ate it. Later he turned up at Hudson's Hope half-starved and crazy. It seemed strange to think that so many years later Fred heard the strange fate of his one pack horse! They told us all about the trails east of here and how we can reach Pouce Coupe prairie, where there are now 300 settlers, in five days, and from there to Grande Prairie City, another five days, – there is a wagon road. So in less than a month we should be home, making our return nearly two weeks shorter than we had planned. So everything seems to be in our favour. They said the war had put an end to the trapping, as marten skins are worth only eighty cents against seven dollars last year, and other skins the same in proportion. Revillon Bros. have closed their stores on the Peace River and have stopped trading on account of the war. They gave us newspapers (Montreal and Edmonton) but though the latest is August 15 (two months old) we are sitting around the campfire devouring every bit of news, – of Thaw being on bail, Huerta's flight from Mexico and the start of the war. This in connection with a big feed of fresh boiled potatoes is enough excitement for one day. Distance 15 miles, altitude 2000 feet. Saw a pair of mallard ducks in the Moberly River.

THURSDAY, OCTOBER 15. WARM – CLOUDY.

We are off today for Hudson's Hope, the last stage of our trip before turning southwards toward home. Before starting, after everything had been packed up and as we were saddling the horses, our Indian friend Joseph turned up.[203] We asked him where the whitefish were and he laughed. He said they were coming and laughed again. No matter what anyone said or what he himself said, he burst into laughter, so that finally we all roared like a lot of kids. It must be pleasant to have such a happy disposition as that, and any man who has for years trapped and hunted in the upper Pine country, as he has, and is still able to laugh like that is certainly to my mind a remarkable character. Soon his little five-year-old boy appeared, his head scarcely coming above the top of the tall grass. He was tugging away at a long moosehide leash on the other end of which was a good-sized dog carrying a pack. It was the first time I had ever seen a dog packed and it interested. me. At a word from Joseph the boy grabbed the dog and held its head between his legs and untied the packs, under which were some spruce boughs serving the purpose of saddle blanket on horse. He produced six beautiful, fresh whitefish, which he was easily persuaded to part with for a little tea and tobacco. Then we packed up and went over to the shack owned by Charlie Poket and Harry Garbitt, after having arranged with Joseph to have his squaw make some large moccasins for us on our return to the lake. At Poket's we left eight horses and all the packs we had no use for in their care, giving them a large chunk of moose meat for which they were very grateful as their diet seems to be mostly hares. At ten o'clock we left for Hudson's Hope, with eighteen miles travelling ahead of us over a high ridge. We made fast time and after several hours reached the top of the ridge and as we emerged from the timber we stopped and gazed at the sight that met our eyes. The whole country for miles lay at our feet like a map. We were at last looking into the valley of the long-looked-for Peace, the river that I had heard of for years and had dreamed of reaching some day. To the west and north were the Rockies, blue in the haze of the afternoon light, and to the east the country was flat to the horizon. It was a lonely, godforsaken sight, a wilderness of timber, yet we knew there, hidden away in the distant timber on the banks of the Peace River, was the Hudson's Bay Company trading post of Hudson's Hope, where there would be plenty of food for us all. So once more we went on, descending the hill rapidly and diving into the timber from which we emerged several hours later to find ourselves on a grassy knoll looking down into the bed of the Peace River, across which on a bench about two hundred feet above the level of the water were several acres of land cleared of timber on which were several log buildings fenced in and a flag pole in front.

Behind, among the poplars, were eight or ten tipis of the post Indians of the Beaver tribe. Not in four months (for we had left Jasper sixteen weeks ago to the very day) had we looked upon anything that gave us so much pleasure. We just sat on our horses silently gazing on this peaceful scene. Except for a few Indians lolling about, there was no sign of any activity.

Once in awhile someone would make some exclamation, but that was all. Our eyes were soon satisfied and we started to descend the sharp hill. Even the horses, tired as they were after the long, hard day coming after two weeks of steady, hard travelling, trotted along for the first time since leaving Jasper. They seemed to realize that we had reached some real place and they couldn't be held down to a walk but trotted on ahead of us. A mile up the river we camped, with grass for the horses and a spring alongside of us, for we were on a bench over two hundred feet above the river at the edge of a perpendicular bank. On one side were three shacks built out of logs which homesteaders had put up this summer. It was dark when we camped. As we ate our supper we heard a cow across the river and a rooster crowing and several lights twinkled. It was all so strange that we could hardly realize where we were. We discussed once more, as we had many times before during the last month, what food we would buy for tomorrow would see us stocked with grub, – all kinds and everything we would want. It was the pleasantest evening we had spent for many a long day for we were glad to have completed the main part of our trip. During two weeks we had come nearly two hundred miles, the previous two hundred having taken two months. I felt well tired out after feeling so poorly and am looking forward to a few days' rest. We turned in for the night and were soon sound asleep, while the river flowed quietly along and the owls hooted from the trees. Saw ravens and black capped chickadees. Distance 20 miles, altitude 1200 feet. End of sixteenth week, total distance 746 miles.

FRIDAY, OCTOBER 16. WARM – CLOUDY.

We were up early as usual and after breakfast Fred sewed his trousers so that they were presentable and together with Bob we started off down the river. We were a hard-looking trio, with clothes dirty and torn and our faces covered with whiskers that would even make Father Time envious. As we only had a little money, which we didn't want to part with, and anyway it would only go a small way toward purchasing all we wanted, our object was to get the man in charge of the post to give us credit and allow us to settle on our way home in Edmonton. The only other alternative was to trade and we were prepared for that, having brought with us every available article useful in that line, from fox traps and guns to articles of clothing. I forgot to mention the result of our bets made on the number of days and hours it would take us to reach our destination. The general bet was won by Fred, as he said sixteen days would get us here, and it took only fifteen. If all goes well he will be presented with a pot of marmalade which he will keep all to himself. The other bet was made between Bob and myself. He bet we would make Hudson's Hope within eighty-four hours on the trail, – he was reckoning on a basis of fourteen travelling days at six hours each. I won, as it took eighty-nine hours and fifty minutes. So on our return to Boston he will have to give me a dinner with wine. Both bets were so close that for several days at the finish it has been very exciting and it was impossible to tell until the last day who would win. We went down to the river but found the only boat was on the other side. A homesteader was close by and he said the only way was to yell until someone came down from the post and brought it over. So at intervals we kept yelling; in the meantime we sat in his house discussing the war. At last someone came down the bank with a wheelbarrow loaded with supplies and dumped them on the shore near the boat. After returning the wheelbarrow he rowed across. He turned out to be another homesteader and his shack is near our tipi. We got into the boat and rowed over. It was a typical, roughly built, straight-sided dory about 25 feet long, good enough for river use. Here the river is about 150 yards wide and being very deep flows slowly. Above us is the end of the rapids and canyon around which canoes and outfit are carried over the twelve-mile portage. Below for hundreds of miles the river is a big, safe, smooth-flowing river. Two boats (sternwheelers) ply up and down the river in summer, one of which belongs to the Hudson's Bay Company and is used to distribute supplies to the various posts. In earlier days, not more than eight years ago, they were brought up in big, square scows, or York boats, which for hundreds of miles were poled and tracked upstream, manned by crews composed mostly of half-breeds and Indians. We went up the steep path and found ourselves in front of the post, which was typical of all Hudson's Bay Company trading places. The buildings, of which there were half a dozen, were built of logs and enclosed by a fence.

There was the store, several warehouses where the bulk of the flour, bacon etc. was kept, the house where the man in charge lived and the Indian house, which is a sort of rendezvous for the Indians who happen to be about the post as well as any white men, – trappers, hunters etc. We found the manager, whose name we later found was Chenier, and he showed us into the store, where we sat about and I told him of our story and how we came to be there without any money. I had two papers on which were placed our hopes of getting credit, one was my appointment as field assistant of the United States Biological Survey, Department of Agriculture, Washington, DC, and the other a letter from A. Bryan Williams, chief game guardian of British Columbia. These I showed to Mr. Chenier and after reading them through he said he was sorry but he would be unable to trade except for cash. It was a disappointment, but I knew there was still a chance of arranging it. He was new at the post, only having been here a month or so. We sat around on the counters surrounded by food of all kinds, a sight that dazzled us, and we didn't keep our eyes off it at all. For an hour we conversed on all kinds of topics, finding that he had come from about sixty miles west of Jasper, so he and Fred knew one or two mutual friends. All the time he was apparently quietly sizing us up and trying to get at us underneath our dirt and whiskers. Finally, he said it would be all right and called his assistant to take our order. I hurriedly pulled out a paper from my pocket on which I had made a list of the things we wanted and we started in. Never before had I spent such an enjoyable hour in a store. I walked around behind the counter picking out what I wanted, eating a cracker out of a box here or grabbing a caramel from some other place. This was an unanticipated pleasure and one that will long last in my memory. Some Indians were lounging about and they must have wondered why a bewhiskered, strange white man should have the freedom of the store such as had never been accorded to them. After our list was exhausted, we racked our brains for other articles and walked about looking for possible purchases. Chenier was a changed man from when our conversation first began, for he was now running about trying to sell us every high-priced article in the store. At last we were through and carrying a few of the necessities, such as tea, sugar, flour, oatmeal, maple syrup, marmalade etc., we returned to camp, greeted by Bob and Jack with indescribable joy. Wood was piled on the fire and cooking began. Our first meal was just as we had planned for weeks, – oatmeal (and we ate an amount fully equal to five or six ordinary helpings at home), maple syrup, pickles, tea, marmalade and bread. A few hours later we had supper, when we had warmed kippered herring and toasted crackers, also tea, marmalade etc. At last we were revelling in the delights of eating and we were now living to eat and not eating to live, as we had been, the difference between pleasure and necessity. Between meals we ate stale caramels steadily, for we craved anything containing sugar we had had so little for months. Then, being so full we couldn't move we lay on our beds laughing over the troubles and hardships we had gone through until we had sufficiently digested our food to give us enough energy to crawl into our blankets, and so ended this eventful and enjoyable day.

SATURDAY, OCTOBER 17. CLEAR – WARM.

Fred stayed at home to do all the washing for the outfit, which was a gigantic task, while the rest of us started for the post with bags, pack straps and stirrup lines to bring back the remaining three hundred pounds of food. As usual, the boat was across, but after howling for awhile someone brought it over and so we soon were at the store completing our purchases. I had my pocket full of caramels and ate them from morning till night. Then we walked over to the "Diamond P" store in the hopes of getting some material to make a tipi, but were unsuccessful. We made a tour through the line of tipis of the Beavers camped among the poplars. There were about eight, only two of which were real tipis. The rest consisted of cloth and hides and brush thrown over poles set up in the same circular form. A whole line of kids and squaws, about twenty, each carrying a pail in each hand, were returning from the river, getting their day's supply of water. They scattered on seeing us and I guess some of the water was spilled during the excitement. In front of each tipi were some kids and inside were the squaws sewing or cooking. The men were lounging about though most of them were at the post store. As a whole, they were a nice-looking lot, though all were, as usual, unclean in appearance. Dogs were in front of each tipi, most of them because of their ferocity were chained, not that they would do any harm to an Indian but they would without any hesitation jump on a white man. They were big, fierce-looking dogs of the husky type, yet beautiful animals. As we passed by and I took pictures they jumped up tugging at their chains, snapping and howling. That was as close a view as I wanted. Then we went on, up on the hill, to the little graveyard where perhaps half a dozen Indians had been buried. It was a typical spot for an Indian's grave, as it overlooked the Peace River and its valleys for miles, as well as the distant mountains to the west where they hunt their caribou. On going down we found Bob, who had been in to see the British Columbia policeman who has only recently been placed here. We returned to make our "official" visit and found him a very pleasant young Englishman but hardly a fit person for such a distant post. It was now the middle of the afternoon and we were hungry, so we returned to the store and made up the packs and rowed across the river. With about eighty pounds apiece on our backs we started up the hills on our way to camp, more than a mile away, glad finally to get there and dump our loads outside the tipi. Then another meal followed, consisting of all kinds of sweets, enjoyable though not the best for our stomachs after our steady diet of meat. Fred was called upon by several Indians from Moberly Lake as they saw our tipi and took us for Indians from the far end of the lake.

He arranged to buy a tipi on our return to the lake, so our last difficulty, we hope, is solved. Daugie, the sub-chief,[204] is camped below on the river, having returned from a successful caribou hunt in which he killed twenty-seven, – bulls and cows – the meat of which he dried for his winter's supply. We plan to spend one more day here in order to dry out our big wash. Soon after dark we heard the tom-toms of the Beavers beating across the river and the noise continued far into the night as their dance continued, inter-rupted now and then by the wolf-like howling of their dogs.

SUNDAY, OCTOBER 18. WARM – SHOWERS.

For the first time this trip Sunday has had the appearance of that day, – the flag was flying at the post – the store was closed and everyone seemed to be loafing about in a leisurely manner. These Indians this fall took treaty[205] from the Canadian Government for the first time, consisting of five dollars apiece and a blanket. Mr. Chenier said that most of them spent it on candy, a bright-coloured handkerchief to wear around the neck, or some little, use-less knick-knack. The squaws' chief wants are coloured calicoes and silk to embroider the moccasins and gauntlets with. Since taking treaty they have the idea the Government is going to support them and so they refuse to do anything but demand credit at the store, saying the Government will pay it to the Hudson's Bay Company next summer. Now that the price of furs has dropped almost out of sight – Revillons have closed their store – the Hudson's Bay Company won't give them credit in advance for furs, and the rabbits, their main winter food supply, have died by the millions from the regular seven-year disease owing to overpopulation, it looks as if the Indians would have a bad winter ahead. Further, with a new man at the post who is a stranger to them and can't talk their language and a young, inexperienced policeman, there is a good chance that there will be serious trouble this year. It doesn't seem likely that the Indians will be willing to stay around and starve in sight of the well-stocked warehouses of the Hudson's Bay Company. Altogether, the prospects are not bright. Fred and I went over again to the post, but our only purchases consisted of a towel and three pounds of stale but delicious caramels, to our taste at least. Prices are high here, – flour sixteen dollars a hundred, sugar twenty-five cents a pound, with all other prices proportionate. We went into the Indian house and joined the crowd there, which consisted of half a dozen Indians, among them Old Man, the Beaver chief, indistin-guishable from the rest except possibly by his being better dressed. A man by the name of Thomas had come over from Fort McLoud[206] by the Pine Pass, a distance of one hundred and eight miles, in twelve days. He said west of the Divide the trail was badly fallen in with big green spruces and east with burnt timber, so it was necessary to follow the river most of the way. It was an easy trip compared to what I had thought and a very different matter from ours. I was glad to see a man who had been over it, however. Everyone confirms the report of no sheep and plenty of big caribou, which undoubtedly are *Osborni*. Two others, one named Copley,[207] [208] had been since April surveying for the British Columbian government the waters of the Findlay and Omineca rivers, travelling by boat entirely, having been up against all kinds of difficult problems owing to the high water of the early summer. They had with them a half-breed and a Chink for cook. They kindly showed us their map, and Antonio, the only Beaver who could talk English, to my surprise recognized the rivers etc. in a very intelligent manner though his knowledge of maps must have been very slight. He knew most of that country, having hunted through it, and gave the men the names of some of the rivers which they had incorrectly named. All the other Indians stood about though they neither understood the map nor the drift of the talk. They just stood and smoked in their usual passive way. It was an interesting collection of men.[209] The country, each person's trip and the war were the main topics. There was no German blood represented, so the talk was very free, no sympathy being accorded the Germans. All our news was fragmentary and over a month old, yet we discussed it and argued over it as if it had been up to date. Finally, the crowd broke up and we went to the river to cross. Copley had brought a twenty-five-foot dugout canoe, which he had made, over the portage and went down to pitch up the seams, as he intended returning to Peace River Crossing several hundred miles down the river tomorrow. He kindly carried some mail for us as he will reach civilization weeks before we shall. It seemed queer to be writing letters home, sitting in the tipi. Saw a water ouzel on the banks of a creek coming into the main river; also Canada jays, great horned owl, black-capped chickadees and downy woodpecker about. A homesteader kindly gave us several papers, the latest being September 12th, as the monthly mail came today. We sat around the tipi all the evening reading aloud extracts of the war news, straining our eyes in the poor light of the fire.

MONDAY, OCTOBER 19. COLD – SNOW.

Awoke to find a wet snowstorm, the first of the year. Another delay for us, as we shall not start out in this miserable weather. We all perused the papers again, gleaning every bit of news possible, but it is all so disconnected that we are more or less uncertain as to what has happened except that Germany with a rush got close to Paris then was driven back and now, surrounded on all sides, is very much on the defensive. Wrote a letter to Chauncey Nash, and Bob and I went over to the post intending to give it to Copley and the other surveyor who planned to go down the river today, but we found they had gone so I will have to carry the letter to Pouce Coupe or Beaverlodge and get someone to take it in for me there. Went in to see the man who is in charge of the so-called post office. He was outside talking to Daugie, the Beaver sub-chief from the west end of Moberly Lake. Mackintosh talked a steady stream of his experiences in the Yukon, for he was in on the big gold rush of '98. He certainly saw some real life, as he was mixed up with the police force. He said Old Man, the chief of the Beavers, was going into a three days' sleep and fast, into a dream so as to make a prophecy as to the winter, what kind of weather there will be and as to the quantity of moose there will be. During his sleep a big fire is kept going and the men take turns in dancing about him. Then he comes out of his dream and tells them what will happen. If his prophecy isn't good he repeats the performance before long. Last year he had to try three times before the men were satisfied. After a good many attempts he can't help hitting it right. Two prospectors arrived from the portage and Miller was going up tomorrow to drag their canoe over. Bob and I returned and as usual found the boat across the river. After yelling some time one of the Indians came over and got us. The weather doesn't look much better, but the barometer is rising slowly. Saw a raven, water ouzel and a western grebe in the river. Bob cooked some delicious pancakes for supper.

TUESDAY, OCTOBER 20. COOL – BRIGHT.

It was not a fine-looking morning, as the clouds were low, but the baro meter had risen three-tenths so we planned to leave. After breakfast Fred, Bob and I walked up the trail a couple of miles to a cabin where a Dane by the name of Hansen lived. He told us yesterday of two fine caribou heads which Daugie, the Beaver sub-chief from the west end of Moberly Lake, had brought in to him and so we went up to see them before leaving. We found he was still asleep but our voices aroused him. Both heads were of good size, one a typical Osborn caribou, the other not, so it is difficult to say what species ranges here. It is very doubtful if it is the same as those we shot at the Porcupine lakes. We left camp about 11.30 and as we climbed the steep bench above the river we turned around to take a last look at

Hudson's Hope, which will always have pleasant memories for us. Living on candy, maple syrup and other sweets has made my wind and muscles so bad that I could hardly walk up the hills on the trail. Camped halfway to Moberly Lake, as it is too far to make in one day with our horses now heavily packed. Distance 10 miles, altitude 2300 feet. Saw golden eagles, black capped chickadees, Canada jays and pine grosbecks.

WEDNESDAY, OCTOBER 21. WARM – BRIGHT.

After our four days' feasting at the "Hope" I feel fat and lazy, a pleasant condition. My arm is healing fast and I feel fit for any kind of work once more, which is a relief. Our plans of going back to Jasper through the mountains from Grande Prairie City, which means getting to Jasper late in November or the first of December, seem too risky on account of the heavy snows we surely will encounter. At this late season it is no time to return to the mountains. The last two years about this time we were returning from our trips and both times were ploughing through a foot or two of snow with great difficulty and horses played out. To tempt Fate a third year seems foolhardy for we undoubtedly would either lose some horses or else they would arrive in such thin condition that they would be unable to go through the winter. So our plans are changed. We shall push on to Pouce Coupe or Grande Prairie City, find a good place and reliable man to take care of the horses and leave them there to winter, then we will get a wagon and harness and take our four strongest horses and drive out over the wagon road to Edson, two hundred and fifty miles from Grande Prairie, and there take the train to Jasper. Some plan similar to this will work out, though the final solution may be somewhat different. By this method we should be at Jasper soon after November 20th. It was a beautiful night last evening and the Northern Lights were magnificent. The corona stretched almost from the east to the west in two large semicircles and the colouring was very fine. Our comet has changed its position a lot since we first saw it and the length of its tail has greatly increased. The coyotes are numerous here and their chorus echoes from the hills night and morning. The horse bells could not be heard when we got up and it looked as if they had gone back over the trail to the good feed we had left. Bob went after them and we sat around the fire waiting hour after hour. It was one o'clock before he returned and in half an hour we had them packed and were started. Bob said they had returned to within a mile of the river. We made rapid time over the familiar trail. As we reached the top of the high hill we looked back and said goodbye to the Peace, of the valley of which we got a magnificent view. Another minute we were over the Divide and looking into the Pine valley, – our old friend. We saw ruffed grouse, black-capped chickadees, ravens, Canada jays, golden eagles and pine grosbecks. As we neared our old camp site we heard horse bells and Bob rode into the timber and found all of our horses. They seemed to be benefited by the rest. We kept on to the lake and camped near its shore. It was a beautiful sight as we approached it. Today there was no wind and it was calm and peaceful looking so that the hills about its sides and the mountains at the far end were reflected on its surface. The whole effect reminded me strongly of the Alaskan shore. We found Joseph busily at work on several log shacks, getting ready for the winter, so our chances of buying one of his tipis are good. He greeted us with a laugh and came over to camp, telling us his boy had shot two moose as they swam the lake. He spoke very little English but we got along sufficiently with a few Cree words. We asked for whitefish without mentioning the trade at all and he sent his little boy over to his tipi and he returned not only with a whitefish but also a nice piece of moose steak. The older boy was sent to the outlet and Bob and I went down and watched him in his fine little dugout canoe as he hauled in the nets, finding only one pike (called jackfish here) and a sucker. The former he brought to us and we had a feast for both supper and breakfast. We gave the little lad a big spoonful of jam for bringing the fish and it was amusing to see the expression on his face as he ate it. He was a fine, manly little lad. Distance 10 miles, altitude 2000 feet.

THURSDAY, OCTOBER 22. COOL – BRIGHT.

The sunset was perfectly beautiful last night as well as the sunrise this morning. "Laughing Joseph" was over again at breakfast. He is an unusual Indian and one that it is a real pleasure to trade with. His boys, both the older and the younger, are polite and have good manners and obey wonderfully. Apparently his squaw is industrious and cleanly, as we saw a lot of washing out on a line today, a rare sight for Indians. We saw a big cottonwood tree away up on the east Pine that had been cut down but had not been used, concerning which we had numerous debates. We asked Joseph about it and he said he had cut it down himself about ten years ago, intending to make a dugout canoe, but the wood was poor and so it was not used. It is interesting the way the solution of such mysteries works out. We gave Joseph a pipe and some tobacco for his squaw and a plate of oatmeal. In a few minutes he returned with the plate, cup and spoon, all of which had been carefully washed. Certainly they are a remarkable family of Indians. Bob Jones and Bob Cross went above to the flat to get the horses and the outfit that we left at Charlie Poket's. The rest of us stayed in camp to try and make some trades with Joseph as we want a tipi, some moccasins and whitefish or moose meat. At first it seemed as though we might be successful. We had Joseph inside the tipi looking at some traps, fish nets, etc., all of which gave him lots of amusement, especially the traps, which he set and sprung again and again, laughing over it heartily. He went to his squaw, for the tipi belonged to her, but she wouldn't part with it. His squaw, who is a big, husky woman with a round, pleasant face, brought her young baby over and sat down by our fire. Another squaw, the one from whom we got the potatoes came too, also the young boy, and all at my request, so that I could photograph them.

Later Joseph took us over and showed us his tipi. Several beautifully tanned moose hides, also some bear skins, hung over poles. The dogs here are a different type from those across the river at the "Hope," which appear to have a lot of "husky" blood in them. These have long, pointed muzzles and long tails, looking more like foxes or coyotes. Bob and I walked up above to our previous camp to see if we could find the notebook containing the small mammal data, as it is missing, but we were unable to find it. Fred and Bob went up to Charlie Poket's to inquire about wintering our horses at Pouce Coupe. Total Distance, end of seventeenth week, 766 miles.

FRIDAY, OCTOBER 23. WARM – CLOUDY.

It was very pretty last night after it became dark, with the glow of the fires coming from the four tipis pitched just behind us on a little rise among the poplars, – certainly a very picturesque scene. Early this morning before getting up, I heard a peculiar noise in the air above the tipi which I thought was caused by a flock of ducks flying overhead. As we were eating breakfast outside around the fire we heard it again and all instinctively looked up, expecting to see ducks in the air above us, but nothing was there. Apparently it was caused by a small whirlwind. Never before had I heard one of these. The air is dead today and heavy snowy-looking clouds are hanging overhead, yet in spite of the bad-looking sky the barometer is as high as I have ever seen it. All of the leaves have dropped off the trees and the foliage is a thing of the past so that the country has a very wintry aspect. The hares are nearly all white now; the last week has produced quite a change in their pelage. Gregory came over to see us after breakfast and kindly gave us some information as to the trail from here. He married a young squaw a couple of years ago and has settled down here, leading an Indian life, – not much of an existence. It was amusing the way he spoke of the laziness of these Indians, considering how indifferent and indolent he appeared to be. He arrived yesterday afternoon, his squaw riding in the lead with one very young baby strapped to her back and another not much older tied to her saddle, then came a heavily packed cayuse, with Gregory himself in the rear on foot. This morning he caught a fine lake trout in his net so that adds to the variety of fish here, – pike, suckers and whitefish being the other kinds. Joseph finally brought over his moccasins this morning and after much difficulty Bob traded his fish net for one pair, rather expensive but Joe wanted money and wasn't anxious to trade at all. They were well-sewn moccasins but the squaw had used as much thread as babiche so there is no telling how strong they will prove. We gave Joseph all our old and worn underclothes, socks, trousers etc., which he seemed glad to have, and all the odds and ends – which we will have no more use for – we either gave to Gregory or left on the ground. Fred and Bob brought in all but two of the horses. Beck and Beaver were missing. In the meantime we packed up the outfit and when Fred finally turned up with the missing cayuses it had begun to rain and was so late that we would only have time to make a short drive, which meant the horses would return here during the night to the good feed, so we decided to stay here overnight and unpacked the outfit. In the afternoon we went up a mile or so with Fred to see a dead fox which he had found hung in a willow tree about ten feet high. Apparently he had sprung at a bird perched in the tree about four feet from the ground and in doing so got wedged in a narrow fork. The more he struggled, the tighter he became wedged. All the bark was chewed off the branches within his reach and two limbs were bitten off and lay on the ground. He must have died a slow, miserable death. It looked as if it had happened within the last month. This is an interesting place, camped alongside of these Indians, with the kids yelling and howling and laughing, and every once in awhile a howl from one of the numerous dogs testifies to its being beaten with a big stick by one of the kids, of whom they stand in great awe. Another family of Beavers came in toward dusk and put up their tipi, so that we have six lodges here now. They built a big fire outdoors later on and all the Indians gathered about, beating their tom-toms, dancing and singing and gambling far into the night.

SATURDAY, OCTOBER 24. WARM – SHOWERS.

Poor Tommy, Bob's saddle horse, has been failing steadily for two weeks now and he is in such poor condition that his strength is not sufficient to allow him to go on, so we shall have to leave him here and give him to Charlie Poket. In this good country, with hay, he undoubtedly will pull through the winter, and if so, Charlie Poket will have a fine stock horse. This was his first trip on the trail and the hard going combined with the poor feed was more than he could stand. Gladys is in rather weak condition and she will be the next to go unless we can reach Pouce Coupe shortly and find a good place to leave all the horses to winter, which is our present plan. All the Indians came out to watch us leave, but Joseph was not around to say good-bye. One of his numerous children, a boy of eleven, is slowly dying of consumption and they thought he would not live through last night, – how he did live through all that noise is a wonder, but he managed to. Our trail led up over one of the hills surrounding the lake and we slowly climbed up over a gradually ascending trail. As we reached the top, fully five or six hundred feet above our camp, we looked back and said good-bye to Moberly Lake, which lay far below us, set among the hills. It was a pretty spot; except for our being anxious to get started for home we hated to leave it. A few minutes in the timber brought us to the east side of the hill and as we emerged from the Jack pine we saw below us the country for miles ahead. At our feet was the old bed of the Pine River, and as it dried up millions of years ago, when its course was changed, a little string of lakes[210] was left so that its old bed was easy to trace from our position. Over the next ridge the low-hanging mists indicated the position of the river of today, and to our right (south and southeast) we thought we distinguished our old friends the valleys of the East branch and South fork.[211] At the lakes we found a well-used campground with many tipi poles and three graves, two of which were very old, for the boards had rotted away and fallen in. The other was quite recent and had a cross at its head which was painted blue as well as the little board shelter over it. A little pile of firewood and a box filled with tobacco, apparently offerings to the deceased, were placed alongside. Our way led east and over open country and a fine trail. A few miles further on, the main trail joined us from the South fork to Fort St. John. At the campground we found several finely made bark receptacles, probably for carrying water, which were well sewn with both sinew and willow roots. These are little used in these days of pots. All along the trail we saw horse tracks going east and they were so fresh that we concluded an outfit was just ahead of us. We saw a ruffed grouse, both Hudsonian and black-capped chickadees and Canada jays, also a small sparrow-like bird which I was unable to distinguish. No water was anywhere to be found in this dry country after this summer's drought, so we kept on and on until finally we heard horse bells, indicating the presence of the camp of the party ahead, which meant water. A mile further we came to a beautiful little meadow (with good grass), half a mile long, surrounded on one side by clumps of spruces and on the other by a dense growth of poplars. It was as pretty a camp as we have yet seen – ideal in every way, wood, water and feed all close at hand, as well as plenty of tipi poles.[212] Fred changed his mind on starting and brought Tommy, who seemed to last the seven hours on the trail very well in his condition. Distance 15 miles, altitude 1700 feet.

SUNDAY, OCTOBER 25. WARM – CLOUDY.

We had for breakfast the whitefish which Gregory kindly gave us on leaving the lake. They were delicious and Bob and I both agree that there is no better flavoured freshwater fish. The outfit of French Canadians moved early to cross the Pine, where they had built a raft, apparently not being used to fording. We started later and on coming to the Pine heard bells and chopping, showing the outfit had crossed and camped. We had difficulty in finding a ford but at last got over where the river was about two hundred yards wide and the water just deep enough to wet the lower edges of the packs slightly. The three bewhiskered men were camped close by but we went on and continued on our way up the Pine, coming to a fine flat which we camped on, with tipi poles and meat racks, with the ground covered with the hide and hair of a moose and a deer recently killed. We passed several graves today and because of them the creek is known as Graveyard Creek. At last we are over the Pine, – our last big river successfully crossed, and in two days we will be on a wagon road, which seems so strange as to be inconceivable at this long distance from Jasper. Saw a golden eagle. Distance 8 miles, altitude 1200 feet.

MONDAY, OCTOBER 26. WARM – BRIGHT.

Yesterday was an eventful day, as it completed our fourth full month on the trail and we crossed the Pine, so the river that has been the cause of all our troubles for the past six weeks is now behind us. Two more days will take us to the settlement called Pouce Coupe, the most northern agricultural settlement in Canada. In these foothills, on account of this summer's drought, conditions are totally different from the mountains, where our trouble lay in finding feed but there was always plenty of water. Here the reverse is the case, – feed is abundant, but water very scarce and what there is (except here on the Pine) very poor. Four-fifths of our trip is over and it looks as if we were well underway on the homeward stretch. It cleared last night and the moon, which is half full, appeared for the first time, owing to the dull weather recently. As we got into our blankets I heard a partridge drumming again and again. This summer and fall on almost every moon we hear them. I don't think I ever heard them drum at home at night in the late fall. For breakfast we fried a tin of our pemmican which we have kept as an emergency supply. It is the same as was made for Peary's trip to the North Pole and is very good indeed. It has grease, meat, raisins and some vegetable matter, besides other indistinguishable ingredients, so that it contains the essential elements and in proper proportion to keep a man's system in healthy condition. Soon after we left we came upon a settler who has homesteaded on the river who gave us further information about the trail and country ahead. Thirty miles, he said, would take us to the wagon road and ten more to Pouce Coupe settlement. Why he settled here on the Pine I can't imagine, as he is four hundred miles from the railroad, but I suppose he thinks there will be a railroad through here some day. Every homesteader thinks the railroad will come by his place and it's lucky they all feel so sanguine; otherwise, the country would be much slower in being settled. The river at camp was about the same width and depth as where we forded yesterday. At the height of water in July we estimated it would be fully ten feet deeper. Saw a deer (doe) on a hill, the first since leaving the Stony River in July. All day we came through beautiful, grassy prairies, the beginning of the Pouce Coupe country. This is a beautiful prairie with grass in abundance but scarcely any water. The creek is dry and only here and there a few pailfuls are left in little pools. It is a pity some of this fine feed couldn't be scattered up in the mountains and some of the water from there brought down to the prairie. We have been trying to size up the three men who have been camped near us. At first we took them to be timber cruisers, but now think they are Grand Trunk Railway men, looking over the country for their prospective through line either via the Pine River or the Peace. The sunset was without doubt the most beautiful and the most brilliant we have seen during all this trip. In the mountains the colours are not fine except in rare cases, probably owing to the extreme clearness of the air, but here we are practically on the edge of the prairie, where the most gorgeous effects at sunset are to be seen quite frequently. There was a group of curiously shaped clouds both large and small in the western sky. They were mostly of the twisted streamer type, – I forget the scientific name given to them. As the sun dropped behind the hill these were edged with gold, which in a few minutes faded and then the whole of the clouds became pink, the colour becoming more and more intense until the effect was simply gorgeous. To make a bromidic remark, it was just such an effect that if on canvas would seem to be more the result of an artist's imagination than a true picture of one of nature's wonderful creations. Instead of fading, the colour changed, first from pink to red, and then to brilliant crimson and thus it stayed for some minutes. Each change seemed more wonderful and more beautiful than the last. The form of the clouds added immensely to the beauty of the whole. Finally, the whole western sky seemed to be on fire and the effect was so vivid as to be really startling. We just stopped work and gazed on this scene so wonderful. The moon, now half full, was in the south and was changing gradually from silver to gold. The air was clear and still and the only sound to be heard was the tinkling of the bells as the horses fed in the meadow below us. Then, as if to make this whole picture more perfect, a coyote from the hill across the little prairie began to howl and another answered with his weird yelping and for a few minutes the sounds resounded back and forth among the hills. Suddenly they ceased and again all was still. In the meantime the brilliant effect in the heavens had faded. The only colour left was the deep purple of the faraway hills in the west. As the light faded more and more, the whole scene changed and nothing was left but the black masses of trees and hills silhouetted against the sky, for the evening had slowly faded and night had begun. Distance 12 miles, altitude 1800 feet.

TUESDAY, OCTOBER 27. WARM – BRILLIANT.

It was a bitterly cold night, not far from zero and several hours elapsed after sunrise before it really was warm. But when once the sun was high up it became distinctly warm so that we rode along with our flannel shirts wide open and sleeves rolled up. The sun rose into a cloudless sky and the warm golden glow before it appeared was a beautiful contrast to the effect last night. Before the horses came in, the other outfit, which has only three pack horses against our fifteen, came along but later we passed them while they were making a midday halt. Then at supper time they again appeared and camped alongside of us. Saw a hawk owl, snow buntings and black-capped chickadees. The trail led all day through open prairies edged with open growths of poplars and willow. Saw an old moose horn, showing there must be a few of them about as well as some deer. We camped alongside of a small pool of water that is so alkaline that it is distinctly unpleasant. Some settlers are camped here also, hunting, as deer is hanging up, so there are three outfits here, – a distinctly populous section of the country, so much so that, unaccustomed to it, we are somewhat shy! Distance 15 miles, altitude 1800 feet.

WEDNESDAY, OCTOBER 28. WARM – BRIGHT.

The Northern Lights last night were the finest we have seen this trip and cold as it was every time I woke up I stuck my head out of the blankets to watch the streamers of light shoot up into the sky, some of which reached entirely across to the southern horizon. It was a wonderful display and I was glad we did not put up the tipi for sleeping out in the open gave us an opportunity to observe this phenomenon which we would not otherwise have had. Again it was bitterly cold. We were up at 5.30, long before dawn, and when it became daylight we were through breakfast, preparing for an early start. The sunrise was beautiful this morning, full of rich, warm colours so typical of the effects on the prairie. We plan to go only eight miles to the Cut Bank River[213] where the trail ends and the wagon road actually begins. The next day of eighteen miles will finish our trip as far as the trail life and packing the horses is concerned. It will be pleasant in a way to no longer have twenty horses to saddle and pack. Making and leaving camp will be an easy matter compared to this. It will take us five days to make the eighty miles to Grande Prairie City, so a week from now we should be there and three weeks should see us back once more at Jasper, our starting point. During breakfast as daylight broke, the coyotes as usual sat around among the little knolls about us howling and yelping, – their morning chorus is getting to be a regular feature now. We were off at 9.30 and shortly came to the Cut Bank River and a couple of miles beyond camped at noon on a little flat. It seemed strange to be in camp so early but we could hardly regret such an occurrence. It was a pleasure to loaf about and doze in the sun for a few hours. We dried out the blankets and I put out all the hides, for though they were in fine shape I thought a final airing would benefit them. Unless they get wet through some unforeseen circumstance the next time they come out of their packs will be at Edson, where we will express them home. Some cabins here were built by the Soto Indians that came from Winnipeg some years ago, about which Treadwell told us on the Pine. Saw Canada jays, black-capped chickadees and hawk owl. Great horned owls hoot about camp regularly every night. Croteau is the name of our friend the homesteader. He came with us today in order to get us to his place, where we will spend a day to rest the horses and get his wagon in shape for the trip to Grande Prairie City. Distance 6 miles, altitude 1700 feet.

THURSDAY, OCTOBER 29. WARM – BRIGHT.

Last night, just as we were going to turn in, the Northern Lights began and the display, which lasted all night, was the most brilliant and the colour effects the most beautiful I have ever seen. At times it seemed as if the whole sky was illuminated as the streamers of light with the brilliancy and appearance of search lights played over the sky, with here and there big masses of light delicately coloured. It was fascinating to watch the continual changes going on and the weird sensation it produced. Sometimes the effect was that of a gigantic stereopticon lantern turned on the sky for its curtain, only instead of pictures we saw fantastic shapes and forms come and go in the zone of light. We planned to make an early start as we had eighteen miles to go so we were up and breakfast was over before the first streak of dawn appeared, and by eight o'clock (shortly after sunrise) we were already on the trail, – our earliest start of the whole trip. Here the wagon road actually begins and before we had gone three miles it was distinctly a good road. After going through open growths of poplar we slowly ascended the height of land and then our descent to the Pouce Coupe prairie, about which we had heard so much. In the distance we saw a rolling, grassy country which we came to by degrees. About this stage we met a wagon, the first we had seen since the middle of June. It was a strange sight and the horses shied as they passed it. All this country is great for hornets and a day rarely goes by that we don't see literally dozens of their nests hanging in the poplars. Shortly, we came to our first homestead, a finely built house of peeled logs, of the bungalow type, behind which was a tipi in which they lived, I suppose, while building the house. The horses, being unused to such a structure, with snorts stampeded by. In the doorway was a young woman of twenty-five or so, the first white woman we had seen for over four months, and, strange to say, she was attractive looking and quite pretty. It must be a lonely life for her to lead while her husband is out working all day in this country, only just being settled up, where only two years ago there were but a dozen homesteaders

all told. Now, over seven hundred homesteads have been filed in the Pouce
Coupe prairie, which is fifteen by twenty miles in extent. Croteau said her
name was Mrs. Goodwin, but being a German we decided not to stop and
ask the latest war news! This part of the prairie was known as the Dawson
Valley because of a little creek of that name running through it, but now
dried up.[214] It was as pretty a little valley as I ever saw, – about three
miles wide and rolling, grassy prairie on all sides. There were practically
no trees except on the hills above and in the creekbed itself, where a few
spruces shot up into the air, – a pleasing contrast to the treeless stretches.
We passed homestead after homestead and everyone stared at us, for an
outfit of twenty horses with five bewhiskered men is a sight of rare occurrence here. No one believes our story of hunting, because they think
such a large outfit must be on a railroad survey or locating tour. Several
of such parties have been here lately, as the railroad is about a hundred
miles east of here and approaching this section slowly but no one knows
just where it will come in or whether it will reach British Columbia via the
Peace or the Pine river. After six or seven miles of this country, trailing
through hayfields, we came to Croteau's little one-room log cabin, where
we unpacked the horses alongside of a big haystack. Croteau didn't have
the key so he broke the lock to get in. When the packs were off I went into
the shack and there was Jack cooking on a stove, his feet shuffling to a rag
being played on the Victor machine in the corner! What a change from
twenty-four hours ago! We had made the 18 miles (altitude 2100 feet) in
six and a half hours, so that we reached here at 2.30, a couple of hours
earlier than we had anticipated. The first stage of our trip home is over;
the first hundred miles, a quarter of the distance from Hudson's Hope
to Edson, is done, taking us eight travelling days. The next stage will be
80 miles, to Grande Prairie City, and the last of 225 miles, to Edson. This
300 miles will be made in a wagon and the probable time will be only 12
travelling days, rather more rapid progress than we have been making.
Some of the horses' shoes are still on though they have been shod for
four and a half months. It hardly seems possible that they could last so
long without hurting their feet. Today was our last day on the trail with
the horses packed, for from now on they will carry only their blankets
and saddles and will run along behind the wagon. After eating, three of
us went several miles to find a man named Tremblay[215] in order to get a
sack of oats. He is an old-timer, having been in this country fifteen years,
and has a store. We were late in returning here and it was quite dark, and
not being used to the prairie we nearly lost our way. Saw black-capped

chickadees, hawk owls and sharp-tailed grouse. End of eighteenth week, total distance 840 miles.

FRIDAY, OCTOBER 30. WARM – BRIGHT.

It looked so rainy last night that Bob and I decided to sleep in the shack though the others stayed outside. As it turned out they were better off, as it didn't rain, was hot inside and the mice were running every which way, with the cat continually after them, upsetting every now and then a pan or a cup, so altogether our slumbers were frequently disturbed. Jack and Fred, being used to early hours, were in here at the first crack of dawn to light the stove, though there was no real need of such an early breakfast, as we have a long day ahead of us with very little to do. We had some fine slapjacks made with sourdough and they were cooked to perfection. It was as mild as could be all day and although stormy-looking at first, the sun later came out. Bob and I went over to Haskell's store[216] and found he had a fine assortment of groceries, – cornflakes, Crosse & Blackwell's preserves etc. We bought a can of honey and three pounds of different cookies, which we consumed steadily all day long. On our return we found Jack had made three cranberry pies so that we are again feasting on sweets. Once more we went through the repertoire of records on the Victor machine. Bob caught three mice at our camp night before last, apparently of the white footed variety, and skinned them. Made up the packs in the afternoon and got all ready to start early tomorrow. In the evening Croteau told us some amusing stories of one of his neighbours named McMillan who is somewhat of a crank. Later he went out to make him an evening visit. While he was gone a neighbour came in here and he finally got started talking of the early days in the Yukon, for he had gone in soon after the first rush. He told us some of the big doings in Dawson of such characters as Swiftwater Bill; of Soapy Smith, who murdered several men and finally had a gunfight with a man in Skagway in which they killed each other; of Alex Anderson, who made a million and spent it as fast as he had made it and today is broke; and of the Malamute Kid. Hundreds of men made fortunes from one hundred thousand to a million and just revelled in spending it as fast as they possibly could, so that it was not long before they hadn't enough left for a grubstake. Altogether it was a very interesting evening, sitting around in the shack. Also a Belgian[217] who has homesteaded here dropped in. He was a young fellow, big and healthy looking, and a boy of considerably more than average intelligence.

JULY 3. LOOKING WEST TO THE HEAD OF THE STONY (SNAKE INDIAN) RIVER.

JULY 7. "THE BIG RAM FELL."

JULY 7. "I WAS SO SUCCESSFUL IN GETTING SOME FINE RAMS FOR THE BIOLOGICAL SURVEY AT WASHINGTON."

JULY 9. "THE MEAT...IS HUNG TO DRY IN THE WIND AND SUN."

JULY 14. FAY AT BIG GRAVE FLAT.

JULY 26. IVAN (EWAN) MOBERLY OUTSIDE HIS HOUSE IN GRANDE CACHE.

JULY 27. "THE MEN...DROVE THE HORSES INTO THE (SMOKY) RIVER."

JULY 27. "BOB AND FRED TOOK THE PACKS OVER IN FIVE LOADS."
CROSSING THE SMOKY RIVER IN IVAN (EWAN) MOBERLY'S DUGOUT CANOE.

JULY 27. "IT WAS BITTERLY COLD WORK WALKING IN THE WATER PULLING THE CANOE." SMOKY RIVER CROSSING AT GRANDE CACHE.

JULY 27. "IVAN (EWAN) AND I CROSSED OVER AS PASSENGERS."

JULY 30. "FRED AND BOB JONES WENT AHEAD TO CHOP THE TREES AWAY."

JULY 31. "THE HORSES....ATE WITHOUT GETTING UP."

JULY 31. "OLD MACLOUD...LAID DOWN AT FREQUENT INTERVALS."

AUG 2. "THE FAMILIAR OPEN SUMMIT COUNTRY OF SHEEP CREEK."

AUG 3. "IT IS A BEAUTIFUL PASS." SURPRISE PASS EN ROUTE
TO SURPRISE (NOW CECILIA) LAKE.

AUG 3. CARIBOU SPECIMEN IN PROVIDENCE PASS.
MT. SIR ALEXANDER IN THE BACKGROUND.

AUG 8. CAMP AT KAKWA LAKE. L. TO R. SYMES, FAY, JONES, CROSS.

PORCUPINE (KAKWA) LAKE.

PORCUPINE (KAKWA) LAKE.

AUG 9. "MT. ALEXANDER APPEARED."

AUG 9. "THE LAKE WAS AS PRETTY AS EVER." (BABETTE LAKE)

AUG 11. LOOKING SOUTH UP EDGEGRAIN VALLEY TO MT. SIR ALEXANDER.
MT. IDA ON RIGHT.

AUG 12. MT. IDA FROM MATTERHORN CAMP.

MT. IDA FROM MATTERHORN CAMP.

AUG 20. "WE STARTED THE HORSES DOWN AN ALMOST IMPOSSIBLY STEEP SLOPE OF SCREE..." THE DESCENT INTO WHATLEY CREEK.

THE FORTRESS, MT. IDA AND THREE SISTERS FROM MATTERHORN CAMP.

AUG 20. "WE STARTED THE HORSES DOWN AN ALMOST IMPOSSIBLY STEEP
SLOPE OF SCREE..." THE DESCENT INTO WHATLEY CREEK.

AUG 28. "WE CAME TO A BEAUTIFUL LAKE...
OF THE MOST WONDERFUL SAPPHIRE COLOR."
THE FIRST RECORDED PHOTO AND DESCRIPTION
OF WAPITI LAKE (SAPPHIRE LAKE).

BOB JONES.

AUG 19. FRED BREWSTER SCOUTING THE ROUTE.

FRED BREWSTER SCOUTING THE ROUTE.

JACK SYMES WITH FRESHLY BAKED BREAD.

CHARLES ROBERT (BOB) CROSS.

SEP 3. "FOUR DAYS OF STEADY CUTTING THROUGH BURNT TIMBER…"
CHOPPING DEADFALL WHILE APPROACHING THE UPPER REACHES
OF THE MURRAY RIVER.

CROSS AND BREWSTER BESIDE THE MURRAY RIVER.

SEP 8. "I NEVER HAD SUCH SPORT IN MY LIFE."
FISHING IN THE MURRAY RIVER.

SEP 13. "HERE IS A HORN THAT BELONGED TO A VERITABLE GIANT
OF HIS RACE." BOB JONES WITH LARGE MOOSE ANTLER.

SEP 18. "HE CERTAINLY LOOKS THIN AND SICK IN SPITE OF
WHAT HE SAYS, BUT HE SHOULD PICK UP SPEEDILY."
AN AILING BOB CROSS RECUPERATING IN CAMP.

SEP 21. "THERE WERE SOME BIG FALLS ROARING AHEAD... CERTAINLY AN
UNEXPECTED SIGHT." THE FIRST KNOWN PHOTOGRAPHS
AND DESCRIPTION OF KINUSEO FALLS.

OCT 1. "TO THINK HOW NEAR AND YET HOW FAR WE ARE FROM
CIVILIZATION AND THE LAND OF PLENTY." SCANNING THE FOOTHILLS
AND PRAIRIE FROM THE SUMMIT OF MT. HERMANN.

OCT 8. "NOT A BREATH OF AIR STIRRED AND THE SURFACE MIRRORED
THE SURROUNDING HILLS." THE FIRST RECORDED PHOTOGRAPH AND
DESCRIPTION OF GWILLIM LAKE (ROCKY MOUNTAIN LAKE).

"A SERIES OF VERY PRETTY CASCADES AND SMALL, SYMMETRICAL FALLS..."
THE FIRST RECORDED PHOTOGRAPH AND DESCRIPTION OF SUKUNKA FALLS.

OCT 15. "LOOKING DOWN INTO THE BED OF THE PEACE RIVER, ACROSS
WHICH... WERE SEVERAL ACRES OF LAND... ON WHICH WERE
SEVERAL LOG BUILDINGS FENCED IN AND A FLAGPOLE IN FRONT."
THE FIRST VIEW OF THE HUDSON'S BAY CO. TRADING POST.

OCT 16. "THE BUILDINGS, OF WHICH THERE WERE HALF A DOZEN,
WERE BUILT OF LOGS AND ENCLOSED BY A FENCE."
HUDSON'S BAY CO. TRADING POST.

OCT 16. FAY, CROSS, JONES, SYMES AND BREWSTER AT
THE HUDSON'S BAY CO. TRADING POST.

OCT 16. SAMUEL PRESCOTT FAY BESIDE
THE HUDSON'S BAY CO. TRADING POST.

OCT 22. JOSEPH CALLIOU AND FAMILY AT MOBERLY LAKE.

OCT 22. JOSEPH CALLIOU FAMILY AT MOBERLY LAKE.

HAIRCUT TIME, BEFORE RE-ENTERING CIVILIZATION.

HAIRCUT TIME, BEFORE RE-ENTERING CIVILIZATION.

SATURDAY, OCTOBER 31. WARM – BRIGHT.

Today we started our three hundred mile walk to Edson. All the outfit, about 1500 pounds, was loaded in the team and Bob Jones drove the horses behind, riding Jimmy, while the rest of us walked except Herb Croteau, who drove the team. After a mile we left the prairie and all day went through an open growth of willow and poplar. About six miles away we stopped at a creek, boiled a pot of tea and ate some lunch and then continued. Bob and I walked ahead of the team and arrived at Bordens' ranch[218] soon after three, where we were to stop for the night. We made the 18 miles at a rate of four miles an hour, for we kept up a good, steady pace all day. The team arrived half an hour later. This is certainly a pretty spot, situated on a lake.[219] Borden has about a hundred head of cattle, lots of pigs and hens, so at last we will see what an egg looks like again. Borden gave us a room in his new house which is clean and neat, for he didn't size us up as hoboes and shove us into the bunkhouse. Some men fortunately have a knack of seeing through a bunch of whiskers. As it turned out, all we saw of the eggs were the shells of those the family had eaten at dinner today. Apparently the hens managed to stop laying just in time so as not to have any for us, so that we were doomed to disappointment. Just as our team pulled in, another "Chatham" wagon, preceded by a buggy in which were two women, came from the other direction. It turned out to be a family by the name of Leroy, – father and mother, a son of eighteen and a very attractive little girl of twenty. Mr. Leroy's health broke down and so he sold his hotel which he owned in Vancouver and is on his way to Pouce Coupe to take up a homestead which he located last spring. Coming from a city to such a lonely place where the people, kind-hearted and nice as they are, are so different from those with whom they have associated at home, they will find it rather hard at first.[220] It was pleasant after over four months to meet some attractive people once more and it resulted in a pleasant evening that will not soon be forgotten. Two other single men coming from opposite directions brought the number up to twelve, but the Bordens were used to a crowd turning up without warning and we not only had two fine meals but had a pleasant stay with the Bordens, who are typical, warm-hearted, hospitable ranchers.

SUNDAY, NOVEMBER 1. WARM – BRIGHT.

After saying good-bye to our hosts and friends we left with the outfit soon after eight o' clock. Bob and I, as yesterday, went ahead, walking fast, but the team kept up such a fast pace that we didn't gain much on them. After going ten miles we stopped and when the outfit came up, half an hour later, we boiled some tea and fried some bacon. It was a warm, beautiful, sunny day and the numerous lakes we passed were covered with ducks as well as muskrats. Saw Canada jays, ravens, black-capped chickadees, mallards, Canada geese and snow buntings. As we ate lunch several large bunches of geese, hundreds in all, flew overhead, honking, bound south. After the horses had a good feed we went on ten miles further and cooked our supper at Horse Lake. Here the muskrats were thick and the water not very tempting as it was full of bugs of various kinds. We passed two teams of homesteaders and two on horseback, so the traffic on this highway is quite heavy. We had a steady, gradual climb over a bare, grassy hill at one stretch and as we came over the top we saw several miles away several little lakes dotted in the prairie and just below us was an Indian camp, the two tipis beautifully set up making a very picturesque scene. Here was a novelty to us, for we saw a wagon, showing that the Indians about here travel differently from those we have been used to. Later we came to a team stuck in the mud in the bed of a little creek. As we could not assist them we told them the outfit would be along before long and help them out. After cooking supper I found that sitting around our small fire I was getting stiff, so Bob and I decided to go ahead of the outfit. So once more we started, just as it became dusk. After an hour the moon, full tonight, appeared through a haze of clouds, so we had plenty of light all evening. Bob and I felt like walking fast, as the air was brisk, yet it was warm enough so that I had to carry my mackinaw on my arm. We were hitting an awful pace after having already walked twenty miles, and on reaching our destination found we had made the last stretch of ten miles in two hours, – at the rate of five miles an hour. It was pretty coming along in the moonlight. The hares were very plentiful and jumped up all around us. It was common to see six or more at once. Most of them were pure white. Finally, we reached Kelley's ranch,[221] having walked 30 miles. Here we put up for the night.

MONDAY, NOVEMBER 2. WARM – BRIGHT.

We had a comfortable bunkhouse, apparently perfectly clean, and slept like logs. Some of the men preferred to sleep outside in the moonlight. This morning we were up early and cooked breakfast with the moon streaming through the small windows. A few fleecy clouds overhead and in the western sky were delicately coloured with pink, making a beautiful effect before sunrise. Bob and I were off soon after the sun appeared, walking ahead of the team. Passed very few homesteads. After going nine miles we came in sight of Johnson's ranch,[222] where we were to stop for dinner. It was situated on a side hill overlooking miles of the valley of the Beaver Lodge River and in the distance rose the foothills of the mountains miles beyond, which we were pushing our way through in August and from where we looked into this very country from the mountain peaks. From here on, along the valley bottom, the land is all taken up and the stubble fields with their piles of chaff indicated that oats are grown here as much as hay. At Pouce Coupe they have only had time to cut the standing hay crops as it has been settled only two years. We found Johnson a typical old-time rancher, who took us in his well-built three-roomed log house. He has been here six years. At first there was no one else and only three people in this whole prairie country, so he was about the earliest settler. A piano in one room testified to the fact that we are rapidly approaching civilization. We went in to eat and sat down to a meal that was more than we could stand. The rancher's daughter waited on us and Bob lost his heart with remarkable rapidity and I can't say I disapproved of his taste. We had first of all eggs (at our request) and they tasted as well as we had anticipated; then fresh pork, turnips, potatoes, little onions, fresh butter, real milk, apple sauce, cake and cream puffs. We just sat in silence and ate to our hearts' content. We all agreed that we would have liked to have spent a couple of days here at least. Once more we started and after going two miles reached a crossroad with one store and a house, – the settlement of Beaver Lodge. Here we stopped and took off some of the load, for this was the parting of the ways, owing to a further change of plans. Bob and I will continue to Grande Prairie in charge of the outfit, about one thousand pounds, and go through with it to Edson in the mail wagon. Fred, Symes and Bob Jones go via the trail to Grande Cache on the Smoky River, where they will leave the horses in charge of Ivan Moberly for the winter, much the most satisfactory arrangement from every standpoint. Then they will cover the 125 miles over the mountains to Jasper on foot. Undoubtedly there will be snow and possibly lots of it, so they are likely to have a hard, miserable trip. So far we have lost no horses though two of them are pretty wobbly. They will pack only four horses, just their blankets and some grub, and the rest will be driven light. It was with feelings of deep regret that we shook hands all around and left the men with whom we had been since the middle of June and undergone all kinds of troubles and hardships. Our parting was brief and as we reached the top of the hill I turned back for a last look and saw them busy at work saddling and packing the cayuses. I felt badly at leaving the horses as many of them were like old friends to us and had done their share of the work wonderfully well, stubborn and troublesome as they usually were, but on looking back on the country we forced them through they were hardly to be blamed for their actions. They were all distinctly individual and as different as people are, some being decided characters. We got to know them so intimately that we knew just what every horse would do under any given conditions. On we went, ahead of the team. As Bob said, it seemed queer to be footing it through this wheat and oat prairie which within a few years will be crossed by several railways and its roads overrun with automobiles. When that day comes I am going to take a trip through here and stop off and see if any of our friends of short standing still remain. The stubble fields as well as some that have been burnt were literally covered in places with snow birds that rose in the air on our approach and wheeled about us in their characteristic restless way, only to alight again near the same spot. We had one amusing incident at dinner at Johnson's. A man came in, a stranger to us, who we later were told was the Presbyterian minister, and his first question was as to what we were doing up in the country, – put in a very abrupt way. Not being customary to enquire people's business by that method in these regions it made me so sore that I was on the point of giving him a sarcastic reply. Fred got ahead of me, saying "Oh, we've been collecting mice and rats and all kinds of things," and seeing the puzzled, doubting expression on the "sky pilot's" face he added "for the Biological Survey." Doubtless he did not know what that was, and collecting mice for a survey outfit, as he must have thought, would seem queer. So the probabilities are that his ideas of our road to Heaven are far different than the circumstances called for. His dinner was ready and he left us, still perplexed and eyeing us sharply, trying to size us up. Later Bob saw him in the store at Beaver Lodge and enlightened him, much to his satisfaction, so that our souls in his eyes at least are temporarily saved. The fourteen miles seemed slow and our feet became weary late in the afternoon and as we saw a man approaching we decided to ask him the distance to the settlement at Saskatoon Lake. He told us it was four miles, which was very encouraging. After we had gone fully a mile we saw two men working on the road about a quarter of a mile apart. We enquired the distance of the nearer one and being employed on the road thought that his estimate of the distance would be accurate. He said it was four and a quarter miles! This was rather startling as after going a mile the distance was a quarter of a mile further than the original estimate. We were so amused that we enquired of the man below and his answer was four and a half miles, and he was sure of it, he said. This certainly was a discouraging situation and we thought perhaps we would be better off to turn about and walk in the other direction. I have often heard stories similar to the above but never before came upon such a perfect example and so have taken particular pains to write this with great accuracy. On we went and after going nearly another mile met two men riding. As a joke more than anything else we again asked the same question, and they said "over four miles"! This seems almost too extraordinary to be true, yet it is, nevertheless. Bob and I burst out laughing and explained our predicament to them, the humorous side of which was not wasted on these two genial friends of the road. They enquired as to where we had come from etc., but in such an open, genial way that it was impossible to take offence as we did with the minister. They advised us to return to Pouce Coupe to avoid having to go to the war, but we said we were from Massachusetts and had nothing to fear from that score. They told us they had only recently come from their home in Utica, New York, so we felt like old friends. After enquiring of us the next stopping place, we parted. It became dark quickly but the moon rose bright and clear, making the last lap thoroughly enjoyable in spite of our weariness. At last we came over a little rise and there in the moonlight was a little cluster of buildings on the edge of Saskatoon Lake. It was a pretty picture to see our first settlement and under such ideal conditions, and it reminded me strongly of a little Cape Cod village built on the shore of a small bay. The likeness was even more so in the morning when we saw little bunches of ducks feeding along the edge in the weeds and here and there small flocks flying back and forth. Herb soon arrived and we had a fine meal at the Empire restaurant, run by an old Hudson's Bay man. We put up here for the night, after having walked 23 miles. Not taking any chance, I unrolled my blankets and slept on the floor, preferring it to the bed.

TUESDAY, NOVEMBER 3. WARM – BRIGHT.

Our breakfast even surpassed our supper. I noticed there was a talking machine in the corner and about fifty records so before leaving I played a few of them. It was a surprise to find this old Hudson's Bay man, who is a cranky bachelor, had some records of Farrar's, Elman's, McCormack's and other noted people. I hardly expected to find anything of that kind amid such surroundings, two hundred and fifty miles from a railroad. Today was our last stretch and we set out a little before nine and walked rapidly. It was a beautiful, warm, sunny morning, just such perfect weather as we have had day after day, and as we went over the rolling prairie we watched with interest the homesteaders at work over their fall ploughing. We looked westward and saw all our mountains covered with snow. There were the very peaks whose summits we stood on in August and looked eastward into this prairie country, a hundred miles away, – invisible to us, but which we knew existed in range of our vision. From the mountains we could not see this prairie, but from here we could see our former vantage points. There, we were mixed up in a miserable country, chopping our way through – here, we were putting miles behind us every hour. It was not necessary to hesitate as to which place we preferred. It seemed strange not to have the horses with us nor the other three men. As we came over a long, rounded hill we saw a cluster of houses five or six miles away on the prairie and at last the long-looked-for and heard-of Grande Prairie City was in sight. Before long we were there, finding a settlement of perhaps twenty-five buildings, houses, barns and stores, either of sawed lumber or logs, on each side of the main street. After looking it over, locating the hotel and telegraph office, I went into the bank and arranged to wire east for money, as we haven't enough to pay our debts. Then we went into the Taft Hotel, a rough board structure and ate our dinner, after which Bob bought the necessary shaving equipment while I telegraphed to Bill and the Old Colony Trust Company. Then, we went to it, washing, putting on entirely clean clothes from head to foot and shaving. As the five months' growth came off by degrees and I saw in the mirror my own original features slowly appear I felt as if I had suddenly met an old friend. It was a curious transition as our pale features emerged. But most amusing of all was the puzzled look of surprise on everyone's face when we made our appearance at supper. Distance 15 miles.

WEDNESDAY, NOVEMBER 4. COLD – CLOUDY.

I startled myself this morning while washing for my hands instead of coming in contact with a bunch of "fur" found a real face. Bob and I laughed over the results of our work. We both had a haircut to complete the transformation. Most amusing of all is the contrast of our pale cheeks with our brown noses and foreheads. I sat next to the telegraph operator at supper last night but he didn't know me and didn't realize it until I went in to see him this morning. An answer came from the Old Colony Trust Company saying the money had been sent, so it should arrive by tomorrow. No word from Bill but he will undoubtedly send a night message, so tomorrow morning will bring forth good news I hope. I certainly look forward to it more than anything else after nearly four and a half months. Most of the outfit was duly weighed and tagged this morning and has started on the mail team to Edson. We should leave on Saturday morning, but the driver is anxious to stay for a big boxing match Saturday evening, so we arranged to stay too. That means we will leave here about midnight instead and drive with a four-horse team all night and the next day with stops only for meals. By Sunday night we should be weary. The driver is a big genial man of about two hundred and fifty pounds and I imagine will not only be full but will have a bottle with him as well, so we look forward to an extremely amusing party. As much as Bob and I have tried to avoid the usual cold contracted from the change of sleeping out of doors to being in heated buildings, we both have developed one. All day we have sat around, legs stretched out, reading, feeling meanly but enjoying to the utmost the relaxation. After our continued hike our feet and legs were rather tired. During three and a half days we walked eighty-six miles, all at an average of four miles an hour, which is pretty steady going. Wearing moccasins made it rather hard on our feet. We have a supply of candy, cookies and cake, so our afternoon is being thoroughly enjoyed. Our express bill to Edson amounted to $86.25 and we have still about two hundred pounds more to go Saturday.

THURSDAY, NOVEMBER 5. COLD – CLOUDY.

An uninteresting day with little to do. We managed to get some good books and spent the day reading, – Bob in the midst of one of Robert Chambers's, while I started Gilbert Parker's *The Seats of the Mighty*. No telegram from Bill, which seems very queer, as I felt sure we should find a night letter from him. Went to the bank and found the money was ready for me and had a long talk with the cashier on the war, for he is a young Englishman. Herb Croteau decided he would start home and left as soon as I paid him. We had to keep him here, paying board for himself and his horses, as we couldn't pay him for the trip from Pouce Coupe, but he was thoroughly agreeable to the scheme. Up to the last few years he has lived in Ontario, an old-time lumberjack, and he turned out to be about the pleasantest man we have met. He has a very quiet, genial way about him and a frank, trustworthy face. Altogether, we have enjoyed his company exceedingly and were sorry to part with him. We tried to persuade him to take us to Edson but he was afraid the roads would be too bad. Went around to the Grande Prairie *Herald* office and gleaned all the latest war news.[223] Then, Bob and I holed up in our room and read all afternoon and evening. My cold makes me feel poorly but it is much better. It seems impossible to avoid catching one on returning from the trail and living inside heated buildings.

End of 19th week, total distance 926 miles.

FRIDAY, NOVEMBER 6. COLD – CLOUDY.

Expecting to get a telegram surely from Bill, I went around to the telegraph office shortly after breakfast. As I entered I heard the machine clicking and saw the man writing down the message as it came. I felt instinctively that it was a wire from Bill and as I waited, listening to the ticks of the apparatus, unintelligible to me, I wondered what news was in store for me, – good or bad. It struck me then how strange it was that such a little machine had within its metal parts the means of causing joy or sorrow. A long minute of suspense ensued, and then a sheet was handed to me. I first looked for the signature, which proved my surmise was right, and then read the news from home, all of which was good except that Bill had just yesterday sprained his knee. Best of all was the news of Chauncey's daughter born four days ago. Much seems to have taken place during my absence. Any feeling of anxiety that I may have had at times as to happenings at home was instantly removed, and now my one thought is to get away and be on the train for home as soon as possible.

THE LAST TWO WEEKS OF OUR TRIP FROM GRANDE PRAIRIE TO EDSON WAS WRITTEN IN JUNE 1956

From Grande Prairie we went on foot via the Edson Trail to Edson and then by train to Jasper, arriving late in November from where we had set out soon after the middle of June. This trail was well known to the thousands of settlers who came in over it from Edson with their entire families in covered wagons and every known conveyance drawn by oxen, horses, even cows, and at times a mixed pair of animals had to be used when others had died on the way. All their worldly goods came with them, as much as they could carry, – pigs, poultry, house furnishings of all kinds, tools and equipment. The trail ran from Grande Prairie due east to Sturgeon Lake, some seventy miles, and then turned south to Edson two hundred miles further. It crossed the Smoky River east of Grande Prairie and south of Sturgeon Lake it crossed the Little Smoky, Baptiste and Athabasca rivers. Over the three larger rivers there were the typical scow ferries found on these western rivers in country where no bridges existed. This trail was cut out in 1911 but was used for only five years, for after 1916 it fell into disuse because it went through, for a good part of its distance, the worst kind of muskeg and dense timber. It was a terrible hardship for the settlers to traverse it, with their wives and young children, even in order to reach this wonderful but isolated fertile farm country. Those who had bad luck, such as loss of their horses or oxen or sickness, took as much as three months to go from Edson to Grande Prairie and Beaverlodge.

In 1911, at the time the trail was opened, there were fewer than 2000 people in the whole Peace River country, which comprises 25,000 square miles, or 16 million acres, of rolling, fertile prairie arable land. By 1950 there were 25,000 families, consisting of approximately 100,000 people. Today there are even more, since oil has been discovered in that area. When we came through the northern part around Pouce Coupe, after we had emerged from the timbered area southeast of Hudson's Hope, and came upon the first settlers, our horses went through mile after mile of this prairie day after day with tall, luxuriant grass reaching up to their bellies, showing how rich the dark loam was of this magnificent new prairie farm country. These earliest settlers which we found here scattered sparsely in their new homesteads were amazed at the extraordinary fertility and enormous yield in bushels of wheat per acre. Without our knowing it at the time we went by the farms of several of these first settlers, who within a few years were to become famous among the wheat growers of the world. One of these, Herman Trelle, won the first prize for three years in succession at the Chicago World's Fair for the finest wheat grown in the world. No one since has duplicated his feat of winning the world's championship for three successive years. Also along our way through the prairie around Beaverlodge, in sight of us yet not known to us until many years later, was the farm of W.D. Albright. His farm was given over to experimental work on wheat, vegetables, fruits etc., so that he became an authority on what types would grow best in that climate. He came to be known as the Luther Burbank of the Peace River country as his fame spread throughout.

Another event of as great and maybe even greater worldwide importance has been the more recent discovery of oil in the Sturgeon Lake area and other parts of this extensive farm land of Grande Prairie. Today test wells are being driven in many places. Little did we dream of such an event as we went by Sturgeon Lake on foot, on our last lap of the trip with 200 miles still to go to reach Edson on the railroad.

To go back to our trip over the Edson Trail, we went out with the mail wagon, which was piled so high with almost the entire equipment carried by our outfit of twenty horses during the past summer, together with all the mail sacks and other baggage, that there was no room for us to ride on the load although we had paid for our passage out. The result was that we had to walk the entire 250 miles or more to Edson. We had already walked fifty miles since we parted with the other three men, who were cutting back across the foothills with the twenty horses on their way back to Jasper via what was known as the old Hinton Trail, which ran from Hinton to Pouce Coupe, crossing the Athabasca, Smoky (at Grande Cache) and Wapiti rivers. As it turned out, walking was preferable to riding perched up on a top-heavy load in a wagon with questionable springs over corduroy roads, frozen ruts, mudholes and streams of all kinds, – largely through timbered country where there was little sunlight, especially in late November as we neared the shortest days of the year with the sun low in the horizon. At least at this time of year we missed the worst of the mud and the terrible hordes of mosquitoes for which this trail was famous. From day to day we saw evidences of what the new settlers went through coming in during the past season. Equipment of all kinds, even furniture, lay along the trail where it broke or was discarded, and many an animal lay where he had dropped from overwork. Fortunately for us the trail was frozen now, as the winter weather was fast approaching and the thermometer each night would go down close to zero. We went about twenty-five miles a day, as at about that interval there were stopping places, consisting of a log bunkhouse and log stable to shelter the horses together with feed for them. Owing to the lack of cleanliness and probable population of lice in the bunkhouses we did not use them but instead cooked our meals on a campfire outside, stretched our bedrolls on the ground under the stars, for except for the three nights we had spent in the Taft Hotel in Grande Prairie we had not slept indoors for nearly five months.

One man, an "old-timer" from the Yukon, laughed at us for our fear of getting lousy. He had his own method of protection and carried with him a ball of worsted and a tube of vaseline and before turning in for the night in the bunkhouse he tied a strand of worsted around each ankle and wrist and his neck and covered the worsted with vaseline. He said the cooties couldn't crawl over such an obstacle! His method apparently worked and so did ours, that is, until the last night on the trail. We had by then reached the Athabasca River and found the ferry, which had been operating all summer, had been taken out for the winter, the ice had formed about twenty feet out from each side, and temporarily there was no way of crossing until, as the ferryman said, the river froze over for the winter. The prospect of a long wait was not inviting. It was cold, down to zero at night and the ground frozen hard, but we slept out comfortably in spite of it all. The next day, however, we woke up buried in snow, for a blizzard had started and lasted for two days, so we were driven into the bunkhouse, which fortunately was much larger than the others on the trail. The bunks were already taken, so we unrolled our blankets on the floor. During the course of those two days other settlers and travellers kept turning up at intervals so that by the second night there was not an inch of space left on the floor for another bed roll. Being packed in like the proverbial sardine was not conducive to avoiding the cooties and so we were not surprised to find on the next day that we had both acquired a few families of lice, which would be with us until we reached Edson, whenever that would be! When I told the old "sourdough" from the Yukon about it, I thought he would die laughing, for he could only think that after all our precautions for nearly two weeks of sleeping out every night, we had finally succumbed to the creatures as a result of being driven indoors by blizzard on our last two nights. Here we had, however, a stroke of luck and the next day as the storm cleared we saw across the river a big wagon with a team of horses. In Edson they had heard of the ice forming in the Athabasca and that the ferry was out so they had sent in a team to bring out the mail. The man at the ferry had a flimsy flat-bottomed boat made out of rough planks and this we managed to launch on the ice, then loaded it with our equipment and the weight broke through the ice and in this way he poled his way across the ice barrier breaking through little by little making a channel for the boat and then by the same method he reached the shore on the other side. In this way we eventually ferried all our duffle, heads, horns, other equipment and the government mail across to the south side of the Athabasca River and loaded it into the waiting mail wagon. The sun came out and the last two days on the trail were pleasant ones although the brilliant light made the glare on the fresh, sparkling snow hard on the eyes. The last fifty miles were covered before we knew it in spite of the fewer hours of daylight, for we were fast approaching the shortest days of the year. At this northern point the sun did not rise until nine and it set soon after three, so we were usually up and off before sunrise in order to cover as much distance as possible and often we did not reach the next stopping place until long after dark. But this was the time of the full moon, so we often, during our two weeks on the Edson Trail, finished the last few miles by moonlight when it was beautiful and absolutely still except for the occasional hoot of the ubiquitous horned owl or the yipping of coyotes in the distance. Finally, late in the afternoon of the second day, after crossing the Athabasca River, a strange sound broke the stillness and we suddenly realized that it was the whistle of a locomotive of the Grand Trunk Pacific Railway at Edson, a sound we had not heard for five months. Nothing could have brought us to the realization with more abruptness that the end of our trip had arrived than the sound of this locomotive whistle as its sound echoed among the hills.

In this small town of Edson, existing solely as a divisional point for the railroad and as the jumping-off place for the settlers going into Grande Prairie via the 250 miles of the miserable Edson Trail, we found several small so-called hotels. After looking them over we chose the "Boston Hotel" as being the most appropriate because of its name, signed the register, and deposited our bedrolls and duffle bags in our room. With a bundle of fresh clothes under our arms, we departed in search of a bathhouse (there were no bathtubs in any of the Edson hotels) and there steamed ourselves with hot water and soap, indulging in a luxury we had not known for five months and thus washed the half-drowned cooties down the drain.

The next day we left by train for Jasper after having shipped our collection of mammals and birds, heads and skins to Washington. We had hoped the men, whom we left at Beaverlodge on November 2nd, nearly three weeks ago, would have arrived by trail with the outfit by that time, as we all thought it would take them about two to three weeks to cover that distance over the "old Hinton Trail." However, after waiting two days we became restless and as we were anxious to get home we left by train for Edmonton.[224] There we looked up R.W. Jones, the head surveyor for the Grand Trunk Pacific Railway, who had been recently in charge of their work in determining the route through the Rocky Mountains. He had been up in the region east of Mt. Sir Alexander and around Jarvis Pass which he had so named. He kindly showed us his maps and on one was marked our Mt. Sir Alexander, labelled "Big Mountain." He said he had never heard of any name given it by the Indians or the trappers he had come in contact with during his ten years of surveying north of the Yellowhead Pass. We asked him about its height and his reply was that, as he was "looking for low passes and not high mountains," he did not attempt to find out. However, he had marked on his map 12,000 feet and he thought it was even higher. As we had obtained the information we sought we left by train for home.

Very shortly after our return to Boston I received the following letter from Fred Brewster from Jasper dated November 27th, which indicated that they had arrived within three days after we had left for home.

JASPER, NOVEMBER 27, 1914

Dear Pete:

A line to let you know that we got in safely Saturday night. The trip
was cold and miserable but without accident or interest. The country
after we crossed the Wapiti River, which was 20 miles or so from
where we left you, is very much the same in character as the country
between the Porcupine *(now called the Kakwa River)* and the Smoky
River and about 80 miles from the Wapiti to the Porcupine, which as
you see is very much farther than we had expected. We scarcely got
Gladys in. Tommy came along all right. We had snow 8–14 inches
from midway "Wapiti to Porcupine" to the Athabasca River. Symes
and Bob Jones left here Tuesday night for the enlisting office.

We made the Beaverlodge bridge the day we left you, only 23
miles; next day 10 miles across to the Red Willow River; 3rd day
10 miles to the south side of the Wapiti River, which was a mean
crossing; 4th day 20 miles to Nose Creek; 5th day 15 miles up Nose
Creek; 6th day 20 miles up Nose Creek; 7th day 20 miles up along
over Nose Mt.; 8th day 15 miles to the Porcupine River, where we
joined our trail of 1912 on that open flat. We made the Smoky in 3
days; the lower ford (visited in July by Bob Cross, yourself and me
on our horses) in one day; layover one day; Moberly's at Grande
Cache in one day by the lower trail; and Solomon Creek in 5 days,
where we left the horses and walked home, getting in here at 11:30
at night – 19 days in all.

The general direction of our trail from Beaverlodge to the
Porcupine River was due south, fine open, level country, until near
the Wapiti, from there to the Porcupine rough and timbered and
of no interest. Very little game beyond rabbit and lynx, one lonely
Indian on the Porcupine. Nose Mt. is a full brother to the mountain
we crossed along the top of just after we left the Porcupine in 1912
only much larger; just as cold, and the day we crossed it there was the
highest wind I ever felt. That evening the wind died down and we got
our first snow storm. It was pretty miserable and we were scared so
we pushed on. From there on in, the snow grew deeper, until when
we reached the Muskeg and Little Smoky rivers it was easily over a
foot deep and was fagging on the horses. We were caught in a young
blizzard just below the Smoky ford and lost one day. Pretty nearly

froze to death ourselves, as we could not put the tepee up and you bet I said good-bye to it just as soon as we got in sight of the Athabasca River. I feel, Pete, that I owe the party an apology for that damned tepee. I don't know how it happened myself. We were out of grub for two or three days before reaching Moberly's, that is, except for flour, of which I took care to have plenty. So I had to buy some grub there from Ivan Moberly, the Indian whose dugout canoe we had used in July to get our stuff across the Smoky River. The old devil soaked me, you bet, as the first thing Jack Symes did was to blurt out that we hadn't had anything to eat for a week, very diplomatic! About 3 miles north of the Hay River we found Beau Gaetz (who was with us on our 1912 trip) with a couple of men building a forestry cabin. He is coming up to spend Christmas with me and expects to continue with the forestry people all winter. In regards to the horses, we got 100 pounds of oats at Beaverlodge and we fed Tommy and Gladys three times a day on a mixture of oats, bannock or mush. Tommy gained slightly although we had a lot of trouble getting him up the hill from the Smoky River. The mare, Gladys, gave us the most trouble, as her side seemed to cause her a great deal of pain and she wouldn't feed the greater part of the night and so it was a close shave to get her through. The others came through all right, although Cigar and Simeon are pretty thin now.

This brings me to the most important part of my letter. Our big mountain (Mt. Sir Alexander) seems to have jumped to the front and is drawing a tremendous lot of interest. I understand Miss Jobe and Curly Phillips tried to make it this fall. He considers it superior to Mt. Robson I believe in many ways and was kind enough to give me a couple of more or less plain pictures of it. I hope you do not intend letting them steal that away from us, as we first discovered it in 1912 and should have recorded it publicly then. I understand they were surprised to hear we had found it in 1912 and camped near it again this summer and photographed it. Our trip has caused a lot of local interest here. Symes spread some extraordinary yarns during the three days he was here before he left to enlist for the war, I mean such as about black wolves killing a moose across a river about a mile wide, and swimming rushing torrents etc., etc.

Later, in December 1914, and again in January 1915, he wrote making additional comments.

Am pleased to see you have dug into it for I think the work you have done in this country needs a little light. Am only sorry I can't be present at some of your illustrated talks before the Appalachian Mountain Club, the American Alpine Club and the Harvard Travelers Club.

I went down to see the horses last week and fed them 30 pounds of salt and will repeat it again next week. I have never seen our horses in such excellent condition at this time of year before, having just returned yesterday from seeing them. The bay mare Gladys of our string this summer is so thin I am having her stabled and fed.

I want to say in closing that I am glad that you could give me a frank view of the trip in such a satisfied way because I particularly wanted it to be a good, resultful trip, as I expect it is my last big trip and will be the one I will always look back to.

Later on in the spring of 1915, before I sailed for France for service at the front with the French, in a letter from Fred Brewster he said that all twenty of our horses had come through the winter. This gave us great satisfaction, as did letters from Dr. E.W. Nelson, assistant chief of the Biological Survey in Washington, thanking us for all the specimens we had collected for him and that he was pleased with the results of our trip in establishing the northern limits of the bighorn sheep (*Ovis canadensis*) and our detailed reports on the fauna of the region between the Yellowhead Pass and the Peace River. Having definitely located our "big mountain" and placed it on the map and having accomplished all of our objectives after five months going through difficult country and living off the land and all this without any accident to ourselves or serious one to the horses gave us the satisfaction of knowing that our trip had ended successfully.

Appendix A

S. PRESCOTT FAY'S REPORT ON WILDLIFE OBSERVATIONS
TO THE US BIOLOGICAL SURVEY, DEPARTMENT OF AGRICULTURE

The editors are indebted to biologist Mark Phinney of Dawson Creek for his research into, and opinions on, the wildlife identified in this report. Some of the common names, and many of the scientific names that Fay used, have changed since 1914. Where the current common name differs from that used by Fay, it is presented here in brackets, in italics.

The absence of white-tailed deer and elk from this list will immediately impress anyone familiar with current large-game distribution patterns. Although the valuable ornithological observations are among the first for the region, some of them appear open to question.

E.W. Nelson, assistant chief of the Biological Survey, thanked him profusely for the collection in December 1914. In a letter of May 1915, after receiving Fay's complete report, Nelson commented: "It is a fine piece of work. I am delighted . . . with the interesting notes which the report contains . . . It is full of good stuff and many of your photographs are gems. You have the sincerest thanks from the Survey as well as my personal appreciation for your kindness in doing such a completely satisfactory job."

EXPEDITION OF 1914
BETWEEN YELLOWHEAD PASS AND PEACE RIVER
BRITISH COLUMBIA – ALBERTA

Early in the spring of 1914 I began to make definite plans for a trip among the Canadian Rockies into a region in which I had been interested for two years. The exact locality lies along the Continental Divide between the 53rd and 56th parallels of latitude. On the south it is bounded by the Yellowhead Pass and the Athabasca Valley, while on the north it is bounded by the Peace River. The mountains here divide the provinces of British Columbia and Alberta for approximately the southern third of this section, then the boundary runs due north along the 120th parallel of longitude. So that, in spite of the fact that our route lay along the east side of the mountains, we were in British Columbia the majority of the time. Though the actual distance was only about 230 miles in a straight line, owing to the difficult nature of the country, we went more than three times that distance to reach the Peace River.

Our main object was hunting and collecting for the Biological Survey, for the purpose of which we had been appointed field assistants, and special permits had been secured for us to hunt out of season and take a limited number of the larger game animals from both provinces. The question that interested us most was as to the distribution of sheep between these two main passes. South were the ranges of Montana sheep (*Ovis canadensis*) and north near Laurier pass, specimens of Stone sheep (*Ovis stonei*) had been secured for the National Museum. The question was, Did either of these two species come into this unknown area and what were the limits of its range, or did both cross their already known borders? If the latter was the case, then there was the possibility of the interbreeding giving rise to a new form. Further, we were interested in determining the species of caribou and as well making a collection of small mammals and birds and taking notes on their distribution and migration. Our route may best be understood by glancing at the map and following the dotted lines. The party, which consisted of five, was composed of Charles R. Cross Jr. of Brookline, Mass.; Fred Brewster of Jasper, Alberta, to whom the outfit of horses belonged; a young Canadian who looked after the horses; an Englishman as cook; and myself. On June 26th we left Jasper, a small town of but a year's standing, on the Grand Trunk Pacific Railway, with twenty head of horses and food for four months, intending to traverse the above described area and return before the heavy snows of October. Our route lay first up the Stony River, over to the headwaters of the Sulphur, then down the Muskeg to the Smoky, across which we swam the horses, up Muddy Water River and over to Sheep Creek, which we followed to its head, then across a high pass which brought us to the head of the Porcupine River. This far we found fairly well-travelled Indian trails but from there on, until we reached the lower part of the Pine River, we struggled without trails of any kind. For two months we cut our way through thick underbrush and green timber but mostly through windfalls and burnt timber, covering a distance of less than a hundred miles in a straight line. Our course here lay across the numerous head streams of the Wapiti River, going across country from one branch to another. Then we found the head of the east branch of the Pine and down this we went nearly to its junction with the main river; then across to Moberly Lake and Hudson's Hope on the Peace River. The return was made by coming east, leaving the mountains and foothills for the timbered plateau region and prairie. In this way we made fast time and avoided any danger of being snowed in. On the last stage it was necessary to return to the mountains in order to get to Jasper by trail, where the outfit arrived late in November. It took four months to reach Hudson's Hope, while the return only consumed five weeks.

In order to give a brief description of the work, for the sake of convenience the trip will be divided into four parts, each one of which represents a geographical division.

First is the area between the Athabasca and Smoky rivers, in which our route lay chiefly through the larger valleys of lower altitude, except for the few days spent among the sheep hills. Of the larger mammals, moose, mule deer, Montana sheep and goat were all common. Grizzly and black bears are in that area but only probably in small numbers. We saw only one caribou track which was very fresh, that of a large bull, and one shed antler, probably from the preceding winter. East of the Muskeg River out of the mountains I have heard caribou reported by several different people. Apparently there are only very few south of the Smoky. The small mammals were well represented but the ground squirrel was by far the most numerous. Birds were found breeding in considerable abundance, the sparrow family being the most conspicuous. Willow ptarmigan were very common. To return to the sheep, we heard from the Indians of their existence here, and the nature of the country made the fact self-evident. The region is ideal for them and the ranges very extensive. Typical sheep hills exist everywhere. Still there are but very few sheep left, for the Indian hunter has been too persistent. Heavy trails showing their former abundance are a conspicuous feature on the mountains. We saw sheep several times and secured specimens which are typical *Ovis canadensis*.

The next area, which is in the higher country, lies between the Smoky River and the head of the east branch of the Pine. Sheep undoubtedly once existed in great numbers along Sheep Creek, and from the signs we knew there must be a few left. North of this we saw no signs of any kinds of them nor any suitable hills. Moose, caribou, goat and grizzly bear were very abundant. Deer did not seem to exist at all. In the first part of this area we saw numerous ground squirrels but then saw no more at all. Of birds, water ouzels, chickadees and jays began to put in an appearance and were seen frequently, as well as sparrows in migration.

The third area is that drained by the Pine River. Here the valleys are very low and the mountains correspondingly so. Timberline is about 5000 feet as contrasted with about 6800 in the first area. The east branch, on which we spent more than a month, was splendid moose country. On the higher mountains were goat, and on the rounded summits that were above timberline caribou were common. Grizzly and black bear were quite abundant, but there were no sheep. Deer began to appear in the lower river valley but in spite of the country being ideal for them they apparently were quite scarce. Near the Peace River the Indian hunter is the main factor in keeping down the game supply, as was the case in nearly all of the first area. But all the intervening country, with the exception of only a very occasional Indian party, has never been trapped or hunted. Even then only a few of the main streams have ever seen the track of man or horse. Small mammals of the same species seemed to be present except ground squirrels, which may have been there only in different places than our hunting took us. Birds were quite numerous, for the migration was at its height, and ducks, shore birds, sparrows and warblers were especially conspicuous.

The fourth and last region lay between the Peace River (east of the Pine) and Edson, which is on the Grand Trunk Pacific Railway about one hundred miles east of the mountains. The country was either a rather level, timbered plateau, sometimes rolling, or level prairie country. It was much less interesting. The only larger animals were a few moose, deer and black bear. Foxes were very common. It was late for birds, being the end of October and November, and the few we saw were winter residents. This accounted for the very few birds seen in this latter region.

MAMMALS

NOTE: On August 12 we left the head of the Porcupine River. Here the boundary between British Columbia and Alberta leaves the Continental

Divide and runs due north along the 120th parallel, so all references made to localities beyond that point or after that date refer to East Central British Columbia. Previous to that we were in West Central Alberta.

MULE DEER

We saw deer only twice, though of course we knew of their existence from their tracks and were able to judge of their distribution in that way. They keep to the larger, lower valleys, preferably where there are bare, grassy hillsides broken up by partially timbered gullies where they may seek shelter. An equally good place to find them is among burnt timber, for here the grass and tender shoots spring up. Their tracks were common in such localities along the riverbanks and bars or in the mud by little swamps and ponds known there as "sloos." Between the Athabasca and Smoky rivers deer are common, especially on both sides of the former river. In other words, they ranged throughout the eastern part of Area 1. We saw no further signs of them until we were halfway down the east branch of the Pine River. There in the lower valleys which were not much over 2000 feet above sea level were bare grassy hills, ideal ranges for them. Still they were rather scarce there. In Area 4, in the rolling, timbered country where the altitude was around 2000 feet, we saw tracks now and then. I believe on the Smoky, Porcupine and Wapiti rivers along the edge of the mountains deer are found quite plentifully. One that we saw near the Stony River was feeding in a willow- and grass-covered flat not 200 yards away from a cow moose with her twin calves. The deer jumped and ran at the instant of our approach but the moose watched us for several minutes before she ran to the shelter of the timber, closely followed by her calves. East of the Pine a deer which we saw appeared rather shy and although at a distance of a third of a mile on a grassy hill above us she ran to the shelter of the burnt timber and willows beyond. On the Sulphur River, where it heads in a grassy willow-covered flat at the other side of which rises one of the branches of the Hay River, was the highest place we saw deer tracks. The altitude was about 6000 feet. Usually they kept to valleys below 4500 feet. The only lick where we saw signs of them was on the Muskeg River, about 4600 feet, in typical moose country. The lick was a circular saline mudhole of about sixty feet in diameter.

MOOSE

Of all the larger game animals moose were the most abundant and the most evenly distributed throughout the whole region. The first few days we saw tracks along the Stony River and it was seldom that there were several successive days during which time we did not see their tracks except in Area 4. They were most plentiful in Areas 2 and 3, for the Porcupine, Wapiti and Pine rivers are all ideal moose valleys. We found several mudhole licks where we found their tracks, more of which will be said later under the head of "Game Licks." On June 29th we saw a dry cow and on the 30th we saw a cow with twin calves, both in the Stony Valley at an elevation of about 4000 feet. The first cow appeared to be very light coloured. On July 11th we saw another dry cow among the willows and scattered spruce groves near timberline at an altitude of 6500 feet. That was the highest we saw one, though we saw tracks of one crossing a pass above timberline at over 7000 feet. The type of country they seemed to prefer lay along the rivers on the willow-covered flats or in burnt timber where the grass and underbrush had a chance to spring up. The shoots and twigs of the willows seemed to be their main food supply. In such localities where there were muddy ponds with good dense spruce nearby for shelter, moose were abundant. At times, along the Wapiti and Pine rivers especially, we found game trails worn down a foot or more in depth along the rivers or leading back to the hillsides. Near the head of the Porcupine River, where several passes not over 5500 feet above sea level led over the Divide into British Columbia, moose were very plentiful and the trails deep. In one particular locality we found numerous "beds" in the grass where they had been lying down. One day we passed through several little dry, grassy meadows not more than an acre or two in extent and in them we found sometimes as many as half a dozen such beds very fresh, for they appeared to have been occupied only within a few minutes. Undoubtedly the moose, alarmed at the sound of the approach of our large outfit, had just left. A large outfit such as ours cannot move quietly and that was one reason why we did not see more game in a country that was so full of it. One day we saw two cows feeding in a "sloo" in the water up to their bellies with their heads under the surface pulling up the aquatic plants. Their calves were playing together in the reeds alongshore. One cow did not seem to approve of her calf playing with the other and several times she rushed out of the water and chased the latter away. Each time, it speedily returned. The first few times, the other cow was entirely indifferent to this treatment of its calf and continued feeding, but finally in disapproval she ran out of the water and took her calf away. Along the Pine River we frequently heard the bulls hitting their horns against the timber as we sat about camp in the evening. Bulls on two different occasions came very near to us. Once, as the men were cutting trail on the bank of the Pine, a large bull appeared on the opposite bank not seventy-five yards away.

He stood there grunting in an excited way, apparently attracted by the noise of the axes. He walked down to the edge of the river and looked as if he intended to swim across. One of the men meanwhile came back to me to get my gun but as I came along the bull disappeared into the timber. Another time, two of the men while camped at 5000 feet on the side of a mountain just about at timberline, hearing a moose grunting and hitting his horns against the trees, ran out. The moose quickly appeared and came to within fifty yards of them, when they shot him. He was a magnificent specimen, in his prime and must have weighed about a thousand pounds. His horns had a spread of 51 inches and his coat was nearly jet black. Curiously enough he was followed very closely by a young bull of only two or three years. All the tracks along the Pine were very large and here we found several shed horns. One pair, the two horns of which lay over a mile apart, but, which, unquestionably, from their shape and size, were mates and probably shed the previous winter, measured very conservatively a spread of 67 inches. One horn was 44 inches high and had a tine 22 inches in length. They were an extremely interesting pair. Further down the Pine at an altitude of about 3500 feet, or 1000 feet above the riverbed, in a small, open spruce swamp or muskeg on the top of a ridge were found fifteen pair of shed horns, none of which were large. All were in good shape and had scarcely been touched by mice or porcupines. This swamp must have been a yarding place for the moose in winter. Further down the Pine near the Peace the moose are not so plentiful, as the Indians are too persistent in their hunting and in Area 4 the same is the case.

CARIBOU

These animals were especially common in Areas 2 and 3. None seemed to exist in Area 4 and only a few in Area 1. Until we reached the region at the head of the two branches of the Porcupine River we saw no real caribou country. There we found fine upland rocky meadows and basins from the edge of timberline to about a thousand feet above, where the caribou seemed to range. Usually these slopes were covered with short grass which gave place to the moss-covered rocky slopes above. Caribou were never abundant, that is, they never appeared in large herds. The most we ever saw together were six, – two bulls, two cows and two calves. This was at the head of the Porcupine River, where we secured a pair. The most we saw at any one time after that was three. More often we saw two or a solitary individual which in most cases was a dry cow or a bull. They were fearless, in fact they were extremely tame. On one occasion one of the men approached so close to a young bull on a high, bare ridge that he tossed a rock on his back. Twice a lone cow fed within a hundred yards of camp and the horses. They never minded seeing either us or the horses, nor did they mind the bells or other strange sounds. It was not until they had circled about and got our scent that they became alarmed. Then their tails would go up in the air and off they would trot until they had gone some distance. Nearly always they would again stop, turn around for a parting look and then run out of sight. We never saw them except above timberline yet we found their tracks two thousand feet or more below and heavily worn trails doubtless used by the moose as well. Whether they stayed in the valley at certain seasons or only used these trails in crossing from one range to another it was impossible to tell. We found a shed antler above timberline on a hill near the head of the Hay River, at 7000 feet, and once saw three, a bull, cow and calf, at about that altitude but usually they ranged on hills at between 5000 and 6000 feet. They seemed to prefer the bare hills just above timberline. I noticed one habit they had, which may, however, have been accidental, and that was of crossing patches of snow when they existed, rather than walking over the rocks. One day I saw a young bull walk along a narrow strip of snow for its full length of nearly half a mile, though it lay at a steep angle on the edge of a bare ridge, and before reaching the end he lay down and, stretching his head out, ate the snow.

GOAT

These animals were abundant in all the country we traversed except Area 4. In all cases they were seen above timberline and often on the most inaccessible kinds of cliffs. Once we saw a billy at an altitude of 3500 feet at a lick with two sheep. The lick was on the side of a very steep, rocky cliff of about 200 feet in height, at the very base of which flowed the Stony River. We first saw the billy at the edge of the cliff above, walking along through the timber. He was in the act of shedding, and his coat, which was a stained cream colour, was "moth-eaten" looking. For a few minutes I lost sight of him. Then a pair of sheep, a ewe and a two-year-old ram, appeared at the base of the cliff just above the river licking the rocks. On seeing me only 200 yards off, they began to slowly ascend and as they neared the top the goat again appeared. The sheep advanced to the same level and they stopped and for a few minutes stood eyeing the goat, which was not over thirty yards away. Then they backed off about a hundred feet, and when they stopped, the goat continued on his way down to the lick by the same route up which the sheep had come. The latter lay down at the top of the cliff until dark, when they disappeared in the timber. When the goat had satisfied his craving for the saline substance, he moved away up the river along the face of the cliff. Just before this episode took place a "she" grizzly and two cubs were seen not 200 yards away from this cliff on the same side of the river. On smelling us they ran into a small patch of timber where they undoubtedly remained until dark for they could not make their escape without being seen. The sheep also were shedding and great masses of wool and hair hung loosely on their flanks. We saw nannies and kids frequently along the head of the Wapiti River. The lowest we saw tracks was on the river bars on the edge of the Pine, at about 2600 feet. They were apparently those of a young billy wandering about, for it was the middle of September, about the time when they start to move around looking up the nannies. In most cases when we approached the billies, either during our climbing and hunting or in moving over high passes with the outfit, they did not seem to mind us greatly. Once, we came within 200 yards of one as we moved along with all the horses. Another time, two came around the side of a mountain and lay down about a thousand feet above camp, which was on a grassy summit above timberline, and paid no attention to us or the horses that were busy feeding among the rocks and ringing their bells. We came upon several very old billies one day. The first one climbed to a little ledge above me from which he could escape in no direction except the way by which he had come, that is, from below, where I was. From any ordinary enemy to which he was accustomed he was secure. He was extremely old, for his horns, hoofs and teeth were all well worn. The former were very light coloured, short and stumpy. His teeth were all loose and one was easily removed with the fingers. He was the largest and heaviest goat I have ever seen and his hide was in magnificent condition. The other goat got a good start and I hurried after him up the rocky slope when I had killed the first one. But apparently he was so fat and so old that he soon gave out and lay down on a ledge and turned his back to me. He allowed me to approach within fifty yards before he arose and turned around. Even then he made no attempt to escape. He was apparently unhurt but it seemed by his actions that he was exhausted. On cutting them up they proved to be the fattest goats I have ever seen. In all their range they kept to the rocky ledges and steep slopes above timberline where there was a dense, weedy growth. I could not make out if they ever ate any of these plants but they were always found in such places and we invariably picked out their ranges and the mountains where we later saw them from that weedy growth. Once, we found moss in their mouths, upon which they had been feeding, – such as the caribou ate. We often saw wonderful exhibitions of their climbing but one in particular stands out above all. As we came over a high pass with the outfit, between Sheep Creek and the Porcupine River, a billy appeared half a mile away. He seemed very much alarmed at our presence and left the slide rock over which he was travelling and started across a steep snow slope. The snow was so deep that he had a hard time making headway, as he sank in at every step. At short intervals he stopped to rest and as we watched him through the glasses we could see him panting and his tongue hung out of his mouth like a dog's. Finally, he reached the rocks and started to climb up the cliffs. By this time we had become so interested in his performance that we stopped the horses, and sat down to watch him with the glasses. As he ascended, the cliff became steeper and steeper. Finally, as he came to one extremely difficult place he put his front feet up to the ledge above and in attempting to pull his hind feet up either he slipped or the footing gave way and he fell over backwards. As we watched him through the glasses we fully expected to see him fall to the rocks below and be dashed to pieces, but in some wonderful way he turned in the air, almost like a cat, and landed on all fours on a little jutting rock only two or three feet below where his hind feet had been. It was a marvellous exhibition and we looked on in amazement, but it only shows what a goat can do when the necessity arises.

SHEEP (*OVIS CANADENSIS*)

Sheep were what interested us especially and so we were continually on the lookout for them. On the hills south of the Athabasca River in Jasper Park they are beginning to come back now that the Indians can no longer hunt there. North of the river we heard from them that there were a few sheep. The third day out we witnessed the goat and sheep episode at the lick described previously. From the same camp eight ewes and lambs were seen several miles away on the hills. Two days later we saw a lone sheep, probably a ram. The next day on the hills on the opposite side of the river were two more. We did our hunting where the heads of the Sulphur and Hay rivers come together as well as a branch of the Stony. We found a flock of eight rams ranging in age from two-year-olds to old rams of nine or ten years. We saw along the bank of the Sulphur River a drowned lamb only a few weeks old. Whether it met its death in trying to cross the river with its mother or lost its footing and fell in was impossible to say. It is the only instance of that kind I ever came upon. Two days later we found a ewe and lamb on the side of a cliff directly above the river bed at a lick. One more young ram along the Hay River was all we saw. As I said before, it was ideal country and fine ranges were everywhere. Under proper protection their numbers will increase rapidly but the Indians hunt them so persistently in this locality that they are becoming very scarce. Along the lower part of Sheep Creek we saw signs of sheep and the Indians said a few were still left, but that is the northern limit of their range. One of the rams we shot, about a six-year-old, had a decided case of lump jaw but there was no indication of any such disease on any of the other specimens. We saw tracks of a band of rams along the Muskeg River at 4500 feet elevation. East of this spot there were no sheep hills but west were fine ranges. At first it looked as if they were crossing from one range to another but more likely they were on their way to some lick. At the heads of the Wapiti and Pine rivers the hills from a distance looked like good sheep ranges but in every case on closer inspection they proved to be rocky, dry moss-covered summits on which we invariably found caribou. North of Sheep Creek we never saw a sign or any indication of sheep; in fact, there were no suitable ranges for them.

BLACK BEAR

There is very little to say about this animal as we only saw one individual and that was on the lower Pine the first day of October at about 4500 feet elevation. He was going through the burnt timber and when first seen was on the bare side of a mountain just below timberline. We saw occasional tracks at regular intervals, so they range through the entire region. On the lower Pine and in the valley of the Peace they are very common.

GRIZZLY BEAR

This bear, except on the lower Pine, apparently was more common than the black. Of course, in the summertime, in the thick brush and timber, it is possible to be in fine bear country and yet not see one single individual. We were more fortunate. They were more numerous, judging from tracks and type of country, in Areas 2 and 3. Area 1 seemed to be only fairly good bear country and Area 4 very poor. We saw a she and two cubs the third day from Jasper along the Stony River and although we saw tracks and indications of where they had been digging out ground squirrels it was not until we got to one of the lakes at the head of the Porcupine River that we saw another, – this time apparently a full-grown he bear. The upper Wapiti and Pine valleys were great berry country and the signs there were frequent. One cave or den was found in which were numerous bones of animals but they were too broken to identify. Another full-grown he bear was seen at 5000 feet above timberline on one of the mountains along the Pine digging for small mammals. At one camp above timberline (about 5000 feet) at the head of one of the branches of the Wapiti River a three-year-old bear rounded all twenty head of horses up and drove them from where they were feeding over half a mile right into camp, where we shot him. His indifference to our scent was very interesting. He crossed a little slope not two hundred yards from camp where we had been walking back and forth within an hour setting traps. When he reached this spot he appeared a little suspicious, judging from the way he stopped and sniffed the air, but he showed no real alarm. It took eight shots, out of which five bullets hit him all in his shoulders and front legs before he stopped running, which shows the great vitality of even a young bear.

BUFFALO

In connection with the former distribution of the buffalo we found evidence of their ranging in Area 1. Along the Stony River at an elevation of 4000 and again at 4200 feet and along the Hay River near timberline at 6500 feet we found old buffalo skulls. It may be of interest to note that in the region between Laggan on the Canadian Pacific Railway and Jasper we have found numerous skulls, one as high as 7500 feet nearly on the top of Wilcox pass, a bare rocky summit. This shows how the buffalo once ranged into the mountains as far as the Continental Divide in the lower passes and crossed the higher passes of great elevation.

GAME LICKS

One of the features that interested us as much as any were the game licks that we came upon from time to time. There seemed to be two different types, – those on the faces of cliffs and those in the mud near streams. The former seemed to be resorted to by goat and sheep, the latter by moose, caribou and deer. The first one we found was along the Stony River at an elevation of 3500 feet. It was along the face of a cliff that rose nearly sheer from the river and was composed of a slaty formation, for here and there were signs of coal. All through this country in the mountains seams and outcrops of coal appear. A few dark spots showed where the moisture oozed out and these were the places to which the goat and sheep went. The second lick was along the Sulphur River at an elevation of about 4500 feet and was similarly situated, – only the rock formation was different, as it was of a limestone nature. Deeply worn trails led under overhanging cliffs and through the timber which had been burnt, for, in contrast to the first lick, the slope was not too steep for trees to grow and here there was plenty of soil covering the rocks. In licking under the ledges and rocks, small caverns had

been formed which had been further enlarged probably by the wind blowing away the small particles of rock broken off. The ground here where the
ewe had been licking seemed dry. A lick about twenty miles south of Jasper
(not in this area) to which the goat resort is in a clayey soil and the animals
have licked out great holes under the roots of trees and under the overhanging bank of the river a hundred feet above the water. On the Muskeg
River at an elevation of 600 feet at the edge of some spruces in a large flat
of several miles in extent covered by willows we found a circular mudhole
of about sixty feet in diameter. Moose, caribou and deer tracks were seen
in the mud. The water oozed out from under the roots of the spruces like
a small spring. An old camping ground nearby with numerous meat racks
testified to the way the Indian kills his game. This was on the edge of the
sheep ranges and nearby on the river bars we found tracks of a flock of half
a dozen rams, so this lick may be resorted to by sheep as well. These three
licks were all in Area 1. In Area 2 we also saw three licks. The first was near
the head of the Porcupine River, in the middle of a large meadow, only a
few feet from the river. It too was a circular mudhole, not over sixty feet in
diameter, from which the water oozed. Two very deeply worn trails in the
hard, rocky ground led down to it from the mountains on both sides, which
led us to believe it was used by goat, of which there were many about. But as
caribou and moose were also abundant it may have been resorted to by all
three species. The second lick, about fifteen miles down the river, was very
similar. Trails from it led up and down the valley but the only tracks we
saw seemed to be those of moose. The elevation of the first was about 5500
feet, – the second, about 4500. Near one of the heads of the Wapiti, close to
timberline at 5600 feet, a similar lick, only smaller, was found. Trails radiated from it in all directions like the spokes of a wheel. As it was in the same
type of country, probably all three of these species used it. In Area 3 we saw
only one lick but it was the largest and most interesting I have ever seen.
It was on the upper part of the east branch of the Pine, at an elevation of
about 3500 feet. The tracks were all of moose and caribou. It differed from
the previous licks of this nature in several ways. First, it was half a mile back
from the river and several hundred feet above it and not near any stream,
and secondly it was in a clayey soil. It was then September, and having had
almost no rain for over two months the ground was dry except in one or
two spots where the water oozing up made it very soft. It was large, fully a
hundred yards long and fifty wide, and was tracked up like a barnyard. As
I took photographs of it the horses all busied themselves licking the mud
and finally had to be driven away. It was surrounded by burnt timber, and

numerous trails worn fully a foot deep in the hard, rocky ground showed the frequency of its use, probably by great numbers of moose and caribou, which were abundant in this region. We never were fortunate enough to see animals of either of these two species at any of the licks.

SMALL MAMMALS

NORTHERN HARE (*SNOWSHOE HARE*)

They were especially common along the Stony, Sulphur, Muskeg and Smoky rivers, – that is, in Area 1. In Area 2 we scarcely saw any at all, being in higher country, and in Area 3 the same was the case until we reached the northern end of it. Then they became very abundant. In Area 4 they simply swarmed in places, so that raising vegetables was almost an impossibility. They preferred the bark of poplars and balm of Gileads, but in their absence ate that of the spruce and Jack pine. A freshly felled poplar would have all its bark stripped off in a few nights in localities were the hares were numerous. At times we came upon acres of young Jack pines or spruces only two to three feet high, every one of which had almost the entire bark eaten off. This was in a region where poplars were not available. The hares were very tame, often never moving out of our way as we went by. In camp they ran all about and would feed within three or four feet of us. They were very destructive in chewing boots, ropes and canvas bags, as well as robbing the kitchen.

LITTLE CHIEF HARE (*PIKA*)

We saw these animals only twice, once on August 19th near the head of the Wapiti among the rocks above timberline at 1500 feet, and again on the 30th near the head of the east Pine at an elevation of 5500 feet, also among the rocks. In the former case they were 1500 feet above timberline, in the latter only 500, owing to the fact that the altitude of timberline changed rapidly in this region. In both cases they were so shy that it was impossible to secure specimens.

PORCUPINE

They were common in Area 1 and in the first part of Area 2. After leaving the Porcupine waters we saw no more, though undoubtedly they must exist there. Sometimes we saw three or four together in an open muskeg where the ground was very wet, and at one time I found one at about 1000 feet, above timberline, on a long, rolling, grassy pass over a mile from the nearest trees. They never bothered us in camp. Sometimes they were very dark coloured but more often were very tawny over the tail, shoulders and head.

LONG-TAILED JUMPING MOUSE (*WESTERN JUMPING MOUSE*)

We saw these mice only twice, – once at 5000 feet, just above timberline on the grassy slopes, where they were extremely common, for their holes were literally everywhere. This was at the head of the Wapiti. A few days previously, on August 20th, at 6000 feet we saw one in the upland meadows.

SHORT-TAILED MOUSE (*MEADOW VOLE*)

In the same locality where we first saw the preceding species we caught one of this variety. These two had their holes along the same slope.

RED-BACKED MOUSE (*RED-BACKED VOLE*)

We caught none of this variety, but in September 1912, they were plentiful near the head of the Porcupine River along the edges of the scattered groves of spruce and balsam. At the head of Sheep Creek in 1913 an Indian caught several and showed us the skins. They interested him and he secured them because they were different from anything he had seen before. We set traps last summer but never saw an individual, though there was plenty of old sign everywhere. Yet, in 1912, we saw them jumping up and running about in all directions. They were then continually inside our tipi at night. In size, as I remember, they were a little larger than the short-tailed variety.

MUSKRAT

These animals were fairly common in the mountains among the lower valleys and outside in the numerous small lakes. In Area 4 they were extremely plentiful. I watched one as he sat on a log only a few feet from me and he seemed to be eating the moss from his floating perch.

WHITE-FOOTED MOUSE (*DEER MOUSE*)

This species we expected to find abundant throughout and were disappointed. The first one we caught was along the Muskeg River at an altitude of 5400 feet. The trap was set in a large hole in the bank, and to our surprise we found only a small mouse as our victim. Here the timber was a dense growth of spruce and Jack pine. Along the Wapiti near Sapphire

Lake at an elevation of 4500 feet in a little open meadow, we caught one in our hands, and at a nearby camp, in a meadow of long grass surrounded by willows at the edge of the river, we caught two. We saw no more until we reached the Peace River. There, on both sides at Hudson's Hope (elevation 1700 feet), we caught several in the log cabins. At Pouce Coupe on the grassy prairie (elevation 2000 feet) we found them also abundant about the cabins.

PACK RAT (*BUSHY-TAILED WOODRAT*)

Only twice did we encounter these pests, – the first time on the Muskeg River (elevation 5400 feet) at the same camp as we caught our first white-footed mouse, and at Hudson's Hope (1700 feet). In the former case he had gnawed some of the straps on the saddles, as well as three large holes in my rubber coat. We found him curled up in the pile of the saddles and outfit. At Hudson's Hope, during the night three large whitefish had disappeared from under the pack covers weighted down with logs at the corners. We found one partly eaten a few feet away, – the others we never saw again. Also a little notebook wrapped up in a white cotton bag had been taken from the inside of the outfit pile. It contained all the measurements of the small mammals and was a valuable record. A pack rat was discovered in the morning under the pile, as in the first instance. He too was killed and to him we laid the blame of stealing the fish and notebook. A thorough search all about revealed nothing, yet in all probability these things were buried in some hole or hollow tree nearby.

BEAVER

Beaver were generally distributed throughout the first three areas. Along the Pine they were very common and we sometimes saw them swimming about the river. They built dams across the small streams and in flooding large areas often made our progress slow and difficult. Their houses as well as their burrows in the riverbanks were a common sight. Often, runways sometimes as deep as two feet extended from the river to their ponds. They preferred poplars, balm of Gileads and cottonwoods and often went a quarter to a half mile away in order to get them. In their absence I have seen spruces cut down by them. I never saw a tree gnawed down by them lodged, for they are expert woodsmen and fell them true. Occasionally cottonwoods twenty inches in diameter were felled by them. In one or two instances they were never used but were left where they had fallen.

GROUND SQUIRREL (COLUMBIAN GROUND SQUIRREL)

We only saw these animals in Area 1. There in localities they were extremely abundant, ranging from 6000 to 7000 feet. They were always below timberline or just at the edge and made their burrows among the spruces or in the long grass that grew in the little meadows and flats along the smaller streams. Often they were a quarter of a mile or more from any water. In 1912 I found a colony of them living along the same bare ridge with marmots. Here they were above timberline and the nearest spruces were fully half a mile distant.

BIG CHIPMUNK (GOLDEN-MANTLED GROUND SQUIRREL)

At the head of the Hay River where we were hunting sheep we found, at an elevation of 7500 feet on the very top of a narrow rock ridge, one individual. As he had gone to the shelter of his hole in the rocks we were forced to dig him out for the collection. Again, near the mouth of the Muddy Water River, at 3500 feet on the edge of a rocky ridge in the burnt timber, we found one. At the southern head of the Wapiti we saw one among the rocks at 7500 feet, far above timberline near the top of a mountain, and again at the northern head at 5500 feet, among the rocks just above timberline. Thus we found them in Areas 1 and 2 and at the beginning of 3.

LITTLE CHIPMUNK

We found these for certain three different times. First, along the Sulphur River (4600 feet) at the edge of a large meadow among some fallen burnt timber; secondly, on the Wapiti (3500 feet) in fallen burnt timber; and lastly, south of Grande Prairie on the way home, in the green spruce timber. Thus they were in Areas 1, 2 and 4. Always they were rather nervous little creatures but at times were very tame and sat quite close by and watched us. They seemed to live in holes in the ground. At 7500 feet on the rock ridge where we dug out the "big chipmunk" above referred to I found three small chipmunks which I tried hard to secure but was unsuccessful. These small ones I at first took to be this species, but after having always found the little chipmunk lower down among the timber I concluded they were probably the young of the big chipmunk, for it was then the first week in July.

RED SQUIRREL

The only statement in connection with this species is that he ranged throughout all four areas and was seen at regular intervals, – always among the spruces or Jack pines, never above timberline, and usually some distance below.

SHREW

We caught only two specimens, one on the upper east Pine along the river-bank in the long weedy growth so characteristic of burnt country.

MINK

Though mink undoubtedly range throughout Areas 1, 2 and 3 we only saw them twice and both times along the upper east Pine in Area 3. At 2600 and 2800 feet respectively we watched one individual swimming and diving from camp. He repeatedly caught small fish, probably trout, four or five inches long, some of which he swallowed whole while others he brought to the shore where he tore them up among the rocks so that he could more easily gulp them down.

MARTEN (*PINE MARTEN*)

Though we saw no marten they are quite common throughout Areas 1, 2 and 3 and are what the Indian trapper is especially after in the wintertime.

WOLVERINE

These animals, though we never saw them, undoubtedly range through Areas 1, 2 and 3 but probably are not common.

FOX

Fox tracks were seen occasionally on the mud bars along the rivers but they prefer lower country and in the valleys of less altitude, especially at the edge of the mountains, so in the foothills they were common. In the northern part of Area 3 and in parts of Area 4 they were extremely abundant. In fact, the Indians trapped almost nothing else. We found one that apparently in attempting to spring through a clump of willows had hung himself in a narrow crotch and thus slowly strangled to death. The twigs, branches and bark were bitten and torn within his reach. As his head was more than a foot above the ground he had no way of escaping.

WOLF

Tracks were not uncommon though we did not see many until we reached the head of the east Pine. Then they became frequent along the river bars. At 5000 feet, on the top of a mountain that rose just above timberline, – typical caribou range – a black specimen was seen. There was a grizzly bear and two caribou on the same mountain at the same time. The next morning as we were eating, a black wolf was discovered sitting on his haunches on a gravel bar on the opposite side of the river about 200 yards away. He sat there watching us, undoubtedly attracted by the smell of the moose meat which was hanging up. He stayed there until I fired and missed, after which he ran off, disappearing in the brush. Very likely it was the same one seen on the mountain top the previous day as it was only a few miles distant. They never bothered our horses, though on the Smoky River the Indians who winter horses there are greatly troubled by them.

COYOTE

Tracks of coyotes were common in the lower valleys but we never saw them in the higher mountains. They were numerous all along the Pine, which seemed to be a great country for them as well as wolves and foxes. In Area 4 they were plentiful and at sunrise and sunset they always sat around the hills near camp howling and yelping as they do on the prairies.

LYNX

We saw tracks only at times but among the lower valleys they were common in Areas 1, 2 and 3. We never passed a trapper's cabin in Areas 1 and 3 without seeing lynx skulls strewn about. Where the hares were plentiful it was a sure sign there was lynx about.

FISH

Although we paid very little attention to the fish, one or two observations we made may be of interest. On only one or two occasions did we bother to try to catch them. In the Muskeg River, at an altitude of 3800 feet, we caught half a dozen Dolly Varden trout of from 1 1/2 to 4 pounds in weight. The stream was fairly clear and water quite cold but not fed by glaciers. Their flesh was firm and the flavour delicate. We never tried again until we reached the upper part of the East Pine River. There in a small side stream in a good-sized pool we caught about twenty trout in half an hour. Their weight varied between one and three pounds. They were a different variety from any I had before seen and I understand they are the so-called Arctic trout, – a name I believe given to a variety that has been found only in waters of the Arctic watershed. They were not a gamey fish at all but swam up slowly and swallowed the hook and bait in a clumsy way, sometimes spitting it out leisurely. They rose to the surface for insects in the same' sluggish manner. They had black backs, a long head, big mouth and large teeth. Underneath they were whitish and on their sides they were silvery with faint spots. The meat was white or a very delicate pink and was soft and poorly flavoured. A week later we returned to this same pool. Then the river was a little lower and the water so clear that it was possible to see the bottom of the pool. At first we saw no fish and then eight trout swam along, all of which we shortly landed with our makeshift tackle. Curiously enough they were all Dolly Varden trout. Between these two times we fished the riffles lower down and as well a large pool at the mouth of this stream where it flows into the East Pine. Here we caught nearly a hundred fish in several trips to the pool, all of which were Dolly Varden except for one Arctic trout. It was interesting to notice that one day while the sun was out the fish bit very poorly, then as it clouded over they bit better, and when it began to rain gently they rose to the surface continually. The reason for this was evident for the rain had brought hundreds of small winged insects out of the air and the surface of the water was covered with them. In one place I was fishing under a long log that extended from the shore far into the pool. Here the surface was covered with bubbles and scum, under which protection the fish were very plentiful. I pushed the log into the stream, and as the scum in consequence cleared, the fish left so that none were seen. The eddy here was such that in a few minutes the log, after making a complete circuit of the pool, returned to its former place. Shortly the scum again accumulated and in a few minutes the fish had returned and were biting as freely as ever. Here there were some big falls over 200 feet in height and in the river below we caught a few trout, all Dolly Varden. Later on in Moberly Lake near the Peace River we found whitefish, lake trout and pike. The former seemed to be in all the larger lakes outside of the mountains and were the main diet of the Indians in winter.

BIRDS

WESTERN GREBE (*AECHMOPHORUS OCCIDENTALIS*)

Peace River, October 19.
  Probably only migrant.

HOLBOELL'S GREBE (*COLYMBUS HOLBOELLI*) (*RED-NECKED GREBE*)

Lake at head of Porcupine River, August 10, altitude 5000 feet.
  Probably breeds.

LOON (*GAVIA IMMER*) (*COMMON LOON*)

Lake between Muskeg and Smoky rivers, July 26, altitude 3500 feet.
  Breeds.

HERRING GULL (*LARUS ARGENTATUS*)

East Pine, September 19 and 25, several flying west.
  Migrant.

RED-BREASTED MERGANSER (*MERGUS SERRATOR*)

East Pine, feeding in river alone, altitude 2600 feet.
  Migrant.

MALLARD (*ANAS PLATYRHYNCHOS*)

Stony River, altitude 4500 feet, July 2, Wapiti River, altitude 4000 feet, pair feeding, August 29.
  East Pine, altitude 2400 feet, September 25.
  Moberly Lake, altitude 2000, pair, October 14.
  Lakes near Grande Prairie numbers feeding.
  Breeds.

GADWALL (*CHAULELASMUS STREPERUS*)

East Pine, three feeding in river, altitude 2300, September 26.
  Migrant.

GREEN-WINGED TEAL (*NETTION CAROLINENSE*)

East Pine, altitude 2600, three seen September 8.
  Migrant.

BARROW'S GOLDEN-EYE (*CLANGULA ISLANDICA*)

Stony River, altitude 4000 and 4700, July 2 and 3.

Lake near Smoky River, altitude 3500, female and four young, July 26.

Lake head of Porcupine River, altitude 5000, female and six young unable to fly, August 8.

Also brood on lake nearby, 5000 feet, August 11.

Breeds.

HARLEQUIN (*HISTRIONICUS HISTRIONICUS*) (*HARLEQUIN DUCK*)

Saw repeatedly throughout Areas 1, 2 and 3 in the small rushing mountain streams at altitudes from 2600 to 6000 feet and from July 3 to September 20. Saw none on lower East Pine after leaving the mountains.

Breeds.

SURF SCOTER (*OIDEMIA PERSPICILLATA*)

Lake at head of Porcupine River, altitude 5000 feet, males, fine plumage, young, well grown, August 10.

Breeds.

CANADA GOOSE (*BRANTA CANADENSIS CANADENSIS*)

Saw several times in all areas and at altitudes from 1600 to 5500 feet.

Found them breeding in July and August along Stony River and lake at head of Porcupine River.

Along East Pine numerous flocks were migrating as well as outside the mountains in Area 4.

Breeds.

TRUMPETER SWAN (*OLOR BUCCINATOR*)

Though the species was not identified, this was probably the one seen.

In upper Stony River altitude 4800 feet on July 3 saw one swan swimming.

In late June 1913 a pair were seen in one of the small lakes near Jasper.

Probably breeds.

WILSON'S SNIPE (*GALLINAGO DELICATA*)

On East Pine in mudhole a pair was seen September 8 and on the next day one was seen, altitude 2600 feet.

Migrant.

PECTORAL SANDPIPER (*PISOBIA MACULATA*)

On East Pine, altitude 2600 feet, several were seen and heard migrating on September 7 and 9.
  Migrant.

LEAST SANDPIPER (*PISOBIA MINUTILLA*)

Smoky River, altitude 3500, two small flocks feeding on mud flat July 26.
  Lake head of Porcupine River, altitude 5000 feet on August 9 three were seen.
  Probably only migrant.

GREATER YELLOW LEGS (*TOTANUS MELANOLEUCUS*)

Smoky River, altitude 3500, a pair was feeding on a mud flat July 26. Saw one catch two-inch fish and spend some time tearing it up with his bill before eating. Head of Wapiti River at small reedy pond above timberline on a grassy pass at 5000 feet saw one bird on August 26.
  May breed but probably only migrant.

WESTERN SOLITARY SANDPIPER (*HELODRAMAS SOLITARIUS CINNAMONEUS*) (*SOLITARY SANDPIPER*)

Near Stony River, altitude 4000 feet, on June 29 found a pair in a muskeg which was surrounded by spruces. They wereevidently nesting, from their actions.
  At head of East Pine, altitude 3600 feet found an adult and one young on August 31.
  Breeds.

SPOTTED SANDPIPER (*ACTITIS MACULARIA*)

These birds were common throughout Areas 1, 2 and 3, being along the streams and at altitudes ranging from 2600 to 6000 feet. The last date we saw one was on September 9, on the East Pine.
  Breeds.

KILLDEER PLOVER (*OXYECHUS VOCIFERUS*)

Near Jasper along the Athabasca River, altitude 3200 feet, saw a pair on June 26.
  Near the Smoky River on a muddy flat along the lake was a pair on July 26.
  Breeds.

RICHARDSON'S GROUSE (*DENDRAGAPUS OBSCURUS RICHARDSONI*)
(*BLUE GROUSE*)

At head of Porcupine River at 5500 feet near timberline saw a female and two partly grown young on August 11. On one of the mountains along the east Pine at 5000 feet at edge of timberline two were seen feeding on berries.

These birds keep near the summit country and are scarce.

Resident.

HUDSONIAN SPRUCE PARTRIDGE (*CANACHITES CANADENSIS CANADENSIS*)
(*SPRUCE GROUSE*)

Common throughout, from altitudes of 2000 to 5000 feet. None seen in valleys from 3500 to 5000 feet.

Resident.

GRAY RUFFED GROUSE (*BONASA UMBELLUS UMBELLOIDES*) (*RUFFED GROUSE*)

Common in the lower valleys from 1200 to 4500 feet. Often heard them drumming at night and on nearly every full moon we heard them up until the end of October.

Resident.

WILLOW PTARMIGAN (*LAGOPUS LAGOPUS LAGOPUS*)

The most common ptarmigan. Ranged from 4700 to 7000 feet. Rarely seen except among the willows, either below or just above timberline. Always seemed to be moulting. On July 19 saw brood of very small chicks above timberline on a high, grassy pass. None seen after August 27 on leaving the Wapiti headwaters, due to not being in right country for them.

Resident.

ROCK PTARMIGAN (*LAGOPUS RUPESTRIS RUPESTRIS*)

On July 11 on a rocky ridge near the head of the Sulphur River at elevation of 8000 feet found a bird and nest of ten eggs. It was not positively identified, however, as a rock ptarmigan.

WHITE-TAILED PTARMIGAN (*LAGOPUS LENCURUS LENCURUS*)

Seen in Areas 1 and 2. They were not as common as the willow ptarmigan. Ranged from 5500 to over 8000 feet. They differed from the above mentioned species in always being above timberline and usually among the rocky slopes, sometimes on the extreme tops of mountains.

Resident.

SHARP-TAILED GROUSE
(*PEDIOECETES PHASIANELLUS COLUMBIANUS*)

Not common except in the lower valleys in the foothills and out of the mountains. Saw them from 2000 to 3700 feet altitude, but only four times. In autumn they gather in large flocks.
 Resident.

MARSH HAWK (*CIRCUS HUDSONICUS*) (*NORTHERN HARRIER*)

Saw only three times, between 5000 and 6000 feet, on July 20, August 8 and 25; in Areas 1 and 2, in the last case above timberline.
 Probably breeds.

GOSHAWK (*ASTUR ATRICAPILLUS ATRICAPILLUS*) (*NORTHERN GOSHAWK*)

In the East Pine Valley below 2000 feet they were seen twice, in October, – each time in localities where ruffed grouse and hares were plentiful.

ROUGH-LEGGED HAWK (*ARCHIBUTEO LAGOPUS SANCTI-JOHANNIS*)

 October 3, along the east Pine, at 2000 feet.

GOLDEN EAGLE (*AQUILA CHRYSAETOS*)

A common bird of the mountains, usually seen soaring high in the air over the mountain slopes. Were throughout Areas 1, 2 and 3 and were seen as low down as 1500 feet on the Peace River.
 Resident.

NORTHERN BALD EAGLE (*HALIAETUS LEUCOCEPHALUS ALASCANUS*)
(*BALD EAGLE*)

Uncommon. Only one bird seen, – along East Pine on September 21 at 2400 feet.

SPARROW HAWK (*FALCO SPARVERIUS SPARVERIUS*) (*AMERICAN KESTREL*)

Seen in July in Area 1 quite frequently from 3500 to 6500 feet but never above timberline.
 Saw one bird on the East Pine September 30 at 2200 feet.
 Probably breeds.

OSPREY (*PANDION HALIAETUS CAROLINEUSIS*)

Upper Stony River, 5000 feet, on July 3, one was seen.
 Probably breeds.

ARCTIC HORNED OWL (*BUBO VIRGINIANUS SUBARCTICUS*)
(*GREAT HORNED OWL*)

A common bird throughout the lower valleys only, occasional in Area 2. Was never seen or heard in valleys above 4500 feet.

On September 28 on the East Pine one bird hooted all the afternoon. Resident.

HAWK OWL (*SURNIA ULULA CAPAROCH*) (*NORTHERN HAWK OWL*)

Seen occasionally in all but Area 1, sometimes near timberline at 5500 feet, as at the head of the Porcupine River and again as low down as 1800 feet in the open poplar timbered country in Area 4. Kept to localities where mice were abundant.

Resident.

BELTED KINGFISHER (*CERYLE ALCYON*)

Frequently seen along the rivers in the lower valleys between 2600 and 4500 feet in all but Area 4.

Breeds.

NORTHERN HAIRY WOODPECKER (*DRYOBATES VILLOSUS LEUCOMELAS*)
(*HAIRY WOODPECKER*)

Along the East Pine, seen three times, on September 12, 14 and 24.

Probably breeds.

NELSON'S DOWNY WOODPECKER (*DRYOBATES PUBESCENS NELSONI*)
(*DOWNY WOODPECKER*)

At Hudson's Hope on the Peace River, October 18.

Probably breeds.

ARCTIC THREE-TOED WOODPECKER (*PICOIDES ARCTICUS*)
(*BLACK-BACKED WOODPECKER*)

On the East Pine on September 24 and 25, altitude 2300 feet.

ALASKA THREE-TOED WOODPECKER (*PICOIDES AMERICANUS*)
(*THREE-TOED WOODPECKER*)

A specimen was taken June 30 at 4400 feet, along the Stony River. Seen along the East Pine on September 29 and October 3, altitude 2300 feet.

Probably breeds.

NORTHERN FLICKER (*COLAPTES AURATUS LUTEUS*)

Seen on July 14, at 6100 feet along Sulphur River and four more times that month down to 3400 feet. Only one other one seen was on the East Pine on September 12 at 2600 feet.
   Breeds.

NIGHT HAWK (*CHORDEILES VIRGINIANUS VIRGINIANUS*) (*COMMON NIGHTHAWK*)

On July 24, near Smoky River, altitude 3500 a pair flew about all after-noon uttering their harsh cries. It was in open country with dry, rocky meadows.
   Probably breeds.

RUFOUS HUMMING BIRD (*SELASPHORUS RUFUS*)

Species not identified but probably the above.
   Smoky River, July 30, 3200 feet.
   Muddy Water, August 1, 4200 feet.
   Wapiti River, August 19, at 6000 feet, above timberline.
   Probably breeds.

LEAST FLYCATCHER (*EMPIDONAX MINIMUS*)

Smoky River, July 26, 3500 feet.
   Sheep Creek, August 1, 4100 feet.
   Probably breeds.

LARK (*OTOCORIS ARCTICOLA*) (*HORNED LARK*)

Sulphur River, July 6, 7000 feet.
   Sheep Creek, August 3, 7000 feet.
   Wapiti River, August 19, 7500.
   Pine River, August 31, 6000 feet.
   In all cases fully 1000 feet above timberline on the rocky slopes and summits. One bird seen each time except the last when several were seen, evidently migrating.

MAGPIE (*PICA PICA HUDSONIA*) (*BLACK-BILLED MAGPIE*)

Muddy Water River, in a narrow canyon on August 1, 4500 feet.
   Porcupine River, August 15, 6000 feet.
   Probably breeds.

CANADA JAY (*PERISOREUS CANADENSIS CANADENSIS*) (*GRAY JAY*)

Common throughout. Not many seen in June and July. Ranged in altitude from 1500 to 6000 feet. Never seen above timberline.
Resident.

NORTHERN RAVEN (*CORVUS CORAX PRINCIPALIS*) (*COMMON RAVEN*)

Seen along the lower Pine and Peace rivers from September 21 to October 21.
One seen November 1, near Grande Prairie.
Keeps to low valleys, never seen above 3000 feet.
Probably resident.

WESTERN CROW (*CORVUS BRACHYRHYNCHOS HESPERIS*)
(*AMERICAN CROW*)

Several were seen near the Smoky River, altitude 3400 feet, on July 24.
Probably resident.

CLARK'S NUTCRACKER (*NUCIFRAGA COLUMBIANA*)

One seen June 23 at Jasper, altitude 3200 feet.
Probably breeds.

RUSTY BLACKBIRD (*EUPHAGUS CAROLINUS*)

Half a dozen seen several times between September 7 and 17 along the East Pine, feeding along the shore among the rocks and on the mud bars.
Migrant.

ALASKA PINE GROSBECK (*PINICOLA ENUCLEATOR*) (*PINE GROSBEAK*)

Seen along the South Pine and Peace, 2000 feet, October 12, 20 and 21.
Migrant.

GREY-CROWNED ROSY FINCH
(*LEUCOSTICTE TEPHROCOTIS TEPHROCOTIS*)

July 11, above timberline at 7000, at source of Hay River several were feeding along a snow bank.
On the 20th at 6800 at source of Muskeg River, six near snow bank.
August 2, head of Sheep Creek, altitude 4800 in a broad meadow with low-growing willows, a few birds were calling.
August 4, at 6500 feet, near Wapiti River.
On the 19th a flock of more than 50 were feeding among the rocks on the top of a mountain 7500 feet, evidently migrating.

Except on Sheep Creek they were never seen below timberline.
Probably breeds.

PINE SISKIN (*SPINUS PINUS*)

On August 8, 11 and 25, between 5000 and 5500 feet along Porcupine and
Wapiti rivers, large flocks were seen flying about and feeding among the
spruces.
Probably breeds.

SNOW BUNTING (*PLECTROPHENAX NIVALIS NIVALIS*)

Not seen until October 27 at 1800 feet elevation some distance east of the
Pine River, in large flocks feeding in a burnt meadow.
On November 1, in Grande Prairie, common in the stubble fields.
Migrant.

WHITE-CROWNED SPARROW (*ZONOTRICHIA LEUCOPHRYS*)

June 30, 4400 feet, and July 1, 4500, Stony River.
On the 6th, head of Hay at 7000 feet, above timberline. Also July 17, 18
and 22.
Breeds.

GOLDEN-CROWNED SPARROW (*ZONOTRICHIA CORONATA*)

Hay River, July 11, 7000 feet, above timberline, in clump of stunted summit
balsams.
July 21 at 6500 feet.
August 8, Sheep Creek, 4800 feet, also on August 9 and 13, head of
Porcupine River, at timberline, 6000 feet.
Breeds.

WHITE-THROATED SPARROW (*ZONOTRICHIA ALBICOLLIS*)

Muskeg River, July 24, 3500 feet.
East Pine, 2400–2600 feet, September 14, 18 and 25.
Probably breeds.

WESTERN TREE SPARROW (*SPIZELLA MONTICOLLA OCHRACEA*) (*AMERICAN
TREE SPARROW*)

Only time was on August 26 at timberline 5000 feet, when a small number
were seen migrating with song and chipping sparrows.
Probably breeds.

CHIPPING SPARROW (*SPIZELLA PASSERINA ARIZONAE*)

Quite common in Area 1, and were in valleys ranging in altitude from 3400 to 6000 feet.

August 3 one was seen and on the 26th they were migrating near the head of the Wapiti with tree and song sparrows.

Breeds.

SLATE-COLOURED JUNCO (*JUNCO HYEMALIS HYEMALIS*) (*DARK-EYED JUNCO*)

Common throughout Areas 1, 2 and 3, both breeding and migrating. Seen from June 26 until October 1 and from altitude of 2000 to 6000 feet, but never above timberline.

Breeds.

SONG SPARROW (*MELOSPIZA MELODIA MELODIA*)

Quite common throughout Areas 1, 2 and 3. Their range varied in altitude from 2600–6100 feet. Never seen above timberline, always in willow flats or along the edge of open meadows. Last one seen September 9 at 2600 feet on the East Pine.

Breeds.

WESTERN TANAGER (*PIRANGA LUDOVICIANA*)

One heard singing at Jasper on June 23, altitude 3200.

Probably breeds.

CLIFF SWALLOW (*PETROCHELIDON LUMIFRONS LUMIFRONS*)

July 16 at 4000 one was seen along the Sulphur River where it goes through a rocky canyon.

On the 24th another was seen at 3400 feet near the Muskeg River.

Breeds.

BARN SWALLOW (*HIRUNDO ERYTHROGASTRA*)

Along the Smoky River, altitude 3200 feet, one flew around the horses on July 30. A few log cabins belonging to the Indians were the only buildings within one hundred miles.

Probably breeds.

TREE SWALLOW (*IRIDOPROCNE BICOLOR*)

One seen at same place as above species, along Smoky River on July 26.

Probably breeds.

BOHEMIAN WAXWING (*BOMBYCILLA GARRULA*)

On September 11, 12, 14 and October 1, along the banks of the East Pine from 2000–2600 feet altitude, several flocks were seen feeding. They perched on the dead spruces, from which they would dart out in mid-air over the rushing stream to catch an insect and then return.
Migrant.

CEDAR WAXWING (*BOMBYCILLA CEDRORUM*)

July 30, along the Smoky River, altitude 3200 feet, several were seen feeding on the saskatoon bushes, which were covered with ripening berries.

On August 1, 2 and 9 at altitudes varying from 4100–5500 several more were seen feeding in a similar way to the Bohemian waxwings above described.
Probably breeds.

RED-EYED VIREO (*VIREOSYLVA OLIVACEA*)

July 30, on the Smoky River, altitude 3400 feet, female and young were seen.
Breeds.

MYRTLE WARBLER (*DENDROICA CORONATA*) (*YELLOW-RUMPED WARBLER*)

June 30, altitude 4400 feet, along the Stony River.
Probably breeds.

WILSON'S WARBLER (*WILSONIA PUSILLA PUSILLA*)

July 20, altitude 6000 feet, pair found breeding in the willows along a small stream surrounded by the dense spruce timber.
September 14, East Pine, altitude 2600 feet, several seen migrating.
Breeds.

REDSTART (*SETOPHAGA RUTICILLA*) (*AMERICAN REDSTART*)

Along the East Pine, altitude 2600 feet, a pair (probably the same) was seen on September 13, 14 and 17 migrating. The male was in fine plumage.
Probably breeds.

PIPIT (*ANTHUS RUBESCENS*) (*AMERICAN PIPIT*)

Along the East Pine, altitude 2600 feet, several were seen on September 9, 16, 20 and 21 feeding on the shore among the large rounded rocks, picking up insects in a similar way as the rusty blackbirds fed.
Probably breeds.

DIPPER (*CINCLUS MEXICANUS UNICOLOR*) (*AMERICAN DIPPER*)

This bird although a permanent resident was never seen until September 16 owing to its secluded habits while nesting, yet we were continually about its favourite haunts.

Seen also September 20, 21, 24 and October 18 and 19, always along some dashing stream, usually a small secluded one. Its haunts varied in altitude from 1500 feet at the Peace River to 5000 feet close to timberline.

Resident.

WESTERN WINTER WREN (*NANNUS HIEMALIS PACIFICUS*) (*WINTER WREN*)

July 26, altitude 3200 feet, an old bird and several well-grown young were seen on an open grassy hillside dotted with poplar trees.

August 15 at 5500 feet near head of Porcupine River among the spruces.

September 1 at 3500 feet along the East Pine; on the 4th at 2800 feet in the deep spruces; on the 9th at 2600 feet among the willows and alders at the edge of the river; again on the 11th, 16th and on the 26th at 2300 feet among the poplars.

Breeds.

RED-BREASTED NUTHATCH (*SITTA CANADENSIS*)

Quite common. Seen in June, July, August and September at altitudes varying from 2500 to 6100 feet, always in the dense spruces and once just above timberline.

Breeds.

LONG-TAILED CHICKADEE (*PENTHESTES ATRICAPILLUS SEPTENTRIONALIS*) (*BLACK-CAPPED CHICKADEE*)

Though these birds undoubtedly were breeding all through this country because of their secluded habits as in the case of the dipper we never saw them until August 22 along the Wapiti among the willows and burnt timber at 3500 feet.

Then during September, but more especially in October, we saw them continually for they are a bird of the lower country.

Breeds.

HUDSONIAN CHICKADEE (*PENTESTHES HUDSONICUS HUDSONICUS*) (*BOREAL CHICKADEE*)

Being similar in its secluded habits to the above, these birds were never seen until August 15. Our only other observations were on the 21st, 24th and

October 24th. They were less common and preferred the higher country. In all cases but one they were seen in the deep spruces between 500 and 5500 feet. The one seen on October 24th was along the Pine at 2400 feet.

Breeds.

HERMIT THRUSH (*HYLOCICOLA GUTTATA PALLASI*)

In July in the deep spruces in the upper valleys between 4500 and 6000 feet, they were found breeding, their wild notes always adding a charm to the mountain sides. They were always shy and difficult of approach. Though only seen during July and in Area 1, they undoubtedly range throughout.

Breeds.

ROBIN (*PLANESTICUS MIGRATORIUS MIGRATORIUS*) (*AMERICAN ROBIN*)

Common. Seen at intervals through Areas 1, 2 and 3 and at altitudes from 2600 to 6500 feet, always below timberline.

In September they were seen frequently seen along the East Pine during their migration, which seemed to be at its height from September 5th until the 18th, which was our latest date.

Breeds.

VARIED THRUSH (*IXOREUS NAEVIUS*)

September 10, altitude 2600 feet, along the East Pine was our only record. A male bird was seen sitting on the branches of a dead spruce.

Migrant.

MOUNTAIN BLUEBIRD (*SIALIA CURRUCOIDES*)

At Jasper, altitude 3200 feet, on June 20th, it was found breeding in a post in the middle of the town. On August 31 one was seen migrating along the top of a bare mountain at 6000 feet. During the years 1912 and 1913 the migration was always seen between September 10 and 15.

Breeds.

SUMMARY

In brief, the results of the trip were satisfactory. Our main object had been to obtain specimens of the sheep between the Athabasca and Smoky rivers, to define their range and determine what species, if any, were between there and the Peace River. We got a pair of sheep in the first named area which proved to be *Ovis canadensis* and found that the northern limit of their range is along the north side of Sheep Creek. Beyond that, we never saw a sign of any sheep nor any possible country where they might range. Although in the distance along the Wapiti and Pine rivers we saw hills apparently suited to them, on closer inspection they turned out to be dry, moss-covered, flat-topped or rounded mountains on which in every case we found caribou. For the latter these mountains were ideal ranges. At Hudson's Hope we found several Indians and white men who had trapped at the heads of the south and west branches of the Pine River and they were unanimous in saying that there were no sheep nor had they ever heard of there ever being any on the Pine waters. Only caribou were found there, – apparently there were not even goat, as the mountains were too low, only a few being over 6000 feet and many scarcely rising above timberline, which here is about 5000 feet.

We obtained caribou at the lakes at the head of the Porcupine River. They are *Ranifer fortidens*, the same species as that described from a single bull taken near Mt. Robson in 1911. Further on along the Pine the tracks seem to be larger, and one bull we saw looked different, so we tried to get specimens here but were unsuccessful, chiefly owing to the fact that our supplies were nearly gone and we could not afford the time, as we had not then reached trails or travelled country and so did not know how long it would take to reach Hudson's Hope on the Peace River, where we could renew our supplies. The moose we found seemed to be an exceptionally large race, but we were unable to bring out a specimen, though a pair of shed horns which we carried along, found in the upper East Pine, measured conservatively, had a spread of 67 inches. Freshly killed they undoubtedly would have been larger. Our collection of small mammals, though small, was representative of the species in that section. Because we so seldom stayed in the same camp more than one night, not often two and rarely more than that, it was very difficult indeed in spite of our efforts to trap many small mammals.

The shells we carried for our collecting gun were so defective that we practically got no birds at all. However, I made careful observations and took many notes on the habits and distribution of the birds so that what we lacked in specimens was partially made up for in this way. If we had had someone in the party who was able to devote his whole time to the collecting end we should of course have had a much more complete series of everything. But continuous travel and the amount of work devolving on all of us with a large outfit of twenty horses going through all but impassable country prevented this. We had wonderful weather, for during the first ten weeks we were never prevented from hunting, climbing or moving with the outfit one single day. During that time we only had two or three bad days but in each instance the rain came after the day's work had begun and so did not interfere with our plans. I never saw such a wonderful stretch of weather before. It made it so strenuous that we finally had to take two days off and rest up before proceeding. It was really entirely due to this wonderful weather that we were able to get through this country, for I believe that in an average summer or during a wet season it would be impossible to make this trip with horses, owing to the dangerous and impossible fords combined with hundreds of miles of burnt timber through a trailless country. Every man reached home well and fit and every horse too. Luck was with us throughout, for we had no serious accidents of any kind though we had one or two narrow escapes that came near being disastrous.

$$Appendix\ B$$

CANADIAN ALPINE JOURNAL 6, 1914–15
"MT. ALEXANDER,"
BY S. PRESCOTT FAY

(READ AT THE ANNUAL MEETING OF THE AMERICAN ALPINE CLUB)

In view of the increasing interest from year to year in the higher peaks of the Canadian Rockies, and especially because of the prominence that Mt. Robson, the highest of them all, has taken, any new mountains worthy of mention should serve to create a new stimulus for further work and exploration by members of this club. For this reason I have written a short paper which Professor Charles E. Fay has kindly consented to read for me as well as to show a few slides.

In 1912 I found myself in a position to take an extended vacation during the summer and I immediately planned to revisit the Canadian Rockies. As I had at first intended doing some climbing I consulted Professor Fay as to what accessible regions were left that needed exploration. However, my plans changed and I determined to take a hunting trip north of the Yellowhead Pass. On August 8th I left Hinton, a station on the Grand Trunk Pacific Railway, with Fred Brewster, from whom I obtained the outfit of horses. Our definite plans were to get as far as possible into the country beyond the Smoky River – a tributary of the Peace – and there hunt. The real object of our trip was to determine the species of sheep existing in the mountains between the Athabasca and Peace rivers. After five weeks of travelling through badly fallen timber, which made our progress slow, we reached the head of Sheep Creek – a stream flowing into the Smoky River. From here we set out from camp on September 12th with packs for a four days' hunt. From the first mountain we climbed, at an elevation of about 8000 feet, we had a magnificent view of the ranges about us. About 25 miles, possibly 30, in a direction northwest from us was a vast region of snow and ice that immediately attracted our attention. From the midst of this rose two high mountains, one of which appeared to be of great height. Our enthusiasm and excitement were so intense over the discovery of this giant peak that we got its exact location by the compass so as to be able to locate it again further on when we should move our camp nearer to it. It rose above all the surrounding peaks, presenting a beautiful sight as its ice-covered summit glistened in the clear September sunlight. We had no way of judging its height at this distance – we only knew we had found a giant mountain. But as it turned out, we saw it no more that year, in spite of the fact that we were camped within ten miles of it as we discovered last summer. It snowed and stormed continually for about ten days after we had moved our camp nearer to it. Our supplies were so low that we spent all of the time hunting. It was then the end of September, and we reluctantly started home, where we arrived late in October, having been seriously impeded by two feet of snow.

Although I was back again in the summer of 1913, owing to an operation the previous spring I could not attempt a long trip, so I spent the time in the country between Laggan and Mt. Robson, from where I returned at the end of November. However, the latter part of June 1914, saw us under way again with an outfit of twenty horses and food for four months on our way north from Jasper, intending to investigate the mountains as far as the Peace River. This time Mr. C.R. Cross Jr., a member of the American Alpine Club, accompanied me. Our main object was hunting and collecting for the Biological Survey of the Department of Agriculture at Washington. However, we had in mind locating the mountain unless it seriously interfered with our work.

On July 13th we caught our first glimpse of the peak from a mountain of about 8000 feet in height along the Sulphur River. It was a rare opportunity to judge its size, for we saw Mt. Robson as well at the same time. The latter, which was south by west (compass direction) from us, was only about 30 miles distant, yet the other mountain was fully sixty-five miles away and northwest by north from us. Even at this great distance, double that to Mt. Robson, our mountain seemed to suffer nothing in comparison with it, which justified our former belief in its great height. These distances are quite accurate, as this section had been partially mapped and some of the meridians have been surveyed. We later found the mountain's location is about ten miles west of the intersection of the 54th parallel of latitude with the 12th meridian of longitude. Our enthusiasm was thoroughly aroused by this magnificent view of these two giants glistening in the sunlight, and we regretfully returned to camp, for we knew it would be fully two weeks before we again saw the mountain. The next glimpse we caught of our friend was on July 31st from the trail high above the Muddy Water River. But it was only for an instant, as the trail, descending sharply, hid our mountain behind the nearer ranges.

From here on, the scenery becomes very beautiful indeed, but space forbids and I shall not attempt a description. A few days later we were crossing the divide between the two forks of the Porcupine River and as we approached the height of land, there arose before us over the grassy summit the snow crest of the big mountain not fifteen miles away. Luck was with us, for at every possible viewpoint we had clear weather, so these unexpected views were pleasant surprises. We camped a few miles below, and from our tipi the ice cornice of the summit was just visible above the glacier on Thunder Mountain. Here we climbed up the slopes above camp after caribou, from where we not only had fine views of the mountain, but as well saw Robson about sixty miles away to the south, giving another fine opportunity for comparison, but with the distances reversed from the similar sight on the mountains along the Sulphur River three weeks previous, where Robson was the nearer of the two. Camp was moved below to the lower of the three lakes, at the head of the north fork of the Porcupine River. This series of lakes is extremely beautiful and, being only a few miles from this high group of mountains, is sure to become a region rivalling that about Mt. Robson and other such places. The lake at the head of the south fork, although not as fine as these others, is certainly worth mentioning, for the first view of it is so unexpected that its beauty strikes one instantly. As we emerge from the timber, suddenly at our feet, perhaps 1000 feet below, appears a lake of about three miles in length of a most beautiful emerald green in colour. Surrounded as it is on three sides by rocky peaks whose lower slopes are heavily timbered with dark green spruce and at one end of which a mass of ice and snow mountains tower, it cannot help appealing to anyone, even though accustomed to beautiful scenery. But the other lakes are grander and wilder, and the mountains, which are higher, rise more abruptly from the shore, making the effect more impressive, especially at twilight when the wind has died down, and the surface of the lake mirrors the surrounding peaks.

From this camp we climbed to a ridge about 7500 feet high and obtained our nearest view of the mountain, which was not more than six miles away. Unfortunately it was none too clear and the top was covered with clouds. The mountain is in British Columbia, not over fifteen miles from the Alberta boundary, and on the west slope of the Continental Divide, so that its glaciers drain into the Pacific Ocean. We could distinguish a stream, which may flow into the Big Salmon River, a branch of the Fraser, which seemed to rise among the icefields on the northeast side of the mountain. It flowed about its eastern and southern faces and disappeared around the western slope, encircling the mountain for probably 180 degrees; so that, on this side, it is separated from the other mountains by a deep valley, from which the rock cliffs of the outlying spurs rise from 1000 to 2000 feet. Whether on the west and north sides it is similarly isolated from the other ranges, or whether it is connected with them, we never found out. This view gave us our best idea of the size and contour of this big mountain mass, whose base is composed of sheer rocky cliffs above which is a large glacier encircling the final peak, which rises above 3000 feet higher. There was a fine hanging glacier, reminding one of that on Mt. Victoria, as its ice in falling resounded like thunder on the rocks below. A curious feature of the mountain was an extraordinary glacier that seemed to be clinging to the steep face of the peak, though its lower part had fallen away, leaving it apparently unsupported. In spite of the immense pressure there must have been from above, it was still clinging there. The peak itself, from some points, presents a pyramidal shape with very steep arêtes, but from this side its summit is a long, generally level ice cornice which looked broken and very steep on the sloping side. It apparently is higher at the northeastern end. No matter from where it is seen it is an impressive mountain, though not as striking as is Mt. Robson seen from across Berg Lake.

We had planned to stay another day in order to make a closer inspection of the mountain, but it was rainy and, as we could not afford to waste a day, we packed the horses going down the Porcupine River. Two days later we caught another glimpse of the mountain, and, as seen through a vista of green spruces at its eastern face glistening in the sun, it was a pretty sight as it towered high up, though it must have been more than fifteen miles away. A nearer view of this face would be extremely impressive. Late that afternoon we emerged from the timber to an open summit, where we intended to camp, and as we turned about, we saw the most impressive sight of all. There, across a narrow valley, towered a very steep-sided mountain whose northeastern arête was as sharp a knife edge as one could imagine. It literally dominated the landscape and dwarfed every peak in sight. Our big mountain, as we later discovered, was directly behind it. We estimated its height at over 11,000 feet and although much lower than the big mountain, I believe it was more impressive. That night I saw it by moonlight, and it was a sight which I shall not easily forget.

The next morning was a fine, clear August day (it was the 12th of the month), and we climbed a ridge 2000 feet above camp, from which we saw one of the most magnificent views I have ever seen in the Canadian Rockies. All the way from the northwest to the south was a region of snow and ice.

In the foreground towered our knife-edged peak and beyond it rose the big snow mountain once more. Both will prove extremely difficult to climb, as well as dangerous, the big one because of its extremely steep and dangerous ice slopes, and, once on top, the ice cornice will be a serious problem. The other, I think, will be even more difficult because the final summit looks unscalable. It is in the shape of an elongated drum set on end and is perpendicular on all sides for the last two or three hundred feet. The base of this cliff probably can be reached by the southwestern arête. This seems to be connected with the final cliff by a dangerously steep-sided, narrow ice slope. Once across this, there is still the perpendicular wall of the drum before the actual summit can be reached. It will certainly prove an interesting climb.

Now, as to the height of the big mountain. Our estimate was 12,500 feet, based on our camp elevations as well as the various elevations of the ridges from where we saw it. We had good opportunities to compare it on two occasions with Robson, and so feel conservative in giving it that altitude. The next day we left here, having satisfied ourselves with locating the mountain, which proved as much of a giant as we believed when we first saw it on September 12th, 1912. We regretted not being able to stay longer to explore it, but time was valuable and, as it was, we were four months in reaching Hudson's Hope on the Peace River. Later, during our climbing and hunting we often saw our old friend in the distance always looming up high above everything else. For many weeks it served as a landmark and aided in our map-making.

A few words in conclusion. Members of the Alpine Club of Canada seemed to have noticed this mountain during their summer camp of 1913 near Mt. Robson, for the accounts read that "many fine snow mountains appear, one of enormous size, some eighty miles away, which rivals Mt. Robson." Apparently this is the mountain they refer to, for the distance they estimated is almost exactly correct. Later on in our trip I heard of trappers who spoke of an enormous mountain at the head of the north fork of the Fraser River. Apparently it was known to the Indians too, but the only other white man whom I have been able to find who has seen it at close range was a Mr. Jones (whose initials I forget), whom I saw in Edmonton on my return. He had spent four years surveying for a suitable pass for the Grand Trunk Pacific Railway, and about ten years ago first saw the mountain. When I asked his opinion as to its height, he said that as he was looking for low passes and not high mountains he did not measure it accurately, but he knew it was at least 12,000 feet, and that was the figure we found on his map. Previous to his trip a man named Jarvis had crossed from the Fraser waters to the

Porcupine through this valley up which we had come, and to the knife-like mountain he had given the name of "Mount Ida."

To return to the big mountain once more, the most likely route to the upper glacier will probably be from the northeast and the route up the final peak to the cornice on the summit will very likely lie by the northeastern or the southwestern arête. I regret that my information is not more detailed. Unfortunately I will be unable to take the time to again make the trip, but I hope that someone will be sufficiently interested to make a serious attempt on the mountain – in fact, on both of them. By this I do not mean to imply these are the only two mountains of interest, for the region is one of high peaks and there should be a number well over 10,000 feet. The region is a worthy rival to that about Mt. Robson, both from a scenic and from a climber's standpoint. The only drawback is its inaccessibility, for it takes over two weeks of steady travelling from the Grand Trunk Pacific Railway to reach it. The only practical route is the one we used, as in that way the outfit can be taken the whole way and camp made at the base of the big mountain amid the most beautiful of surroundings. In absence of any name for this new high mountain we called it "Mount Alexander," after that most intrepid explorer, Alexander Mackenzie.

Appendix C

APPALACHIA XIII, 6, 1915

BY S. PRESCOTT FAY

READ APRIL 14, 1915

For the last 20 years the Canadian Rockies have offered a wonderful field for mountaineering activities and exploration has been energetically carried out by climbers from both this country and abroad. The names of many of the important peaks testify to the number of world-famous climbers and mountain explorers who have been lured into this fascinating field but comparatively recently opened up. At first all the exploratory work was limited to the country contiguous to the main line of the Canadian Pacific Railway, as there were plenty of interesting regions close at hand. But as the more important of the virgin peaks were conquered one by one, and valley after valley was explored and new glaciers discovered, it became increasingly difficult to push into new lands, more and more time being wasted in getting through the already known area. However, by the year 1909, in spite of the great distance and the amount of time consumed on the trail, all the country up to the Yellowhead Pass, including that around Mt. Robson, the giant peak of all, was explored, and much valuable work had been done in mapping and surveying.

But further than this it was impossible to go until the Grand Trunk Railway started building its extension to the Pacific coast via the Yellowhead Pass. When the steel had been laid only as far as Wolf Creek, about one hundred miles east from the pass itself, pioneer exploration into remoter regions was begun from this side, and on July 17, 1910, Prof. J. Norman Collie and Mr. A.L. Mumm with their party started with pack horses to get into the new country to the west. They spent some time about Mt. Robson; but there was so much snow on the mountains and the weather was so stormy that climbing was almost out of the question and they were able to ascend only some of the lesser peaks. They returned down the Smoky River, then over to the Stony and down this stream, along which they found interesting mountains and glaciers. The next summer (1911) they made another trip, this time going in by the Stony River and over a high pass to the Smoky, then up it to Glacier Creek, which they ascended to Mt. Bess, at the base of which is one of the largest glaciers in the Canadian Rockies. Here they spent most of their time climbing and exploring this region of high mountains, fine snow fields and big glaciers. An attempt was made to go down the Smoky, but fallen timber and bad muskegs in the face of a limited amount of time changed their minds. So a return was made to Mt. Bess, where the remaining days were spent before being compelled by the lateness of the season to return once more to the Athabasca River by nearly the same route that they had come. However, they accomplished much and brought back information of this unexplored country that aroused much interest in alpine circles. Professor Collie's party was therefore the first to go into this new land to the north of the Athabasca for the sake of exploration and climbing.

In the early summer of 1912 I planned to revisit the Canadian Rockies, and at first thought of a trip into the mountains between Laggan and the Yellowhead Pass to do some climbing. Yet, in spite of the fascinations of such a trip, it meant going into a region already known and mapped. That summer the Grand Trunk Railway had completed its line to the Yellowhead Pass, and trains were being operated as far west as Jasper, – the center of the new park of that name. This presented a rare opportunity to make a trip north of the Athabasca Valley into new regions, now made accessible, where mountains, lakes and rivers unknown except to a few trappers and prospectors could be explored. Then, too, the possibilities for hunting were great, and finding game in a new country is so much more interesting than going to a locality already known to the guide! The idea of investigating the fauna of this area, of locating and defining the ranges of the larger game animals interested me very much. There was a question as to the variety of the mountain sheep north of the Athabasca River. Here was a chance to solve this situation and determine whether it was the same variety as on the south side or an entirely new one. For this reason my plans changed, and on August 8 we set out from Hinton, which is located on the eastern edge of the mountains. Fred Brewster and Beau Gaetz, who had come in here only recently, though they had not as yet been north of the railroad, comprised the other members of the party. We had seven pack horses, as we intended to be gone about eight weeks, and our plan was to get across the Smoky River, where we would hunt as well as investigate the mountains as much as possible between its valley and the Continental Divide.

The first few days were spent in going up Solomon Creek and the Hay River to Rock Lake, where we got our best view of the inside ranges. Though only about 8000 to 9000 feet high, they were very effective in the afternoon light seen from across the lake. Then the Stony River was reached, and the next few days were spent along its valley, from which we got fine views of the very interesting rocky ranges on its southern side. One or two side streams that join the main river opened up their valleys to the glaciers and peaks beyond, making a vista effect that was very fine indeed. It was difficult to make an accurate estimate of the height of these mountains, but probably they range between 9000 and 10,000 feet. Owing to the very warm days, the snow and ice of the glaciers were melting rapidly, causing the rivers to rise and flooding the meadows all along this valley, so that the effect was that of a long, serpentine lake of a beautiful greenish colour, in which the mountains and glaciers were reflected. The trail was extremely bad, necessitating endless chopping, because of the amount of fallen timber, -the usual after-effect in burnt-over country. The mosquitoes also were troublesome, but the beauty of this valley fully compensated for all our discomforts. I do not advise anyone who is seriously troubled by these pests to visit it without head nets and sleeping nets, for all three times that I have been through it mosquitoes have proved a terrible nuisance. Last June they were absolutely unbearable and we were glad to leave as speedily as possible, – though we had to stay longer than we intended.

Further on, as the trail goes over a ridge, Mt. Bess appears, its upper part only being visible; yet it is very inspiring seen in this way, towering as it does above the mountains at the further end of this fascinating meadow-flooded valley. Unfortunately the view is only momentary, for the trail descends rapidly, and Bess soon disappears behind the nearer ranges. One of our prettiest camps was among the spruces on the edge of these meadows. From it we looked across the marshy pools to the head of the valley, where a beautiful glacier backed by a rugged mountain gives rise to the Stony River. The icefield is extremely large, and we were anxious to explore it; but us we had other plans in view and a long trip ahead, we could not afford the time. Its beauty and the wonderfully effective picture it made, with the peak towering behind it, impressed us all.

After crossing the summit between the waters of the Stony and Smoky Rivers – which we always referred to as "Marmot Pass" because of the endless number of these animals in the upland meadows – we dropped down rapidly to Twin Tree Lake, so called because of two rocks in the middle, on each of which stands a solitary spruce. It is a beautiful sheet of water nearly two miles long, the colour of which is a soft green. Seen from above the effect is even finer, as in general the colour of these lakes is more intensified when one looks down from an elevation. Twin Tree Lake is set in a deep basin, surrounded by mountains of between 9000 and 10,000 feet. At its head is a green meadow, or muskeg, and the stream flowing in carries so much mud and dirt from above that quite a delta has been formed at its mouth. The subsequent discoloration of the water extends far into the lake, causing a blemish on its exquisite coloured surface. From its southwestern shore the green timber extends far up on the mountain sides, until it gives place to the lower rock-slopes and slides of scree under the cliffs. Then comes the snow and ice of the glaciers above, from which protrude the rocky peaks themselves. Altogether the composition of lake, mountains and glaciers is very delightful, suggestive as it is of peace and solitude.

From here, as we dropped down to the valley of the Smoky, we came to a little, rocky, partly timbered ridge, on which we stopped a minute to take in the view. Behind was our pass, on one side of which the range seemed to be set on end, for the strata were perpendicular and presented a saw-toothed outline. Among these peaks was Mt. Hoodoo, which Professor Collie climbed in the summer of 1911. In front across the valley, to our surprise, we saw a high range, the summit of which was a towering mass of snow and ice. Mt. Bess, situated at the head of Glacier Creek and presenting a dazzling sight under the brilliant sun, was speedily recognized. The mountains about it seemed even higher and a large amount of snow and ice was in evidence. A few minutes later we forded the river, here a stream of about 50 yards in width and now very deep and swift, for the glaciers were melting fast under the hot August sun. We noted that in the early afternoon it would start to rise, and sometimes during the night over a foot would be added to its depth; then, about the middle of the morning, it usually had subsided to its low level of the day only to repeat the same performance. Just below was a mountain, very similar in outline to Cascade at Banff, probably not much over 9000 feet in height, but nevertheless impressive with its rugged rocky buttress and cliffs. On a blazed tree near its base was a register of Professor Collie's party, recording the height of this peak, which they had ascended.

From the minor peaks, that we climbed during the next few days in the course of our hunting, we were able to size up the country about us very well. East of the river the mountains are low and insignificant, while of those on our side some were interesting and rather bold in outline, though none seemed any higher than the one just mentioned. From the valleys up which we hunted it was possible to see some interesting country, but no high peaks appeared. At the head of Wolverine Creek, which is south of Mt. Bess, are some fine-looking mountains carrying a vast amount of snow and ice, also two large glaciers; but as it snowed all the time, it was impossible to form any estimate of their height. Although we did not on this trip follow the Continental Divide sufficiently closely to make accurate observations, what we saw in the summer of 1913 and 1914, and what we heard, led us to believe that north and northwest of Mt. Bess and its neighbouring peaks the mountains become lower. Here rises the Jack Pine River, flowing some distance in a northerly direction. Where it turns easterly another fork comes in, whose source is quite close to the headwaters of the Muddy Water River. We later hunted all over this last-mentioned region, finding no high mountains, but having fine views of Mt. Bess and its surrounding peaks.

We continued down the Smoky River, spending weeks chopping our way, though it was only a comparatively short distance; but the valley has been burnt over, the fallen timber obliterating all signs of any trail – if at any time one did exist – and making it all but impassable. During that fortnight of steady going we saw no signs of anyone's having been down that part of the valley before us. In one small side valley, up which we hunted, we found a beautiful lake over a mile long, which we called "Cascade Lake." At its head was an open meadow, dotted here and there with clumps of spruces, beyond which the stream on its way down cascaded over a high rocky wall. On two sides rose the mountains, some with much snow and ice, – probably the northern end of the Mt. Bess range.

Finally we came to the Muddy Water River and an old trail, the first we had seen for several weeks. This we followed, finding it crossed the river a day above its junction with the Smoky and led over to Sheep Creek, another tributary of the latter. Two more days took us to the head of Sheep Creek, where we planned to give the horses a few days of rest, – much needed after their continuous two weeks' travelling, – while we climbed and hunted.

From the first mountain, at an elevation of about 8500 feet, we saw to the northwest and about 30 miles away a view that gave us a great surprise. There, from a vast field of snow and ice, rose two large mountains, one of which was of enormous size. What a contrast was this group to the small mountains, insignificant in comparison, that lay at the head of Sheep Creek and Muddy Water River! Between Mt. Bess and the region ahead there were no large mountains nor any snow and ice of consequence. We got the exact direction of our high peak, and, estimating the approximate distance, felt confident of being able to locate it further on, so as to camp close by and explore the surrounding region. Unfortunately we saw it no more that year; for after we had moved over the intervening passes and camped beyond them, it snowed and stormed continuously for nearly two weeks, hiding all the mountains from us. Though our camp was not over ten miles from this elusive peak, we did not realize it until we returned there two years later.

As our food supply was extremely low, all our time was spent in hunting, in vain as it turned out, and we had to continue our trip without fresh meat. It was then the end of September and we had already been out the length of time planned for the entire trip; so we started down the Kakwa River, endeavouring to find a different way home which would avoid the high passes now covered deep with snow. After much difficulty and detention from the two feet of snowfall that we encountered, we reached Hinton at the end of October with our food supply completely exhausted.

Unsuccessful as our trip had been we had roughly located this new high mountain and, in spite of the bad weather, had been able to appreciate the beauty of the surrounding country, which, with its fascinating lakes, charming valleys and high mountains, so delighted us that we made up our minds to return to explore it further at the first available opportunity.

In 1913 I was back again, but being unable to take a long trip, I contented myself with several shorter ones in which we covered nearly all the country from Mt. Robson and the upper Smoky (including the exploration of nearly all its tributaries) to Laggan on the line of the Canadian Pacific Railway. Still we kept in mind the country to the north, and on my return home from the mountains in December vague plans were made, but nothing definite was done until the next spring. In the May number of *Scribner's Magazine* I noticed an article on the Mt. Robson region by Mrs. Elizabeth Parker entitled "A New Field for Mountaineering." Speaking of the view to the north, seen in the various climbs made thereabout by members of the Alpine Club of Canada, who held their annual camp of 1913 on the shores of Berg Lake, she said, "Many fine snow mountains appear, one of enormous size some eighty miles away which rivals Mt. Robson." This naturally further aroused my interest, as there was no doubt that our peak was the one referred to, the distance of eighty miles being quite correct.

Our trip was speedily planned, and soon after the middle of June 1914, C.R. Cross Jr. (a friend of mine from Boston), Fred Brewster of Jasper, Alberta, two other men and myself were under way with twenty head of horses and food for four months, intending to go through the mountains to the Peace River. Our primary object was hunting and collecting for the Biological Survey of the Department of Agriculture at Washington; but we planned to investigate the mountains as thoroughly as possible on our way, and particularly to locate exactly the big peak and explore the surrounding country, provided it did not interfere with our collecting. To hunt the mountains for sheep between the Athabasca and Peace rivers in our effort to determine the variety that ranged this region was no small task, and it meant slow, careful work, especially if the sheep were scarce. For that reason our time was limited and every day was valuable.

On July 13 we caught our first glimpse of the big mountain from an elevation of about 8000 feet on the range along the east side of the Sulphur River. It was readily recognized from its size, shape and location as the peak first seen by us on September 12, 1912, from the mountains at the head of Sheep Creek. We at once concluded it must attain a great height, for we had a rare opportunity to compare it with Mt. Robson, which loomed up in another direction. The latter was about south by west from us and a little more than 30 miles distant, while the former, which lay northwest by north, was more than 60 miles away.

Even at this distance, which was fully double that to Mt. Robson, the big mountain, looming up supreme above everything nearby, seemed a worthy rival to the highest peak of all. It was a wonderfully clear day, and the sun gleaming on both mountains made them very beautiful indeed. Our enthusiasm was thoroughly aroused by this magnificent sight, and it was with regret that we descended the mountain and returned to camp, for we knew it would probably be more than two weeks before we should see our friend again. We continued on our course, swimming our horses over the Smoky River, which was at its highest stage of the year, then following it to the Muddy Water River. From the trail high up on the south side of the valley, on July 31, we again caught a glimpse of the big mountain, – a pleasant surprise, for it was entirely unexpected. It was but the shortest kind of a glimpse, because the trail, descending rapidly lost it immediately from view. This trail took us to the head of Sheep Creek. Although it was from the mountain opposite to the camp in this place that we first had seen this peak two years previously, we resisted the temptation to repeat the ascent, as it meant losing a day and days were precious now.

Leaving this camp, the scenery becomes extremely interesting. As we turned north, keeping just on the east side of the Continental Divide, we slowly ascended a pass, – the divide between the waters of Sheep Creek and the Kakwa River. The trail led through park-like groves of spruce, which gradually became fewer and fewer until only scattered clumps were left; these in turn were superseded by masses of stunted spruces, so characteristic of all summit country. We looked across the grassy alps to the actual pass itself a few miles beyond, – a bare, rocky ridge connecting the range which lay exactly on the Continental Divide with the range east of it. A bold, smooth-faced rock mountain, which we named Mt. Guardian, stood on our left, like a sentinel at the entrance of the pass. At its foot was an exquisite little lake, over half a mile long, of a beautiful emerald-green colour, which changed to a turquoise blue as we later looked back on it under a different light. It sparkled so brilliantly under the sun and its colours were so ever-changing that we called it "Rainbow Lake."

The ice began to appear on the higher basins beyond the top of the pass, which rapidly fell away to the valley below. These glaciers form the source of the south fork of the Kakwa River. This stream we followed for several miles, and then the trail once more entered the dense growth of spruce. All of a sudden the timber opened out and we found ourselves at the very edge of a steep descent, and to the complete surprise of those of us who had not been there before, at about 1000 feet below us lay a magnificent lake. The name of Surprise Lake was so appropriate that it was instantly christened. It is nearly four miles long and of a deep green in colour. At the southwestern end are bold mountains surmounted by snow and ice, while the other sides are surrounded by rock mountains whose lower slopes, heavily timbered with spruce contrasting with the cliffs and peaks above, make an ideal composition. In some ways it reminded me strongly of Emerald Lake near Field.

After descending an exceedingly steep trail nearly to the edge of the lake and then ascending through the tall spruces, – many of which had fallen and necessitated many detours and much chopping, – we emerged from the timber to an open grassy summit, the divide between the two forks of the Kakwa River. The meadows were covered with a luxuriant growth of flowers; but of all the varieties the mountain forget-me-not was the most fascinating, giving a tinge of blue to the slopes on which it grew in great abundance. Here another surprise awaited us, for as we approached the height of land, there arose ahead, over the grassy summit and not much over twelve miles away, the white, icy summit of the big mountain. A short distance below we camped, with just its top visible over the glacier on Thunder Mountain (Mt. Cross), another one of our friends from 1912. We climbed up on the slopes east of camp to a basin above to get some specimens of caribou, and from there obtained a fine view of the mountain. Another day, from higher up still, Mt. Robson was visible over sixty miles away. Seen from the Sulphur Hills on July 13 this mountain was twice as distant from us as Robson. Here the conditions were reversed, for Robson was now far away and the big mountain near at hand. This new chance for comparison, fully confirmed our belief in its great height. Camp was moved further down, to a little stream that connected the two lakes at the head of the north fork of the Kakwa River.

This series of lakes is extremely beautiful, and the region, being only a few miles from the group of high mountains, would surely become a rival to the country about Mt. Robson were it not for its inaccessibility. The upper lake of the three, small as it is and not particularly fine in colour, still is beautiful, for with the groups of spire-like spruces that line its shores and the towering form of Thunder Mountain (Mt. Cross) beyond, it composes as an impressive picture. We usually saw it when it was calm, with the reflection of the mountain in its surface, and so called it Lake Wapumun, which in Cree means "mirror." The lower lake, which is fully three miles long, is of a pretty turquoise blue, at least as viewed from above. A range composed of several different peaks rising rather abruptly from this body of water gives it an appearance of wild grandeur. Last, but by no means least, is Bear Lake, which lies hidden in a big basin in the deep timber surrounded on all sides but one by the mountains. This is one of the most ideal spots I have ever seen. Although it must be nearly a mile long, it so nestles down at the base of The Fortress that it appears much smaller. It is of the most exquisite emerald-green colour, and the contrasting formation of its shores adds greatly to its unique beauty. On one side the spruces grow to the water's edge, on another a big rock slide has forced its way into the lake, while at the further end is a green meadow dotted with clumps of spruces, behind which abruptly rise the cliffs of The Fortress several thousand feet above. We first saw this enchanting spot in 1912, discovering it by accident, and as far as we know no other white man has ever visited its shores.

The big mountain's location, as nearly as we could tell, was about ten miles west-northwest of the intersection of the 54th parallel of latitude with the 120th meridian. It is situated in British Columbia, not over ten miles from the Alberta boundary, and rises on the western side of the Continental Divide, so that its icefields all drain into the Pacific Ocean. Rising among the glaciers on the northeast slopes and flowing around the east and south sides, thus encircling the mountain for probably 180 degrees, we could distinguish a stream, which may flow into the Big Salmon River, a branch of the Fraser. Thus on this side the great massif was separated from the intervening ranges by a deep, narrow valley from which in places the cliffs of the outlying spurs rose sheer for 1000 to 2000 feet, their vastness adding greatly to the grandeur of the mountain. As for the north and west sides, we could tell nothing from here. Whether the mountain is in turn separated by a stream from the ranges beyond or whether it is connected with them we had no way of discovering. This view gave us a wonderful idea of the size and contour of the mountain. Above these vast cliffs and partly isolated buttresses is a magnificent series of glaciers, some of which are hanging. Then above this encircling mass of the upper glacier rises the main peak itself – its steep sides and slopes a mass of névé, while its eastern face was streaked here and there by the sliding snow. On the steep face of the peak was seen clinging a curious small glacier, the lower part of which had fallen away, leaving this mass of ice seemingly unsupported. The eastern face appears nearly sheer, but the northern and southern arêtes are not very steep until nearing the summit, when the angle increases greatly. There also seemed to be another arête, a very steep one, on the eastern side. The summit as viewed from this direction is a long, fairly level ice cornice which, viewed through the field glass, presented an irregular broken outline and under a bright sun was extremely fine. It is unquestionably narrow and doubtless slopes at a very steep angle on its western side. At all events it appeared extremely dangerous, and a traverse from one end to the other did not look very inviting. The highest point seemed to be at the northern end. But beautiful as this mountain is, from nowhere is it as striking as Mt. Robson seen from across Berg Lake.

We planned to stay here longer so as to make another trip nearer to the mountain, but as the following morning was rainy and every day valuable, we reluctantly broke camp and went down the Kakwa River. The following day we left all signs of trails behind and started on the strenuous part of our journey to the Peace River. In following up a small tributary of the main stream, after going through the dense growth for a long time, we came to an opening in the timber giving us a long vista to the west, and there to our surprise towered our mountain (now southwest from us) magnificent in the light of the afternoon sun. Though it was probably twelve miles away, we got an excellent idea of this side, which was pyramidal in shape. A nearer view would have been very impressive.

Two hours later, as we emerged from the green timber to the scattered spruces that led to an open summit above, we turned around to view our surroundings and found an even greater surprise. There, across a deep, narrow valley, towered above us not two miles away a steep-sided mountain, – a wonderfully striking peak, the top of which seemed so vertical as to be unscalable. It was in many ways a more impressive, certainly a more startling peak than the big mountain, though not so high. We estimated it was over 11,000 feet. Our camp was more than 6000, timberline here being much lower than further south on the other side of Wilcox Pass. That night we saw it by moonlight, and it was a sight I shall never forget. Its setting is extremely fine as it stands out by itself, well isolated from any other peak. On its western side, several thousand feet below the summit, is a large glacier whose melting ice cascades in innumerable little streams over the cliffs, disappearing into the deep valley below, – the water forming one of the head streams of the north fork of the Fraser River. This peak, which we afterwards found to be Mt. Ida, has a stream in the upland valley east of it which drains big icefields beyond, from which rise several interesting snow mountains. One of these, which is probably over 10,000 feet high, we named "Mt. Koona," the Cree word for "snow." It may also be seen towering above The Fortress from south of Lake Kakwa. Just beyond the glacier west of Mt. Ida is a range of three peaks which bear much snow and ice. All day, as well as all night, ice fell from these glaciers to the rocks below in the most terrific avalanches I have ever heard, but unfortunately they were hidden from our view.

The next morning was a fine, clear August day (it was the 12th of the month) and we climbed a mountain east of camp, for we assumed that from a point sufficiently far along on the ridge our big mountain would open out from behind Mt. Ida. In this we were not deceived, for as we continued along on the arête at about 2000 feet above camp, the big white summit slowly appeared. For more than two hours we looked at this wonderful view examining every peak in sight, as well as every visible aspect of the two important mountains. West of us were some large snow-fields with glaciers innumerable, for this region of ice extended for many miles to the northwest.

To return to the two big peaks, both will prove difficult to climb, the higher one because of its extremely steep and dangerous ice slopes and the ice cornice at the summit. Mt. Ida will be, I think, even more difficult. Indeed it appears to be unscalable from all sides, except the southwestern arête. To reach a point within 500 feet of the top may not be too difficult; but, once here, great trouble will be experienced in reaching the actual summit. The final peak is in the shape of an elongated drum set on end, some 300 to 400 feet in height, on top of which is an icy cone dangerously steep on all sides. At the upper end of the southwestern arête is a rocky knob which is connected with the base of the drum by a narrow, steep-sided ice slope. The gap between the knob and the base of the drum is filled with the accumulating snows, which it might be dangerous to cross. Once over this, there is still the perpendicular cliff and the steep icy cone. Undoubtedly it will prove an interesting climb as well as a dangerous one – fit only for a skilled mountaineer.

Now as for the height of the big mountain, our estimate was 12,500 feet based on the elevations of our camps as well as of the various ridges from which we viewed it. In all cases it appeared a giant peak and we felt safe in placing its height at this figure. Later on in our trip we found a man who informed us that he knew of trappers who had been on the upper waters of the north fork of the Fraser River and had spoken of an enormous mountain near the Continental Divide, – apparently this same one. On returning to Edmonton at the end of November at the conclusion of our trip I also met Mr. R.W. Jones, who had spent four years surveying for possible passes for the Grand Trunk Railway extension to the Pacific coast. He had seen the mountain on one of his survey trips about ten years before and had made frequent use of it in his work. We asked his opinion of its height. His reply was that, as he was looking for low passes and not high mountains, he did not triangulate it, much as it had interested him; but on his map he had marked it 12,000 feet, which figure he considered extremely conservative. Previous to his trip, a man named E.W. Jarvis crossed from these waters of the Fraser to the Kakwa River, going through the valley from which we first saw our second high mountain. It was he that had named it Mt. Ida, and Mr. Jones who named the divide between these two watersheds Jarvis Pass. Undoubtedly the big mountain has been known to the Indians who in the past have hunted and trapped in this region but who now seldom penetrate this far from the outskirts of the advancing civilization. But Jones, previous to us, was probably the first white man to see it at such close range. In the absence of any name we called it "Mt. Sir Alexander" after that intrepid explorer Sir Alexander Mackenzie, who was the first white man to cross the Rocky Mountains.

I am sorry that because of previously laid plans we were unable to explore this region more thoroughly, and that I can not give more definite information as to the most likely side from which to make the ascent. Probably the approach from the northeast will prove the most practicable, at least the best side from which to reach the icefields below the main peak, which can itself best be scaled either from the northern or southern arête. Unfortunately it will be impossible for me to return to that region again, in the near future at least, but I hope someone will be sufficiently interested to make a serious attempt on both of these mountains. The only drawback is their comparative inaccessibility, for it takes over two weeks of steady travelling to reach their bases from Jasper. But good trails, with only occasional fallen timber, lead to the lakes at the head of the Kakwa River, and camp can be made at the very base of Mt. Sir Alexander. To recapitulate: the route we followed was to Grand Cache on the Smoky River, by the well-known trail which the half-breeds and Indians still use. There, the only difficulty is having to swim the river, but, if every care and precaution is used, it can be done safely. Once across, the trail leads upstream a few miles, then up the Muddy Water River and over a divide to Sheep Creek, then up that to its head and over the pass to the waters of the Kakwa River. So far as I know, our party is the only one of white men to go in by this way, which I consider the only practicable route, certainly the only one by which the base of the mountains is accessible with pack animals.

The following night after leaving the camp near Mt. Ida, which we always referred to for the sake of convenience as the "Matterhorn Camp," we came to a stream, – the north branch of the Kakwa River. We could not have been more than a very few miles from its source, yet it was quite a powerful torrent and, judging from its colour, was glacier fed. Undoubtedly it drains the eastern side of the icefields we saw north of Mt. Sir Alexander and west of our previous camp, and the volume of water testified to the immense size of these glaciers. This convinced us that the névé must be on the Continental Divide, though we previously had thought it was on the west slope.

As our hunting for sheep and caribou kept us skirting the ranges a short distance east of the Divide, our knowledge of the mountains along it was derived entirely from what we saw during our climbing at these times. But, as we continually had fine, clear weather, the opportunities were excellent for extended views in all directions. Often we could look seventy-five to a hundred miles in every direction: far east beyond the foothills into the prairies; west across the Divide to range upon range of mountains beyond the western slope; south to the high region now familiar to us; and north and northwest, where the mountains, though carrying some snow and ice, were much lower. North of Mt. Sir Alexander the big glacier area recently mentioned seemed to extend for fully 20 miles, and from it rose several beautiful and interesting snow peaks, one in particular that repeatedly aroused our interest was in the form of a large dome. Its smooth, white summit gleaming in the sunlight made it the most conspicuous mountain of all in that region. From here as well as from our climbs near the big mountain, we got some fine views of the Cariboo range west of us in British Columbia. No one has yet penetrated their inhospitable valleys, though the height and beauty of their peaks fully justify an expedition. One mountain composed of several peaks seemed to tower above everything else and always attracted our attention.

At the head of the Wapiti River, which apparently has four branches, the mountains fell away rapidly. The southern branch seemed to rise at the end of the big icefield, and the mountains there probably were the northernmost peaks of that high section. For a distance along the heads of the other branches the country seemed lower. Some distance below the source of the north middle branch is a lake fully two miles wide and four miles long. It is set among the rocky peaks and on two sides high cliffs rise boldly from its waters. The colour was very unusual for a mountain lake, being a deep sapphire blue, – a vivid contrast to the dark green of the spruces that lined its shores. Altogether it was extremely effective and the composition was very different from anything we saw during the summer. Its colour suggested the name and we called it "Sapphire Lake."

Further along we came to the head of the east branch of the Murray River, at the upper end of which are two small lakes. Judging from the snow mountains to the southwest and the colour of the stream, as well as its size, for it was the largest since leaving the Smoky River, it undoubtedly drains extensive icefields. Only a few miles below, another good-sized fork came in. The valley was low, not more than 2500 feet above sea level, yet we were not far from the Continental Divide. There were no mountains of any size west or northwest. Beyond, the two largest are Hunter's Peak, lying near the head of the south fork of the Pine, and Canoe Mountain, further northwest at the source of the west branch. Though these are on or near the main watershed and are the most prominent and conspicuous peaks for miles around, they only rise to a height of about 6500 feet. The altitude of the so-called Pine Pass, on the Divide at the head of the west fork, is only slightly over 2800 feet. Between here and the Peace River the mountains become lower and there are none of any consequence, although Mt. Selwyn, close to where that river forces its way through the main chain of the Rockies, rises to a height of about 6200 feet. Consequently, north of the area of the large icefield beyond Mt. Sir Alexander there is nothing of interest to the alpinist.

On our way down the Murray River, what interested us most were some beautiful falls which we came upon very unexpectedly. A loud roar fell on our ears and in a few minutes we saw the river cascading ahead of us. Soon we came to a rocky point from which we looked down on the falls and to a big pool below; but from this outlook we had no idea of their beauty. An hour later, as we emerged from the timber at the edge of the river a short way further on, their full beauty was before us and we gazed on an impressive picture. The total drop was about two hundred and fifty feet, but not sheer. The entire stream cascading over the cliffs, the whole effect was much more varied and interesting. The contrast of the clouds of spray that rose and fell and of the white foam with the black cliffs along the sides of the gorge was very beautiful. That night we camped at their base and went to sleep with the roar of the water in our ears. As the pools in the river were full of Dolly Varden trout, on which in the absence of anything else we had subsisted entirely for more than two weeks, we appropriately named these falls the Kinuseo Falls, from the Cree for "fish."

Trouble after trouble in the endless maze of down timber hindered our progress from here on, but finally we reached the Peace River and the trading post of Hudson Hope, where we obtained supplies for the return trip. It was not until late in November that we arrived at Jasper, where our trip had begun in June.

Appendix D

Editor, *Outdoor Life*:

I have been reading with much interest the articles by Major Townsend Whelen and Mr. Frank Conger Baldwin on their hunting; trips west of the Smoky River in Alberta. and with even more interest still the comment and criticisms of Mr. Val A. Fynn, Mr. J.A. McGuire and Mr. Donald Phillips.

My interest lies in the fact that I spent a large part of the summers and autumns of 1912, 1913 and 1914 in that region, – my last and longest trip covering the entire distance from Jasper to Hudson's Hope on the Peace following close to the Continental Divide a large part of the way. This trip took five months. To the best of my knowledge my trip of 1912, lasting nearly three full months, was the first trip west of the Smoky made by a white man primarily for hunting mountain game. Naturally I have no definite proof of this but I believe it to be so. Anyone who has spent a large amount of time on the trail in the mountains knows very well that there are very few spots left that have not been visited by trappers or prospectors. These are what one might call the silent records which seldom come to the notice of sportsmen. All through our trips we saw signs in isolated places testifying to this fact, as I will explain further on.

In order to back up Mr. Fynn in not allowing sportsmen and others to get a false impression as to the virginity of this country I will give the names of men who I know personally to have been north and west of the Smoky and the approximate dates of their trips. No doubt there are many more of which I do not happen to know.

One of the two men who accompanied me in 1912, named Beau Gaetz, after the Klondike rush of 1898 attempted with several other prospectors to reach that country via Grande Prairie and the Wapiti River. Needless to say, they failed, owing to the impossibility of such a trip and, after eighteen months and spending two winters on the Wapiti River (the largest northern branch of the Smoky), during which time they all got scurvy and lost most of their horses, they returned home.

Mr. R.W. Jones of Edmonton spent four years (I imagine he referred to summer seasons) surveying for possible passes for the Grand Trunk Railway for its Pacific coast extension. As I remember, this was between 1900 and 1905. He had therefore used, and doubtless had made, many of the trails up the tributaries of the Smoky, which we saw and which will be explained later. He told me that he had done much surveying around the Porcupine Lakes and had used Mt. Sir Alexander Mackenzie in his work, owing to its height.

Previous to his first trip, a man named Jarvis had crossed from the Fraser waters to the Porcupine River by the valley which runs east and west on the north side of the slopes of Mt. Ida, Mt. Koona and the Three Sisters. This valley, – a deep canyon-like affair – Mr. Jones named Jarvis pass. Mr. Jarvis gave the name to Mt. Ida, which is one of the most beautiful peaks (as well as difficult to climb judging from appearances) I have ever seen.

In 1907 Prof. A.P. Coleman of Toronto, his brother and the Rev. George Kinney made a trip from Laggan via Wilcox Pass to the headwaters of the Smoky in an attempt to climb, but without success. Again in 1908 they went into that region, this time starting from Edmonton. Once more they failed to reach the summit of Mt. Robson. These two were notable trips and well known to the mountaineering world.

Finally, a third trip in 1909, made via the latter route by Mr. Kinney and Donald Phillips, resulted, after many severe hardships and dangers, in the conquest of the highest peak in the Canadian Rockies.

That same year, and also in 1910 and 1911, Prof. J. Norman Collie, Mr. A.L. Mumm, Mr. Amery and Mr. Hastings, members of the Alpine Club (London), made long expeditions into the country west of the Smoky, doing a lot of pioneer mountaineering work, recording a number of first ascents of difficult peaks. Accounts of all these trips from 1907 to 1911 have been written and published.

I outfitted with Fred Brewster, the pioneer guide in that region. He was a graduate of a college in eastern Canada, having taken an engineering course. But his love for the mountains caused him to take up the outfitting business, especially as he saw the future prospect in Jasper Park. In 1912, the year of my first trip, he was located at Hinton (now called Entrance) which was then at the "end of the steel." At that time he was the only outfitter in that country. The next two years I went with him from Jasper, where he is still located outfitting more hunting, tourist and government surveying parties than anyone else. He has now been in that country since 1912, except from March 1915 to July 1919 when he saw active line service at the front, being continuously in the Ypres sector for three and a half years, having an enviable war record, being twice decorated and twice promoted. To him I owe the success of my three trips, which were made in what was then much more "virgin" country than it is today, although we did not then call it such.

To give my three trips, they were as follows: in 1912 we started the first week of August, returning the end of October. Leaving Hinton, we followed the trail up Solomon Creek, the Hay River, to Rock Lake, referred to in the recent articles by Major Whelen and Mr. Baldwin. Then up the Stony River and over a high pass we came to the Smoky near Thin Tree Lake, where we forded this river.

Our objective for this trip was to get as far beyond the Smoky as possible, as we wanted specimens of sheep well in that country in order to determine the species that ranged between the Athabasca River on the south and the Peace River on the north. As sportsmen then knew, *Ovis canadensis* ranged south of this region and *Ovis stonei* was found north of the Peace. No specimens had ever been brought out from the intervening country of over two hundred miles north and south. As no one knew whether one or the other of these species ranged here or whether by interbreeding a new species existed, the problem to be solved was an interesting one. Particularly so as this region was almost the only one in Canada at that time where the existing species of sheep was undetermined.

On the west side of the Smoky we found no trail so we struggled in a mess of down timber and muskeg, backwaters from beaver dams, and a heavily swollen river, – in fact we encountered every possible obstruction. During this stretch of not over 25 miles (which consumed over two weeks of continuous travel and trail cutting until we reached the Muddy Water River) we saw neither trail nor evidence of man except for what looked like cutting by a trapper at the mouth of the Jack Pine River. Major Whelen could more correctly have termed that "virgin" country at that time. I understand that today there is a trail down the Smoky on the west side, so I presume someone in later years followed in our footsteps and opened up our old trail. At the Muddy we followed the old Hudson's Bay Co. trail, the same one Major Whelen followed and which the Indians go over every year getting into their hunting country around Sheep Creek. In fact we found Indians camped in here. It was then a well-worn trail all the way to the Porcupine Lakes, needing only some cutting here and there from windfalls.

We hunted the head of Sheep Creek, the Muddy Water and Jack Pine rivers and later spent two weeks on the lakes at the head of the Porcupine River in the vicinity of Mt. Sir Alexander Mackenzie. Then we went home going down the Porcupine River over a pass to the Smoky and home through the foothills and the Grande Cache trail, travelling the last week in nearly two feet of snow and with supplies entirely exhausted.

In 1913 we spent our time near the headwaters of the Smoky around Mt. Robson and down close to Mt. Bess, crossing the Smoky there and returning to Jasper. Owing to an operation, I was unable to take a difficult trip, so the next two months I contented myself with a trip from Jasper to Laggan via Wilcox Pass, doing some easy sheep hunting around Brazeau Lake. On our return in November we took our outfit of horses in to Fortress Lake after caribou but the snow piled up to a depth of two feet, which made the hunting as impossible for us (being without snowshoes) as grazing was for our cayuses.

The last trip, which was made in 1914, we started in June and returned in November, going all the way from Jasper to Hudson's Hope on the Peace River. A large part of the way north was made close to the Continental Divide and the high mountains. On our return we came over good trails via Grande Prairie and the lower country owing to the lateness of the season. The trip was primarily for hunting, and although it was my personal trip, it was made in the interests of the Biological Survey of the Department of Agriculture in Washington. We brought them such specimens of skins, ranging in size from mice to caribou, as we were able to collect. Our detailed report relative to the mammals and birds found in that region is on file at Washington. We also made a map of the region lying between the Yellowhead Pass and the Peace River, copies of which have been on file at Washington and Ottawa with the Geographical Survey of the Department of the Interior for the last ten years. I will gladly send copies of these to anyone interested in the region. Naturally the maps were not very accurate, as we had neither the time nor the proper facilities for making them. My article entitled "The Canadian Rockies between the Yellowhead Pass and the Peace River" in *Appalachia* vol. XIII, no. 3, for June 1915, might be of interest to those who are contemplating a trip into that region, as its illustrations and descriptions give a good idea of the country.

My outfit consisted of five men (including Fred Brewster and myself), twenty horses and supplies (excepting meat of course) that would last with care nearly four months. Of course we were our own guides and had to lay out our own route, as no one could tell us of the country we were to traverse. Naturally we were familiar with the country up to the Porcupine Lakes but from there on to the Peace River we had to depend on our own resources.

Had we known what difficulties lay ahead for us I doubt if we would have attempted the trip, for after leaving the Porcupine Lakes we spent two months of steady travelling, cutting our way for the most part through a jumble of fallen timber, making actually in distance not over a hundred miles in a straight line. Here we had only snatches of game trails to help us but these often caused more trouble than help by misleading us. But here let me state that at the heads of several of the branches of the Smoky (in particular the Wapiti) we saw signs of old travel, either in the nature of very old cutting or of faint trails. This was because white men and Indians, particularly the latter, had hunted, trapped and prospected up these streams. But as they had come from the prairie country to the east, they reached this region by ascending a stream to its head in the mountains, and either returning the same way or crossing a high pass to another nearby tributary and then descending to their starting point. Anyone knowing these Indians realizes that they stick close to well-known trails and do not wander off much into country unknown to them. They have pretty well-defined routes of travel which they take on their annual hunting trips. These snatches of trails we encountered, therefore, ran in an easterly or northeasterly direction, but as our route lay roughly northwest, they were of no use to us. In most cases they had not been used for years and in no places did we see tepee poles or any old camp sites. In recent years the fallen timber resulting from forest fires was probably the cause of this cessation of travel.

Opposite page 247 in the issue of *Appalachia* in which my article above referred to appears, the reader will see at the top a picture of our Mt. Guardian, which the major called Mt. Pippins, not realizing it had been named twelve years ago and was already on the maps. The same may be said of his Greenwater Lake, which Mr. Fynn refers to as Surprise Lake, showing he had seen our maps or our article and knew it had been named years before. Incidentally, a rereading of the major's Part III in the February *Outdoor Life*, page 92, will show why we named it Surprise Lake. In fact, his description is perfect and serves as a most fitting introduction to our name. Our feelings were identical with his and I find in my diary a similar description of that scene.

We went through a great deal of beautiful scenery all the way from Sheep Creek to the Pine River. At the heads of the various branches of the Wapiti we found many beautiful lakes but the finest of all was Sapphire Lake, near the head of the Callohoo River, one of the largest branches. As for Kinuseo Falls on the Pine River, which are over two hundred feet high, they proved to be scenically finer than anything we saw after leaving Mt. Sir Alexander Mackenzie.

Major Whelen briefly mentions Miss Jobe's short, hurried trip of 1914 to the above mountain, to which the Geographic Board of Canada officially gave our name of Mt. Sir Alexander Mackenzie. He erroneously says "which has since been called Mt. Sir Alexander." Miss Jobe in her ignorance did not know it was already named and that we had located it and camped in its vicinity on three trips previous to hers. The major then says (in Part I of his story) "this in brief is the history of the Country so far as it was known when I entered it." The falsity of his statement is only too apparent.

I have endeavored to show what a false impression sportsmen have been given of this country by the major's article, for if the reader will recapitulate he will see that I have mentioned fifteen different important trips made by white men into the heart of the mountains west and north of the Smoky River for surveying, climbing, hunting and prospecting previous to Miss Jobe's short trip of 1914.

As it happened, only once did two of these trips occur in the same year (1909). In fact, from 1899 up to and including our last trip of 1914 only two seasons went by when the familiar sound of a white man's axe was not heard echoing in the mountains as he cut out his trail.

This country, marvellous as it is for its beautiful scenery and its wonderful hunting, could not even have been called "virgin" country when we first entered it twelve years ago. Prospectors, surveyors, trappers and even hunters do a lot of work and cover an extensive amount of mountainous and almost impenetrable country, undertaking the greatest of hazards and risks and encountering all kinds of hardships and dangers entirely unknown to the general public. To find truly "virgin" country today is virtually impossible.

THE BEAVER
MAGAZINE OF THE NORTH
"THE GREAT MOUNTAIN"
PART 1
SUMMER 1957
BY S. PRESCOTT FAY
WITH BRADFORD ANGIER

The mountain rose high above a vast region of snow and glaciers, presenting a beautiful sight as its ice-covered summit glistened in the clear September sunlight. There was no way of judging its height from where I was, sheep-hunting some 30 miles to the southeast. I only knew we had found a giant mountain, a mountain we felt convinced would prove to be one of the highest peaks of the Canadian Rockies.

As it turned out, we saw it no more that year, for after we had moved over the intervening passes and camped beyond them, it snowed and stormed continually for nearly two weeks, hiding all the mountains from us. When we finally managed to get back out to Hinton with our horses, our food supply entirely exhausted, it was the end of October.

Unsuccessful as our trip had been we had roughly located this new high mountain and, in spite of the bad weather, had been able to appreciate the beauty of the surrounding country which, with its fascinating lakes, charming valleys and lofty peaks, so delighted us that we made up our minds to return to explore it further at the first available opportunity. Although I was back at Jasper the next year, I was unable to take a long trip, so contented myself until nearly Christmas with several shorter ones in which we covered nearly all the country from Mt. Robson and the upper Smoky to Laggan on the Canadian Pacific Railway.

However, the latter part of June the following year, 1914, saw us once more under way, this time with an outfit of twenty horses, food for four months, and the added intention of investigating all the mountains along the eastern slope of the Continental Divide between Yellowhead Pass and the Peace River. We also bore authorizations from Alberta and British Columbia authorities to hunt and collect for the Biological Survey of the Department of Agriculture at Washington. Our party consisted of Charles R. Cross, Jr., a Boston friend and neighbour of mine, together with Fred Brewster of Jasper and two other men, making five in all, a good practical number for a long, difficult trip.

Although summer was at its height, I had arrived at Jasper in a howling snowstorm, so that the appearance of the mountains was scarcely unlike that of December last when I had left for the east. The skies soon cleared and the weather became very hot, so that the melting of the fresh snows turned already swollen rivers into roaring torrents, making them higher than they had been for years.

Our horses were a picked lot, fat and in good condition, but, not having been used since the previous fall, were rather wild. One mare had never before been packed, and she caused an endless amount of trouble even to the end of the trip. It was slow work inducing her to stand quietly, and at first it was necessary to blindfold her. Even then she would often buck and tear about, shaking off the packs if they were not securely tied on.

Another mare caused us almost as much annoyance in a different way. She always stood docilely while her packs were lashed on. Then, perhaps not until all the other horses were loaded and we were under way, she would start her exhibition, which was never anything but an exasperating performance, for it was impossible to do anything but watch until she had finished. This she invariably did either by breaking the cinch or by loosening the load, with the end result that packs, ropes and gear would be strewn over the landscape. Finally, we discovered that the trouble lay in her cinch being so far back that it worried her into a nervous state. This difficulty was easily enough remedied, and she made no more trouble in that direction.

And so we got used to our horses, one by one, and began to understand them as if they'd been human beings, for they were all different and some of them real characters. Later if there was any disturbance in the line behind, it was often possible to tell which cayuse was the cause of it without turning around to see.

We started up the Snake Indian River, then the Stony, away from the Athabasca Valley and the Grand Trunk Railway. That day – June 28, 1914 – we said good-bye to the sound of engine whistles echoing along the valleys. It was five months later before a similar sound broke the stillness and reminded us that we had returned once more to civilization.

The second night in camp we had been regretting the coming of the railroad, with its old construction camps and stables left about the river flats disfiguring the landscape, when we discovered outside one of these an immense quantity of enormous field mushrooms. In a few minutes we had filled two large copper pots and for several meals feasted on delicious, juicy, fried mushrooms. I think this in a way compensated, temporarily at least, for the injury to the landscape.

As we followed the old Indian trail up the Snake Indian River over a high ridge, we looked back for a last view. To the eastward rose the rectangular cliff of Roche Miette, located just inside the present Jasper National Park gate, one of the most notable landmarks along the old Yellowhead route made famous in the 1800s by the traders and explorers of the Hudson's Bay Company. Beyond this guardian of the Athabasca Valley were the lower peaks of the outside ranges. In the other direction was a prettier sight, for the fresh snows had given a touch to the higher mountains that was very refreshing indeed under the hot June sun. Pyramid Mountain towered above its surroundings in a beautiful, sharp peak, a far more impressive sight than the view of it as seen from Jasper.

The sun, however, did not last long, for the clouds quickly rolled up – stormy-looking ones, too – and in a few minutes the wind began to howl and whistle through the standing dead timber. Then it began to hail, and big stones driven by this furious blast stung both men and horses. The latter liked it the least and turned tail into the wind, so it was with great difficulty that we forced them to move on. Now and then a tree crashed to the ground with a loud report, reminding one that travelling through standing burnt timber is not always the safest place during a heavy blow.

We were directly in the center of the storm, and the vivid flashes of the lightning accompanied simultaneously by deafening peals of thunder were none too pleasant, threatening as they did to stampede the horses any minute. However, it soon cleared, and the sun speedily dried out our clothes and warmed us up. The effect of its rays was certainly beneficial, for during this brief storm the temperature had dropped rapidly and it had turned bitterly cold.

That night we had an interesting time and for reasons which will soon be seen we always referred to it as the menagerie camp. No sooner had we put up our tipi on a little grassy flat along the Snake Indian River than literally dozens of varying hares (snowshoe rabbits) began hopping all about. One man dropped his buckskin gloves while working on a wet knot. Not long afterward, only the metal buttons remained. Still, these hares were merely an incident.

About supper time we heard a squeal, and looking across the stream saw on the opposite bank, not two hundred yards away, a she grizzly bear and two cubs just disappearing into the thick bushes. Apparently the mother had struck one of her youngsters over the head which had caused it to give vent to its feelings.

When the excitement of this had worn off, I wandered up the river not more than two hundred yards and stood gazing at the almost perpendicular cliff of slate at the foot of which the river flowed. As this country has many outcropping coal seams, I was intently examining this formation when before my eyes, harmonizing in colour with the background, materialized two sheep, a ewe and a yearling, busily licking the face of the rock. As I moved away to tell the men, the sheep saw me and started slowly to ascend the almost sheer cliff. As one of our objects was to procure specimens of sheep, all this was of special interest to us.

Then as we stood and watched the bighorns climb slowly upward, there on the upper edge of the cliff appeared a goat. Both he and the sheep were moth-eaten specimens, as they were in the midst of shedding their winter coats and large pieces of hair and wool hung on their flanks ready to be pulled off by the bushes. To say the least, they were far from being attractive-looking individuals. This certainly was an interesting moment, for the goat evidently was headed for the same lick from which the sheep were returning.

However, he stopped on the upper ledge and stood looking down at the sheep, who continued ascending until they were on the same level. Then the question was, who would give way to the other! There they stood, eyeing each other, while we momentarily expected some sort of a fight might ensue. Neither seemed to like the looks of the other. Finally the sheep backed off about 30 or 40 yards and gave the goat a chance to go below to the lick, which he proceeded to do unmolested.

Nothing more was seen of the bears. It was a great chance for her to have killed a sheep, and unless it was because of our scent we could not understand why they never reappeared. Some say that sheep and goat are never seen on the same mountain, but this is not true. Although their ranges are separate, as the types of mountains each inhabit are so distinctive as to be readily discernible, both sometimes do range over the same country and cases of this kind are not rare. Because of their keeping apart, they are apt to have separate licks as well, but in this case the goat and sheep mountains were almost part of the same range so this incident was easily accounted for. To have seen grizzly bears as well as goat and sheep all within three hundred yards of one another, and at precisely the same time, was extremely unusual.

The first few days of our trip being through the lower valleys, the pre-dominating trees were poplar and balm of Gilead, with some spruce and pine; but as a little higher country was reached, the latter two trees became more and more numerous until finally the poplar and balm of Gilead were no longer seen. For some time we travelled along good trails formerly used by the Cree Indians on their hunting trips, at times crossing big open flats covered with long grass still brown, for the spring snows had only just gone. These stretches would be succeeded by beautiful parklike groves of Jack pine. It was ideal travelling, and as the warm sun brought out the perfume of the flowers that grew everywhere in abundance, while the fragrance of the balm of Gilead filled the air and the birds flew about singing, it seemed that nothing could be more perfect.

One thing only spoiled the effect. The mosquitoes swarmed at times, especially toward sunset, and for the first part of the trip before the nights became sufficiently cold they were terrible. The air was so full of them that it was a source of wonder how it contained them all at once. Our head nets helped us to sleep, but the incessant hum nearly drove us frantic. However, they were not with us continuously, and sometimes for several consecutive nights we were free from the miserable pests.

Since the menagerie camp we had seen goat and sheep several times, but we continued for ten days further through unfamiliar country. After a mis-erable long day on the trail, through endless muskeg, in a driving rain we made camp among the wet spruces, a forlorn looking place at the time. But when the weather cleared that afternoon it proved to be an ideal spot, and later on we often looked back on it as one of the snuggest camps of the whole trip. It was fascinating to be back among the sheep hills once more, especially as, although it was during the closed season, we had special per-mits to collect for what is now the U.S. Fish & Wildlife Service, much of this country being – as the Geographic Board of Canada expressed it in a letter to me – "a large blank on our maps."

Seldom have I enjoyed anything more than the following few days. When we left camp in the early morning for the day's hunt, the hermit thrushes were singing in the big spruces, and as we reached timberline the simple little notes of the golden crowned sparrows greeted us. Flowers of endless kinds carpeted the hillsides, but of all the different varieties we saw that day or in fact during the whole trip, none seemed quite as fascinating as the dainty little mountain forget-me-not. It grew everywhere above timberline and seemed to flourish among the rocks as well as in the grass. The remem-brance of climbing over those grassy hills, the slopes of which were blue with these little flowers, while the notes of the golden-crowned sparrows filled the air – that remembrance will never fade.

A few days later we again hunted, for a ewe this time, as we now had fine specimen rams. As we reached the summit of one of the typical sheep mountains on the Sulphur River, a sight greeted us that caused considerable excitement and speculation. From our elevation of about 8000 feet we had a magnificent extended panoramic view of the mountains for miles and miles around. About thirty miles away south by west (compass direction) rose the superb head of Mt. Robson shimmering in the morning sunlight.

Looking further around, we saw more than sixty miles off in a direction northwest by north another tremendous mountain, immediately recognized as our big peak which I'd first seen in September 1912. Even at this great distance, double that to Mt. Robson, our mountain seemed to suffer nothing by comparison, which justified our former belief in its great height.

Realizing the length of the trip ahead, we thought it inadvisable to hunt for a ewe, deeming it wiser to trust that we'd be lucky enough to get one as we went along. So down the Sulphur River we went on our way to the Smoky, bagging our museum ewe from the canyon of the Sulphur, as it happened. On July 27 we swam the horses across the Smoky, up which we headed.

So far, nearly all of the way had been through country unfamiliar to us, but now we came to the trail on which I had been in 1912, and so for several days we passed by mountains and through valleys that seemed like old friends, with our old camps serving as landmarks. On July 31, from the trail high above the Muddy Water River, we caught a glimpse of our big mountain to the northwest. It was only momentary, however, for a sudden, rapid descent hid the snow peak behind the nearer ranges.

From here on, the scenery becomes very beautiful indeed, and each day its attractiveness increases until, finally, the climax of high, rugged mountains of snow and ice and beautiful lakes of ever-changing colours is reached. This spot is the region I will dwell on, for to my mind it rivals some of the finest scenic points in the Canadian Rockies.

The summit at the head of Sheep Creek, which creek provides a low pass of about 5000 feet over the Continental Divide to the waters of the Fraser River on the British Columbia side, we reached through country that became more and more open until finally we emerged from park-like groves of spruce onto a big expanse of open meadows miles in length. These extended all the way across the valley bottom, which was more than half a mile in width, and here, as on the slopes of the mountains, flowers of endless variety grew in abundance. We camped in an open grove, finding as the only intruders since we had been here two years before an Indian hunting party of the previous summer.

Our site was an ideal one, for the valley which ran east and west commanded an extensive view of open meadowland backed by rugged rock mountains of moderate height. It was not wonderful or even highly impressive, but it was distinctly an ideally lovely spot, for the composition was nearly perfect. The sun at this time of year did not set until late, and after supper we sat about the campfire listening to the simple tuneful notes of the sparrows which were occasionally interrupted by the chuckling call of a willow ptarmigan flying past on set wings. The bright rays of the late afternoon sun, followed by the afterglow, made a setting which long remained in our memory.

From the mountains opposite this camp we first saw the big mountain in September 1912, but as we were now sure of its general location it seemed inadvisable to waste a day in order to get just another view of it, for days were precious now.

PART 2

AUTUMN 1957

During the two years it took me to return I only knew that we had found a giant mountain, a new high peak I felt convinced would prove to be one of the highest in the Canadian Rockies. Now I was back with Charles R. Cross Jr., a Boston friend and neighbour, together with Fred Brewster of Jasper and two other men, making five in all; a good practical number for a long, difficult trip. We camped 2nd August 1914 at the same site where, from the heights opposite, I'd first spied in 1912 the lofty new mountain that still drew me onward.

The following morning we continued on our way as usual, going over a high pass of about 7500 feet that led north. The upland meadows, sparsely covered with the stunted balsam and spruces, were bright with flowers, the little mountain forget-me-not predominating. As we reached the top of the rocky pass, the view behind opened out to the south for many miles.

All the higher mountains at the head of Jack Pine River appeared one by one, and we thought we could distinguish Mt. Bess far away. On two sides the mountains rose nearly sheer for several thousand feet, shutting in the pass, while on our left was a rugged, smooth-faced rock wall at whose base was an exquisite little lake. Its colour, which changed with the light, was, as we first approached, an emerald green; then, as we looked back, it had changed to a delicate turquoise blue. It looked like a gem in its wild setting of rugged mountains.

At the top of the pass we halted to watch a goat as he laboriously worked his way along the other side. He showed an unusual amount of alarm, for goats as a rule do not exhibit such fear at the distance of half a mile which separated us. The snow through which he was ploughing was deep and the going heavy, so that he became winded and his tongue hung out of his wide-open mouth like a dog's. After making frequent stops to get his wind, he finally reached the rock wall and in the next few minutes gave a remarkable exhibition of climbing.

The sheer walls gave him considerable difficulty, and once, as he reached far up with his front feet in order to pull himself to the ledge above, he slipped and fell over backwards. We instantly thought he would be dashed to pieces on the rocks below, but in falling he turned in the air like a cat and dropped nimbly on all four feet on a narrow, jutting rock below. It was an astonishing sight, and we could hardly believe our eyes. However, even those of us who were not watching him with glasses saw it as plainly as those with the binoculars.

As we crossed the divide between these two forks of the then Porcupine River – whose name at my suggestion was later changed to Kakwa River, now used on the maps – there arose before us over the grassy summit this same day the snow crest of our big mountain not over 20 miles away. Luck was with us, for at every possible viewpoint we had clear weather, so these unexpected glimpses were pleasant surprises. A few miles below we camped, and from our tipi the upper part of the peak and the ice cornice were just visible above the glacier on Thunder Mountain, later named Mt. Cross, for my friend who accompanied me. Through an error this was later changed to Mt. Wishaw.

Camp was moved again, to the lower of the three lakes at the head of the Kakwa River. Here we had been two years before. But at that time, because of the continued stormy weather, no one had realized that we had been within ten miles of the big peak. Not a person had intruded during the interval, not even Indians, and everything was unchanged, even to the tipi poles that still rested against the spruce trees as we had left them.

This series of lakes is extremely beautiful, and being only a few miles from this group of high mountains, needed, I realized, only accessibility to make it a rival to the country around Mt. Robson and other such places. The upper lake of these three, small as it is, though not particularly well coloured, is still beautiful, for the composition it forms with the groups of spire-like spruce that line its shores, and the towering form of Mt. Cross beyond, makes the whole an impressive picture. We usually saw it when it was calm, with the reflection of Mt. Cross on its surface. and so called it Lake Wapumun, which in Cree means "mirror." This name was later officially accepted.

The lower lake, which is fully three miles long, is of a pretty turquoise blue, though the colour cannot be appreciated unless one climbs the nearby mountains and views it from above. A range rising rather abruptly from this body of water gives it an appearance of wild grandeur.

Last but by no means least is Bear Lake, which lies hidden in a big basin in the deep timber, surrounded on all sides but one by the mountains. This is one of the most perfect spots I have ever seen. Although it must be nearly a mile long, it so nestles down at the base of a mountain called the Fortress that it appears smaller than its actual size. It is of the most exquisite emerald-green colour, and the contrasting formation of its shores adds greatly to its unique beauty. On one side the spruce grow to the water's edge, on another a big rock slide forms the shores, while at the farther end is a green meadow dotted with clumps of spruces, behind which the cliffs of the Fortress abruptly lift. We first saw this enchanting spot in 1912, discovering it by accident, and as far as we knew two years later no other white man had ever visited its shores. We were so delighted with it that I took especial pains to revisit it. Seen under a warm sun on a bright, calm day, with its ever-changing colours, the effect is perfection itself, and we always look back on it as the most beautiful spot during the whole summer's journey.

From this camp we climbed to a ridge and obtained our best view of the big mountain which was then not more than six miles away. Its base, we saw, is composed of sheer rocky cliffs, above which is a large glacier encircling the final peak, which rises what appeared to be 3000 feet higher. There was one hanging glacier, reminding us of the one on Mt. Victoria, as its ice in falling sounded like thunder on the rocks below.

A curious feature of the mountain was an extraordinary glacier that seemed to be clinging to the steep face of the peak though the lower part had fallen away and left it apparently unsupported. In spite of the intense pressure there must have been from above, it was still clinging there. The peak itself presents from some points a pyramidal shape with very steep arêtes, but from this side its summit is a long and generally level ice cornice which looked broken and very steep on the sloping side. The highest point seemed to be at the northeastern end. No matter from where it is seen, it is an impressive mountain.

Late in the afternoon two days later we emerged from the timber to an open summit where we intended to camp, and as we turned about we saw the most impressive sight of all. There across a narrow valley towered a very steep-sided mountain whose northeastern arête was as sharp a knife edge as one could imagine. Our big mountain, as we later discovered, was directly behind it. Although this other mountain, which we later found to be Mt. Ida, was much lower than the big mountain, it was in its shape and isolation very dramatic. That night I saw it by moonlight, and it was a sight I shall not easily forget.

The next morning was a fine, clear August day, and we climbed a ridge 2000 feet above camp from where we saw one of the most magnificent views I have ever looked at in the Canadian Rockies. All the way from the northwest to the south was a brilliant region of snow and ice. In the foreground towered the knife-edged peak of Mt. Ida, and beyond it the big white summit of our giant snow mountain appeared.

Both, we could see, would prove extremely difficult as well as dangerous to climb, the big one because of its unusually steep and hazardous ice slopes and because of the serious problems to be offered by its ice cornice on top. The most likely route to the upper glacier seemed to be from the northeast and then up the final peak to the cornice on the summit by the northeastern or the southwestern arête.

Mt. Ida, it was evident, would be even harder to climb. To reach a point within 500 feet of the top might not be too difficult, but once there, great trouble would be experienced in reaching the actual summit. The top peak is in the shape of an elongated drum set on end, some 300 to 400 feet high, atop of which is an icy cone perilously abrupt on all sides. At the upper end of the southwestern arête is a rocky knob which is connected with the base of the drum by a narrow, steep-sided ice slope. The gap in between is filled with the accumulating snows, which it might be unduly dangerous to cross. Then there is still the perpendicular cliff and the steep, icy cone.

A few words in conclusion . . . . Members of the Alpine Club of Canada seemed to have noticed our giant mountain during their summer camp of 1913, for the accounts read that "many fine snow mountains appear, one of enormous size, some eighty miles away, which rivals Mt. Robson." Apparently the giant we'd first glimpsed in 1912 is the mountain they referred to, for the distance they estimated is almost exactly correct for this.

Later on during our 1914 trip I heard of trappers who spoke of a tremendous mountain at the head of the north fork of the Fraser River. Evidently it was known to the Indians too, but the only other white man

I had been able to find who has seen it at close range was R.W. Jones, whom I saw in Edmonton at the conclusion of our 1914 trip. He had spent four years surveying for possible passes for the Grand Trunk Railway extension to the Pacific coast. He had seen the mountain on one of his survey trips about ten years before, but as he was looking for low passes and not high mountains, he did not triangulate it, much as it interested him.

Previous to Jones's trip, E.W. Jarvis and his party had crossed here in the winter of 1874–5 on a survey expedition for a low pass for the CPR. It was Jarvis who named Mt. Ida, seeing it when he crossed from the Fraser watershed to that of the Kakwa River through the valley up which we had just come. But Jones, previous to us, was probably the first white man to see the great new mountain at such close range.

This hot, brilliant 12th of August, 1914, that we spent here by the great mountain, was a day in a thousand. Snow and ice, glacier and peak stretched far to the south, west and northwest, while to the east and south lay bare, rocky ridges, a perfect succession of them. Far below us lay our string of six lakes, the longest over two miles and of the most exquisite emerald green. As the day lengthened to late afternoon, the colour of these changed to a beautiful sea green. This day, I felt, was the most perfect I had ever spent among the mountains.

I looked about me at the four others, who, after breakfast beside the campfire, had climbed with me to the ridge 2000 feet above our horses and tipi, to where the giant appeared white and clear without even a cloud to obscure it. It was entirely owing to their experience, loyalty and hard work, I realized, that the success of our trip had been possible.

Major Fred Brewster (still at Jasper) was the most resourceful man I have ever met. You always had the most complete confidence in him under any conditions, no matter how bad things ever got. He was indefatigable, had remarkably good judgment, and his many years of experience with trail life in difficult country made him absolutely invaluable. As for C.R. Cross (killed in France September 1915) I can say just as much. As a friend of mine back home in Boston, he had originally interested me in hunting and exploring in difficult and inaccessible parts of the Northwest. He had hunted big game early in this century from Newfoundland to Alaska and had climbed in Switzerland as well as on this continent. He and Fred Brewster were as perfect a pair as any man could want to be with in the wilderness. The three of us together worked out our plans, and every decision was in our hands jointly.

Bob Jones (drowned in 1955, in the Snake Indian River, east of Jasper) was in charge of our outfit of twenty horses, and he was an ideal man for that very important job. No one could have been more loyal or devoted to all of us nor more interested in the success of our trip. He was always calm and quiet around the animals, an ideal helper around the camp, and a tireless worker on such jobs as cutting our trail, which was a daily chore.

Jack Symes, a former member of the Mounted Police (killed near Ypres, June 1916 [near Arras, May 1917], soon after receiving his commission as an officer), had come along as cook and general helper in any way he might be needed, which meant every day and in innumerable functions. We could always count on him and Jones. Furthermore, both were good companions, and no hardship or difficulty ever bothered them for long. It was an altogether fortunate group of men. Never once had there been any misunderstanding or unpleasantness between any of us during our five consecutive months in the bush, during three of which we saw no other human being.

The next morning we headed down the Kakwa River. We regretted not being able to stay longer to explore the big new mountain, but time was valuable, and utterly trailless country lay ahead through which we were to journey almost continuously through the daytime except when we rested the animals and climbed on foot to some eminence where we could lay out our course ahead. As it was, we were four months in all in reaching Hudson's Hope on the sunny north bank of the Peace River. During our climbing and hunting, however, we often saw our old friend in the distance, always looming high above everything else. For many weeks it served as a landmark and aided us in our map-making.

In the absence of any name for this big new mountain, we called it Mount Sir Alexander after that most intrepid explorer Alexander Mackenzie, who in becoming the first white man to get through the Rocky Mountains, had passed only a few miles to the west of it. This name was later approved by the Geographic Board of Canada. Three abortive attempts to climb the mountain were made, and not until 1929 did a party of climbers finally reach the summit, 10,740 feet high.

Fay Party Biographies

SAMUEL PRESCOTT (PETE) FAY

Pete Fay was born at Boston on May 27th, 1884. He was a member of a long-established New England family descended from a whaling magnate. (Presidents George Bush Sr. and Jr. belong to another branch of the family.) He had a lifelong association with Martha's Vineyard and established his summer home there in 1952. He graduated with a bachelor of arts degree from Harvard in 1907 and eventually worked as an investment counsellor.

Fay visited the Rockies and climbed in the Lake Louise and Lake O'Hara areas in 1906 and following years. In 1912, he made a three-month exploration with Fred Brewster from Jasper north to Kakwa Lake, through country that was almost unknown. He returned in 1913, but because he was recuperating from surgery, he was unable to make an extensive trip. Instead, with Fred Brewster, he made a number of shorter trips over several months, to the Mt. Robson/upper Smoky River area, to the Brazeau country and to Fortress Lake. They ended their season at Lake Louise. In 1914, he undertook the expedition that is the subject of this journal.

On learning of the outbreak of war in Europe, he volunteered with the American Ambulance Field Service as an ambulance driver in France and was cited for bravery. When the United States joined the war in 1917, he was commissioned as a first lieutenant and later served as an aerial observer with the 91st Aero Squadron.

There is no record of further climbing or exploration after his return from war service. However, he was an early member of the American Alpine Club and remained a member until his death. He later became interested in Arctic exploration and sponsored an expedition and was a member of the Arctic Institute.

Pete Fay and Fred Brewster remained lifelong friends and maintained a correspondence until Brewster's death in 1969. There is a family photo of the two of them together at Jasper in 1940. Fay also kept abreast of activities in the area of his 1914 expedition and maintained a file of related articles, which fortunately have been preserved. In 1957, Fay and well-known outdoors writer Bradford Angier co-authored two articles about the expedition, which were published in *The Beaver* magazine.

Fay was instrumental in having several geographic names officially accepted, including Mt. Sir Alexander, Kinuseo Falls, Kakwa and Babette lakes and Mt. Cross.

Fay and his wife, Hester, had two daughters and a son. Members of the family have been helpful in providing information and photographs.

Fay suffered from frail health in later years. He died on August 11, 1971, at his home in Chestnut Hill, a little more than six months after the death of his wife. Fay Lake, near his "Matterhorn" camp, across the valley from Mt. Ida, preserves the memory of his pioneering exploration.

FRED BREWSTER

Frederick Archibald Brewster was a member of the well-known Brewster family, whose tourism businesses have been a part of the Canadian Rockies since the 1880s. Fred, the fourth child of John and Bella Brewster, was born in Kildonan, Manitoba, on December 21st, 1884. (There are minor discrepancies in the dates given in various sources. This date is from Fred's enlistment for war service.) The family moved to Banff in the winter of 1887–88, where Fred's father had started a dairy. Fred and his brothers got to know the mountains on trips with Native guide Walter Twinn and, while still in their teens, began taking visitors on fishing trips. This was the start of the tourism empire that Fred's brothers founded in Banff.

Fred, however, went off to school, completing his early education at St. John's College in Winnipeg in 1905. Two long exploration trips through the wilderness of northern BC followed, in late 1905 and 1906, the first almost a year in length. He then continued his education at Queen's University in Kingston, graduating in 1909 with a degree in mining engineering. He briefly prospected in BC in 1910. Then, with his brother Jack and their brother-in-law Phil Moore, he established a freighting business for the construction of the Alberta Central Railway into the Nordegg coal fields between Banff and Jasper, in the winter of 1910–11. When construction of the Grand Trunk Railway approached the mountains, Fred moved north in the spring of 1911, to haul freight for construction crews. In 1912, anticipating a boom in tourism, he established an outfitting and guiding business in Jasper. It was in the fall of 1912 that Fred made his first trip with Pete Fay, exploring as far north as the Kakwa Lake area.

Fred volunteered for military service in 1915 and, because of his education as a mining engineer, was commissioned as a major in the Second Tunnelling Division. He was decorated for his company's work in demolishing a German observation post.

After the war, Fred expanded his business, establishing a tent camp at Beauvert Lake and a series of camps and chalets known as Fred Brewster's Rocky Mountain Camps. The tent camp was bought out by the Canadian National Railway, and Jasper Park Lodge was built on the site. He also continued outfitting and trail rides and, each fall, guided hunting parties into areas north of Jasper National Park. In time, he also owned a hotel in Jasper and boat operations at Maligne and Medicine lakes. Although some of his brothers, particularly Jack, worked with him for a while in the early years, Fred operated separately from the Brewster family business in Banff.

During the 1950s, Fred was active in the campaign to protect the area north of Jasper National Park through which he had travelled with Pete Fay, and on many subsequent hunting and outfitting trips. Willmore Wilderness Park was the result.

On his return from war service, Fred married Azalia Adams of New York and built a log home which still stands in Jasper. His wife was seriously ill for many years and predeceased Fred. They had no children.

Fred retired from his business in 1962 and died at Edmonton on March 4th, 1969.

CHARLES ROBERT (BOB) CROSS JR.

Cross was born at Boston on June 17th, 1881. He was a friend and neighbour of Fay and a fellow graduate of Harvard, where he obtained degrees in fine arts and law.

A lawyer by profession, his passion was the outdoors – climbing, canoeing, exploring and hunting. During his college years, he spent four summers climbing in the Swiss Alps and was an early member of the American Alpine Club. After law school, he spent four summers in the northwest, visiting the Stikine country of BC, the headwaters of the Mackenzie River and Alaska on hunting trips. He hunted caribou in Newfoundland during the fall months of 1911, 1912 and 1913.

In 1913, he was part of an expedition sponsored by the US Biological Survey that searched for wild sheep in the Babine country near Smithers, BC (the expedition report is preserved at the Smithsonian Institution).

Like Fay, Cross volunteered for humanitarian work on the battlefields of Europe in 1915, two years before the United States joined the First World War. Two months after his return from the 1914 Rockies trip, in January 1915, he went to France, where he drove an ambulance. This was followed by several months in the Balkans with the American Sanitary Commission, which was fighting typhus in the region. He returned to France in July of 1915 and offered his services to the American Distributing Service, which distributed supplies to military hospitals. He was killed in a vehicle accident while working for this agency and died at Dinard, France, on October 8, 1915. He was unmarried.

In memory of his friend's war service, Fay submitted Cross's name to the Canadian Geographic Names Board. Mt. Cross, in the heart of the Kakwa area and in sight of Mt. Sir Alexander, is his memorial.

BOB JONES

Robert Boydell (Bob) Jones was born at Winnipeg on March 23, 1893. He was an early guide and packer in Jasper and was part of the group that supported the Alpine Club of Canada's 1911 trip to Mt. Robson. He was responsible for the horses and equipment on the Fay expedition. He enlisted for military service in January 1915, less than two months after returning from the expedition.

He worked in the mountains throughout his life, first as a packer and guide and from 1940 as a warden in Jasper National Park. He was a keen photographer.

In 1954, he was posted at a warden station near Devona, northeast of Jasper townsite. He drowned in the Snake Indian River (the Stony River of the journal) on December 4 of that year, when he slipped on the ice while collecting a pail of water. He was unmarried.

After his death, his sisters in the United States donated his photo album of the 1914 trip to Fred Brewster, who in turn ensured its preservation at the Jasper–Yellowhead Archives. Some photos in this book are copied from Jones's album.

JACK SYMES

John Barnes (Jack) Symes was born at Tunbridge Wells, England, on March 26, 1891. No information has been found about his immigration to Canada. Before his arrival in Jasper, he was a member of the North-West Mounted Police for two years. Symes was responsible for the camp during the Fay expedition. Like Jones, he enlisted for military service in January 1915. He became a captain in the London Regiment, Royal Fusiliers, 2nd Battalion and was killed in action on May 3, 1917. He is buried in the Commonwealth War Graves cemetery at Guemappe in northern France. He was unmarried.

Access to Fay's Route

The southern half of Fay's route is mostly protected in national and provincial parks and can be experienced much as Fay and his party did. The information in this section is current to January 2006. Up-to-date access information should be requested from the agencies listed at the end. The access points are as follows:

1. Fay started his expedition at Jasper, which is the headquarters town in Jasper National Park and provides a full range of visitor services. Highway 16 (Yellowhead Highway) runs east–west through Jasper, from Edmonton to interior British Columbia. The Icefields Parkway (Highway 93N) connects Jasper with Banff and the Trans-Canada Highway to the south. Jasper can also be reached by Via Rail passenger trains. From Jasper, the Celestine Lake road follows the west side of the Athabasca River to the start of the North Boundary trail, which heads north up the valley of the Snake Indian River (Fay's Stony River). This is Fay's route.

2. Northeast of Jasper is the town of Hinton, from which Highway 40 heads northwest to Grande Cache and Grande Prairie. West of the highway is Rock Lake–Solomon Creek Wildland Provincial Park, reached via a secondary road. A major trailhead is located at Rock Lake, providing an alternative departure point for the North Boundary trail in Jasper National Park and for trails in the southern part of Willmore Wilderness Provincial Park. The trail joins Fay's route at Snake Indian River. A little way upstream, a side trail follows Fay's route northward through Eaglenest Pass to the well-established trail system in Willmore Park.

3. Grande Cache is a modern town on Highway 40 with all services and is a major entry point to Willmore Wilderness Provincial Park. A trail enters the park at Sulphur Gates, just outside the town (where the Fay party crossed the Smoky River) and follows the river upstream. A tributary trail heads north up the Muddywater River, following Fay's route to Dry Canyon and Sheep Pass.

4. An eastern access to the Kakwa area is available from Grande Prairie. Forestry roads head southwest toward Kakwa Wildland Provincial Park (in Alberta), with the trailhead several kilometres outside the park at the Deadhorse Meadows staging area.

5. From the west, the main access to the Kakwa area is Walker Creek Forest Road, which leaves Highway 16 between Prince George and McBride. This route provides vehicle access as far as Bastille Creek (75 kilometres) near the boundary of Kakwa Provincial Park (British Columbia). A 29-kilometre hike on an old mining track leads to the Kakwa Lake area and to Mt. Sir Alexander and Mt. Ida, all part of Fay's route.

6. From Crescent Spur, west of McBride on Highway 16, the Morkill–Forgetmenot Forest Road heads toward the south side of Intersection Mountain. The availability of this route depends on forestry activities. Depending on where the road terminates, it is possible to reach a rustic trail in the valley on the southwest side of Intersection Mountain; this route leads over an alpine ridge to Sheep Pass on the Alberta–British Columbia boundary.

For current road and trail access information on the southern section of Fay's route, contact the following:

1   Jasper National Park
2   Alberta Parks
3   BC Parks
4   Grande Cache visitor information centre
5   Grande Prairie visitor information centre
6   McBride visitor information centre
7   Alberta Forest Service
8   BC Forest Service

NORTHERN SECTION

From Kakwa, the Fay route passes successively through the four major tributaries of the Wapiti River system. The first of these, the Narraway River, is remote. Access to the next three valleys, Belcourt Creek, Red Deer Creek and the Wapiti River, is via the Wapiti Forest Service Road and its branches. This is an increasingly busy radio-controlled road with lots of industrial traffic. The turnoff south onto this road is 50 kilometres from Tumbler Ridge along the Boundary Road. Twenty-four kilometres along the forest service road there is a major fork.

From this fork, the left branch is the Red Deer Forest Service Road. After 12 kilometres, it forks into east and west branches. Keep left, on the east branch, which crosses Holtslander Creek, then Belcourt Creek, and then forks. The right fork allows difficult access to the Fay route via an ATV trail to Belcourt Lake. The Fay party noted the lake on their map but did not visit it, as they left the valley a few kilometres upstream from the lake.

The area around Belcourt Lake is part of a coal property, and is therefore potentially subject to mining, depending on the price of coal, infrastructure development and the presence of a willing long-term buyer. From here on, the Fay route lies parallel to the coal beds and properties, which form a virtually continuous band. Initially, the route lies west of the coal seams. In the Murray River section the Fay routes crosses the coal bands, and beyond Tumbler Ridge the Fay route is east of the coal.

From the fork described above, the right branch continues as the main Wapiti Forest Service Road, and crosses the Wapiti River and Red Deer Creek. The terminology is confusing, as Red Deer Creek is larger than the Wapiti River. Access to parts of the Fay route is possible up both of these valleys.

To get from Belcourt Creek to Red Deer Creek, the Fay party had to ascend through a pass and traverse through the streams of Whatley Creek. In the process, they descended the steep scree slope that provided one of their most evocative photographs. This area forms a fascinating destination for the adventurous hiker.

It is reached via an old exploration road along the north side of the Red Deer valley, starting on the Wapiti Forest Service Road about four kilometres before the bridge across Red Deer Creek. This track provides a nine-kilometre (one way) trip to Red Deer Falls. The old road continues and crosses Red Deer Creek via a ford a few hundred metres upstream from the falls. From here, it becomes more overgrown and leads into the upper reaches of the valley and the Warner Lakes in Warner Pass. Four kilometres beyond the ford, "Fay territory" is reached at the point where the party left this drainage and crossed to the Wapiti Valley via the low pass to the west. Their route can be approximated for the next four kilometres upstream (this is where Fay commented that they encountered an old Indian trail) up to the point where the creek from Warner Lakes joins the Red Deer from the west (17 kilometres from the trailhead). This was the site of one of the Fay camps.

At this point, a branch of the track leads up west through a pass into the Whatley Creek drainage. The Fay party descended via this route, so that following it traces their footsteps in reverse. Once through the pass, the track curves sharply to the right and straightens out for over three kilometres. About a kilometre along this straight section a smaller track branches off to the right, heading south up the most southerly tributary of Whatley Creek. This leads up a beautiful valley into the alpine and crests a pass after another seven kilometres (29 kilometres from the trailhead). Looking back (north) down the valley from the approach to this pass, the telltale skyline of the scree descent photograph can be identified on the ridge to the right. The col through which they passed and the steep scree slope they then had to descend to enter the valley are apparent, raising the question of why they chose that particular route.

One caveat with regard to this hike is the Red Deer Creek crossing at kilometre nine. After heavy rain this can be unfordable. If worse comes to worst and torrential rain threatens to maroon the hiking party in the upper reaches of Whatley Creek, an escape route is feasible over the high ground to the north, through a short section of forest into the highest clear-cut, and onto the extension of the Wapiti Forest Service road. This can then be followed over the bridge across Red Deer Creek and back to the trailhead.

Access to the Wapiti River section is more developed and is via the Wapiti Lake hiking trail in Wapiti Provincial Park. The trailhead is reached by turning right at a fork a few kilometres before the Wapiti Forest Service Road crosses the Wapiti River. This trail leads to an overnight cabin on Wapiti Lake after 19 kilometres. This cabin is on the Fay route.

From the cabin, the hiking trail continues north to Onion Lake. The first few kilometres roughly follows the Fay route; then the Onion Lake trail climbs north through a pass, while the Fay route continues northwest west up the valley and over two passes to enter the Murray valley.

The extensive Murray River section of the route is accessed from Tumbler Ridge, by driving 14 kilometres along the Boundary Road, turning right, past the old Quintette mine site, crossing the Murray River, then turning left onto the Murray Forest Service Road, which leads to Monkman Provincial Park and Kinuseo Falls (65 kilometres from Tumbler Ridge). Beyond the turnoff to the falls, and just before the provincial park campground ,there is a turnoff to the left. This is the start of the Bulley Creek Forest Service Road, which leads further into the mountains for over 40 kilometres and provides access to the upper section of the Murray River. The hiking trail to Monkman Lake begins at the park campground and leads along the Murray River for seven kilometres, then crosses it by means of a suspension bridge and leads south into the heart of the park.

The Fay party struck the Murray River downstream of its confluence with Bulley Creek. This area is about 15 kilometres up the Bulley Creek Forest Service Road, and the pass by which they entered the valley is visible to the southeast. They crossed the Murray River close to the site of the suspension bridge on the hiking trail and made camp a short distance on, maybe close to the backcountry campground just downstream from this bridge.

From here, they headed north along the west bank of the river, whereas the Monkman Lake hiking trail follows the east bank. Cross and Brewster then went on a reconnaissance trip and climbed the Albright Ridge at its eastern end. It is possible to scramble up this aspect of the ridge from the Imperial Creek Forest Service Road, which branches off the Bulley Creek Forest Service Road a couple of kilometres from Kinuseo Falls, and soon crosses the Murray River. This access is trailless and involves bushwhacking and crossing Hook Creek. The more usual access to the Albright Ridge is from its northwestern end via the Wolverine Valley at kilometre 53 of the Wolverine Forest Service Road.

Once the members of the expedition had reassembled, they proceeded down the Murray, crossing it, then recrossing it near the pool at the bend in the river that is skirted by the short stretch of road between Kinuseo Falls and the Kinuseo Falls Campground. When they came upon Kinuseo Falls they were on the west bank, whereas the viewing platform and current trails are all on the eastern bank.

From here, they followed the Murray River all the way toward present-day Tumbler Ridge. Part of this section is approximated by the Murray Forest Service Road between kilometre 0 and kilometre 19, where the road is on the west bank. En route they paused to climb Mt. Hermann. A road climbs up the western aspect and over much of the top of this flat-topped hill, and a short walk leads to the small tower on the summit. From here, it is possible to enjoy the view of the prairies in the distance as described by Fay. To get onto Mt. Hermann, after crossing the Murray River on the way to Kinuseo Falls, turn right on the road to the Mesa pit of the Quintette mine, and after nine kilometres turn left and drive up the Mt. Hermann road.

What Fay called the Big Flat, just below present-day Tumbler Ridge, is the floodplain surrounding Flatbed Creek before it enters the Murray River. He called it the finest flat he had seen in the mountains, and it must have changed a lot in the intervening years, for it is now well wooded. It is accessible via trails on either side of the creek and from the Flatbed campground.

From here, they ascended the Wolverine River for about five kilometres, then over the hill to the north (approximating the original, and no longer fully passable, Tumbler Ridge–Chetwynd road) until they came across the middle reaches of Bullmoose Creek close to the site of the Bullmoose Marshes, where a hiking trail (with interpretive brochure) now leads through the wetland area.

From Bullmoose Creek to Moberly Lake, the Fay route can be more or less followed by road. Highway 29 leads past Gwillim Lake Provincial Park.

The Fay party visited the western end of the lake, a few kilometres west of the provincial park campground. Their route from here to the Sukunka River, following trappers' cabins, lies close to Highway 29.

Once in the Sukunka valley, Fay and his men incorrectly veered upstream and passed Sukunka Falls, before retracing their steps. Sukunka Falls Provincial Park is reached by leaving Highway 29 and following the Sukunka Forest Service Road for 21 kilometres up the valley along the approximate route Fay took. This is another narrow, busy, unpaved, radio-controlled road with lots of industrial traffic; it leaves Highway 29 some 69 kilometres from Tumbler Ridge and 23 kilometres from Chetwynd.

Highway 29 along the eastern side of the Sukunka Valley follows the route Fay followed along the existing trails, crossing the Pine River just below the confluence of the west Pine and Sukunka rivers, then leading past Chetwynd to Hudson's Hope via Moberly Lake. From Moberly Lake to Hudson's Hope, the Fay route was northeast of Highway 29, and crossed the Peace River at Hudson's Hope.

To get from Hudson's Hope to Grande Prairie, Fay followed the existing trails. This route led them first back to Moberly Lake, then on a direct trail to the Pine River via Jackfish Lake. They crossed the river north of where Highway 97 crosses it today. After crossing the Kiskatinaw River, their route lay close to today's Highway 97 and then Highway 2. Wagon trails took them through the valley of Dawson Creek to Pouce Coupe, then past Swan Lake to Stony Point near present-day Beaverlodge, and then to Grande Prairie via Lake Saskatoon. From here, they took the Edson Trail and caught the train from Edson back to Jasper.

For current road and trail access information on the northern section of Fay's route, contact the following:

1   Tumbler Ridge visitor information centre
2   Hudson's Hope visitor information centre
3   Dawson Creek visitor information centre
4   BC Parks
5   BC Forest Service

1   Jack Brewster, Fred's brother.

2   Lewis Swift was an early homesteader in the Jasper area, well known to early visitors.

3   Photos from Fay's 1913 trip.

4   See for example J.G. MacGregor's *Overland by the Yellowhead*.

5   Moberly Flats is north of the town of Jasper, where the Athabasca River turns to the northeast. The family moved to Grande Cache when Jasper National Park was designated.

6   Fay consistently used this spelling. Later he would amend parts of his journal by hand and change "tipi" to "teepee."

7   Now known as Snake Indian River.

8   Pyramid Mountain overlooks the Jasper townsite on the north side.

9   More usually spelled "coulees." The term denotes narrow, deep draws.

10 Merganser.

11 Mt. Robson, the highest peak in the Canadian Rockies. Fay visited the area in 1913.

12 Rock Lake is just outside the boundary of Jasper National Park, northwest of Hinton. It is a popular starting point for trips into Willmore Wilderness Park.

13 Spruce grouse.

14 Gray jay.

15 Still named Deer Creek.

16 James Beaumont (Beau) Gaetz (1857–1922) was a rancher, trapper, outfitter and guide in the Red Deer area of Alberta. His photos of the 1912 trip with Fay and Brewster are in the museum in Red Deer.

17 Kakwa Lakes. Fay later was responsible for the official name change from "Porcupine" to "Kakwa."

18 Snake Indian Pass.

19 The Smoky River originates in the glaciers on Mt. Robson and flows north through Willmore Wilderness Park to Grande Cache, then northward to join the Peace River.

20 More usually spelled "slough." The term refers to a backwater or flooded side channel.

21 Probably the Calumet Mountain area east of Mt. Robson.

22 The Sulphur River is a tributary of the Smoky River, which it joins at Grande Cache.

23 The US Biological Survey, which sponsored scientific expeditions throughout North America and other parts of the world between the late 1800s and 1940s. Reports are archived at the Smithsonian Institution in Washington, DC.

24 The Athabasca River is the main river flowing through Jasper National Park.

25 They had reached Mowitch Creek, which turns to the east and drains via Rock Lake.

26 The Cree were likely the hunters attached to the Hudson's Bay Company post at Jasper House in the 1800s.

27 The Brazeau River, in the southeast part of Jasper National Park, was visited by Fay and Brewster in 1913.

28 Moss campion.

29 Columbian ground squirrel.

30 Hudson's Bay Company.

31 The Klappan River is a tributary of the Stikine River in northwest British Columbia. Bob Cross had hunted in the area in 1908.

32 The "Ashcroft Trail" is the Yukon Telegraph Trail, which ran north from Ashcroft in southern British Columbia and was in use until the 1930s. There is only one record of cattle being driven over the trail, in the days of the Klondike Gold Rush.

33 Only the woodland caribou is found in the region through which they were travelling. The Osborn is a more northern subspecies, possibly encountered by Cross while hunting in northwest British Columbia. The barren ground caribou is found in the Arctic.

34 Golden-crowned sparrow.

35 A number of trails followed the main valleys northwestward from the Hudson's Bay Company post at Jasper House to the hunting country of the Smoky River watershed. This would have been a direct route from the Snake Indian valley into the Sulphur River valley and beyond.

36 American kestrel.

37 Rock Creek, draining southeast to Rock Lake. In his diary, Fred Brewster referred to it as the west branch of the Hay River. At this point the party had left the modern-day Jasper Park and crossed into what is now Willmore Wilderness Park.

38 Buffalo were found in the mountains, particularly during the summer, until their extirpation from the Prairies in the 1880s.

39 They appear to have been in the Persimmon Range, north of Eaglenest Pass.

40 Fay uses the term "balm of Gilead trees" to denote aspen. Gilead was a town in Israel that produced copious amounts of soothing balm in Biblical times, and the "balm of Gilead" is referred to in Jeremiah 8. Modern-day balm of Gilead is produced from buds of the aspen tree, and is used mainly to treat upper respiratory infections.

41 Fred Brewster (and later travellers) referred to it as Big Grave Flat.

42 Mt. Sir Alexander.

43   Sheep Creek is a northwest tributary of the Smoky River, to which they were headed again.

44   Mt. Robson, at 3954 m, is the highest peak in the Canadian Rockies, which is why it is used for comparison. It is much higher than all surrounding mountains and is visible over long distances from high vantage points.

45   CNR is the Canadian Northern Railway, a competitor of the Grand Trunk Pacific through Yellowhead Pass. During the First World War, the two railways were amalgamated into the Canadian National Railway and one set of tracks was torn up for use in Europe.

46   They reached the Sulphur River at its head and were already past the Eaglenest Pass connection when they started downriver.

47   Eaglenest Pass.

48   Edgartown is on Martha's Vineyard, in Massachusetts.

49   They had now reached the Wild Hay River.

50   Northern harrier.

51   The Muskeg River is farther north. The river they had reached was the South Berland.

52   South Berland River.

53   They had crossed the pass from the South Berland River to the North Berland River. The Muskeg is the next drainage to the north.

54   Deer mouse.

55   They had now reached the Muskeg River.

56   The trail from Hinton to Grande Cache.

57   À la Pêche Lake.

58   Grande Cache and Victor lakes, near the modern-day town of Grande Cache.

59   See note 5. Descendants still live in the area.

60   Probably Mt. Louie.

61   A mountain in the White Mountains of New Hampshire, elevation 3475 feet.

62   Spelled Ewan but pronounced Ivan. He was a well-known guide and hunter in the area.

63   Adolphus was also a well-known guide who accompanied numerous groups exploring and climbing mountains in the Jasper and Mt. Robson area. Adolphus Lake in Jasper National Park is named for him. It is just across the boundary from Berg Lake in Mt. Robson Park.

64   A coastal town at Cape Cod, Massachusetts.

65   Sulphur Gates, at the entrance to Sulphur Canyon, near Grande Cache.

66   The Jack Pine River is a west tributary of the Smoky River.

67   Kakwa lakes.

68   Kvass Creek and Monaghan Creek are tributaries of the Smoky River named for these well-known trappers.

69   Mt. Sir Alexander.

70   Mt. Sir Alexander was also noted by the Amery/Hastings/Mumm party while on the Kain Face of Mt. Robson in 1909. (See Amery, L.S. *Days of Fresh Air*.)

71   Mt. Sir Alexander is 10,720 feet high.

72   Fay was right in this assumption. Mt. Sir Alexander and nearby Mt. Ida are the most northerly 10,000-foot mountains in the Rockies.

73   Now known as Dry Canyon.

74   According to Fay's July 27 entry, Mason was heading for the Jack Pine River, which would have taken him southwestward from Grande Cache, not up the Sheep River.

75   Sheep Pass is a large expanse of open alpine country on the BC/Alberta boundary. They were now crossing from modern-day Willmore Wilderness Park in Alberta into modern-day Kakwa Park in BC.

76   Probably Intersection Mountain, where the interprovincial boundary leaves the height of land along the spine of the Rockies and follows the 120th meridian.

77   Kakwa lakes.

78   Mt. Bess, 3212 m, is a little north of Mt. Robson and close to the BC/Alberta boundary.

79   Surprise Pass.

80   Rainbow Lake.

81   Porcupine River is the Kakwa River and the tributary is Cecilia Creek.

82   Cecilia Lake.

83   The trail runs northwestward toward Providence Pass to avoid losing over 1,000 feet in a descent to Cecilia Lake.

84   Providence Pass.

85   Mt. Sir Alexander.

86   The seven visible lakes are probably Broadview, La Glace, Kakwa, Babette, Wapamun, Mariel and Wishaw.

87   McGregor Pass.

88   The Porcupine lakes are Kakwa and Wapamun lakes, with a short channel separating them.

89   Babette Lake was named by Fay for "a young cousin who took an interest in my travels."

90   Jarvis Pass and the easterly of the Jarvis lakes chain.

91   Wishaw Mountain. The eastern extremity is Mt. Cross, named by Fay in memory of his friend and expedition member Bob Cross, who was killed in France in 1915 (see biographical note).

92   Holmes River, near McBride, BC. The mountain is not identified but is possibly part of the Premier Range, south of the Holmes River and the Fraser Valley.

93   The copper pot was possibly a relic of hunting parties from the Hudson's Bay Company post at Jasper House. In 1915, the Jobe party reported finding the lid of a copper kettle near the base of Mt. Sir Alexander and whose origin they attributed to the HBC. (See Taylor, William C. *Tracks Across My Trail*.)

94 A large lick is found nearby on the route to La Glace Lake.

95 This "ideal campsite" is the main campsite in Kakwa Park, BC, located adjacent to the park ranger's cabin, on the short creek from Wapamun Lake to Kakwa Lake.

96 Babette Lake.

97 The unnamed pass is on the west side of Mt. Ian Monroe. Fay and Brewster followed it around to McGregor Pass.

98 Subsequently named Mt. Sir Alexander. This is the first reference to what is now the official name. Previously, it was referred to by Fay as the "Big Mountain" and by Jobe as "Mt. Kitchi."

99 The official name is Mt. St. George, named in a fit of silliness by boundary surveyor A.O. Wheeler. Adjacent peaks are Mt. St. Andrew, Mt. St. David and Mt. St. Patrick. They are named after the patron saints of the British Isles. "Fortress" would be a much more appropriate name for the impressive cliffs towering several thousand feet above Babette Lake.

100 Mariel and Wapamun lakes, draining to the east of McGregor Pass; Wishaw Lake, draining to the west.

101 Red-necked grebe.

102 Jarvis Lake chain.

103 The party was heading west in Jarvis Pass. The lakes drain via Jarvis Creek and McGregor River into the Fraser River.

104 Mt. Ida, named by Jarvis and Hanington during their February 1875 crossing of Jarvis Pass.

105 The view is south, up the Edgegrain valley.

106 Mt. Sir Alexander is 10,720 feet high.

107 Jarvis valley, downstream of Jarvis lakes.

108 Mt. Ida is 10,472 feet high.

109 The first ascent was in 1954.

110 Possibly Mt. Hanington, depending on how far they went. The peak above camp which they all climbed is unnamed.

111 Blue grouse.

112 Moonias Creek valley.

113 *Pinus albicaulis.*

114 The "good-sized stream" is the Narraway River, which originates in the glaciers of the Mt. Petrie/Mt. Ovington massif to the west. It is the southernmost branch of the Wapiti River.

115 The party left the river and headed north through the valley on the west side of Nekik Mountain.

116 After crossing the pass, they were on the upper part of Belcourt Creek, which is another tributary of the Wapiti River.

117 Muinok Mountain on the west side of Belcourt Creek.

118 Mt. Secus.

119 Boreal chickadee.

120 Murray River.

121 The party crossed the ridge on the west side of Belcourt Creek, south of Mt. Belcourt.

122 They were looking toward the Red Deer Creek valley, a major tributary of the Wapiti River.

123 Mt. Belcourt.

124 Pikas.

125 The photograph of the party and horses descending this scree slope is haunting and evocative, prompting the desire to identify its location. From the journal text and map it appeared most likely they were entering the valley of Red Deer Creek, one of the three major southern tributaries of the Wapiti River. Fay's party had already traversed the upper drainages of the other two, now known as Belcourt Creek and the Narraway River. Each of these carries a larger flow than the northern branch, which is nonetheless known as Wapiti River. After passing through some formidable canyons, the rivers reach their confluence near the BC–Alberta boundary, and their combined flow is still known as Wapiti River, until it joins the Smoky River. In 2003, Kevin Sharman, president of the Wolverine Nordic & Mountain Society (Tumbler Ridge's outdoor group), explored the upper reaches of the Whatley Creek drainage. Thanks to the distinctive horizon evident in the 1914 photo, he was able to conclusively identify and photograph the "impossibly steep scree slope."

126 Red Deer Creek.

127 The Delaware grape (*Vitis labrusca 'Delaware'*) is named for Delaware, Ohio. It is a unique grapevine, originally from Europe, which developed its characteristics by chance.

128 Grand Trunk Pacific Railway surveyors led by Robert W. Jones had travelled through this country in 1905–06, investigating possible railway routes through the Wapiti, Herrick, Paksumo and Warner passes.

129 Probably a western jumping mouse.

130 Headwaters of the Wapiti River.

131 In addition to First Nations groups, there are three known candidates for the blazing of this trail:
Beau Gaetz had accompanied Fay on his 1912 trip, and had visited Wapiti Lake in 1898, while searching for a route to the Klondike. With a few other prospectors, he had spent two winters in the Wapiti, during which they lost most of their horses and developed scurvy (Fay mentioned this in his 1925 article in *Outdoor Life*).
R.W. Jones, surveyor for the Grand Trunk Pacific Railway, whom Fay visited in Edmonton at the end of the expedition, had explored the region for railway routes through the mountains in 1905 and 1906.
Spencer Tuck, an English timber cruiser from Jasper, wrote a harrowing account of his crossing of the Wapiti Pass with a guide in 1907.
In his *Outdoor Life* article Fay expands on how these trails, likely made by First Nations hunters, were of little use to his party, as they began in the prairie country to the east, ascended a valley, and would usually peter out. Typically these trails therefore were perpendicular to Fay's line of travel.

132 Fay called this lake "Sapphire Lake" on his map and in his subsequent writings. By the 1920s, it was already widely known as Wapiti Lake. The 16,837-hectare Wapiti Lake Provincial Park was proclaimed in 2000, preserving the lake and surrounding mountains.

It also includes Fossil Fish Lake, an internationally renowned paleontological site, where exquisitely preserved specimens of Triassic fossil fishes and marine reptiles are exposed.

133 This speculation was incorrect; they were leaving the "north branch of the Wapiti" behind at Wapiti Lake, and would enter the drainage of the Murray River, then known as the east branch of the Pine. Fay believed that the north branch lay ahead of them, and that their "Sapphire Lake" lay on the "north-middle branch" (as he wrote in *Appalachia* XIII, 3. In his 1925 article in *Outdoor Life*, he calls this the "Callahoo River." On their map they inserted a non-existent branch of the Wapiti farther to the north. They may have been aware that the Wapiti River system had four main branches. Their map confirms they had not recognized in the headwaters of the Narraway River, the southernmost of these four branches.

134 Now the hamlet of Lake Louise.

135 The west branch of Fellers Creek, south of Mt. Comstock. Somewhere north of this, John Holzworth, also exploring for the US Biological Survey, secured a bighorn sheep specimen in 1923.

136 Upper reaches of the Murray River ("east branch of Pine River").

137 Mt. Comstock, 6483 feet high.

138 The most northerly bighorn sheep are found in the Narraway area, which the party had passed through, though there are occasional reports of individuals as far northwest as Wapiti Lake. The next sheep are Stone sheep at Mt. Selwyn on the south side of the Peace River. The gap between the two ranges is about 300 km. Others followed Fay, trying to resolve the issue whether the ranges of the two species overlapped or were separate: Holzworth in 1923–25, Gray in 1927 and 1928, and Borden and Sheldon in 1932.

139 They reached the river some kilometres downstream from the confluence between the Murray River and Bulley Creek, its first major tributary. The "creek" is actually longer than the "river," and the substantial unnamed peak at its source, crowning the Bulley Glacier, is the highest in the Tumbler Ridge area (2630 m, or 8600 feet, above sea level). Tumbler Ridge has the possibly unique distinction of its highest mountain being unnamed. Fay makes no mention in the journal of the lakes upstream on the Murray River, now known as Upper and Lower Blue Lake. However, in his article in *Appalachia* XIII, 3, which was read to the American Alpine Club on April 14, 1915, by Charles Fay (no relation), in mentioning this river he notes "at the upper end of which are two small lakes." Brewster's handwritten diary provides the answer: on their August 31 mountaintop reconnaissance, the two lakes had been observed, and he indicates them in one of his diary sketches.

140 The confusing and variable nomenclature of the Pine River system has been a nightmare for historians. Fay at this stage was seriously underestimating the distance ahead. It would be over five weeks (October 11) before his party would realize with certainty which branch of the river system they were on, and which one they had been following.

141 Monkman Creek.

142 Imperial Creek. According to Brewster's diary, they struck it a few miles upstream from its junction with the Murray River, as they had left the latter in order to pass through green rather than burnt timber.

143 From their summit vantage point of August 31, they would have been able to look straight up the valley of Hook Creek and see Hook Lake in the distance. It appears they initially planned at least to get to Hook Lake. If they had followed this route, they would doubtless have continued on into the headwaters of the Sukunka River and descended in this valley all the way to its junction with the Pine River.

144 In reality, they were 80 miles in a straight line from Pine Pass.

145 Copies of the map have survived in archives and it was indeed used by subsequent explorers.

146 Fay's original journal, wildlife report, photos and map are preserved at the Smithsonian Institution in Washington. Copies of some of the material are held in archives in western Canada.

147 Rusty blackbird.

148 Although Fay's ornithological identifications usually appear plausible, the description of pectoral sandpipers as "grass birds" is puzzling, and on the wing they are not readily identifiable to non-experts.

149 Arctic grayling.

150 A popular diner in Boston at the time.

151 Wilson's snipe.

152 Ruffed grouse.

153 Hairy woodpecker.

154 Archaeological sites dating back probably a few thousand years have been discovered a few kilometres away near Imperial Creek.

155 This spot is close to the hiking trail to Monkman Lake, a few kilometres downstream from a beautiful swing bridge, constructed by BC Parks, which enables hikers to enter the splendid backcountry of Monkman Provincial Park. Few visitors nowadays would likely choose the epithet "godforsaken."

156 American dipper.

157 Due to Cross's illness and the terrible weather, little had been accomplished in the eight days. Brewster's diary makes it clear that they headed north from the camp and ascended the southeastern end of Albright Ridge. On the second day, Brewster climbed to the top of one of the ridge's eastern summits. On the penultimate day, another summit was reached. Had they enjoyed better weather and health, they may have come across some of the limestone caves that dot the Albright Ridge, or been able to comment on its remarkable coral fossils.

158 This mistaken theory held sway until October 11.

159 This was likely close to the site of the current Kinuseo Falls campground. Because they briefly left the river here, skirting it through the forest on the eastern bank, they did not record the sizeable Hook Creek joining the river from the west.

160 This beautiful, cliff-lined bend in the Murray is well known to visitors to Monkman Provincial Park: between the sideroad to Kinuseo Falls and the Kinuseo Falls campsite, the road winds above this bend. At the downstream end was a popular campground that has been closed by BC Parks. A tragic drowning occurred there in 1995.

161 This is the first written description of Kinuseo Falls, and the photographs taken were also the first. Despite the wet weather the Fay party had endured for the preceding two weeks, the water level is clearly very low, and the sight of the burned timber on the horizon immediately strikes modern-day viewers of the photos as odd. The 1906 map produced by Robert W. Jones for the Grand Trunk Pacific Railway shows a 215-foot-high falls at the site, constituting the first written record. Jim Dixon mentioned in passing to Tumbler Ridge matriarch Janet Hartford that he had seen the falls in 1907. They were known to prehistoric peoples: archaeological sites have been discovered a few kilometres above the falls near Imperial Creek. After the Fay party, the next recorded visitor was Prentiss Gray in 1927; he took the first motion picture of Kinuseo Falls, which miraculously has been preserved. Fay's 1915 article in *Appalachia* had prompted Gray's interest, and some time after Gray's trip the two men met and Gray was able to show him the movie of Kinuseo Falls.

Fay was not aware of any First Nations name for the falls, and therefore felt comfortable naming them Kinuseo, for the abundance of fish both above and below them. By 1927, Gray was able to report a mellifluous traditional name, Kapaca Tignapy, "the place of falling waters"; the date of origin of this latter name is not known.

Fay's height estimate is accurate – the falls are currently listed as 225 feet high. Janet Hartford free-climbed the cliff to the left of the falls (looking upstream) in 1939, and the first winter ascent was led by Al Tattersall in 1997. One dog has survived a tumble off the falls.

Fay displayed great persistence in having the falls officially named, and the final letter of confirmation arrived in 1920. He may have experienced some chagrin at one disdainful comment of the Geographical Board of Canada in 1925: "I may state that Mr. Fay is lucky in having these names accepted, as the Board generally looks with disfavour on names suggested by tourists."

Fay maintained an abiding interest in the area his party had traversed. He sent a letter to the editor of *Natural History* magazine in 1941 describing Kinuseo Falls, in response to an article on the world's highest waterfalls.

162 Southeastern end of Albright Ridge.

163 This state of mind may have been at least partially responsible for Fay's impending (and totally uncharacteristic) harsh criticism of Jack Symes.

164 Black-backed woodpecker.

165 Issidore (or Isidora) is also a prominent Kelly Lake name. This Métis settlement was founded around 1910 to the east near the BC–Alberta border. Although its inhabitants rapidly developed an outstanding knowledge of the mountains and valleys, it seems unlikely that one of them would have been at this site as early as 1910.

166 This ridge, which culminates in Pyramid Peak, is prominent on the drive back to Tumbler Ridge from Kinuseo Falls, and characterized by a symmetrical high col.

167 Again, this was optimistic thinking – they likely had seen the Wolverine Valley, but no lake is visible from this ridge.

168 One of Brewster's sketches indicates that this camp was a short distance up Tentfire Creek.

169 Also referred to later by Fay as the Alaskan three-toed woodpecker, this is now known simply as the three-toed woodpecker.

170 Both the Murray and the Sukunka rivers swing north after flowing east. The party still believed they were descending the Sukunka (Middle Pine).

171 Known as Delavan's Comet after a famous early-20th-century comet hunter, this comet of 1914 is distinguished in having the longest orbital period of any known comet: 26 million years.

172 Although Fay's journal does not specify which summit they had reached (or even suggests Mt. Babcock) it is evident from Brewster's diary that they had ascended Mt. Hermann.

173 The most prominent semicircles of peaks seen from this summit are the Castle Mountain–Shark's Fin–Boone Taylor Peak complex, or else the Bulley Glacier–Mt. Bulley area. However, the Fay party had not explored any of these peaks, so he must have been referring to lower summits.

174 This is an intriguing observation – there are no recent records of sharp-tailed grouse from the Tumbler Ridge area. In Brewster's diary, they are recorded as "prairie chicken," a common misnomer to this day.

175 Flatbed Creek; the trail led through the foothills to the Wapiti River.

176 Flatbed Creek.

177 Wolverine River. In his diary, Brewster noted astutely: "probably Wolverine."

178 The Big Flat clearly refers to the low-lying area just below and to the west of Tumbler Ridge, through which Flatbed Creek meanders past the Lions campground to its junction with the Murray River, and flanked to the north by Tumbler Point. There has been a significant vegetation change since 1914: the flat is now covered with mature deciduous or mixed forest. Brewster wrote "Promised Land" in big letters in his diary to describe it.

179 If they had continued just one mile farther downstream, they may have come across a cabin, and the first settler. Victor Peck arrived in 1913 or 1914. He married Kathleen Shepard in 1916, and together they stayed until 1924, raising four young boys in this most isolated spot, before moving to Hudson's Hope. They established a trapline from Kinuseo Falls down to the Murray Canyon (20 kilometres downstream from their cabin). Their descendants are still active in the Peace Region.

180 Brewster recorded in his diary that they went seven miles up what he correctly thought was the Wolverine Valley, then swung north over the hills into the Bullmoose Creek Valley. Around this time, Kate Edwards, the lone pioneer of the Wolverine, established her ranch a few miles further upstream.

181 Bullmoose Creek, possibly at Bullmoose Marshes/ Bullmoose Flats.

182 Brewster recorded that Nelson was a Dane. The correct spelling is likely Neilsen, as this name is recorded in the Calverley collection (www.calverley. ca) as belonging to one of the very first trappers in the region. "Nielson" is also used. Brothers Hans and Nels Neilsen trapped in the Rocky Mountain Lake (Gwillim Lake) area until at least the late 1930s.

183 The First World War had broken out in the first week in August. Within six months of their encounter with Nelson, Fay and Cross, the Americans, would join the American Ambulance Field Service (two years before the US officially joined the war) and would

be assisting the Allies in ambulance service in France, where Cross lost his life in an automobile accident within his first month of service in 1915. Symes was killed in action near Arras in May 1917, soon after receiving his commission. Brewster became a major and was decorated with the Military Cross and Bar.

184   Gwillim Lake, named after Prof. J.C. Gwillim, who first surveyed the area for oil and gas in 1919 on behalf of the Geological Survey of Canada and the BC Department of Lands.

185   These eloquent lines form the first known written description of Gwillim Lake. There are numerous archaeological sites around the shores of this large lake, some of which have been radio carbon dated to around 3,450 years ago. Gwillim Lake Provincial Park was expanded in 1999 to 22,461 hectares, and is a regional favourite for camping and fishing.

186   It was probably in one of these cabins near Martin Creek that Hans Neilsen died in a freak accident in 1939 or 1940. His brother Nels found him with a bullet hole in the forehead – Hans's rifle, which he had left in his pack, had accidentally gone off when he threw down the pack in the cabin.

187   As becomes apparent, they were already on the "South Fork" (Sukunka River). The mention of the "mouth of the South fork" must refer to a smaller tributary valley visible upstream, probably Boulder Creek.

188   This is the first written description of Sukunka Falls, now preserved in a small provincial park, and the Fay party took the first ever photographs of this feature. It is interesting to compare those images with the falls as they are today, and realize the degree of erosion that has taken place in 90 years.

189   Salteaux.

190   In 1967, at the age of 82, Fay wrote a letter to Brewster, reminding him of this encounter and mentioning that Treadwell was mentioned in Peace River Chronicles, the well-known anthology that was published in 1963. The only indexed mention of "Frank Tredwell" is that he arrived at the Hudson's Bay Company post in Fort St. John on May 9, 1919, from the Sukunka, where he had been trapping for the winter. Papers in the Calverley collection (www.calverley.ca) make it clear that Treadwell was a revered old-timer with legendary feats to his name. He was also known as Twidwell, hence Twidwell Bend, where the Pine and Sukunka rivers join, and nearby Twidwell Creek.

191   We can but wonder how far the party would have continued, and with what consequences, had they not come upon Treadwell.

192   This anecdote probably refers to the epic of Jack Thomas, as recorded in The Peacemakers of North Peace, in which he and "Red River" MacDonald chose to cross the mountains in 1912, Thomas with one horse, MacDonald with six. As there was no obvious trail, they disagreed on the route, and split up. Thomas chose the Pine Pass, and had a very tough time. Starving, he ended up eating his horse. MacDonald ended up on the Clearwater River and also had to resort to eating horsemeat.

193   Pine Pass.

194   Sukunka River.

195   From here on in the journal, there are occasional statements that strike 21st-century ears as being intolerant and prejudiced. Suffice it to say that within the context of their age, such comments were the norm amongst non-First Nations writers.

196   This confluence is just upstream from the bridge on Highway 29, about ten kilometres south of Chetwynd.

197   Brewster identifies him as Knuttson. This was probably Ernie Knutson, pioneer trapper, also known as "Silvertip," reputedly the best musher and snowshoe man in the district..

198   Their route from the forks of the Pine to Moberly Lake appears to approximate, or lie slightly east of, the current highways. In describing the Kakwa area, Wapiti Lake, Kinuseo Falls, Gwillim Lake, Sukunka Falls, and now Moberly Lake, Fay had seemingly unerringly provided early or first accounts of the region's treasures that would in time become the major features of British Columbian provincial parks. The only exception is the less impressive Bearhole Lake, which was first described by Prentiss Gray in 1927.

199   Frederick Vreeland, a US inventor and manufacturer already in his forties, explored the northern Rockies from their western flanks over the course of three summers between 1912 and 1915. His most notable first ascents were Mt. Vreeland and Ice Mountain. Fay and Vreeland were interested in each other's exploits, corresponded and probably met in 1916, and tried to correlate the geographical features they had recorded from their respective sides of the Rockies. A recently discovered copy of Fay's map has barely legible pencilled notes by Vreeland. Following their correspondence, Vreeland travelled to the Kakwa area in the summer of 1916, and reached the icefield on the western side of Mt. Sir Alexander. He identified a likely route of ascent, which was used by the 1929 summiting party. His pictures of Mt. Sir Alexander appeared in the Canadian Alpine Journal account of the ascent.

200   This man was the Scotsman Harry Garbitt, a renowned pioneer of the Peace region. He had come to Canada in his youth. He operated the trading store of Revillon Frères in Fort St John. He was both packer and guide for Vreeland's 1912 hunting expedition to Laurier Pass in the country north of Hudson's Hope. He moved to Moberly Lake with Charlie Paquette in 1914, where he married and had three children, and opened a trading store. He stayed at Moberly Lake for many years, living to the age of 86.

201   In handwritten amendments to this part of the journal, Fay used the spelling "Pauquette." Charlie Paquette came to the Peace region from Quebec in 1887, and packed and trapped all over the north. He filed a squatter's claim in 1912 on what is now downtown Hudson's Hope. Paquette and Garbitt moved to Moberly Lake in 1914 to raise cattle on the Salteaux Indian Reserve, but were removed by the Indian agent after a few years. Paquette stayed on at Moberly Lake; he died in 1937.

202   The Finlay River and Parsnip River join at Finlay Forks to form the Peace River.

203   Although Fay simply named him as Joseph, Brewster wrote "Joseph Cayou" in his diary. Joe Calliou was the eldest of three remarkable brothers. Joe, Pete and Sam guided the 1927 and 1928 Prentiss Gray expeditions, and Pete assisted Sheldon and Borden from Moberly Lake when they explored the Sukunka in 1932. Joe, Pete and Sam Calliou were still listed as guides out of Moberly Lake in 1947. They inevitably impressed those that wrote about them, and were regarded as the finest guides.

204 Probably Dokie. The Dokie family is still prominent in the Moberly Lake area, and there was at least one Chief Dokie.

205 Treaty 8, still in effect.

206 Fort McLeod, on the far (western) side of the Rockies, had been established in 1805 by Simon Fraser. It is the oldest continually occupied settlement west of the Rockies north of California.

207 George V. Copley produced one of the first maps of northeastern British Columbia, along with N.F. Murray, after whom the Murray River was named after he was killed in action in France.

208 The other was Frank C. Swannell, who went on to have a long and distinguished surveying career, and who was a veteran of both world wars. In the 1950s, Fay scribbled Swannell's name into his journal. Forty years after the expedition, he had read an article by Swannell in *The Beaver* magazine entitled "Ninety Years Later." The name meant nothing to him, but in reading the article he discovered that it dealt with the survey of the Finlay River in 1914, and that his assistant was Copley. Fay and Swannell (and Copley) became friends and regular correspondents. On October 18, 1964, 50 years to the day since he and Brewster had first crossed the Peace at Hudson's Hope, Fay, aged 80, started a letter to Swannell, summarizing those days in which their paths had first crossed. It is a beautiful letter of a man in his twilight years reminiscing on and glorying in a well-spent youth.

209 In a letter written in the early 1960s to the editor of the *Alaska Highway News*, Fay wrote that during his few days in Hudson's Hope he had also met a trapper who had homesteaded there. In 1953, he sent a photograph, which he had taken at the trading post in 1914, to a friend in Hudson's Hope. The trapper was identified as Dudley Shaw, who subsequently became a correspondent for the *Alaska Highway News*. Fay and Shaw made contact and Shaw would send him batches of this newspaper at frequent intervals, thus allowing him to keep in touch with the Peace River country.

210 Probably Jackfish Lake.

211 Fay later amended these by hand in his journal to Murray River and Sukunka River, respectively, in keeping with their new names.

212 This camp was probably at Sundance lakes, a popular camping site because of the good water.

213 Kiskatinaw River.

214 Dawson Creek.

215 Hector Tremblay was the first permanent white resident of the Peace District. He had arrived in 1899, bound for the Klondike, but been intrigued by the possibilities of the area and got a job running the pack outfit for the team that was surveying the Peace River block for the first time. He then bought its 25 horses, machinery and supplies and settled at what became Pouce Coupe, trapping, trading and farming. He has been called the "Trailmaker of the Peace" for the numerous trails he cut. In a 1957 interview described in the Calverley collection (www.calverley.ca) Hector Tremblay's son describes how his father had cut the first half of the trail the Fay party would now travel along, and of how arriving settlers would have little option but to stay at the series of stopping places that Fay now goes on to describe: the Borden, Kelly and Johnson ranches.

216 Fred Haskin operated a store in Pouce Coupe.

217 According to Dawson Creek historian Gerry Clare, this was likely Frank DeWetter. They might not have realized that his brother Joe had worked for Brewster in Jasper. DeWetter's age matches this description. The only other Belgian candidate is Richard Vanhove.

218 Ellis and Mary Borden had arrived from Stettler in 1910.

219 Tupper at the south end of Swan Lake.

220 John Leroy died in 1916, and his widow, Katherine, took over the homestead and proved it up.

221 Kelly (Kelley) was apparently a nickname for a rancher named Sunderman.

222 Oliver "Rutabaga" Johnson of Stony Point, near Beaverlodge. He had been the second settler in the district in 1907 and was one of the creators of the Hinton Trail. He was known as Rutabaga because his first crop was Swedish turnips.

223 This must have been more than just a one-way conversation, for the Grande Prairie *Herald* published a glowing account of the expedition's achievements.

224 The Edmonton paper also featured their expedition in a November article, focusing on the fact that they had heard of the war only two months after it had broken out.

Major sources

The original of Fay's journal is in Record Unit 7176 at the
Smithsonian Institution in Washington, DC (U:\Fay\
Record Unit 7176 Series 2 – United States Fish & Wildlife
Service, Field Reports, 1860–1961.htm; Box 117, Folder
29), from whom permission to publish the journal was
obtained. For this book, the editors used the copy which
was kindly made available by the Jasper–Yellowhead
Museum & Archives in Jasper, Alberta (Fonds 84.167).
Other copies are held by the Whyte Museum of the
Canadian Rockies in Banff, Alberta; the Glenbow Archives
in Calgary, Alberta; and the British Columbia Provincial
Archives in Victoria, BC.

The wildlife appendix is from Record Unit 7176 at the
Smithsonian Institution.

The photographs are reproduced from Fonds 84.87 at the
Jasper–Yellowhead Museum & Archives. The source is the
photo album which belonged to Bob Jones, the wrangler
on the expedition.

The maps are from the BC Provincial Archives (CM/B2019
and CM/C2046) and from the Whyte Museum of the
Canadian Rockies (Fonds M53/V86).

Some useful trail location information was obtained from
Fred Brewster's diary of the trip, which is located at the
Whyte Museum of the Canadian Rockies (Fonds M53/V86).

The Fay biographical material is from an obituary in the
American Alpine Journal 18(46), 1972, p. 244, and from the
American Alpine Club Journal 11(33), 1959, p. 256.

The Cross biographical material is from the *American
Alpine Club Journal 6*(20), 1947, p. 357.

The Brewster biographical information is from the
Brewster fonds (84.167) at the Jasper–Yellowhead Museum
& Archives.

Biographical information about Jones and Symes was
obtained from their First World War enlistment records
in the National Archives of Canada, available for Jones at
www.collectionscanada.gc.ca/databases/cef/001042-119.01-
e.php?&id_nbr=340257&interval=20&&PHPSESSID=bki8
p957n84bcrt9l2i1cokpq1

and for Symes at www.collectionscanada.gc.ca/databases/
cef/001042-119.01-e.php?&id_nbr=261793&interval=20&&
PHPSESSID=ogkoucuip3l1hsvr5id96otra4

References and works cited

BOOKS, REPORTS AND PERIODICALS

American Alpine Journal VI (20), 1947. 357. (Cross biographical information)

American Alpine Journal 11 (33), 1959. 256. (Fay biographical information)

American Alpine Journal 18 (46), 1972. 244. (Obituary for Samuel Prescott Fay, by Henry S. Hall Jr.)

Amery, L.S. *Days of Fresh Air.* London: Hutchinson Universal Book Club, 1940.

Andrews, G.S. *Métis Outpost: Memoirs of the First Schoolmaster at the Métis Settlement of Kelly Lake, B.C., 1923-1925.* Victoria: Pencrest Publications, 1985.

Baldwin, Frank Conger. "With Pack Train and Teepee in the Rockies of Alberta." *Outdoor Life,* June and July 1924.

Borden, Richard. "Trip into the Peace River Region, 1931" and "British Columbia, 1932." In Theodore J. Holsten, Jr. et al., eds. *Spirit of the Wilderness,* chapters 3 and 4. Missoula, Mont.: Boone & Crockett Club, 1997.

Brewster, Fred. Diary of 1914 Fay Expedition. Whyte Museum, M53/21.

Cautley, R.W., and A.O. Wheeler. Report of the Commission Appointed To Delimit the Boundary between the Provinces of Alberta and British Columbia, Parts IIIA and IIIB, 1918 to 1924. Ottawa: Office of the Surveyor General, 1925.

Dawson, George M. Report on an Expedition from Port Simpson on the Pacific Coast to Edmonton on the Saskatchewan River. In *Geological and Natural History Survey of Canada,* Report of Progress for 1879-80. Montreal: Dawson Brothers, 1881.

Fay, S. Prescott. "The Canadian Rockies between the Yellowhead Pass and the Peace River." *Appalachia* XIII(3), 1915.

————. "Mt. Alexander." *Canadian Alpine Journal* VI, 1915, 170-177. Alpine Club of Canada.

————. "Some Pioneer Explorations in Alberta." *Outdoor Life,* January 1925.

Fay, P., and B. Angier. "The Great Mountain (Parts I and II)." *The Beaver,* Summer 1957 (pp. 34-39) and Autumn 1957 (pp. 42-47).

Grande Prairie Herald, Nov. 4, 1914. Copy in Fred Brewster fonds, M53/V86, Whyte Museum of the Canadian Rockies.

Gray, Prentiss N. *From the Peace to the Fraser: Newly Discovered North American Hunting Journals 1900 to 1930.* Theodore J. Holstein Jr. and Susan Reneau, eds. Missoula, Mont.: Boone & Crockett Club, 1994. 209-330.

Helm, Charles. *Beyond Rock and Coal: The History of the Tumbler Ridge Area.* Tumbler Ridge, BC: MCA Publishing, 2000.

————. *Tumbler Ridge: Enjoying its History, Trails & Wilderness.* Tumbler Ridge, BC: MCA Publishing, 2001.

Heuer, Karsten. *Walking the Big Wild: From Yellowstone to the Yukon on the Grizzly Bears' Trail.* Toronto: McClelland & Stewart, 2002.

Holzworth, John M. Report on Trip Taken in August, September and October 1923 in Northeastern British Columbia in the Interests of the United States Biological Survey on the Subject of Mountain Sheep and Caribou Distribution. Smithsonian Institution Archives Record Unit 7176, Series 2, Box 118, Folder 8.

————. *The Wild Grizzlies of Alaska.* G.P. Putnam's Sons, The Brickerbacker Press, 1930. 388-408.

Jobe, Mary. "The Expedition to 'Mt. Kitchi': A New Peak in the Canadian Rockies. *Canadian Alpine Journal* VI, 1914-15.

Lamb, W. Kaye, ed. *The Journals and Letters of Sir Alexander Mackenzie.* Published for the Hakluyt Society by Cambridge University Press.

MacGregor, J.G. *Overland by the Yellowhead.* Saskatoon: Western Producer Prairie Books, 1974.

Moberly, Henry John. *When Fur Was King.* London and Toronto: J.M. Dent, 1929.

Phillips, Donald. "Winter Conditions North and West of Mt. Robson." *Canadian Alpine Journal,* VI, 1914-15.

Rich, E.E., ed. Colin Robertson's Correspondence Book, September 1817 to September 1822. Toronto: The Champlain Society, 1939.

Rindsfoos, W. Report of Wm Rindsfoos to Provincial Game Warden of B.C., Smithsonian Institution Archives Record Unit 7176, Series 2, Box 117, Folder 18.

Robinson, Mike, and Dave Hocking. *The Monkman Pass and Trail: A Brief History.* Calgary: Petro Canada Coal Division, 1982.

Sheldon, William G. *Exploring for Wild Sheep in British Columbia in 1931 and 1932.* Clinton, NJ: Amwell Press, 1981.

Smith, Cyndi. *Off the Beaten Track: Women Adventurers and Mountaineers in Western Canada.* Jasper: Coyote Books, 1989.

Stacey, E.W. *The Monkman Pass Highway.* Beaverlodge, Alta.: Beaverlodge & District Historical Association, 1974.

Taylor, William C. *Tracks across My Trail: Donald "Curly" Phillips, Guide and Outfitter.* Jasper: Jasper–Yellowhead Historical Society, 1984.

Townsend, Chris. *High Summer: Backpacking the Canadian Rockies.* Sparkford, UK, Oxford, and Seattle, Wash.: Cloudcap, 1989.

Truax, Madelon Flint, and Beth Flint Sheehan. *People of the Pass: A Human Interest Story of the Monkman Pass.* Beaverlodge, Alta. : Beaverlodge & District Historical Association, 1988

Tuck, Spencer H. "Through the Wapiti Pass," in *Peace River Chronicles.* Edited by Gordon Bowes. Vancouver: Prescott Publishing Company, 1963.

Ventress, Cora, Marguerite Davies & Edith Kyllo. *The Peacemakers of North Peace.* Fort St. John, BC: Davies, Ventress & Kyllo, 1973.

Whelen, Townsend. "In Virgin Game Mountains of the North." *Outdoor Life,* December 1923 and January, February, March 1924.

CORRESPONDENCE

BETWEEN S. PRESCOTT FAY AND:

Charles Sheldon, 1913

Theodore Lyman (Harvard Travelers Club), 1913.

E.W. Nelson (US Dept of Agriculture, Bureau of Biological Survey), 1914, 1915.

Bryan Williams, BC Provincial Game Warden, 1914.

A.O. Wheeler, 1914–1916.

E. Deville (Geographic Board of Canada), 1915.

A.H. Whitcher (Geographic Board of Canada), 1915, 1916.

Frederick Vreeland, 1916.

Editor, *Outdoor Life* magazine, 1924.

R. Douglas (Geographic Board of Canada), 1925, 1926.

C.F. Hanington, 1926.

H.F. Lambart (Topographical Survey of Canada), 1930.

E.A. Goldman (US Biological Survey), 1933.

Natural History magazine, March 1941.

G.M. Munroe, Canadian Board of Geographical Names, 1956, 1957.

G.S. Andrews, 1939.

Frank Swannell, 1964, 1965.

Fred Brewster, 1967.

OTHER CORRESPONDENCE, BETWEEN:

E.W. Nelson and Bryan Williams, 1914.

Charles Cross and Bryan Williams, 1914.

G.M. Munroe and W.R. Young (Chief Geographer, BC Dept. of Lands & Forests), 1957.

ADDITIONAL SOURCES

Bob Jones. Photos of Fay 1914 Expedition. Jasper–Yellowhead Museum & Archives.

Calverley Collection, www.calverley.ca.

01–142. An Incident in the Life of Old-time Trapper Frank Treadwell.

3–039. Story of a Freighter on the Peace and Pine rivers.

8–06. Hector Tremblay: Trailmaker, by Dorothea Calverley.

18–094. Mr. Bob Tremblay remembers his father.

Edmonton Paper, 1914. Copy in Fred Brewster fonds, M53/V86, Whyte Museum of the Canadian Rockies.

Maps by Robert W. Jones for the Grand Trunk Pacific Railway, 1906. American Geographical Society Library, University of Wisconsin–Milwaukee Libraries, Milwaukee, Wis. USA

Personal communication with Gerry Clare, Dawson Creek Historical Society.

Report on Various Proposed Railway Routes for a Western Outlet to the Pacific from the Peace River District by a Joint Board of Engineers of the Canadian National and Canadian Pacific Railways, 1929. University of Northern British Columbia Library Special Collections.

Index

Other titles available from RMB

Where the Clouds Can Go

Conrad Kain

ISBN 978-1-897522-45-5 $26.95

Of all the mountain guides who came to Canada in the late 19th and early 20th centuries, Conrad Kain is probably the most respected and well known. In this internationally anticipated reissue of *Where the Clouds Can Go*—first published in 1935, with subsequent editions in 1954 and 1979—Rocky Mountain Books has accentuated the original text with an expanded selection of over 50 archival images that celebrate the accomplishments of Conrad Kain in the diverse mountain landscapes of North America, Europe and New Zealand.

No Ordinary Woman: The Story of Mary Schäffer Warren

Janice Sanford Beck

ISBN 978-0-921102-82-3 $24.95

Artist, photographer, writer and explorer Mary Schäffer Warren overcame the limited expectations of women a century ago in order to follow her dreams. In 1903, Mary embarked upon a series of explorations in the Canadian Rockies that were far more extensive than was thought proper for a woman at the time. Her most famous trips, in 1907 and 1908, led to the rediscovery of Maligne Lake and, later, her highly regarded book *Old Indian Trails of the Canadian Rockies*.

Jimmy Simpson: Legend of the Rockies

E.J. "Ted" Hart

ISBN 978-1-897522-25-7 $24.95

This book is the story of Jimmy Simpson's 80-year epic as one of the most important guides, outfitters, lodge operators, hunters, naturalists and artists in the Canadian Rockies. The story takes him from blazing trails in the valley bottoms to ascending some of the highest peaks in the range, from guiding scientists, mountaineers, big-game hunters and world-famous artists through some of the most unimaginable scenery on earth to entertaining thousands of visitors over the years at his famous lodge at Bow Lake with his tales—both true and tall—of the pioneer days.

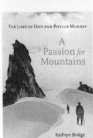

A Passion for Mountains: The Lives of Don and Phyllis Munday

Kathryn Bridge

ISBN 978-1-894765-69-5 $26.95

Don and Phyllis Munday are western Canada's most famous mountaineering couple. Active members of the Alpine Club of Canada, they climbed for almost four decades throughout the Pacific Northwest as well as in the Selkirks and the Rockies. The Mundays were ahead of their time. They are chiefly renowned for their tenacity and environmental awareness, as well as for their scientific contributions in exploring and documenting the little-known Coast Mountains. Their joint climbs from the 1920s through the 1940s included scaling 150-plus mountains, more than 40 of them in first ascents.

New illustrated editions available in 2010

⇓ ⇓

The Canadian Rockies:
New and Old Trails
A.P. Coleman
ISBN 978-1897522509 $19.95

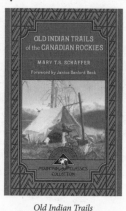

Old Indian Trails
of the Canadian Rockies
Mary T.S. Schäffer
ISBN 978-1897522493 $19.95

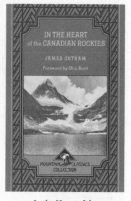

In the Heart of the
Canadian Rockies
James Outram
ISBN 978-1894765961 $22.95

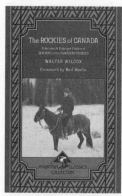

The Rockies of Canada
Walter Wilcox
ISBN 978-1897522141 $19.95

Climbs & Exploration in the
Canadian Rockies
Hugh E.M. Stutfield &
J. Norman Collie
ISBN 978-1897522066 $19.95

On the Roof of the Rockies
Lewis R. Freeman
Illustrated Edition
ISBN 978-1897522462 $19.95

THE MOUNTAIN CLASSICS COLLECTION is a series of important reprints documenting historic explorations in the mountain West. These are the first-hand tales of the brave souls who were drawn to Canada's majestic, pristine landscapes. Experience the wonder and excitement of these early adventurers as they negotiate treacherous rapids, encounter wild animals and endure severe weather in unmapped territory.